The Film Handbook

The Film Handbook examines the current state of filmmaking and how film language, technique and aesthetics are being utilised for today's 'digital film' productions. It reflects on how critical analysis of film underpins practice and story, and how developing an autonomous 'vision' will best aid student creativity.

The Film Handbook offers practical guidance on a range of traditional and independent 'guerrilla' film production methods, from developing script ideas and the logistics of planning the shoot to cinematography, sound and directing practices. Film professionals share advice from their creative and practical experiences shooting both on digital and film forms.

The Film Handbook relates theory to the filmmaking process and includes:

- documentary, narrative and experimental forms, including deliberations on 'reading the screen', genre, *mise en scène*, montage, and sound design
- new technologies of film production and independent distribution, digital and multi-film formats utilised for indie filmmakers and professional dramas, sound design and music
- the short film form, theories of transgressive and independent 'guerrilla' filmmaking, the avant-garde and experimental as a means of creative expression
- preparing to work in the film industry, development of specialisms as director, producer, cinematographer or editor, and the presentation of creative work.

Dr Mark de Valk is Senior Lecturer in Film and Television Studies at Southampton Solent University. He specialises in guerrilla-/indie-filmmaking processes and continues to produce, direct and write productions in documentary, drama and experimental formats.

Dr Sarah Arnold is Lecturer in Film and Digital Media at University College Falmouth and is author of *Maternal Horror Film: Melodrama and Mo*

Media Practice

Edited by James Curran, Goldsmiths College, University of London

The *Media Practice* handbooks are comprehensive resource books for students of media and journalism, and for anyone planning a career as a media professional. Each handbook combines a clear introduction to understanding how the media works, with practical information about the structure, processes and skills involved in working in today's media industries, providing not only a guide on 'how to do it', but also a critical reflection on contemporary media practice.

The Advertising Handbook
3rd edition
Helen Powell, Jonathan Hardy, Sarah Hawkin and Iain MacRury

The Alternative Media Handbook
Kate Coyer, Tony Dowmunt and Alan Fountain

The Cyberspace Handbook
Jason Whittaker

The Documentary Handbook
Peter Lee-Wright

The Fashion Handbook
Tim Jackson and David Shaw

The Film Handbook
Mark de Valk with Sarah Arnold

The Graphic Communication Handbook
Simon Downs

The Magazines Handbook
3rd edition
Jenny McKay

The Music Industry Handbook
Paul Rutter

The New Media Handbook
Andrew Dewdney and Peter Ride

The Newspapers Handbook
4th edition
Richard Keeble

The Photography Handbook
2nd edition
Terence Wright

The Public Relations Handbook
4th edition
Alison Theaker

The Radio Handbook
3rd edition
Carole Fleming

The Sound Handbook
Tim Crook

The Television Handbook
4th edition
Jeremy Orlebar

The Film Handbook

Mark de Valk with
Sarah Arnold

Routledge
Taylor & Francis Group

LONDON AND NEW YORK

First published 2013
by Routledge
2 Park Square, Milton Park, Abingdon, Oxon OX14 4RN

Simultaneously published in the USA and Canada
by Routledge
711 Third Avenue, New York, NY 10017

Routledge is an imprint of the Taylor & Francis Group, an informa business

British Library Cataloguing in Publication Data
A catalogue record for this book is available from the British Library

Library of Congress Cataloging in Publication Data
De Valk, Mark.
The film handbook / Mark de Valk with Sarah Arnold.
    pages cm. — (Media practice)
    Includes bibliographical references and index.
    1. Motion pictures—Production and direction. I. Arnold, Sarah. II. Title.
    PN1995.9.P7D42 2013
    791.4302'3—dc23
    2012035856

ISBN: 978–0–415–55760–3 (hbk)
ISBN: 978–0–415–55761–0 (pbk)
ISBN: 978–0–203–14644–6 (ebk)

Typeset in Helvetica and Avant Garde
by Florence Production Ltd, Stoodleigh, Devon

Printed and bound in Great Britain by
TJ International Ltd, Padstow, Cornwall

Contents

Figures

Contributors

John Brice has worked as an assistant film editor and as a writer/producer/director in film and television. He has also worked as a story consultant to a major feature film company and has taught screenwriting/story structure at UCLA extension, Southampton Solent University, De Montfort University, Bournemouth University, and the London Film School.

David Church is Associate Instructor in the Department of Communication and Culture at Indiana University Bloomington, USA.

Roger Deakins, ASC, BSC, is an English cinematographer best known for his work on a number of films, including *The Shawshank Redemption*, *The Assassination of Jesse James by the Coward Robert Ford*, and *O Brother, Where Art Thou?* He has also worked as visual consultant on films including *WALL·E* and *Rango*. He is a member of both the American Society of Cinematographers and the British Society of Cinematographers.

Paul Rutter (MProf) is Programme Group Leader in Music at Southampton Solent University. He is a musician, producer, writer, music industry educator, and author of *The Music Industry Handbook*, published by Routledge in 2011. Paul has an extensive 30-year professional background as a music content provider, having written and produced music for synchronisation in film and television for broadcasters such as STV, BBC, and the ITV network in the UK. Paul has also created solo popular music compositions for international artists, such as 'Heaven Can Wait' (covered by Paul Young), and has also created music content for the commercial advertising sector. Paul guests regularly as a music industry consultant on BBC radio in the UK and acts as a professional adviser for programmes concerning the narratives that surround the creation, use, and exploitation of musical work.

Acknowledgements

'The DI, Luddites and Other Musings' by Roger Deakins is reproduced by permission of the author and American Society of Cinematographers.

'Notes Toward a Masochizing of Cult Cinema: The Painful Pleasure of the Cult Film Fan' by David Church was published in *Offscreen* online journal, Vol. 11, Issue 4, April 2007. Reproduced by permission of the author and *Offscreen*.

'Screenwriting: From Script to Screen' by John Brice incorporates elements of 'How to Write a Compelling Story—in 4 Easy Steps (Really!)' by John Brice and 'Why We Need the Devil in Our Stories—The Role of the Antagonist' by John Brice, both published in *ScriptWriter Magazine*, 2008. Both articles reprinted with permission.

For my daughter, Brigitte de Valk . . . who showed me the way.

Foreword

Roger Deakins, ASC, BSC

THE DI, LUDDITES AND OTHER MUSINGS

As a film-school student, I sought any and all information I could gather from everywhere and anywhere. American Cinematographer was a primary authority because the information in its pages came through the patronage of the American Society of Cinematographers. It is the same today.

From my many sources, I learned a lens operated to its best advantage at an aperture of T4-5.6. I learned lighting involved the use of a keylight, a backlight, a fill light, an eyelight and something referred to as a kicker. I learned my negative needed to be meticulously exposed so as to print at a mid-light of 25, and that a true cinematographer used Brute Arcs to light a set and a geared head (operated by a specialist) to achieve smooth camera-panning shots.

But I also learned Raoul Coutard operated the camera himself and that he would often shoot with a handheld Camiflex camera and sometimes light his shots using household bulbs and tinfoil reflectors. I learned John Alton, ASC was ostracized in his time for his radical approach to lighting, eschewing the use of greenbeds and declaring, "It's not what you light, it's what you don't light" that's important. I learned Conrad Hall, ASC overexposed his negative by some 2½ stops to achieve the stunning anamorphic images in Abraham Polonsky's *Tell Them Willie Boy Is Here* (1969) – a technique he repeated for the exteriors in John Huston's 1:85:1 feature *Fat City* (1972).

I had seen Peter Watkins' films *Culloden* (1964) and *The War Game* (1965) before the latter was banned by the BBC for something like 20 years. Both films had a profound effect on me, the first for its contemporary reportage-style re-creation of the battle of Culloden ("They have created a desert and called it peace," declares a reporter while viewing the historic battle and its aftermath), and the second for depicting what, in 1965, could very well have been our imminent, all-too-possible future. Both films were made for the BBC in grainy black-and-white in a 1:33:1 aspect ratio; *Culloden* was photographed by the late, great Dick Bush, BSC, and *The War Game* by Peter Bartlett and Peter Suschitzky, ASC. Both films were handheld and sometimes out of focus, they lacked any sense of artifice, and they were the most powerful films I had seen, both then and perhaps since.

In 1968, I saw *Once Upon A Time in the West*, and in 1969, *The Wild Bunch*. At the National Film School, I learned the latter was shot by Lucien Ballard, ASC using 35mm film in the anamorphic format and blown up to 70mm for projection at the larger theatres, whilst the former, shot by Tonino Delli Colli, AIC, was photographed in Techniscope, a 2-perf pull-down system with a negative area of just 9.47mm x 22mm. (That would be a poor man's Super 35mm, I suppose!) I loved both films then and still watch them often. In his 1974 philosophical study of the concept of quality, *Zen and the Art of Motorcycle Maintenance*, Robert Pirsig never seems to come up with a definition of quality, but both *Once Upon A Time in the West* and *The Wild Bunch* defined and still define quality for me. Stylistically, they are quite different, a product of the opposing systems of image capture the filmmakers used, selective depth of field against deep focus, et cetera, but they are equal works of – and I use the word cautiously – art.

The messages for this student of cinematography remained confused. What was the right way to approach cinematography? What was the best way to create an image? Why was there no test I had to take before I became a cinematographer?

Many years after I left the National Film School, I visited Conrad Hall on his island paradise off Tahiti and spent evenings talking with him over dinner at our home in Santa Monica. My wife and I rebuilt our house in 1999, and I was keen to show Conrad my new darkroom; after a break of some years, I had become keen on taking still photographs again, and the darkroom had been a prerequisite of our new home. My expectations were shattered when Conrad pronounced the photochemical process "antiquated." Why wasn't I using a digital stills camera? All those messy chemicals! You could not predict what Conrad would do, certainly not when it came to his cinematography. He talked at length and with great enthusiasm about the opportunities digital manipulation would create, after he had seen a small example of the technology whilst shooting *Road to Perdition* (2002). Conrad's mantra was always, "Story! Story! Story!" I would never presume that he would have failed to embrace the digital-intermediate (DI) finish or any other new technique that might have helped him develop as a visual storyteller and would have benefited the project.

I remain an avid, though amateur, black-and-white stills photographer and I continue to shoot on film. The other day, I was in Samy's Camera buying some developer when the cashier referred to me as a "mad scientist," or maybe it was a "Luddite!" "I own a Leica M8 digital as well," I muttered as I left.

Not that I don't sympathize with the Luddites. Napoleon was on the rampage in Europe, his continental system of blockade was threatening to strangle the economy, there was the small matter of a war against a former colony, and the stirrings of the Industrial Revolution were threatening to take their jobs. But, for all their protests, the Luddites were no match for the mechanical loom. Invented in 1801, the Jacquard Loom, which used punch-card controls, was the conceptual precursor of the computer. It is not such a stretch to say that it was an ancestor of the DI. So much for history!

Some time ago, I was privileged to see a newly restored print of *Citizen Kane* (1941) that had been made from a negative found in Belgium. The film is universally (well, on this planet, at least) acclaimed for its innovative and masterly cinematography. Watching the film again, in awe of its visuals, I was drawn to study the variations in image "quality" from scene to scene. The print was excellent, so good that variations – caused, I imagine, by stock inconsistencies, uneven or deliberately forced development, variation in lens resolution at different apertures, and the optical manipulation of certain images – were quite apparent. What, I wondered, would Gregg Toland, ASC have thought of modern film stocks, the T1.4 Arri Master Prime lenses, the Steadicam and the remote head, let alone digital compositing? With all our modern inventions and innovations, there are few films that manage to achieve the "quality" of *Citizen Kane*, though there are many that have far less grain and considerably higher resolution.

I would not for a moment suggest a Super 35mm image scanned at 4K or even 6K would approach the resolution of an anamorphic image produced photo-chemically today. It might be interesting, though, to compare the resolution of a release print of an anamorphic film from the '60s or '70s, generated from an internegative, with a release print of a contemporary film shot in Super 35mm on Kodak Vision2 200T 5217 using a Master Prime or a Cook S4 lens and scanned, timed and recorded out at 6K/4K. So much for resolution, as well as history!

But what do we mean by "quality?" Isn't that what we're concerned about?

Was *There Will Be Blood* (2007) a stunning achievement in cinematographic "quality" because it was shot in anamorphic, or did its exceptional shot conception and exquisite sense of composition and the meticulous execution of it all by the camera operator play a part?

Is the current nostalgia for the "look" of the films of the '60s and '70s due to their picture quality (and here I do mean resolution) or to the direct and simple way their visual construction helps tell the story?

There is nostalgia, too, for a time when the cinematographer's craft was less transparent, something of a mystery known only to a few.

Today, there are many more toys and more people who want to play the game. A majority of films are probably finished digitally, 4K has become something of a standard, and 6K imaging is no longer an impossible goal. Yes, the DI is a powerful tool, but it holds no threat to the filmmaker, only opportunities. How quickly we forget that when fast lenses and film stocks were introduced, some producers said lights were no longer necessary! Since then, I managed to overload and blow out the transformer at Wilmington Studios, and we've seen the development of the 18K HMI, the 12K Par, the 100K SoftSun, and so on.

O Brother, Where Art Thou? (2000) could well have been shot in anamorphic and finished photo-chemically. Would it have been a better film? Would its images have been of a better "quality"? It certainly would not have looked the same.

Contrary to popular belief, the manipulation of images in the digital world takes a great deal of skill. It offers no easy fix for those who are careless with their exposures, and there is no software that can compensate for poor lighting or shot conception. The closer the photographed image is to the filmmaker's intent, the more control the DI suite avails the cinematographer.

I have just completed the digital timing of a scene that involved covering a long walk-and-talk over two days of variable weather last January. On the first day, the forecast promised us the cloud cover we wanted, but we arrived to find a bright blue sky. So we waited, and then we waited some more! As is often the case, the light began to fade as we began shooting the scene, and the time inevitably came when I could no longer expose my negative "correctly." We were using a Steadicam and were at T1.4 on the 40mm lens, and my assistant certainly had to perform a minor miracle. But the scene was not just about the shots – it seldom is. The performances were mesmerizing, and, like the director, I wanted to shoot while the actors were on top of their game. I knew with the combination of the larger negative (I was shooting Super 1.85:1), the resolution of the Master Prime (even at T1.4), and the controls I would have in the DI, I had a chance to make the shots match in an acceptable way.

The closer angles we shot on a subsequent day under rather different cloud conditions were also a challenge. There was no alternative – we had no more time and no other days in the schedule. Was I to refuse to shoot? Yes, I made a deliberate compromise in terms of image quality, but not, I suspect, in terms of the quality of the completed film. Every shot I have ever made has been a compromise in some way. That's a sweeping statement, but true nonetheless. No image has ever been as good as the one I envisioned in my mind's eye. Maybe that's what keeps me going: just once, I want to see that image onscreen!

Is it so wrong that the DI process is used to soften a few wrinkles? It is certainly easier to make a selective "fix" using contemporary digital software without compromising the whole frame; with digital tools, any cut between shots can be made less jarring than a cut to a shot that utilizes the complete coverage that traditional lens diffusion or Vaseline has to offer. Is any so-called "interference" by an actor so new? Marlene Dietrich was not alone in dictating the way she was lit, after all. What if the story involves a flashback in which the actress appears 20 years younger than she is in the main body of the film? Is digital retouching acceptable in that situation?

From time to time, it crosses my mind that I am somehow cheating, until I remember how I dodge and burn my darkroom prints, or that the widely admired photographs of George Hurrell owe as much to their retouching as they do to the original negative. Personally, I prefer the grainy street photography of Roger Mayne, but that's another story. But I will own up to progressively adding grain to a recent film. Yes, I did say "adding grain." Blame who you will, but for better or worse, Pandora's Box has been opened.

Some years ago, I was asked to oversee the timing for a new DVD of *Sid and Nancy* (1986). Apologies were made that this would be done using reels from a number of prints because no one pristine copy could be found. Naturally, I objected, and eventually, an interpositive was struck from the original cut negative, which, fortunately, still existed in the vaults of the lab. There has always been a disregard for preservation, whether it's preservation of a historic site, the Dodo, the polar bear, or a film like *Sid and Nancy*.

Only last week, it was announced that a 16mm copy of Fritz Lang's original cut of *Metropolis* (1926) had been found in Argentina, revealing 20 minutes of unseen footage. Why is there so much more concern for archiving a film just because it has been finished digitally? Any number of negatives can be recorded out from the digital master, as can any number of separations. Whilst I would agree that a print taken from an inter-negative made from the output negative of O Brother . . . will not have the resolution of the original negative, things have changed in the years since that film was finished. It is both less expensive and faster to record out "original" negatives, and it might not be long before a scan of an original camera negative will retain more information than any photochemical copy. (Maybe that's true right now if the scan were 6K or 8K.) A print taken from a 4K master of a Super 35mm negative is surely superior in terms of resolution and saturation to one taken from an inter-negative of the same original.

And I have not touched on the number of films, from *Napoleon* (1927) to *The African Queen* (1951), that have been restored digitally! Is that not incongruous? I look forward to seeing another digitally restored version of Lang's iconic film in the not-too-distant future. So much for resolution, history and preservation!

Then there is *WALL·E* (2008). I was privileged to be involved in a very minor way in the making of that film, and I learnt a great deal about the process behind what Pixar refers to as an "animated" film. The animators who "photographed" the film worked in a three-dimensional world and covered the action in much the same way as a live-action film, but the directors of photography, Danielle Feinberg (lighting) and Jeremy Lasky (camera) – separate positions you might note – used no emulsion, no Fresnel lamps or diffusion, no Steadicam, no geared head, nor any other live-action tool. Nevertheless, theirs was a stunning cinematographic achievement. It's true they had an advantage – they never had to battle fading daylight, conceal a light's source or hide dolly tracks – but I would not hesitate to recommend them for ASC membership.

There are all sorts of techniques and technologies we cinematographers can use to create our images. Some are new, and some have been in use since *The Robe* (1953) was photographed, or even longer than that. Some of us migrate to one way of doing something rather than another. A video artist might choose to use film and a filmmaker might choose to use video, but is it not diversity that makes any form of human activity interesting?

It's been awhile since I was a student, but information continues to come at me from a variety of sources professing a variety of certainties, whether in regard to the role of the operator, digital capture, or other thorny issues. If you believe cinematography is more than a craft, then there can be no formula for shooting a film. There can be no rules. Just as we have no definition for what we mean by "quality," we can't say what really gives an image resonance, but I'm sure there is more to it than technique.

I'm not suggesting for a moment that film should be consigned to the history books anytime soon, or that anamorphic is redundant (one recent blockbuster has disproved that idea); at the same time, I would not dissuade the use of 16mm or a cell phone to capture an image if that medium were appropriate. Only change is a certainty, and as members of the ASC, we need to encourage students of cinematography to find their own ways of seeing and their own ways of creating images in our changing industry. If there is a threat to the role of the cinematographer in the future, it will surely be the lack of vision.

There is *Culloden* and there is *The Wild Bunch*. I'm so very glad we have both.

Roger Deakins, North Devon
www.rogerdeakins.com

SELECTED FILMOGRAPHY

Rango (2011) (Visual Consultant)
True Grit (2010)
WALL·E (2007) (Visual Consultant)
In the Valley of Elah (2007)
No Country for Old Men (2006)
The Assassination of Jesse James (2006)
Jarhead (2005)
The Village (2004)

A Beautiful Mind (2001)
The Man Who Wasn't There (2001)
O Brother, Where Art Thou? (2000)
The Big Lebowski (1998)
Fargo (1996)
Dead Man Walking (1995)
The Shawshank Redemption (1994)
Sid and Nancy (1986)

Reprinted with the permission of Roger Deakins and American Cinematographer

Introduction

A film is – or should be – more like music than like fiction. It should be a progression of moods and feelings. The theme, what's behind the emotion, the meaning, all that comes later.

Stanley Kubrick, *Stanley Kubrick: Interviews*

Simplicity is absolutely essential to creation.

Jean Renoir, *Renoir on Renoir*

The Film Handbook is for students. It is a portable reference volume for you to thumb through when you need creative inspiration and as a reminder exemplifying a range of theory and practice elements. The handbook serves to underpin theoretical modes of film thought and production across a range of filmmaking processes. Keep this handy compendium with you throughout your time studying film and refer to it to motivate and stimulate your own story themes and cinematographic ideas. With over 100 years' worth of cinematic experiences to draw upon, *The Film Handbook* highlights, and offers, a rich series of aesthetic choices, story decisions, theory, creative processes, films and filmmakers for you to draw upon in furtherance of encouraging and inducing the development of your own creative *personal signature*.

Throughout the book, you will come across the names of many directors and references to films. I implore you to note down the film titles and filmmakers in this volume (and from your studies), then seek them out to view and study. As a filmmaker, you must be able to communicate and 'talk the talk' with your industry counterparts. Having the wherewithal to discuss, and be cognizant of, a broad range of filmmakers and their aesthetic choices and practices is essential within film production circles. Otherwise, you will be 'left in the dark' as industry etiquette demands such interiorised knowledge of its own creative dynamics and practioners; this film knowledge forms a type of integrity test, as it were, to your cinematographic 'mettle'. Being passionate about viewing and studying a vast range of films, filmmakers, and cultural concepts is essential to not only developing a knowledge of cinema, but in appreciating how you can draw from theoretical film models in furtherance of cultivating creative and aesthetic influences and choices as a path to assist you in developing your own individual creative 'voice'.

Historically, cinema developed at the dawn of the twentieth century as a novel means of communication. Within a short time frame from its inception, filmmakers began to draw their ideas from social and artistic 'modernism'. Modernism is the notion connoting changes in society and in social relations: expanding cities, industry, new technology, capitalism, new social classes. Modernism described a culture of society; that being the culture of social relations, and artistic culture. The culture of the arts, to that time, included painting, literature, poetry, music, photography, sculpture, dance, and theatre. However, within a short period after its establishment, the cinema was solidly influenced by modernism's societal shifts, social relations, and its art culture. To understand more, modernism, as represented within the visual arts, spans a 100-year period from approximately 1860 to the early 1960s. During this historical time, the artist's philosophical aims and goals mattered at its heart, which developed in a way so that their creative output acted to confront and challenge not only its audience, but particular societal conventions and norms. Examples include impressionism, cubism, surrealism, and abstract expressionism. Surrealism and abstract expressionism are of particular note to early cinema language experimentation as two seminal cinematic works can be cited, which should be (and are) studied to this day: *The Cabinet of Dr Caligari* (Robert Wiene, 1920) and *Un Chien Andalou* (Luis Buñuel, 1929). Modernism represents an era of examination and experimentation where the arts and cinema developed and explored various creative processes and capabilities to express and mirror the tumultuous societal events and moods indicative at the dawn of the twentieth century and the ensuing decades. Modernism reflects an ideological and creative shift that artists embrace in terms of what a particular work of art can express and in the form that creative expresion takes.

The relevancy of applying, considering, and studying how theory underpins film construction can be read in how cultural assumptions incorporate the understanding of an assemblage of cinematic elements and signs (or signifiers), which seek to express meaning and stir emotion. In order to ensure that the film's intended message is received and understood by the audience, there needs to be a representational comprehension between the filmmaker and the viewer. Therefore, the nature of the visual elements within the frame (which draw from cultural familiarity to generate awareness on the part of the viewer) are only valid if the intended meaning is created, or drawn from, a universally understood language structure. Thus, in order to affix signification to a particular film, it is central to recognise, understand and introject the cultural model that it was produced from.

FILM AS A LANGUAGE

Why is film considered a language? Can the signs and symbols, within the cinematic frame, actually 'speak' or communicate to an audience? Yes, they can and do. As filmmakers, we need to consider the subject of film grammar and develop an appreciation and understanding of why cinematic language is imperative to comprehend and study. Let's consider how invoking a theoretical model will help us down this path. Christian Metz (1931–93), a prominent contemporary French film theorist, draws his hypotheses from studies by Swiss linguist Ferdinand de Saussure (1857–1913), who considered the social significance that the role of signs (that of an object/space or confluence of objects/spaces) represent within society; thus, the term *semiotics* (or 'sign system') was subsequently born. Concentrating on narrative construction, Metz promotes, in *Film Language: A Semiotics of Cinema*, the concept of the 'Grand Syntagmatic', which is an approach to classify film scenes, whether connotative or denotative, in terms of infusing a particular shot's motivational nature. To be denotative, the shot or scene literally *shows* or *demonstrates* meaning, while connotative *suggests* or *implies* meaning. Metz also explores cinema as a signifier reflecting our flawed reality by invoking psychological concepts as argued by French cultural theorist Jacques Lacan, who developed the notion of the 'mirror stage', and Sigmund Freud, whose psychoanalytic theories focused on the human dream state and traits of the unconscious. By considering Christian Metz as an example of a theorist who has applied semiotic and psycho-analytical hypotheses to cinema, we begin to grasp the potential, and understand the relevance, of exploring and applying theoretical concepts to our filmmaking practices.

Expanding on this theme, it was Russian filmmaker Lev Kuleshov (1899–1970), in the early part of the twentieth century, who first applied elements of de Saussure's notions of semiotics to associate meaning to camera framings, objects and elements within the cinematic image, and its subsequent assemblage through editing. Kuleshov argued that different camera shots could (and did) act like letters of the alphabet, in a way that one could immediately decipher, similar to how we understand words. Kuleshov worked and associated with prominent Russian filmmaking pioneers Sergei Eisenstein and Dziga Vertov to develop and apply their theories of how signs operate in terms of image construction and montage editing (which will be discussed later in detail). Here, the notion of 'metaphor' takes hold, and shape within the filmmaking process and the conceptulisation of a 'cinematic vocabulary' takes root.

How is it, then, that the concept of filmic 'letters' and 'words' can be translated through the various cinematic shots displayed on the screen? Although Metz doesn't agree that the smallest cinematic component constitutes a particular word, and that the initial establishment of cinema was nothing more than a 'mechanical' process, he does argue that it was the development of *narrative* that comes closest to creating a *visual sentence*, one that is understandable to the audience as a form of language. This sustained form of visual linkage (or narrative storytelling) is argued, by Metz, to be first fully demonstrated, and realised, in the film *The Birth of a Nation* (1915) by American director D.W. Griffith. Here, Metz suggests that this particular cinematic narrative was the earliest film to emulate, most closely, verbal language.

We have heard that Metz relates a linguistic sentence to a shot; however, he does later problematise his cinematic notions of shot connection to the common word by pointing out that there are a finite number of dictionary words that we use as opposed to the unlimited number of shot potentialities that can be created. Additionally, he argues, words are already present in a form of a pre-existing pool, which we draw upon to invoke our verbal language, while cinematic shots are newly *formed* and fashioned, at-hand, by the filmmaker for a particular film. As such, shots have a far greater potential denotative and connotative range.

Metz also modified his initial viewpoint on the cinema's connection to verbal language by suggesting that while film constitutes a form of language, it isn't drawn from a concrete or fixed language structure (as we have constituted our word system); he calls this *langage sans langue*, a 'language without a language system'.

Thus, we can see that the earliest cinematic presentations were constructed and advanced with an analytical eye towards understanding and developing a *grammar of film*, which cultural theoreticians have examined and argued, across the decades, as a means to decipher and decode cinema as a form of social signifier. The study of, and experimentation with, metaphor, representation, and the signification of images will serve you, the student filmmaker, well in terms of developing your own creative autonomy. By considering how theory underpins practice, you will not only attain a richer understanding spanning a range of cinematic social debates, but you can draw from those deliberations to infuse the thematic ideas you wish to bring to the screen.

Part I

Film language and aesthetics

CHAPTER 1

Renaissance of (digital) film

FROM FILM PRINTS TO FILM FILES

Filmmaking today thrives as an independent, personal and industrial form of creative expression within today's global digital, web-based and television environment. Until recently, the use of 35 mm film stock has been utilised in over 95 per cent of productions destined for the cinema theatres. Currently, with the advancement of digital projection systems, the prohibitive cost of 35 mm film stock, and the resolution capabilities of evolving camera and lens systems, 'film-image' digital capture practices have transcended the silver halide emulsion process. In 2012, the UK distributed over 80 per cent of its movie productions digitally. Within the next few years, distribution companies will not be making available any film prints and all cinemas will have completed the transition to full digital projection. The great cinematic camera companies, such as Panasonic, are no longer developing 35 mm technologies and are now focused on advancing high-definition digital image capture and lens quality to suit. What we are witnessing in cinema today is the grandest technological shift since the advent of the voice and soundtrack that transformed spectator experience. This contemporary transference is more than this new technology's software and hardware upgrade; it stimulates convergence and diversity for filmmakers and audiences while contributing to social development and practices. It can be readily argued that with the range of digital equipment at our disposal, from student to Hollywood studio, the aesthetic concepts of how film stock captured its image, *mise en scène*, light and character has been transferred to its digital counterpart. Thus, the term 'digital film' is an applicable notion and moniker, for today, that represents the amalgamation of traditional cinematic concepts (as originally achieved on celluloid) with today's digital formats and practises, including 3D holographic and IMAX systems.

Conversely, however, in today's 'digital film' world, independent, transgressive (and some studio – Oliver Stone's *JFK*, 1991) filmmakers employ a widening range of retro camera formats to capture their imagery. These include 16 mm, Super 16 mm, Standard 8 mm, Super 8 mm, Fisher-Price, VHS, and Hi8 formats in conjunction with current mobile phone and computer technologies to create and experiment with image, narrative, and structure. In fact, today, many filmmakers utilise cross-platform formats (digital and film), including varied ratio aspects, to affect particular creative and aesthetic outcomes. For example, Kodak has recently re-released both Standard 8 and Super 8 mm film formats. A fantastic range of 8 mm and Super 8 mm cameras can be found for sale on Internet sites, with dedicated websites advocating and discussing 8 mm film practice, equipment, and processes.

As filmmaking shifts into direct digital capture and digital projection at our local cinemas, the resolution (and economic viability) of such digital capture and projection has not yet matched the richness and depth of image as captured on 35 mm and IMAX film (70 mm) formats. The exception is high-definition 'Red Cinematography', which has surpassed the resolution of 35 mm. However, the editing platforms and high-resolution monitors and screens required to handle the massive amount of digitised information have not been developed sufficiently to display the Red camera's ultra-high-end resolution capabilities due to its prohibitive economic cost. But the time is coming when the prohibitive cost of digital production, storage, and display capabilities will no longer be an obstacle or barrier to experience the richest and most detailed image resolution. Through all of this, what will endure will be filmmaking's concepts, aesthetics, and vernacular of practice, which will live on to inspire as digital moves into the future. Thus, *film language* (and its study) will remain relevant and viable regardless of the technological and mechanical forms created for image capture and dissemination. Hence, the pursuit and goal of the filmmaker will remain one of developing and creating an individual and unique *personal signature* in furtherance of carving out a particular creative 'voice' through cinematic language, a cinematic language that needs to honed, crafted, and broadly debated.

FILM GRAMMAR

Grammar is broadly defined in the dictionary as:

- an examination of how words and their constituent parts combine to form sentences;
- an examination of structural relationships, including pronunciation, meaning, and linguistic history;
- a system of nuance, syntax, and word formation; and
- a system of rules implicit in a particular language, viewed as a mechanism for producing all probable sentences.

Drawing from this definition, we can now distinguish what constitutes the language of film and its corresponding grammar. We need to be able construct our *visual sentence* by working to understand how imagery relates to its perception and reception by an audience. This may be entirely a subjective position as the old adage posits, 'what speaks to one person may not speak to another'. It is true that a particular film we may enjoy, which speaks to us intellectually or emotionally, may not resonant with others at, or on, the same level. How many discussions, arguments, and debates have we had with friends and family over a particular film on whether it was a fulfilling emotional experience or one of indifference or boredom? How can it be that a filmmaker has worked so diligently to present the strongest and most dynamic imagery, dialogue, and acting, yet the film may fail to spark, or speak to, an audience? Is it that the filmmaker has not understood film language? This question cannot be answered fully as all forms of artistic endeavour and storytelling artefacts are formed from a limitless arrangement of factors (including those personality traits of the individual filmmaker himself or herself) that constitute expression even though they are drawing from a set number of hardware factors as all films are shot and displayed utilising a uniform set of technological and mechanical parameters (for example, cameras, lenses, lights, dolly, Steadicam, editing platforms, projection, screen). The core hardware is uniform to the production medium, whether film or digital, much in the way that that there are endless ways to create music but its production emanates from a set number of notes, again like our alphabet with its 26 symbols that our spoken language derives from. It is not the amount of notes (or letters) that change, but the arrangement of these notes, which can be composed infinitely. The same principle applies to film. The capture and dissemination apparatus for motion imagery is predetermined but the assembly of film grammar that expresses that imagery is boundless.

We may call this *mise en scène*, a French cinematic term indicating *what elements the director consciously arranges within the camera frame*. This *populated* frame is what the filmmaker utilises to project to the audience information, or an intended emotion, through a particular shot, scene, or sequence to send its message, whether coded by shared social signifiers such as politics, civics, customs, norms, dress, speech and/or implanted through shape, colour, character positioning and movement, depth of horizon, object placement, lighting, and frame size. The notion that a cinematic *visual sentence* is demonstrated through a narrative construct is witnessed in the shooting script where each shot is (and should be) notated and meticulously planned out. This 'sentence' is then transposed into a series of storyboards, which function to visually *pre-write* the shot, scene, or sequence in a way that the director wishes to realise on screen.

Counter to Christian Metz's considerate focus on symbolic representation in cinema is French theorist, philosopher, and essayist André Bazin (1918–58), who wrote a series of seminal works on film as a reflector of 'realism', including an essay on cinematic grammar entitled *The Evolution of the Language of Cinema*, where he expounds on the notion that filmmaking, being 'mechanical' in nature, is innately a purveyor of the 'real world'. Bazin argues that cinema is but a technical advancement developed to promote 'realistic' ideas and that cinema functions as an evolutionary superior form to that of the painted image and photography; as such, filmmaking constitutes a 'fingerprint' or 'imprint' of our reality where the film image is but a 'transfer' of that reality to the screen. Bazin argues this superiority results from motion film's ability to capture events and scenarios that depict and convey durations of time that paintings and still photos cannot replicate. Later, we will examine Bazin in further detail in relation to Eisenstein and explore, as a case study, the notion of the *realists* and the *montagists*. For now, we can outline Bazin's effective notions of film language and grammar in furtherance of understanding his argument that cinema functions to capture reality. These cinematic practices, he suggests, include:

- *Mise en scène* – that which is physically placed within the scene, the collective of situated elements that convey the shot.
- The long take – allowing the scene to play out, generally in a master shot, without resorting to short edited takes or shots.
- Camera movement – physical camera motion throughout a particular shot (for example, the tracking shot).
- Deep focus (depth of field) – all elements within the frame are, and remain, in focus.

Bazin highlighted these cinematic elements as historically occurring in the early 1940s, emanating with director Jean Renoir's *La règle du jeu* (*The Rules of the Game*) (1939) and Orson Welles's *Citizen Kane* (1941), along with the Italian neo-realists, such as Luchino Visconti's *Ossessione* (*Obsession*) (1943), Roberto Rossellini's *Roma, città aperta* (*Rome, Open City*) (1945), and Vittorio De Sica's *Sciuscià* (*Shoeshine*) (1946). Bazin identifies and argues that these particular films and filmmakers, among others of that period, have developed, undergone, and represent an evolutionary stylist shift from the Soviet-based (and silent cinema's) *imagist* film language form to one of a *realist* film language form that fulfils the medium's genuine narrative capabilities (we will discuss *imagist* and *realist* in more detail further on). Alternatively to Bazin's concepts, Russian filmmaker V.I. Pudovkin (1893–1953) argues that each shot requires an original aim to maintain value and integrity, while extended shots (long takes) were not effective to induce 'true drama' in a way that the juxtaposition of images is capable of achieving on screen. These debates continue to this day as filmmakers draw from these divergent theoretical models in terms of how these film grammar models can, or should, inform one's own creative aesthetic and shot choices. As students, it would be wise to experiment with these concepts as you make your initial films and develop your personal creativity.

EXERCISE FILM GRAMMAR

Construct and shoot a particular scene from a script you are writing, collaborated on or have commissioned, with a mind to creating a myriad of shots that can be juxtaposed together to create a particular emotional response you would like the audience to experience. Then try planning out a one-shot master take of the same scene and arrange all the elements within the frame that are required to be shown on the screen to create the story information your audience will need to conjure the emotional response you seek to project from what has been place in the frame.

What did you find worked and didn't work for you in the two divergent film theories in terms of potential ways and choices of shooting the same scene? Was the exercise helpful in demonstrating where your strengths might lie in terms of developing scene construction and working with objects, spaces, and characters to create particular imagery for, and within, the scene? Can the two competing theories, Bazin's and Metz's, be combined to produce imagery and, thus, a form of *combined languages*?

Today, film grammar continues to develop and progress; however, the core systems of cinematic language continue to be constantly sourced by filmmakers around the world. Some of these time-honoured grammatical film notions include:

- *Screen direction* – The 180° rule; characters' eyelines must be maintained to authenticate direction of gaze, otherwise actors will come across as looking in opposing areas of the frame; this applies to characters coming in and out of the frame margins as well.

- *Seek a structural connection* – Visual linkages between shots require corresponding elements.

- *Time manipulation* – The reality of time can be compressed by utilising a range of varying shot types and sizes.

- *Each shot equates to new information* – Each individual shot is required to convey some form of original knowledge to develop the narrative.

- *Shot matching* – Edit shots together that are equivalent in frame size and focal length.

- *Edit static shot to static shot and motion shot to motion shot* – Steer clear of editing a still shot to a moving shot, cut on the relative implicit action or inaction.

- *Pace* – Use of transitions and strategic edits to control the film's tempo.

- *Editing on action* – Masking invisible transitions involves cutting on a particular action or movement within the shot.

- *Silence* – The subtraction of sound within a scene can add an alternate depth and function to draw, or focus, the audience's attention.

Theses film grammar paradigms represent a century's worth of rules that have advanced film language to our current day. As with all sets of rules, breaching them has its place, as filmmakers will work to break with convention so as to experiment with how imagery can be created or manipulated to affect a specific scene result or progress a particular point of story information. Additionally, directors and editors will work to conceive their own language formulas and work to mine dynamic and innovative forms of film grammar.

THE EFFECTS ON FILM GRAMMAR

Metz argues that the film industry is not only institutional in nature, but embodies a form of 'mental machinery'; that being an acclimatised spectatorship, which has cultivated (and consumes) an 'internalised history' of cinema. In other words, repeated film consumption has led to audiences acquiring a 'learned' ability to understand cinematic language construction. A way to understand that this 'learned' cinema language is, in fact, tangible can be exemplified by those moments (whether a particular scene or sequence) when you are watching a film and you find yourself confused or perplexed by what you are seeing on the screen. If the *film grammar* is not able to be recognised, then the audience questions, either internally or verbally, why it is that what has just been viewed doesn't make 'sense'. In other words, film language constitutes a form of *visual perception*, which works and acts to link the individual still frames to create the illusion of movement. In turn, the viewer *suspends disbelief* and attributes and draws a cognitive meaning to the 'moving' images projected on to the screen. These cinematic images, as we know technologically, are captured and projected at a speed of 24 frames per second, which also includes the black spaces between each individual frame. Thus, it can be argued that *film grammar* functions to link those *invisible* spaces as a means to create, articulate, and impart a *knowledge* of the filmmaker's intentions and ideas. These intentions and ideas are created through *mise en scène* to convey, and strike, an emotional cord within the viewer and function to progress the film's particular theme. Cinematic language has been honed and constructed over the decades through experimentation and miscalculation. The intricacy and detail of visual information that is presented (and must be understood) on screen is a testament to the ability of human intellectual and emotional capacities. Consequently, it is crucial that you continue to study and labour to master film grammar and language skills in furtherance of creating your own individual dynamic cinematic voice so that what you offer up on the screen is grasped and of significance.

FURTHER READING

Bazin, André (1967) 'The evolution of the language of cinema', in André Bazin
    What is Cinema? Vol. 1. Berkeley, CA: University of California Press.
Bordwell, David (2012) *Pandora's Digital Box: Films, Files and the Future of
    Movies*, available at www.davidbordwell.net/books/pandora.php (accessed
    19 March 2013).
Metz, Christian (1990) *Film Language: A Semiotics of the Cinema*. Chicago, IL:
    University of Chicago Press.
Metz, Christian (1986) *The Imaginary Signifier: Psychoanalysis and the Cinema*.
    Bloomington, IN: Indiana University Press.
Spottiswoode, Raymond (1950) *A Grammar of the Film: An Analysis of Film
    Technique*. Berkeley, CA: University of California Press.

CHAPTER 2

Developing *mise en scène*

For the filmmaker, *mise en scène* is the grand key to generating a personalised cinematic signature. Composition, framing, lighting, colour, camera movement, time and space rhythm, placement of actors, the relationship of objects within the frame, special effects, and sound all contribute to materialising what can be termed *visual logic*. The construction of shots is boundless and it is here, through *mise en scène*, that the film practioner can infuse notions of theory (both cultural and film) to create further depth, or layers of meaning, within the spatial components of the frame. As such, the confluence of these elements (that is, the expression and structure of the space(s), objects, and characters within the frame) function to not only propel the storyline, but serve to act as metaphor to denote and convey a deeper narrative meaning, one that operates beyond what any particular dialogue can articulate or relate. The entirety of the frame's image constituents factor into its signification and, here, the notion of the cinematic author or auteur comes to the fore. Coined in the 1950s by French film critic and *Nouvelle Vague* director François Truffaut (and subsequently embraced by American film academic Andrew Sarris), the concept of *auteur theory* relates to his argument that the central acumen of creativity is formed by one person: the director. The caveat being that only those films exemplifying directorial authority over their creation, inclusive of the script, can be considered as genuine forms of artistic expression.

Hence, the director's *oeuvre*, or the overall body of work, can be collectively considered in support of one having an individual creative signature. Of interest to note is that the earliest examples of Hollywood filmmakers to be bestowed the accolade of demonstrating an auteurship by their oeuvre, as argued by the French critics and essayists writing for the influential *Cahiers du Cinéma* magazine in the 1950s, were directors Alfred Hitchcock, Howard Hawks, and Nicolas Ray. These filmmakers were deemed to have encompassed a 'personal cinematic vision' that transcended and circumvented the staid and formulaic big-budget studio pictures of the day. Following on into the 1960s, what has been termed 'The New Hollywood' brought forth a plethora of new independent and vibrant filmic voices. These include directors such as Mike Nichols (*The Graduate*, 1967), Arthur Penn (*Bonnie and Clyde*, 1967), Dennis Hopper (*Easy Rider*, 1969), Bob Rafelson (*Five Easy Pieces*, 1970), Robert Altman (*MASH*, 1970), Brian De Palma (*Carrie*, 1976), and Martin Scorsese (*Taxi Driver*, 1976), who embraced the concepts and notions of the French New Wave to carve out their non-conformist personalised film signatures, where the *mise en scène* connoted and denoted narratives of societal alienation and emotional isolation.

To consider, when we watch a film, our eye scrutinises not only the foregrounded performers, but scans the background of the frame for additional signs, objects, and their meanings. This two-pronged approach, by the eye, works to conjure within the audience an overall emotional resonance and the transference of story information. An example would be if you had four characters playing poker in a dimly lit, grungy warehouse strewn with rusting machinery and looming windows in contrast to four people playing poker in a warmly lit, suburban pale-coloured lounge with a comfy crackling fire, and snow gently wafting down outside the windows. Here, the divergent scenes radiate a contrasting emotional reading of the characters, one threatening, and the other not. Compared to *montage*, where significance is produced through continuous picture edits, *mise en scène* denotes a stylistic practice or method that concentrates on creating meaning through the elements within the scene; this 'meaning' percolates and surfaces through extended scene takes and the use of uninterrupted camera movement, such as utilising a tracking shot or a handheld shot. The camera in motion is one of the foremost dynamics of *mise en scène* as it allows the navigation and marking out of space. The moving camera can re-characterise space. It functions and operates at a level that allows space its totality (that is, the spectator experiences a *realistic* representation and sensation of space). As such, this *realism*, as argued by Bazin, lends itself to a closer interpretation of the actual world around us, something that cutting, arguably, is incapable of achieving. As an example, the authority of a particular character can be manipulated depending on the chosen angle and camera movement. Characters can be followed from behind by the camera or from the front where the camera tracks back with a leading sense of motion.

Master filmmakers who traverse space with the camera include Martin Scorsese, particularly *Raging Bull* (1980), and Stanley Kubrick, particularly *Full Metal Jacket* (1987); in these examples the camera winds and negotiates various environments, worming its way along with the trajectory of the characters. In *Full Metal Jacket*, for example, Kubrick's camera tracks forebodingly from behind, and in front of, a company of American soldiers who traverse a torched-out cityscape during the Vietnam War. This camera movement emulates the first half of the film where the young recruits are continually berated and denigrated in their barracks by a demanding and demeaning drill sergeant; here, the travelling frame follows in front of, and behind, the marauding officer as he navigates his charges meting out the 'wrath' of military authority. By the final sequences of the film, the soldiers are now the 'marauders' snaking in and out of the 'shell-shocked' and decimated buildings spewing forth their wrath on the Vietnam landscape and its inhabitants. By creating multifarious spaces for the camera to navigate, the viewer becomes ensnared or swept along into the murky and threatening world that the characters find themselves immersed in. Another example is the poignant pre-boxing match scene in Scorsese's *Raging Bull*, where a Steadicam shot follows the main character (a boxer), in one continuous shot, from prepping for the fight in his dressing room then following him out through the arena's meandering hallways out into the crowd tracking down a gangway and up into the boxing ring, where the camera next perches on to a crane that extends and hovers overhead. The aforementioned scenes are also strong examples of the extended take, where the director and editor permit no cuts to interrupt the flow of the performers or the observing audience. Moreover, the travelling camera and extended shot function to inject potency and weight to the characters' objectives and goals as the narrative unfolds.

Although the attention to, and experimentation with, *mise en scène* in studio films has been atypical, in reverse relation with independent and underground filmmaking practices, many current-day directors have developed identifiable or discerning visual techniques and methods. Here, two good examples are directors Mike Leigh (*Secrets & Lies*, 1996; *Naked*, 1993) and Michel Gondry (*Eternal Sunshine of the Spotless Mind,* 2004; *The Science of Sleep,* 2006). Leigh's *mise en scène* involves character types who are drawn from working-class backgrounds; here, the frame is also populated with the habitat and habits of those people including their topographical surroundings. Interpersonal relationships and dynamics are a particular construct in Leigh's visual realisations, and the imagery captures, and resonates with, the trials and tribulations of family and personal emotional trauma and upheaval. In Leigh's *oeuvre*, family anxieties create a palpable mood that permeates the frame. For Michel Gondry, notions of surrealism and Freudian dream and memory analysis are fused to create eccentric images to create the quirky worlds in which the characters inhabit. In particular, within many key scenes, Gondry places his characters within a frame that adopts a *forced perspective* (that is, the set design includes props and objects larger, or more exaggerated, than one would in 'real' life). This perspective highlights or suggests a 'child-like' state of mind (Figure 2.1).

Gondry's aesthetic, arguably, entails treating the filmmaking process as a 'toy' or 'dream' (that is, in terms of having 'child-like expectations' where the filmmaking process is experimented with by 'enjoying the whole process', much like a child who pushes the limits or range of a toy's capability) (Figure 2.2).

In terms of underground filmmakers who push 'boundaries' even further, transgressive filmmakers, such as New York City director Nick Zedd, challenge and subvert *mise en scène* conventions. For instance, in *Police State* (1984), Zedd creates a 'de-

FIGURE 2.1
Stephane (Gael Garcia Bernal) 'floats' past an imploding cityscape

FIGURE 2.2
Protagonist and lover escaping from the 'mainland' (reality)

populated' (16 mm) frame whereby minimalist (and found) settings, props and 'actors' are disarranged and placed antithetical to Hollywood traditions.

Historically, the central motivation to put emphasis on *mise en scène*, arguably, originates from a filmmaker's resistance to emulating the fundamentally indistinctive method of studio-type film production processes, which utilise imperceptible and fast editing techniques. As such, the foundation of an expressive and sound *mise en scène* signifies a method and process to creating a personal film signature. This notion is witnessed, for example, in Italian director Federico Fellini's (1920–93) mythological tales of morality and avariciousness that define his characters' worlds, in such films as *La Dolce Vita* (1960) and *8½* (1963), to the French New Wave-inspired cinema of Alain Resnais, whose modernist approach to filmmaking challenges conventions and classical forms of cinematic storytelling.

L'ANNÉE DERNIÈRE À MARIENBAD (*Last Year at Marienbad,* Alain Resnais, 1961) ## Practice/theory *mise en scène*

As a case study, let's consider Alain Resnais's avant-garde *L'Année dernière à Marienbad* (*Last Year at Marienbad*), which is an excellent example to illustrate the manipulation of time and character as constructed through *mise en scène*. To understand these notions within the film, for example, we witness the actors functioning in a deliberately artificial way, giving stilted performances in furtherance of countering notions of what is termed naturalism (that is, the concrete, observable, verifiable elements of which we live with on a day-to-day basis). The concept of naturalism denies the existence of anything mystical or spiritual and relies only on what actions, events, or objects that we can witness occurring in nature (e.g. the four seasons, snow, rain) or in a natural form (e.g. gravity, genetic codes). For Resnais, he cinematically explores the antithesis of this concept through a 'refusal of naturalism', whereby he sets the story within a synthetic and theatrical environment, including the two main characters, who have no formal names, only going by the monikers 'A' (the female) and 'X' (the male).

Thematic notions of time are also experimented with as there is no tangible chronology of events to discern along with the uncertainty of about the transpiring of time, itself, as it could be taking place in hours, a day, a month. *Last Year at Marienbad* has staked itself out as a good representative case study that scholars and feminist academics have studied and one where theoretical models of time and trauma are read as underpinning Resnais's film practice.

In considering Resnais's filmmaking, the French philosopher Gilles Deleuze (1925–95) is instructive. He wrote two seminal works on film as an artistic practice: *Cinema 1: The Movement-Image* and *Cinema 2: The Time-Image*. Deleuze divides our cinematic history into two periods of analysis: *Cinema 1* explores the pre-World War II period and *Cinema 2* considers the post-World War II era. In 'The Time Image', Deleuze theorises that the imagery in

C@SE STUDY

C@SE STUDY

Last Year at Marienbad embodies the *notion* of time as opposed to the typical 'movement image' of conformist cinema. Here, Resnais's images are 'expressive rather than representative' of time (that is, the images convey 'shocks of force' to communicate time rather than utilising imagery that 'carry' or 'imply' time in terms of structuring the film's narrative). Hence, the film challenges notions of cinematic time and memory by rejecting an understandable chain of narrative events (that is, Resnais 'refuses' traditional *film grammar* – which we considered earlier in this chapter – to construct his *personalised* cinema).

Deleuze argues that Resnais's film denotes time as a cinematic element to be considered in of itself and not as a way to gauge or calculate the movement or flow of the narrative. As a consequence, the utilisation of this time conceptualisation for *Last Year at Marienbad* can (and does) have repercussions for an unsuspecting audience as its *learned film language* is called into question and challenged. As such, the storyline comes across as distorted or dreamlike, full of repetition. This is the essence of Resnais's thematic, the exploration of our notions of what time is, what constitutes it, and how it is (and can be) applied to cinema. The infeasibility of affixing sense to what the story is all about derives from the instability of attaching or excavating the various characters' viewpoints or even who they are. Consequently, we are not clear who, in fact, is telling the story or who the narrator is. As far as decoding *Last Year at Marienbad*, it is a production entirely envisioned in terms of its form (i.e. shape and structure), as there is no referencing to an external society. In terms of the plot, it can be understood as a kind of puzzle or game, where gratification is not in figuring out how the pieces fit together, but through participating in the game itself. We also see the recurring use of mirror images and the theatre-play-within-a-film motif that populates the *mise en scène*, here indicating or reflecting the dual nature of time perception, memory, and 'reality' of character. Resnais was inspired by the 1950s *nouveau roman*, a term coined to identify 'the new way of a novel', which represented during that decade an alternate style of French writing – an approach that deviated from traditional literary storytelling modes, techniques, and characters. Resnais adopted this concept to conceive this surrealist cinematic fable for the nuclear age, an early 1960s trend that concentrated prevailing societal fear and anxiety over the nuclear bomb and the potential for the wholesale destruction of the globe. Here, the frozen ethereal appearance of the characters is instructive of this point.

In terms of feminist scholarship, Ginette Vincendeau (*The Companion to French Cinema*) relates that a closer look at Resnais's film text unearths the significance of the 'play within the film'; a production called 'Rosen' (which is a shortened version of Ibsen's *Rosmerholm*). It is a play about a man and woman who have conflicting views of what happened in the past and the past's connection with repressed sexuality and intonation of sexual violence/rape and the denial of the female character in the film that comes out of a these traumatic events; the play-within-the-film functioning, arguably, as a way of talking about trauma and, as such, instead of a cold intellectual game, the film can be read awash with emotion. Through the personal decision to select angles, position the camera, how objects and characters are placed, and how the scene is lit comprise the core elements that filmmaking demonstrates as no other particular art form can replicate. This collective of aesthetic choices demonstrates the prominence of cinema in fashioning reasoned and complete fictional worlds that the spectator is immersed into.

Much as in the cinema of Swedish director Ingmar Bergman (1918–2007) and Italian director Michelangelo Antonioni (1912–2007), during this same time period of the late 1950s and early 1960s, this collective western European *mise en scène* is resplendent with 'ghostly' figures that permeate the frame. Review these directors' films from this era and compare to Renais's work, such as Bergman's *The Seventh Seal* (1957), *The Virgin Spring* (1959); Antonioni's *L'avventura* (1960), *La note* (1961). In terms of expressionistic filmmaking, and the breaking with conventional film grammar codes, the cinema of Michelangelo Antonioni is instructive and relevant to consider within the context of pushing *mise en scène* boundaries. In *The Optical Unconscious*, Rosalind Krauss posits that Antonioni inverts the forefronting of characters in relation to a particular background. Here, the setting or milieu is foregrounded much in the way particular painters of that time period were working and experimenting with abstract expressionism, where the *image* of the human figure becomes indefinable in relation to its surroundings. As such, Antonioni considered his actors' physical positioning and actions as being but a single element within the frame; one that also encompasses a consideration of the physical elements and objects that surround the characters, the actual geographical position where they find themselves, and the camera's observation of their movements, dialogue, and interaction.

Spaces and the structural design of buildings infuse Antonioni's positioning, and personal dilemmas, of the film's protagonists. Here, traditional narrative plotting is not utilised to denote any of his films' thematic intentions; rather, the characters' inability to articulate their situations, or social alienation, is represented by the spaces they occupy. To grasp the director's use of foregrounded barren and isolated landscapes, and expressionist technique, and multifaceted *mise en scène*, it is best to watch Antonioni's *oeuvre*, including *Il Grido* (1957), *L'eclisse* (1962), *Red Desert* (1964), *Blow-Up* (1966), and *The Passenger* (1975). By studying these films, you can begin (and continue) to attain an understanding of how a director works to create a personal signature; a signature that is interested in expanding the breadth of cinematic language and one where developing and experimenting with *mise en scène* comes to the critical fore in terms of developing an individual form of artistic expression and creativity in filmmaking processes and practices.

Historically, *mise en scène* has engrossed a range of European and American film directors throughout the twentieth century. Emanating during the early post-World War I period in Germany, *expressionism* arose, crafting a cinema that depicts a terrifying, apprehensive, and murky visual terrain in films such as *The Cabinet of Dr Caligari* (Robert Wiene, 1920), *Nosferatu, eine Symphonie des Grauens* (F.W. Murnau, 1922), and Fritz Lang's *Dr Mabuse: The Gambler* (1922) and *M* (1924). These German directors construct a *mise en scène* that communicates their protagonists' chaotic psychological disposition through the disquieting settings and spaces they occupy or dwell in. As expressionist films proved a commercial success and an artistic triumph for European audiences, many of the directors who invoked these alarming and distressing cinematic portrayals were either brought over directly to Hollywood by the major studios or had their conceptualisations 'adopted' by American directors. These include such classics as *Dracula* (Tod Browning, 1931), *Frankenstein* (James Whale, 1931), *The Bride of Frankenstein* (James Whale, 1935), *Citizen Kane* (Orson Welles, 1941), and the 1940s era of *film noir*, from *The Maltese Falcon* (John Huston, 1941) and *Double Indemnity* (Billy Wilder, 1944), Alfred Hitchcock's *The Wrong Man* (1956) and *Psycho* (1960), through to Bernardo Bertolucci's *The Conformist* (1970) and Martin Scorsese's *Taxi Driver* (1976). These directors' cinematic constructions are influenced, to varying degrees, by the original German expressionistic films of the 1920s.

Many filmmakers, such as Alfred Hitchcock, also drew from the psychoanalytic theories as propagated by Sigmund Freud to construct characterisations and exploit narrative scenarios that explore unsettling psychologies and the torment of social alienation; these elements were then woven into the character construction. An interesting example is Hitchcock's *Spellbound* (1946), which draws from Freudian psychoanalysis to create a narrative that explores the relationship between psychiatrist and patient. Of note is that the surrealist painter/filmmaker Salvador Dalí (see *Un Chien Andalou*, Luis Buñuel, 1929) was hired to create the set design for the film's dream sequence; the *mise en scène* encapsulates the main character's disquieting neuroses.

EXERCISE **CHARACTER AND STORY CONSTRUCTION**

Research a number of academic cultural theorists who delve into the role of the psyche/body and society. Drawing from these models, construct a protagonist with a troubled or dark past that can act as metaphor to a particular societal concern, today, and devise a scenario where these 'disturbing' elements could play themselves out through the 'flawed' character you have created.

So, to re-cap our understanding of *mise en scène*, we can remember it in this way: it is simply *all* that is transpiring inside and throughout the cinematic frame. You, as the filmmaker, must be cognisant and take the responsibility to consciously populate your film frame. This requires your undivided attention and thorough creative thought to compositional detail and visual nuance. The concept of *mise en scène* is the path you must traverse to attain and develop your creative personal directorial signature; it creates the shots, and marks out and builds the place of the narrative to point up relevant knowledge in furtherance of relating the world of the storyline. We see that the greatest of cinema artists have strived (and not always to a successful degree) to develop their craft by expanding and experimenting with cinematic vocabulary through the invocation of their particular creative sensibilities and desire to re-imagine cinematic language.

You can cultivate your directorial craft by considering the following physical attributes and actionable points as you develop and write your screenplay or when working with another screenwriter's completed script:

1   *Locale or stage design*: Will you shoot on location or on a set? How will the surroundings, background, foreground, and props be incorporated into the action? What shot composition will you consider in conjunction with your setting (e.g. horizontal and vertical lines, doorways and windows, light and shade, reflective surfaces, object and character placement)? How does your chosen location (e.g. cityscape, forest, internal rooms) function as denotative and connotative signs in to convey narrative and ideological information? How will you make use of colour (or black and white)?

2   *Acting method*: Will you choose actors who have the ability to 'unfold' a character, with the audience as an onlooker 'overseeing' the protagonist's personal journey (that is, the story as focus and not the characters – Brechtian approach)? Or powerful and psychologically driven characterisations where the spectator 'experiences' the emotions of the character(s) (Stanislavsky's 'method' approach)? Or less exaggeration focusing on 'naturalness' and the use of 'silence' (Meisner's technique of 'relaxation' and 'behaving' in the moment with the ability to 'listen')? Through auditions, you will choose actors that have their own recognisable style or type that you will need to select in terms of their appropriateness to how you've constructed, or *see*, the script's character(s). In what way will you handle audience anticipation of how your actor will interpret his or her character? Will your performers bring 'truth' to their characterisations? Will you cast against type and physical audience expectation for your characters?

3   *Camera movement and position*: Will the camera track in or out, pan or tilt? Will it dolly along with the action? What shot-size composition is appropriate for the scene or sequence? What focal length and lens size will contribute to creating emotional information? What aspect ratio will you choose for your frame to frame your perspective: 16:9 (widescreen),

4:3 (television), 2.35:1 (anamorphic)? Will it be shot from a particular character's point of view or the audience as voyeur?

4 *Painting with light*: Hard, soft, obscured or chiaroscuro lighting? How do you envision the luminosity of the film, daylight or artificial? You can 'paint' with high-key lighting (generally placed at a 45° angle to your character); a fill lighting (placed in the region to the side of your character for highlighting areas not reached by the key light); low-key lighting to construct shadows and add depth and contrast to a set or location space; use of top or hair light; the use of filters, colour gels for effect, or diffusion materials to soften light.

5 *Costume and personality patterning*: How will your characters be distinct from each other and their surroundings? How will you address the fashion, physical habits, and grooming of your protagonist/antagonist? Will you invoke behaviour archetypes?

FURTHER READING

Deleuze, Gilles (2009) *Cinema I: The Movement Image*. London: Continuum.
Deleuze, Gilles (2005) *Cinema II: The Time Image*. London: Continuum.

CHAPTER 3

Directing the actor

As a student or indie filmmaker, it is imperative to invoke your directing skills during the casting session. An old adage proposes that 80 per cent of a director's talent is witnessed through their casting choices. This may be an arguable point, but it is crucial that you choose the actor(s) with greatest connection to the role(s) you are casting. As you will be working with an absolute minimal budget, it is of the essence to cast the strongest performers you can find for little or no money. You will find that many up-and-coming actors and those with just a few secondary production credits will be more than happy to extend themselves to be involved with your production. Another well to draw from, in terms of finding actors with a bit more experience, are those who have done only television commercials and are looking for an opportunity to gain a film credit and further experience. These actors are worth pursuing as they have on-set know-how in front of the camera. Other actors can found with theatre backgrounds and training. Bear in mind that theatrical acting and film acting are two very different forms. If you find a theatre actor who has little or no camera experience, it will be your job as filmmaker to keep that performer's craft in check, as theatrical training involves grander body gesture and the projection of voice due to the nature of stage performance to a live audience. It is best to study up on some of the great actor teachers, including Stanislavsky, Brecht, and Meisner. As such, you can learn and appreciate how an actor learns and hones his or her craft. This will be indispensable knowledge, and is required reading, if you as the filmmaker want to be able to relate to an actor and his or her processes. Of course, the key will be finding that right actor for your production at no upfront cost. Keep in mind that if you do find an experienced actor that you feel is right for the part, and he or she is interested in being in your film, that you can always negotiate a contract stipulating future payment for acting fees if, in fact, you are able to garner any sales or broadcast fees at some future date. This generally works well for young filmmakers without a budget.

Turning now to the audition process, you will need to have what are referred to as 'sides' (a particular scene from the script) for your actor to demonstrate his or her ability to grasp and project the character and scenario at hand. Actors are versed in receiving these 'sides' on the day of their audition as this affords you the chance to conduct a 'cold read' to test their craft and ability to conjure their character quickly. Or you may choose to send them the scene in advance to get a more polished or nuanced audition. Also helpful in advance is providing a character summary and plot outline. The more information actors have of character and plot dynamics for the casting session, the more chance for an enhanced audition performance will be had. These elements should also be available to give out as they arrive to the actual location of the auditions, preferably with an additional separate room or space where the actor can prepare. Another good idea is to have a few props available for the actor to use so that you can also get a sense of his or her ability to physically interact with various elements. Overall, you should plan on 20 to 30 minutes with each actor to get a solid grasp of his or her capabilities and personality. It is best not to hasten the casting session, if at all possible, so as to facilitate the auditionees having the opportunity to demonstrate their skills at a relaxed and calm pace for your evaluation. It is also best to determine, at this stage, what other skills your actor may particularly have. This is important if the script calls for specific qualities the character must have (for example, a driver's license, the ability to speak another language, certain athletic abilities).

Some directors also choose to have an 'improvisational' casting session where you will ask your actor to create dialogue and characterisation after you've discussed some of the story background. You will obviously rely on an actor's résumé and show-reel to invite him or her to the audition, but you must have something tangible for him or her to work with. Additionally, you need to record all your auditions so that you can judge how the actors come across through the camera and on to the screen. It is also recommended to designate a script reader to engage the actor during the scene audition. This will allow you to assess the reaction and interaction aptitude of the auditioning actors. You should direct your reader to give the actor the time and space so that you get a clear sense of his or her responsiveness and range of craft. The key is to determine competency and rapport between yourself and the actors. Keep your audition personnel to a minimum, that is, yourself as director, the producer (if applicable), the cinematographer, and a reader will suffice. Provide each auditionee an overview of the story's theme and how you envision the character at hand. Discuss briefly the emotional moment that the character finds himself or herself within the scene at hand and what his or her thoughts are of any other characters he or she is interacting with (these the reader will play). Don't over-complicate the session by giving too much detail or over-rationalising; keep it clear and succinct. Make clear that the actor has a couple of chances to do a read-through before you commit to video-recording his or her performance and ask if he or she has any questions. If not, you can ask him or her a question or two about what he or she thinks of the scene at hand or the character's motivation. Allow the actor to express potential other ways to approach the scene or character. When delivering his or her performance, it is imperative that you pay complete attention to the performance and not be distracted or distracting by scribbling down annotations while the camera is turning. This can be done after the audition is completed.

It is vital to note that at this point of the audition eliciting, a definitive performance is not essential. The strength and intensity of performance will develop as you work with the actors in discovering various methods to excavate their characters. Even small differentiations in approach can enrich the characterisations. Once the audition is completed, ensure that their schedules are clear or flexible for your proposed shooting dates. Additionally, let them know that they will have to sign a release form to appear in the film, which will stipulate their credit and title placement. Being a student or indie filmmaker, your budget will not include the ability to pay your actors, however it is good etiquette to be able to cover their transportation costs and provide meals during the shoot as well as a DVD copy upon completion of the film. Most aspiring actors will agree to these conditions, but make sure you are clear on these points at the outset so as to avoid any disappointment or miscommunication.

Upon the actor's departure from the audition, it is best now to jot down, or record on video, relevant notes for later reference. Briefly garner any additional comments from your crew, if applicable, and continue on with the next audition. By the end of the audition process, you will have an 'instinct' of who is right for what particular roles you are casting for. Be confident of where your beliefs take you but keep an open mind as you mull over your decision. In some cases, filmmakers may do what is known as a 'call-back', where two or more actors will be asked to return to do another read-through, this time likely with a different scene. This is not uncommon and will help you settle you thoughts as to whom the part should go to. Once you've made your decision, it is best to let your successful actor(s) know first that they have secured the role, then make courtesy calls or send personal emails to the rest. Without saying, keep your second choice actor(s) ready in your mind in case your first choice performers, for any reason, have to bow out of your production. Contingency plans will serve you well as preparedness for unseen circumstances are indicative of your professionalism, as production obstacles are more than a common occurrence within the world of filmmaking.

PRE-SHOOT REHEARSAL

Working with and prepping the actors before the shoot is as crucial as your production schedule and shooting strategy. Building in a rehearsal period affords the occasion to develop a solid rapport with your actors. Before working out your scene blocking (that is, how you position and move the characters within a particular shot or scene in relation to your camera position, movement and lighting), it is beneficial to concentrate on fully comprehending your character's background, which includes their strong and weak points and their needs and convictions as you identify them. Encourage any feedback from your actors who may have creative character ideas to contribute; the rehearsal period is the right time to test their veracity in furtherance of making a judgement as to their use or not. Head into your rehearsals having a solid grasp of what it is you want to execute, intensify, or observe functioning. Consider your script's backstory: discuss with your actors the relationship of the characters, their lives before the film begins, their desires, aims and goals, how they come to meet, and why they will travel or traverse the narrative simultaneously or in relation to each other. Draw from improvisation to supplement these notions, as they can be very constructive and valuable when you are shooting.

THE SHOOT

As a student or indie filmmaker, you are operating with a minimal budget, however you will generally have more time to produce your film than usual industry schedule dictates. Plan carefully what your study schedule and timetable allows for your shoot and use it effectively. On each shooting day, give your actors a run-through of the entire scene and action to be filmed. Provide an encouraging environment and work positively with your actors if they are not giving the performances you require. Your role on set with the actors is to: (1) *create* an inspiring space; (2) *explain* the emotional context of the scene to be filmed; and (3) *block* (or choreograph) the actors' movements in relation to the camera and lighting. Allow your actors, and their craft, to interpret the scene at hand after discussing the characters' motivation within the scene (that is, the aims and desires of the character at this particular moment in the storyline). If your actors struggle, take a few minutes to allow them to re-compose and shoot the scene again. Utilising action verbs are best for motivation. Never tell an actor 'how' to act; that is his or her job. Finding the right vocabulary and language to express the nuances of character with your actors is a skill you will develop over time. Before you shoot begins, write out a list of action-orientated verbs that you can draw from to stimulate your actor in relation to his or her character's disposition in the scene being filmed. By developing this practice, you will come to have a lexicon of vocabulary at your fingertips to spur on, and as incentive, for your actor's performance and finding the scene's emotional 'moment'.

CHAPTER 4

Cinematography
Painting with motion

Derived from the Greek *kinema* (movement) and *graphien* (to record), cinematography simply denotes *lighting in movement*. It is also correspondingly known as 'writing' or 'painting' with light. In addition to the selection of light fixtures and their placement, the cinematographer (or director of photography – DOP) creates the 'appearance' or 'look' of the film through frame space, perspective, camera motion, texture, and tone. As film production students, at post-graduate and graduate level, you will have already attained an understanding of core *coverage* terminology and practice of basic three-point lighting (the use of key, back, and fill lights to create high/low contrast; for instance, a silhouette shot or to demarcate background, object, character separation). At this stage of your cinematic development and early career, it is now important to be particularly conscious (as director and/or cinematographer) of creating an independent dynamic visual look to suit (and develop) your *personal signature*. Your shot planning must take into account a range of cinematographic practices and histories that should (will) inform how you translate the written script to pictorial life on the screen. Hence, a cognisance of visual language principles pertaining to: rhythmic patterns and perspective line; proportionality and relationship of objects within the frame; field of vision or use of depth (between characters, objects, and horizon); compositional sizing and balance; and shade and shadow to demarcate space and mood are required to be cinematographically addressed for each scene.

In furtherance of these aesthetic aims, lighting is crucial to cinematography and to the creating of 'sensation', or emotional/psychological resonance, within the frame. The use of light serves to create and attach a range of meanings to your film's storyline (for example, to heighten atmosphere, affect perception, create character and set tension). Objects and spaces can also have awareness brought to them by the direction of diverse light sources arranged in a myriad of creative ways. In addition to a attaining a solid grasp of traditional lighting modes of studio-produced films or those emanating from particular European or international cinematographers, experimentation, here, is useful to pursue when planning your own scenes. Nothing is cast in concrete and you may adapt and combine a range of shooting and staging techniques to visually craft and light your scenes.

DEEP-FOCUS SHOOTING

A good technique to get a grasp of, particularly when shooting on a low budget, is the ability to shoot your scenes in master-shot takes, which involves a full playing out of the continuous actions as written in the script; in other words, a prolonged shot of a scene's action that doesn't resort to shooting close-ups or changing camera position. This can be accomplished through the concept of filming in *deep focus*. Deep-focus cinematography is a practice utilised to keep a series of shot-planes (foreground, mid-ground, and background) all simultaneously in focus and allows for a range of concurrent actions to unfold within the frame. Deep-focus cinematography affords you the potential to develop a unique style in contrast to that of creating action through the intercutting of discrete shots. Conjoining elongated takes with deep-focus *mise en scène* removes the need for editing, as you will choreograph character placement, movement and interaction within a set frame. As mentioned in Chapter 1, theorist André Bazin has argued and championed that this form of shooting closest represents the 'real' world around us and, as such, 'realism' reflects a 'greater' form of cinematic practice through its non-use of intercut shots. We will consider Bazin further in Chapter 10. What films have you studied in which you recall the use of deep focus? Most of you have doubtlessly viewed Orson Welles's *Citizen Kane* (1941) as a prime example of deep-focus cinematography. What other films can you think of that employ this technique?

EXERCISE DEEP FOCUS

Construct and shoot a one-minute scene whereby a series of actions take place across the three focal planes as listed above. What challenges did you observe when planning and shooting the scene? Were you successful in maintaining focus? What would you do different on future shooting projects when employing the use of deep focus?

MASTERING LIGHT

It is of the essence to create a lighting plan before you shoot. You need to assess the source of light for each scene, then resolve the following queries:

1   Where does the original light emanate from?

2   What light fixture or element is literally viewed in the scene, whether interior or exterior (for example, candle, cigarette lighter, lamp post, moon)?

3   Where is the light located (for example, streetlight angling in through a window, a crackling fireplace)?

4   How strong is the light (vivid or faint)?

5   Is the light warm or cool (daylight or fluorescent)?

6   Is there a light action (for example, room light turning on, the lighting of a gas barbeque)?

7   Is there a particular lighting characteristic (flat, harsh, varied)?

8   What style are you trying to create (for example, high-key, low-key, colour, black and white, tonal greys)?

As you are aware from your studies and workshops, a diverse range of lighting styles are available for you to emulate and experiment with. To review, the style you choose for the shoot is done in collaboration with the director (and the production designer if your project entails as such). You will need to review the script and make notations on the story's atmosphere, where it is set, and the characterisations of the protagonist and antagonist. The three core lighting styles are 'high-key', 'low-key', and 'graduated tonality'. High-key scenes employ soft lighting techniques that have minimal or no shadowing, often shot with filters, scrims, or gauze to diffuse the light. Hence, the scenes are vivid and clear on screen, with a minimal differentiation between lighter and darker aspects within the frame. In contrast, low-key shooting involves severe shadows, muted colours, richer blacks, and brighter whites. In other words, the ratio of dark and light is much more defined and stark (as you have studied, for example, in the film noir period). The third concept is the notion of *graduated tonality*, which is obtained through soft light sources to generate subtle shadows, generally from a solo fixture or natural source (for example, daylight reflected from a bounce board). Graduated tonality can also be created in the set construction or through the characters' outfits and face make-up, with certain areas of the set or parts of the actor crafted to be deliberately obscure or opaque. Your overall aim is to *paint with light* in order to produce texture and depth, to delineate shape and form, to obscure or illuminate; in other words, to create atmosphere to signpost the emotional and thematic world of your storyline and characters. Experiment with your lighting by positioning fixtures to the sides and back of your characters or objects in the frame. To heighten scene depth and create tone, test out a range of colour gels and flags to accentuate, for example, facial form and

SPICE chart

		Result to obtain	Method to accomplish
Source	Where is light being generated from?		
Position	Location/placement of light source		
Intensity	High, mid, low, warm, cold		
Colour	Or black and white		
Effect	Particular light casting (for example, reflecting water, striking match, candlelight)		
Quality	Hard or soft, opaque, muted		
Style	High-key, low-key, master painter/influence		

shape. As a helpful guide to remembering what lighting elements need to be addressed for your cinematographic practice, the above industry-standard 'SPICE chart' is a useful resource to keep handy when you are at the stage of breaking down the shooting script. It would be wise for you to keep a copy of this chart with you when you are planning your shoot or breaking your shooting script. You may also add other questions that may be relevant for your production or those that address your own personal lighting methodology.

INFLUENCE OF REMBRANDT AND VERMEER

Two seventeenth-century Dutch painters, Rembrandt and Vermeer, have been recognised as the foremost masters who began to prolifically work with natural light and shadow. Vermeer, for instance, analysed how rooms and faces were affected by natural sources of light and where shadows fell (Figure 4.1). His subjects were usually placed by windows, which provided the impetus to render the effects of daylight that streamed in over the subject and spilt into the room at hand. Light in Rembrandt's paintings, too, is sourced from a particular window, entrance, or fireplace, and exemplifies the direction of light from its source (Figure 4.2).

An excellent example of cinematography that was shot using only original source light (of which special low-light NASA shooting lenses were adapted to fit 35 mm cameras) is Stanley Kubrick's *Barry Lyndon* (1975) (Figures 4.3 and 4.4).

FIGURE 4.1
'The Glass of Wine' 1661/62 (courtesy of SMB Gallery, Berlin)

FIGURE 4.2
'The Holy Family' 1645 (courtesy of the Hermitage Museum, St Petersburg)

FIGURE 4.3
Cinematographer John Alcott utilises only the actual candlelight (and fast lenses) to illuminate *Barry Lyndon*'s interior scenes

FIGURE 4.4
Alcott's use of natural light, which harks back to Vermeer and Rembrandt

View this film to see how British cinematographer John Alcott interpreted the storyline's eighteenth-century texture and atmosphere by utilising original source light. Kubrick's film is a rare, one-of-a-kind big-budget production that relies on no artificial interior light fixtures for its on-location shots, an almost unheard-of reality within the industry at studio level, and is a prime example of *chiaroscuro* technique (that is, the high contrast between dark and light).

Here, the painterly works of Rembrandt and Vermeer have influenced motion picture cinematographers around the world who emulate and impact this lighting technique to create atmosphere within the frame. Emanating with the German expressionistic film period, in the early part of the twentieth century, the concept of chiaroscuro was further developed and honed during the American *film noir* period of the 1940s and 1950s and continues on to today, where high-contrast lighting is utilised in studio, independent, and experimental productions. An interesting note is that many current-day films adopt this aesthetic and are referred to as *neo-noir*, in that they draw from a combination of noir iconography, conventions, and chiaroscuro lighting technique, itself. For example, Robert Rodriguez's *Sin City* (2005), Ridley Scott's *Blade Runner* (1982), and Bernardo Bertolucci's *The Conformist* (1970) all are cinematographically drawn from the roots of Rembrandt and Vermeer's original use of light and shade source technique as a means to invoke a textured and layered high-contrast *mise en scène*; this is known as 'low-key' lighting. Can you think of other films that utilise the relationship between dark and light, shadow and shade, to construct particular scenes or sequences? Will you adopt this technique for your current film projects in furtherance of creating a dynamic atmosphere? Working with high-contrast, low-key lighting set-ups will (should) produce, in the audience, a resonant emotional reaction that 'takes hold' of the viewer to create a depth of drama, one that is created without the use of exaggerated action or an exploding soundtrack; here, subtlety is the key to create atmosphere and style, and to intimate movement within the frame.

In further considering Rembrandt's striving for natural light authenticity (in terms of how it illuminates the body), he noticed that when light fell at a particular angle on one side of subject's face, it created a small upside-down 'triangle' of light underneath the eye on the opposite side of the person's face. Rembrandt adapted this observation to his painting style and it has been largely adopted by directors of photography around the world. This technique has become known, in cinematography circles, as the 'Rembrandt Triangle' and is utilised extensively in film lighting set-ups. It is a time-honoured technique that serves to create depth and nuance to a character's face (in conjunction, shadow can also be created underneath the nose to create further dimension). I would now suggest you look for this triangle of light in all your favourite films. You'll be amazed (and now conscious) that it is present in many scenes and sequences in the majority of films produced since the 1920s, particularly studio-shot productions.

EXERCISE **LIGHTING**

Sign out a light kit, find an actor, then in a blacked-out room or studio work out how the lights can be arranged to produce the 'Rembrandt Triangle'. What angle did the light fixture have to be placed to facilitate the triangle on the face? By understanding how light can add atmosphere to a character, you have now mastered one of the main tenants of professional cinematographic practice.

FRITZ LANG AND THE COEN BROTHERS
From expressionism to (neo) noir

From his German-produced expressionist films, *Dr Mabuse: The Gambler* (1922), *Metropolis* (1926) (Figure 4.5), and *M* (1931) (Figure 4.6), through to his American-produced noir films, *You Only Live Once* (1938), *The Woman in the Window* (1944), and *The Big Heat* (1953), director Fritz Lang embodies an excellent example of a filmmaker transitioning from the early roots of European expressionism through to American noir.

FIGURE 4.5
The 'soul' of Maria is passed to her 'corporate' counterpart in *Metropolis*

FIGURE 4.6
Hans Beckert (Peter Lorre – top left) is 'trapped' by three figures

C@SE STUDY

His practice offers a perception of society that conspires against, engulfs, and ensnares individuals. Lang creates a *mise en scène* and lighting design that creates a world that distorts and schemes, pitting the populace either against each other or directed at a particular individual, luring them further and further into an inescapable entangling void. In Lang's work, lighting fosters a visual style that delineates a series of overwrought characteristics in order to sustain an atmosphere of anxiety (for example, an unstable frame, disturbed composition, the dominance of shade and shadow, a high-contrast relationship between dark and light, skewed camera angles, a sharp depth of field). These elements are not utilised as flashy exaggerations but shape the essence or core of his films' various narratives. In Lang's noir world, violence, menace, and immorality invoke a nightmarish form of existence, a bad dream that the main character never wakes from. The protagonist is an ill-fated person traversing a crime-ridden netherworld that deceives and betrays. This irrevocable disloyalty is generally embodied by a *femme fatale* character, a woman who the protagonist has become infatuated with. Here, the high-contrast, low-key lighting stratagem of expressionism, the foreboding sets, and tight or skewed camera angles create an entrapped claustrophobic atmosphere for Lang's protagonists to navigate the storyline. In terms of style, his films express a (male) volatile psyche, ambiguous ethics, and inherent mistrust of those around him. The *mise en scène* in his films portrays unstable and eerie surroundings, with characters with little self-control or harmony in their lives. Shadow, silhouette, and reflective surfaces imply a twisted psyche or a secondary alter ego that haunts or overwhelms the story's protagonist. Furthermore, the femme fatale, or 'perilous woman', in Lang's noir films can be read as representing internalised sexual anxiety or dread as psychologically experienced by the male protagonist; here, the main character struggles to suppress and restrain these fears.

This original classic period of film noir has been argued to have ended in 1958 with the release of Orson Welles's *Touch of Evil* (Figures 4.7 and 4.8), which embodies all the remnants of chiaroscuro lighting, radical angles, and a shadowy underworld of corrupt characters.

Why is Welles's film considered as the end-point of the film noir period? In *The Maltese Touch of Evil: Film Noir and Potential Criticism* (2011), Shannon Clute and Richard L. Edwards argue that Welles constructed the film in a completely self-conscious manner (that is, by the period of the mid-1950s filmmakers were over-drawing from noir techniques as a means in of themselves). During this time period, film noir had been written about and praised by the French publication *Cahiers du Cinéma*, as promoted by their writers and film critics (including François Truffaut and Jean-Luc Godard). This self-reflexive approach to (re)produce noir technique and style during

FIGURE 4.7
Deep-focus shot of Detective Hank Quinlan (Orson Welles) 'calling' in a
murder before it happens!

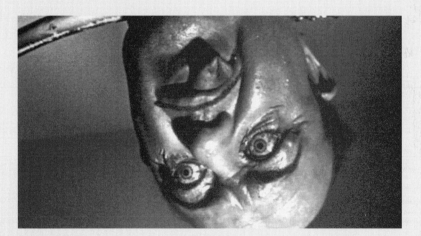

FIGURE 4.8
Quinlan's 'handiwork' after the call to police headquarters

C@SE STUDY

the mid to late 1950s, Clute and Edwards argue, negates the cinematic ability
to 'tell a straight noir tale' and that '[Welles'] film is so self-conscious that
it is no more a narrative than it is a demonstration of how to create a film
narrative'.

Today, the influence of expressionism and noir continue to infuse cinematic
storytelling techniques. As mentioned earlier, these stylistic atmospherics
have been adopted by a myriad of directors and cinematographers, and the

films are described as neo-noir. Hence, spates of current-day neo-noir films adopt brusque editing, an off-balanced frame, and distinct travelling shots or camera movement to craft style. A strong example of these practices can be seen in films such as Roman Polanski's *Chinatown* (1974), David Lynch's *Lost Highway* (1997), and Joel and Ethan Coen's *The Man Who Wasn't There* (2001), which was shot by British cinematographer Roger Deakins. Deakins's work on *The Man Who Wasn't There* is quite poignant, as the film utilises black and white cinematography (it was originally shot on colour negative with black and white inter-positive negatives struck for the film's release) complete with high-contrast, low-key lighting as a dynamic homage of noir-style films. The scenes in the film were shot with an extended depth of field, which allows for all elements within the frame to be in complete focus (see our discussion of deep focus earlier in this section). Additionally, the camera position is generally set at the same horizontal as that of a particular character's eyeline. In the film, light streams in through window blinds or is uniformly segmented in curvilinear patterns (Figure 4.9) when striking a surface such as a floor or walls, with faces in half-shadow or obscured (Figure 4.10).

Here, Deakins has drawn from the early German expressionist chiaroscuro techniques, as further developed during the American film noir period, to reflect the cold and alienated world of the protagonist. Overall, the film's *mise en scène* has been argued to represent the thematic of post-World War II American imperialism, paranoiac science fiction anxieties, and Heisenberg's 'uncertainty principle', all of which have been atmospherically heightened

C@SE STUDY

FIGURE 4.9
Interrogation scene in the Coen brothers' *The Man Who Wasn't There* (2001)

C@SE STUDY

FIGURE 4.10
Billy Bob Thornton as small-town barber Ed Crane

through the well-planned and detailed use of chiaroscuro lighting to paint a dynamic portrait of the 1940s.

VISUAL CONFIGURATION

In order to create a *symmetry of perception* within the *mise en scène* (that is, to visually contribute to imparting a character's emotional disposition and/or to suggest a particular thematic thread), you can work with film frame's *depth of space* and the use of compositional lines, whether vertical, horizontal, or angled. By planning a particular scene's use of space to arrange characters, settings, and objects (props), you can accord the narrative by drawing from, and invoking, a series of linear perspective techniques that will add subtext resonance and information that the audience will glean from the visual field of the frame. We discussed Alain Resnais's *Last Day at Marienbad* earlier, which we can now consider as a prime example of the use of perspective. A key exterior scene in the film is set in sprawling ornate palatial gardens, where the director and cinematographer have created a deliberate series of perspective and horizon lines (Figures 4.11 and 4.12).

Here, you can follow the outer vertical lines of the garden walkway through to what's referred as the *vanishing point* at the top centre of the each frame. In Figure 4.12, we can also see the horizontal line of the intersecting marble balcony balustrade, which can be thematically read, for example, as representing the 'division' between the two characters. Notice, too, the use of angles, particularly the triangular-shaped shrubbery and the relationship of the characters to each other;

FIGURE 4.11
Filmed in Munich, the surreal palatial gardens cast no shadows

FIGURE 4.12
Cinemascope framing enhances perspective, space, and distance

they are distanced but are 'connected' by straight diagonal lines. Additionally, the compositional lines between the characters in Figure 4.11 are also constructed in triangulation form to each. These *triangle configurations* are a mainstay of visual structure and they function, at optical level, to create a dynamic moving frame. This occurs due to the reflexes of the human eye, which naturally 'moves' across or 'scans' these perspective lines in an effort to glean information or affix meaning. The use of compositional lines in graphic art can be traced back to the classical Greek period, where artisans developed these linear tenets to create equilibrium and unanimity between subject and object in their artwork. These triangles within the frame are a common occurrence in most films. Another compositional code to consider and utilise for your *mise en scène* is the use of *sinuous* lines. These 'meandering' lines appear as a form of 'snaking river', which are visualised on screen in the shape of a 'backward S' (Ƨ) (Figure 4.13) and are influenced and drawn from naturally occurring lines in nature (Figure 4.14).

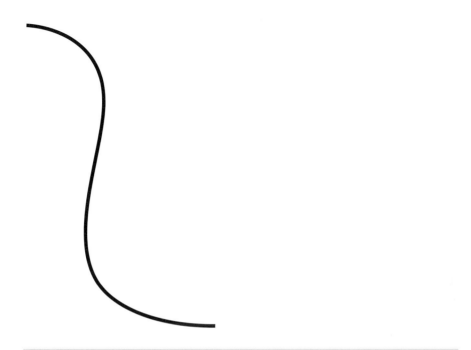

FIGURE 4.13
The 'reverse S' (Ƨ) perspective line utilised by many filmmakers to denote character division and narrative obstacles

FIGURE 4.14
The 'reverse S' (Ƨ) snaking river in John Boorman's *Deliverance* (1972)

This linear perspective provides a visual symmetry or flow between characters and their environment within the *mise en scène*. If you pay close attention, you will see that in many films the placements of characters within the frame are positioned in relation to each other along these sinuous lines. These naturally occurring perspective lines are sought after by filmmakers and cinematographers to set their scenes in so as to metaphorically represent the division either between characters or the internal 'division' within a particular character's psyche (for example, the protagonist may have a troubled mind due to a particular guilt they harbour or perhaps the protagonist is in a conflicted emotional state due to witnessing a traumatic event). A strong illustration of this can be found in Francis Ford Coppola's Vietnam War film *Apocalypse Now* (1979) (Figures 4.15 and 4.16), where the main protagonist, a military assassin, has to 'travel' up a precarious Vietnamese river in furtherance of his mission to terminate another military leader.

Here, the cinematographic use of the river represents not only the main character's physical struggle to traverse the obstacle-filled jungle terrain to realise his goal, but

FIGURE 4.15
In *Apocalypse Now*, a Navy Patrol boat 'snakes' through the 'heart of darkness'

FIGURE 4.16
Captain Willard (Martin Sheen) emerges 'snake-like' to execute his mission

as a visual signifier demarcating his conflicted emotional 'inner' struggle (Figure 4.16) to come to terms with his own morality and the murderous actions he is ordered to undertake. In a frame from the film (Figure 4.17), we can see that the placement of the actors follows a reversed sinuous S-pattern (Ƨ).

EXERCISE **PERSPECTIVE**

As an experiment, get a blank sheet of paper and pen. Starting at the frame's centre point, represented by the character wearing the bandana (in mid-frame background), draw a line to the right to the character wearing the beret, following along to the character with the jungle leaf affixed to his head, then curve over to Dennis Hopper in the red bandana, and then along to the point of the Martin Sheen character in the foreground.

FIGURE 4.17
Dennis Hopper (frame left) explains the byzantine mind of Col. Kurtz (Marlon Brando) to Willard

The line-image on your piece of paper should appear in the shape of a reverse S (Ƨ); this positioning of characters within the frame is the line your natural eye-reflex travels to determine information about the image it is processing. This perspective concept is a useful creative tool for you to be cognisant of when you are breaking down your script at the storyboard stage. Practise arranging and framing your characters in this manner during the rehearsal stage, where you can position your actors along a sinuous axis then test-record the scene to see how dialogue and action can be affected by invoking an inverse-S pattern. Remember to keep a lookout for naturally occurring sinuous, horizontal, and vertical lines within the environment you are shooting (for example, beach or coastal frontages, street curves/pathways, shrubby and tree/forest edges, fencing, walls, whether they are exteriors or interiors). Carol Reed's *The Third Man* (1949) exemplifies the precise use of cinematographically framed natural surroundings (Figure 4.18) to accentuate perspective lines; here, note the dual tree lines, road lines, pathway line (left frame), building line (right frame), the tree-stump cart, the suitcase – all draw your eye to the vanishing point in the centre of the frame. Additionally, these perspective lines are intersected with the horizontal lines of tree shadows and the vertical (height-line) stance of the two characters and the tree trunks.

It is good practice getting into the rhythm of searching for linearity during the pre-production location scout stage to incorporate and heighten perspective in your film work.

In terms of interior sinuous 'S' lines to plan as part of your *mise en scène*, a staircase or curved hand-rail are effective set-pieces to utilise. Alfred Hitchcock was a master at the use of stairwells, staircases, and balustrades to create tension, and indicated a 'divided' or alienated mind or emotional disposition in films such as *Suspicion* (1941) (Figure 4.19) and *Vertigo* (1958) (Figure 4.20). Steven Jacobs writes in *The Wrong House: The Architecture of Alfred Hitchcock* (2007, p 200), 'Staircases pervade in Hitchcock's oeuvre. Conveying ordeal and moral change, they punctuate crucial narrative elements'.

Another exemplary film on this account is Robert Siodmak's *Spiral Staircase* (1945), a thriller about a serial killer who targets a disabled woman in an old mansion. Here, the key action and thematic play themselves out, literally, on a gothic staircase (Figure 4.21). The sinuous line of the staircase comes to represent the terror and anxiety that the disabled character experiences. Here, we have a creative combination of noir chiaroscuro lighting technique and the dynamic use of the reverse-S pattern to create an atmosphere of tension and dread.

FIGURE 4.18
Holly Martins (Joseph Cotton) awaits Amanda Schmidt (Alida Valli) after the death of her lover Harry Lime (Orson Welles)

FIGURE 4.19
Cary Grant bringing a glass of 'milk' to an ailing Joan Fontaine in *Suspicion*

FIGURE 4.20
Hitchcock's chapel-tower stairwell, in *Vertigo*, triggers the protagonist's acrophobia

FIGURE 4.21
The 'reverse S' (Ƨ) of the stairwell suggests the characters' anxiety

COMPOSITION – THE RULE OF THIRDS AND FRAMING THE FRAME

In filmmaking, the cinematographic frame can be divided into three separate composite elements, running both horizontal and vertical, to create nine sub-sections in furtherance of demarcating subject and object positions to form the *mise en scène* (Figure 4.22). This concept of compositional frame breakdown is drawn from photography's *rule-of-thirds* rule, which suggests a way to line up a character or characters at the junctures that the horizontal and vertical lines intersect.

This visual methodology is utilised to place a character, for instance, at the point of one-third of the way inside the frame area. This can be accomplished by using the right- or left-hand side of the frame or else from the bottom or top of the frame. As such, the aim is not to position the subject in the middle section, as this will be less gratifying to the viewer's eye reflex, which naturally gravitates towards the centre of the frame. By composing your shot adopting the rule of thirds, you will be able to create a more dynamic image that satisfies the spectator to a greater degree due to the eye's perception of a more coherent balance as it scans film's rectangle frame. It is of interest to note that the rectangle functions as the core aspect ratio that the film (and broadcast) industry utilises to record and screen images, whether it's the 35 mm film frame of cinema (and still photography) (Figure 4.23) or the 16:9 format of HD widescreen television sets.

You will have to make a concerted effort to plan and compose your shots so that characters are placed within the frame in an asymmetrical or off-centre position.

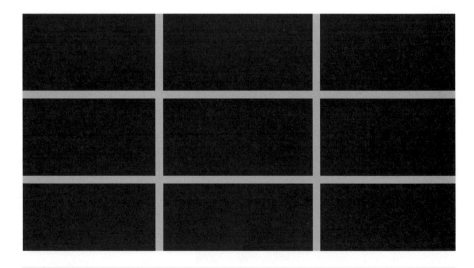

FIGURE 4.22
The cinematic frame in thirds – the rule of thirds

An example of the notion of thirds can be seen in Martin Scorsese's *Shutter Island* (2010) (Figure 4.24).

Here we see the two main characters sub-divided on either side of the screen. Their goal to 'solve' the mystery on Shutter Island is 'divided' (thwarted) by the policeman (an alternative 'authority'). This will be of significance later into the narrative where a later revealed character twist is revealed. As such, Scorsese and his cinematographer (Robert Richardson) utilise the rule of thirds as a form of foreshadow in terms of how really 'divided' the two main characters are by the film's end. In Figure 4.25, you can also see the rule of thirds at work without the imposed dividing lines; here, Leonardo DiCaprio's character is mid-height between the other two and a visual symmetry unfolds as the eye scans from the tallest character to the shortest.

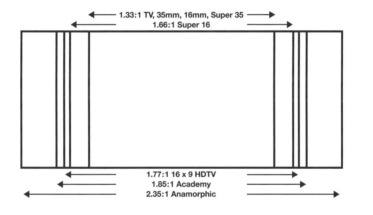

FIGURE 4.23
Film and television industry-standard frame aspect ratios

FIGURE 4.24
2.35:1 screen ratio divided into thirds; the two main characters bi-sected by a third

FIGURE 4.25
US Marshall Teddy Daniels (main protagonist Leonardo DiCaprio) framed as the 'centre' of attention

Another important compositional form to consider is the use of *frame within a frame*. This perspective device entails the utilisation of an alternative aspect ratio set within the main frame. Examples of this would include, for instance, the use of windows, doorways, building arches, sewers, rooms within a house, and mirrors; in other words, the setting off of a particular framing device, as an element of the *mise en scène*, to further suggest a character's emotional disposition and/or as a thematic device. A classic example of frame-within-a-frame composition technique occurs at the end of John Ford's western *The Searchers* (1956). Here, a point-of-view shot inside a darkened home depicts the protagonist (John Wayne) exiting through the doorway (back to the camera) to a fully lit sprawling exterior desert landscape. The signification of the door frame within the film frame alludes to the character's incapacity to find a stable home environment and he knows that his destiny is to wander, unable to put down the roots of traditional home life. In this final scene of the film, the interior home and his silhouette are in darkness until he 'passes' through the doorway (Figure 4.26) out into the 'harsh' (light) existence of whence he came. In other words, this framing thematic device suggests a number of eternal anxieties that can haunt an individual and society; these notions are foreshadowed and posed in the film's opening title song, where the lyrics include the following questions: '*What makes a man to wander? What makes a man to roam? . . . And turn his back on home?*'

In conclusion, your protagonist's emotional and physical challenges and obstacles (or 'divisions') can be visually signalled in the *mise en scène* through the creative and vigilant planning and utilisation of darkness and shadow, linear perspective, and composition to create a dynamic engaging narrative, one that compels an audience to travel along with, and experience, the emotional journey of your characters and the themes you want to visually explore and express.

FIGURE 4.26
Ethan Edwards (John Wayne) shuns 'home' in the film's final scene

EXERCISE **VIEWING**

Watch some of your favourite films again and make a note of these cinemato-graphic concepts; you'll be amazed at their frequency. If you make a conscious effort to invoke and experiment with these visual models, your film will gain a depth of resonance that will serve your creative aspirations well.

Here is a helpful list of cinematographic terms that you need to fully grasp, compre-hend, and consciously implement for your *mise en scène* as you progress in your filmmaking practice:

Angle and level of framing: The positioning and height of the camera frame so as to psychologically represent or indicate: the relationship of the characters to each other; the relationship of character(s) to object(s); the relationship of character(s) to the setting; the relationship of object(s) to the setting (for example, low, high angle, skewed). Hence, a compositional technique to create a visual field in furtherance of portraying a character's psychological perception.

Aspect ratio (Figure 4.23): The relation of an image's vertical edge to its horizontal edge and offered in varying rectangular quotients. The most common frame ratios utilised for the film industry include: 1.66:1, 1.85:1, and 2.35:1. HD widescreen television monitors are 16:9 ratio to accommodate both the rectangular film frame and the widescreen digital frame. These varied shooting ratios are available to afford filmmakers and cinematographers greater creative compositional latitude to impact the narrative's thematic through the psycho-logical and tangible space of the frame.

Colour: Employ to demarcate character and emotion and for aesthetic design.

Contrast: The proportion of light to dark within the frame. 'High contrast' denotes a large variance from the darker elements to the lighter elements within the scene and 'low contrast' exists when the ratio between light and dark is minimal. Natural scene lighting is considered low contrast (that is, 'high-key' lighting, particularly used for drama, action, and comedy) while high-contrast ('low-key') lighting is generally utilised for suspense, neo-noir, or horror films to create a stark, foreboding *mise en scène*.

Deep focus: Where important scene components are spread over a broad area of the film plane. These varied plane depths, and the various elements that populate the frame, remain in focus.

Shallow focus: In direct opposition to deep focus, where the depth of field is limited, generally with only a single plane within the frame or a particular scene element maintained in focus. This technique is used, for instance, to indicate a character's narrow emotional field or, perhaps, an unconscious state of mind or ignorance of the setting he or she finds himself or herself in or occupies.

Depth of field: The actual range or distance of the represented space within the frame that is in full focus. Here, the greater distance of focus required in the scene, the greater amount of light required to maintain sharp focus. Wide-angle lenses are useful for this purpose (as opposed to long or zoomed-in telephoto lenses to maximise focal depth). To create a more specific area or element of the frame that you want to draw your audience to, then you would adopt a shallow depth of field where the other frame elements are soft or out of focus. Remember not to misperceive depth of field with focus, as the later demarcates how sharp a subject or object is and the former is the distance available within the film plane to maintain such focus.

Exposure: The camera aperture control that regulates the amount of light coming through the lens. Exposure can be experimented with in order to darken or lighten an image, hence the terms 'over-exposed' and 'under-exposed'.

Rack focus: Manual operation of the camera's focus ring to alternate or shift the focus from one subject or object to another within a single shot; this produces the effect of guiding the viewer's awareness as a means to connect or associate an element on one focal plane to another.

Scale: The placement of a character or object, within the frame, relative to its surroundings (for example, a protagonist lost in the desert might be filmed as a small figure on a distant horizon subsumed by the vastness of an empty and never-ending landscape). Counter to that, placing your actor in close foreground can promote an intimate connection to a character's disposition. Hence, scale is an important compositional device in furtherance of crafting the inner emotional nature, mood, and temperament of your character.

In terms of a film that exemplifies an overall engaged cinematographic practice, David Lean's *Lawrence of Arabia* (1962) is instructive (Figures 4.27 and 4.28). In these two frames from the film, we witness a confluence of the ideas discussed in this chapter: the use of scale; varying focal lengths; depth of field, focus, linear perspective, the rule-of-thirds; the Rembrandt light triangle; and the use of aspect ratio.

FIGURE 4.27
T.E. Lawrence (Peter O'Toole) contemplates 'not minding' the pain

FIGURE 4.28
Appearing on the horizon, a mysterious figure emerges from the desert heat

EXERCISE *MISE EN SCÈNE*

Script out a 30-second scene, in the genre of your choice, and design a lighting and perspective plan; one that incorporates at least three cinematographic practices as discussed in this chapter.

FURTHER READING

Jacobs, Steven (2007) *Wrong House: The Architecture of Alfred Hitchcock.* Rotterdam: 010 Publishers.

CHAPTER 5

Sound underpinning image

CONTEXTUALISING THE SONIC EXPERIENCE

Physiologically, the eye registers and remembers objects and elements even after only viewing them for a first or second time. The ear, however, is considerably challenged in terms of identifying and distinguishing our surroundings. To the greatest degree, it is through the eye that we navigate our surroundings and determine the veracity and safety of our environment as a means of survival and societal interaction. If we had only the benefit of hearing, and no use of sight, the world would elude us to a vast extent. Scientifically, however, it has been argued that the ear has the ability to extricate a greater range of subtle sensory distinctions than even sight allows for. Hence, the eye's ability to discriminate colour, hue, tint, tonality, and light's intensity pales against the far greater capacity of the ear's range to experience noise, sound, and frequency vibration. What is of interest here is that the divide between the recognition of where a sound emanates and the discernment of a sound is substantial. As such, an individual can discern a range of diverse sounds before figuring out where actually a sound emanates from or who/what is responsible for its origin. Contrary to this, it takes greater effort for the eye to comprehend what it is witnessing, but once acknowledged, it is far easier to identify and recollect. It is interesting to note that the sounds that we experience provide us with no definitive interpretation on objects or environments under our observation; however, our visual field and all the elements it contains are able to be concretely identified. In terms of cinema, however, the use and manipulation of sound's secondary sensory role in understanding or verifying our surroundings can be used as an effective device to create tension and emotion within a film. For example, in a horror film scene, we may hear on a film soundtrack the sound of a squeaking noise in a dark room creating an air of eerie suspense, a terrified face squints from a dark corner to an open window, suddenly a light turns on and the audience breathes a sigh of relief when it 'sees' that the noise was emanating from a loose window shutter flailing in the breeze. Sound creates depth within the frame and gives it its 'realness'.

However, it is to your advantage to be creative with your sound design and experiment with the aural elements. A particularly poignant 'sound' that can be effectively utilised is silence. Here, silence has the ability to suggest closeness or distance (for example, you might have your protagonist driving a car but with all exterior sounds removed and, perhaps, just the light sound of their breathing). This type of silence technique can suggest the closed or cut-off world of a character or one where he or she is in a moment of introspection about a personal problem he or she is experiencing. The point, here, is that you must take into conscious consideration your aural elements and how you can be creative with them to enhance and drive the narrative and provide dimension to construct depth of character. Cinematically, the use of silence is wide-ranging and dramatic and has its own 'voice' to project action, information, and signals. Silence allows a character's face to draw the audience further into his or her world, one which may be in turmoil, in torment, in pain, or, conversely, a moment of relief, sublimeness, or self-pity. Soundless gestures and fleeting looks can emphasise threat, anxiety, warmth, and compassion as part of the *mise en scène*, to amplify a scene's power and veracity. The use of silent moments or beats within a film will not impede narrative momentum, but, rather, can bring a deeper, richer, and a more inventive palate to create mood, atmosphere, and drama. The use of sound as an integral part of the cinematic process confronts our prejudiced understanding that filmmaking is but an image-centred form of expression, void of any other sensory elements. What other films can you think of that utilise silence as a narrative or character device? Will this technique be of relevance to utilise in your current film project? Work to be imaginative and innovative when planning and constructing sound effects, music, and narration to create dynamic associations between the audio and visual elements.

SOUND AND IMAGE RELATIONSHIP

The rationale for the use of sound in filmmaking practice is to create an aural milieu and ambient representation of the acoustic world that surrounds us. From talking to nature to the whirring of engines to the gentle ticking of a time bomb to the silence of the midday desert sun, the film image's interdependency and relationship with sound is vital to the projection of a scene's meaning. Hence, an audience's understanding of a character's emotional disposition and their perspective and perceptions of the world around them is guided by the signification of sound elements, whether they are inherent and emanate from a particular object or are manufactured in post-production to effect, enhance, or imply a particular feeling or sensation from the action or image on the screen. With the timbre of voice and the invocation of nature's or an object's sound, you can create a dynamic particular *physiognomy* (that is, you can project the 'character' or 'face' of your protagonist, a scene, or sequence to affect a desired resonant 'colour' for the spectator to experience). The use of 'sound colour' in the filmmaking process is similar to how a painter will apply varying layers of paint to create an overall blended colour effect as a means to convey an emotion or message within the frame. When you are planning a scene's *mise en scène*, be conscious of how you can utilise sound or layers of sound to compliment and enrich the visual elements. During the pre-production phase, ask yourself these questions on how the script will be best realised:

- Is it stronger to include original sound(s) only?
- What additional sounds or sound elements are required for each scene?
- Are there any particular points or moments in the narrative where silence is required?
- When and where should music be utilised?
- What type of emotion does each scene require to fulfil the narrative's potential?
- What nexus of sound and picture is required to construct a unified emotional resonance and balance between the aural and the optical in each scene, sequence and the overall film?

At this stage, it is worth viewing a number of films that utilise sound, specifically as signifier of theme and as a crucial element of plot.

EXERCISE **AURAL TRACK**

Watch Francis Ford Coppola's *The Conversation* (1974) (Figure 5.1), Brian De Palma's *Blowout* (1981) (Figure 5.2), and Wim Wenders's *Wings of Desire* (1987) (Figure 5.3). Take note of two key scenes from each film and discuss how the use of sound contributes to an understanding of the protagonist's emotional disposition, *mise en scène*, and each story's thematic. Here, consider the notion of 'eavesdropping' in the films and how it relates to theoretical notions of voyeurism that you have studied. Write out in the form of a chart and compare how all three directors and the sound designers have constructed and interwoven the aural and optical elements of the scenes you have chosen. You should now be applying this form of sound analysis, consideration, and planning when you are developing a script, both at the story development stage and at the pre-production phase of your film production.

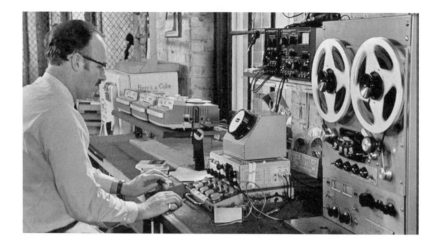

FIGURE 5.1
Harry Caul (Gene Hackman) as a tormented government snoop

FIGURE 5.2
High-angle shot of an overwhelmed Jack Terri (John Travolta) engulfed by his strewn recording tapes and equipment

THE 'IMAGE' OF SOUND: VOYEURISM AND EAVESDROPPING

It is useful, at this point, to consider an example of how cultural theory underpins film practice. As you have surely studied and come to understand notions surrounding the 'gaze' and 'voyeurism', these terms are relevant in the analysis of the relationship between spectatorship and audience. Here, we can discuss how these ideas correlate not only as a consideration of the visual 'lure' of a film, but also as to its aural lure. If the eye is correlated with voyeurism, then it can be argued that the ear correlates with eavesdropping, both indicating a type of 'clandestine' or 'distanced' desire to anonymously experience a particular unfolding event or action. In film terms, eavesdropping can also be read as a form of 'privacy incursion'. This is clearly demonstrated in the films listed above, *The Conversation* and *Blowout*, where the narrative is constructed so that the viewer is 'spying' or 'listening in' on the protagonist who's character, themselves, are eavesdropping. In *The Conversation*, for instance, the eavesdropping perpetrated by the main character becomes the central motif (the role of technology) that the director explores (that is, questions of society's implication and complicity in sanctioning the technological processes that the security forces and government utilise to monitor and control its own population). Here, the film's protagonist descends into paranoia and a deepening crisis of consciousness in direct relation to his rising guilt about his complicity as an operative working for the state's security apparatus, one that surveils and conspires against its own citizens. As the narrative progresses, we witness the main character's 'soul' destruction. It is also of interest to note that the protagonist's surname, (Harry) Caul, is a pun on sound (aural communication) and is indicative of the emotional obstacles he must navigate. That is, metaphorically, Harry has no one he can trust to 'call' for help or assistance to extricate him from the quandary at hand and, additionally, Harry is not the type of individual who is approachable *to* call, as he is selfish and incapable of seeing beyond his own desires and job obsession.

Another eavesdropping technique is the use of 'off-screen' sound to effectively create or enhance tension and suggest hazard. Hence, a dramatic moment or the impending appearance of a character can be foreshadowed before that particular action occurs or a figure appears on screen. Of course, horror, suspense, and war films use sound effects and design to instil atmosphere and intensify conflict. Here, the audience is overhearing information that the character(s) in a particular scene or sequence are unaware of or are yet to experience. Hitchcock uses this technique to great advantage, as he presents visual and aural information to the audience that the film's characters were unaware of in order to create a 'foreboding intimacy' to heighten suspense; in other words, for example, being privy to a terrible secret or the impending demise of character. Hence, we can argue that this aural technique acts as a form of 'presaged eavesdropping'. In Wim Wenders's *Wings of Desire*, the protagonist, an angel unseen by others around him (Figure 5.3), travels around Berlin 'listening' in to the musings of the city's citizens; the film is a strong example of how the director invokes sound/voice as a crucial element of the *mise en scène* to propel the narrative and develop character.

Eavesdropping sound techniques are used in many narrative scenarios and locales. View these further examples of where the thematic and dynamic of regulated and institutionalised aural monitoring is an integral element of plot and character development: church confessionals (*True Confessions*, Ulu Grosbard, 1981); patient/ psychiatric therapist (*One Flew Over the Cuckoo's Nest*, Miloš Forman, 1975); addiction group meetings (*Fight Club*, David Fincher, 1999). When you're developing

FIGURE 5.3
Bruno Ganz's angel surveys Berlin high atop the city

your story ideas, be mindful of how sound can be utilised for your production. Take conscious note of how your film can be more dynamic and stimulating by creating an acoustic experience that contributes either directly to the plot or as a suggestive or subliminal signifier of character or place. What knowledge can be created through the application of sound design and eavesdropping technique for you film? What can it disclose or expose? Can sound contribute to developing your individual *personal signature* as a filmmaker?

SOUND FORM

A film's audio track is comprised and constructed from two core constituents, diegetic and non-diegetic sound. These aural concepts are drawn from the Greek word *diegesis* ('narration'). Non-diegetic sound refers to aural elements emanating from a source or sources not viewable in the film, nor directly connected to a scene's action. This would include: atmospheric music, manufactured sound effects to enhance intensity, and voice-over narration, where the sound's origin is independent of the narrative's physical events on screen. Conversely, diegetic sound refers to acoustics directly attributable to viewable material sources or to sources tacitly linked to particular actions within the narrative. This includes: music emanating from instruments within the scene, objects that produce a naturally associated sound or noise, and character voices; hence, any sound that directly correlates to a physical object or subject, whether inside or outside the frame. Diegetic and non-diegetic sound work together to create *ambience* within a scene, which creates or contributes to a particular setting or location's mood and feeling. Ambience represents a psychological rendering of the frame, its contribution to generating an emotional resonance that the audience experiences.

An excellent use of diegetic and non-diegetic sound is exemplified in William Friedkin's *The Exorcist* (1973) (Figure 5.4). Watch the film and pay special attention to the soundtrack, which interweaves a dynamic range of manufactured effects, speech, and classical and experimental music to create an acute presence of eeriness, suspense, and pathos. How did the auditory experience sit with you? Do the analogue sound design and techniques employed still hold resonance in comparison to today's advanced digital effects age? Is there room to create original sound effects from found objects to add to your own film's sound mix? What films can you identify whose soundtrack deeply resonates with you and how is this accomplished? Acoustically, *The Exorcist* is constructed to echo and counterpoint the severe interchanges between high-key and low-key lighting that occur from one scene to the next.

The soundtrack ambience of *The Exorcist* works to authenticate the narrative and compose the *mise en scène*. Editorially, ambience assists the picture-cutting and image juxtaposition through its sonic consistency across each individual shot that comprises a scene or sequence. Equally, if the ambient atmosphere suddenly deviates at a particular picture edit, the spectator instinctively understands that a scene change has occurred. *The Exorcist* also well exemplifies the concept of *sound motif*, which constitutes either a single effect or mixture of auditory effects related to theme, place, time, circumstance, or individual within the narrative. For example, the character of the young priest's self-doubt and guilt is heightened by the voice of his deceased mother (as verbalised through the demonic incantations

FIGURE 5.4
Father Merrin (Max von Sydow) arrives to administer holy rites

of the possessed young girl) whom, earlier in the film, he had committed to an institution against her will. The film's sound mix also encompasses what are known as sound bridges, whereby a sound effect or voice effect crosses from one scene to the next as a linking device. By working with sound motifs and bridges, you can subconsciously intensify a spectator's emotional response to a character, setting, or event, as well as indicate narrative links and character connections. Again, it is imperative that as a creative filmmaker you consider how sound can be used for your production at the planning and pre-production stages. It is good practice to invoke a creative sound design for your film. Re-watch some of your favourite films and think how effects, music, and voice can act as motifs throughout the narrative, then think seriously what it is aurally that you want to project to audience. Creating sound motifs and ambience will assist you to forge and structure storyline and theme.

FURTHER READING

Philip Brophy (2000) *Cinesonic: Cinema and the Sound of Music*. Sydney: AFTRS Publishing.

CHAPTER 6

Editing
Temporality and structure

As we discussed in the Introduction, concepts of editing practice moved from the static collection of moving image actions and occurrences to an ability to manufacture and re-arrange dramatised events with regards to place, topography, and time, as first witnessed in D.W. Griffith's *The Birth of a Nation* (1915) (Figure 6.1). As such, Griffith's silent film has demarcated the filmic concept of narrative and editorial construction since that time.

FIGURE 6.1
'The South vs. the North', Griffith's American Civil War monumental battle sequence

Hence, the editing was such a cinematic progression, for that time period, that it prompted the first ever written film theory text to be published, and this material, today, is considered a seminal essay work. Hugo Munsterberg, considered the 'father of applied psychology', who taught at Harvard University, published *The Photoplay: A Psychological Study* in 1916, a year after the release of *The Birth of a Nation*. Munsterberg had been overwhelmed at how the cinematic manipulation of time and space had occurred under Griffith's direction. It is important to re-state that up to that point in the mid-teens in the early part of the twentieth century, the use of cross-cutting, flashback, and other techniques Griffith developed had not been witnessed by the public in the cinemas of the time.

Munsterberg classified and theorised on several self-proclaimed terms and techniques that he applies to *The Birth of a Nation*. Although we take these editing language terms and their meanings for granted, today, back in 1916 these concepts were the first theorisations to be published on editorial film construction and they produced an immediate impact on directors and film studios in how they perceived, conceived, and re-aligned their cinematic storytelling practices: (1) 'cross-cutting', where two different storylines, both occurring in the same time frame but at differing locales, are constructed interchangeably before merging into a single storyline; (2) 'close-up', the positioning of the camera lens in tight proximity to a character or object to emphasise the spectators' gaze; (3) 'continuity editing', the construction of 'natural' movement or action across scenes, movement which is not interruptive and functions seamlessly and imperceptibly to an audience; (4) 'flashback', a technique of memory imitation, a sequence depicting an incident or experience that a character, in a reflective mode, recollects from a prior time; and (5) 'special effects', the exploitation of the film frame (for example, double exposure, frame masking) or the use of light to craft a character's fantasy or demonstrate their dreams. Munsterberg separated out these (what he termed) 'devices' through his understanding and application of psychology to the viewing of the film. Today, these 'devices' form the key film editing and structure practices used in our digital post-production platforms and software. In his treatise, Munsterberg expresses the virtues and merits of film editing, where 'the photoplay tells us the human story by overcoming the forms of the outer world ... space, time, and causality ... by adjusting the events to the forms of the inner world ... attention, memory, imagination, and emotion' (Munsterberg, 1992: 356).

RHYTHM, TIME, AND PACING

When you're planning your editing strategy, it would be wise to review a range of prolific directors' films and pay close attention to how scenes and sequences have been constructed and paced out. An excellent example of a director who has carefully considered the editing process in his practice is Russian filmmaker Andrei Tarkovsky (1932–86), whose films explore thematic notions of time and memory –

for example, *Ivan's Childhood* (1962) (Figures 6.2a and 6.2b) and *Stalker* (1979) (Figure 6.3).

Tarkovsky argues that the most influential dynamic of the cinematic image is rhythm, which conveys the progression of time within each shot. He works with what he terms 'time pressure' in order to determine the rhythm of the editing. In other words, it is not the duration of the edited elements, but the inherent pressure of

FIGURE 6.2a
'Externalising' perspective lines; current reality as lived experience

FIGURE 6.2b
'Internalising' perspective lines; fractured reality sustained by memory

FIGURE 6.3
A menacing and disturbing landscape in *Stalker*

time that courses through them. Here, time becomes the underpinning value and is the primary foundational component of a completed film. Of course, other directors have varying views on cinematic construction, but here Tarkovsky is instructive as a filmmaker who forges a distinct personal signature (or 'individuality') through the editing process and its creative significance. It is of interesting note that Tarkovsky had a certain contempt for the *montage* editing practices as developed by Eisenstein and Vertov, as he felt that the rapid intercutting of imagery inhibits a spectator's accessibility to his or her own personal emotional reaction to what he or she is viewing. In other words, the rapidity of cuts and the juxtaposed images that comprise montage editing distracted or disengaged the viewer from his or her own reactions to the a particular scene or sequence. Instead, as he suggests, the audience's emotional response is influenced by the image construction itself.

Thus, we can consider rhythm in editing to that of the beat in music, where the imagery and sound are woven in lyrical tandem. Time in film is controlled by pace, which can be conveyed by: (1) the length or duration of a shot within a scene; (2) the manner in which a sequence of shots are cut and organised; and (3) a particular shot's motion or action within the frame. By working with rhythm and pace, you will be creating what is known as the film's *arc*, which denotes the association of the story's core actions or events throughout the film. The arc of film represents how scenes and sequences are structured or arranged throughout. We will explore later, in further detail, the two main editing methodologies as theorised by Bazin and Eisenstein (that is, 'realism' versus 'montage'). Try experimenting with realist and montage methods in your production. What works best for your script and narrative flow? It is also quite common, today, to combine these editing methods. Is there a way to formulate your own personal editing signature to express time through the tempo of your film?

TWO-DIMENSIONAL EDITING

Other than if you are making an abstract or avant-garde production, generally, films are editorially constructed so that the narrative is continuous, flows seamlessly, and is visually logical. This practice is known as continuity editing and is the classical form that most filmmakers learn and adopt. However, in recent times, directors and editors have begun to develop and advance a much more vibrant and experimental approach to structuring and linking imagery and still be able to have an accessible and palatable narrative for an audience to experience, but one that breaches time-honoured editorial conventions of continuity. This concept is called *two-dimensional editing* and involves the following cutting techniques that you may consider utilising for your film edit.

(1) The use of movement in a shot to draw the viewer's eye to a focused position within the frame then edit to the next shot with a similar movement in the same frame area.

(2) The use of contrast, where the eye is enticed by anomalies in the image such as a distant lighthouse on a dark coastal horizon or an investigative flashlight – both used to good effect as a thematic device in Roman Polanski's *Death and the Maiden* (1994) (Figure 6.4). In terms of colour, contrast can also be utilised to broach conventional technique (for example, a black and white object positioned within a colour frame or, conversely, a colour image set within a black and white frame). A good illustration of this concept is demonstrated in Steven Spielberg's *Schindler's List* (1993), where the entire film is in black and white other than one sequence that depicts a little girl traversing, oblivious to her surroundings, through a terrifying military intervention (Figure 6.5). This 'distraction' is utilised for editorial

FIGURE 6.4
Sigourney Weaver confronts her suspected torturer (Ben Kingsley)

FIGURE 6.5
Spielberg's only use of a muted red 'colour' (paint effect, applied by CGI process, rendering the child's coat red) in *Schindler's List* draws the eye

effect to create an emotional response and to affect narrative flow, as the eye discerns movement and colour quicker than the brain can form a particular message or meaning from the visual field the spectator is presented with. It is the calm figure (here, the girl) within the panic that draws the eye. Thus, 'visual diversion', as editorial technique, is most effective to cover or disguise the breaking of generic editing continuity methods in furtherance of allowing you to experiment with, and forge, image construction and structure. Additionally, sound can and should be used on this account as a means to foster a two-dimensional editing aesthetics.

(3) The insertion of white flash frames between actions in a scene to bridge a range of differing shots; here, the eye and mind 'forgive' what would otherwise be considered a jump cut in conventional editing, thus taking the viewer out of the 'reality' of the moment. A good example of flash frame use in editing occurs in Oliver Stone's *JFK* (1991), where varying shots and actions are 'connected' by flash frames usually by use of light or sun hitting a characters glasses. Scorsese is well known for technique (through his excellent editor, Thelma Schoonmaker) in the film *Raging Bull* (1980) where there is dynamic intercutting resultant from the 'popping' of flashbulbs from news photography cameras (Figure 6.6).

(4) Finally, the use of a swish or whip-pan where the camera, or the effect thereof, suddenly and jarringly pans, blurring the image; this results in an almost invisible or seamless cut to another shot, which finishes the swish-pan movement to complete edit. Scorsese also uses this technique in *Raging Bull* in a number of the boxing fight scenes. Watch the film and carefully note how scenes are constructed, editorially, by Thelma Schoonmaker. What other techniques does she utilise to create two-dimensional editing and create dynamic and highly charged sequences? Does she invoke sound edits, and to what degree?

FIGURE 6.6
Jake LaMotta (Robert De Niro) knocks out his opponent

EDITING CHECKLIST

When you plan and progress through the editing stage, address the following questions as you formulate and refine your scenes and sequences from the rough cut to fine cut to picture lock:

1   *Does your attention drift?* A potential warning that particular segments require re-working.

2   *At what point does the film engage you?* Is it the first scene or a scene or two further in? Is the beginning too lax? Is it a delayed start? Be clear on when you feel the film really commences and begin from that point.

3   *Gauge rhythm and pace. Divide your film into a series of sections and demarcate temporal flow and 'time pressure'.* Determine what timing corrections are necessary in each section; this will help determine where crucial shots and moments can be tweaked to work out and form the *shape* of the film. When working towards your first rough cut, it should be approximately no more than a third of the film's envisioned completion time. Shot, scene, and sequence length is a subjective and personal course of action during the edit stage. As such, you must focus to get in tune with your materials and allow them to take on a 'natural flow', without forcing square pegs into round holes. Don't force preconceptions as to how a scene should be constructed or, perhaps, as you might have initially planned for. Be adaptive and flexible and allow the film to take on a life of its own, for it is by following your intuitive creative process that you will develop your personal signature as a filmmaker.

FURTHER READING

Anderson, Joseph (1996) *The Reality of Illusion: An Ecological Approach to the Cognitive Film Theory*. Carbondale, IL: Southern Illinois University Press.

Bordwell, David (2012) *Film Art: An Introduction*. 10th edition. New York: Addison-Wesley.

Bottomore, Stephen (1990) 'Shots in the Dark', in Thomas Elsaesser (ed.), *Space, Frame, Narrative*. London: BFI.

Eisenstein, Sergei (1970) *Film Form and Film Sense*. London: Faber and Faber.

Jónsson, A. Gunnlauguir and Óttarsson Á. Thorkell (2006) *Through the Mirror: Reflections on the films of Andrei Tarkovsky*. Newcastle: Cambridge Scholars Press.

Murch, Walter (1992) *In the Blink of an Eye*. Sydney: Australian Film Television and Radio School.

Reisz, Karel and Gavin Millar (2009) *The Technique of Film Editing*. London: Focal Press.

Part II

Film theory in practice

CHAPTER 7

Reading the screen

HOW FILM CONSTRUCTS MEANING – SEMIOTICS

Does the filmmaker act on instinct or does the filmmaker consciously consider a set of rules and organising principles when constructing a shot, scene, or film? It may be the case that some framing devices, camera moves, lighting scenarios, or performances might seem obvious, natural, or inevitable. One might carefully consider the colour coding of a particular character through choice of costume, setting, or lighting. One might also consider the place and pace of the edit. All of this contributes to the careful construction of meaning within the text. The filmmaker wishes that the film convey meaning to the audience. Therefore, the filmmaker is concerned with making films mean something. However, even beyond this, film carries much more meaning.

So far, you have developed your knowledge of specific filmmaking techniques that will allow you to improve your skills as a practitioner. These skills will help you to become competent and confident in the shoot. Putting these skills into practice is essential to the process. All too often, students pay far too little attention to *mise en scène*, cinematography, sound, and performance. Instead, evident in many student films is story and dialogue. Part I is designed to help you to progress from this. Part II is designed to give you the theoretical underpinning that will enable you to make intelligent, critically aware films. This section will outline some of the main schools of thought and disciplines that have shaped film studies and film theory. Film studies courses quite often split film studies into film theory and film practice, and it is the student's responsibility to bridge the two. This section will help you to apply theory to practice. Each strand of critical thought will be followed by a suggested shooting task. These are intended to be short exercises that will ask you to demonstrate your knowledge through film.

HOW FILMS *MEAN*

In order that the audience understands the meaning conveyed, film must contain a system of recognisable codes. This is where we enter the terrain of semiotics, the study of codes and their meaning. Many of the codes in film come from the extra-filmic world. For example, most audiences will presumably understand when a film is set in the past. The film may not indicate through titles that the film is set in the past; there are simply enough codes within the text to illustrate this. An opening long shot may reveal a town or city. Here, the architecture instantly reveals that the town is not contemporary. Likewise, the fashion of the characters would equally reveal the historic time period, as might the language of the characters. In other words, all of these signs (architecture, fashion, language) take on specific meanings. In the context of the film, the meaning is that the film is set in the past. In the most basic sense, this is semiology. We come to understand the world through the interpretation of signs. Understanding these 'real-world' signs is necessary to our ability to make sense of the world around us. Yet, again, in the context of the film, there are other codes in operation that are the product of film and filmmaking itself. These cinematic codes enable us to understand what is taking place within the film. In a sense, this is what film theoreticians often call the language of cinema. So, we can begin to think about these two types of codes that give film meaning: codes of the everyday world and filmic codes.

Before we move into a discussion of how the filmmaker engages with semiotics, we will trace the development of semiotics from linguistics to cinema. While the latter might seem more pertinent to the film practitioner, both are inherently interlinked and speak to each other. While the initial detour into linguistics, anthropology, and cultural studies might seem unnecessary, it is interesting to trace the semiotic field from one discipline into another. In fact, in the early years of film, Russian formalist filmmakers were already considering the notion of the sign. Many of their theories and filmmaking practices were directly shaped by semiotics. It is, perhaps, no surprise that these films, filmmakers, and theorists are still held in high esteem among practitioners and academics alike. Thus, this first section will outline briefly the influential strands of thought that have shaped the development of film scholarship, while the remaining sections will focus on the resulting film scholarship itself, and reframe this scholarship to speak to you, the film practitioner.

SEMIOTICS AND LANGUAGE

While the study of semiotics can be founded in the work of Aristotle and Hippocrates, the modern study of signs emerged at the turn of the twentieth century through two key theorists, Charles Sanders Peirce (1931–58) and Ferdinand de Saussure (1916). Peirce coined the term 'semiotics' for the study of systems of signs. He formulated a theory of signs based on a triadic model: that of the sign, the object, and the interpreter. What was particularly unique about this theory was the inclusion of the interpreter. In other words, signification only takes place through the interpreter. The sign does not convey the object until the interpreter reads it as such. As an example, let's take the birth of a baby. Commonly, the colours blue and pink are associated with boys and girls respectively. So, a girl's bedroom might be painted pink and a boy's blue. Yet, the connection between pink and the female is arbitrary. This association only 'makes sense' to those who are already familiar with the code. An outsider would not initially understand the codification of sexes in this way, but would eventually learn it. In this sense, we can see that the interpreter is at the heart of the sign's meaning. And the sign means something beyond itself. Pink denotes the colour but when a baby is clothed in pink it connotes femininity. This has relevance for film too. Film is governed by whole myriad of codes and signs that only take on meaning through the interpreter. For example, we are probably all familiar with the now clichéd line uttered by a secondary character of the slasher film, 'I'll be right back'. Ordinarily, this sentence seems straightforward in its meaning. However, in the context of the slasher film, the sentence takes on a different meaning. Those who understand the codification of the slasher genre will inevitably interpret this as the impending death of the speaker. Again, we can see that meaning is only produced through interpretation.

While Peirce placed semiotics within the field of science, de Saussure saw what he termed 'semiology' as an element of linguistics. The terms are often used interchangeably, although the more common term now used is 'semiotics' (Stam *et al.*, 1992: 4). De Saussure was to become a key figure in the development of structuralism (the study of structures, in this case of language) and a number of other fields, including psychoanalysis, and film theory. De Saussure proposed a dyadic model of signified and signifier, the signifier being the actual form of the sign (for example, a picture of a cigarette with a cross through it), and the signified being the meaning or idea produced from the signified (for example, 'you cannot smoke here'). The system at work is referred to as the sign. The sign only functions when both signified and signifier are apparent. For example, a signifier must mean something to someone in order to become a sign. In the case of the 'no smoking' sign, if a person has no experience of signs, the cross will not take on negative connotations, and the meaning will be lost.

In his examination of the structure of language, de Saussure (1916) differentiated between *langue* (language) and *parole* (speech). *Langue* is the pre-existing system of rules and organising principles used within a particular group or society. *Langue* contains the various elements that can be coordinated to produce meaning through *parole*. *Parole*, therefore, is the individual use of aspects of *langue* at a particular point to convey a concept or idea. This has proven particularly significant in the study of film. If we think of cinema as the *langue* (language), we can then understand films as individual expressions of the cinematic *langue*. In other words, films draw from a pre-existing set of conventions and rules in order to convey specific meaning. For example, how does the filmmaker know to cut from one shot to the next at a particular point? How does a filmmaker know how to cut between locations without confusing the temporal and spatial organisation of the text? The filmmaker knows this because he or she understands how to 'speak/write' in the film language. The audience understands it because they know how to 'listen to/read' film language.

EXERCISE **FILMMAKING THROUGH CODES**

Make a one-minute film (with no dialogue) that produces meaning through a series of codes. These codes can be filmic codes (lighting, sound, *mise en scène*) and/or cultural codes (behaviour, customs, setting). You might consider the following:

1   What meaning are you trying to convey?

2   What effects will you use to convey that meaning?

3   What do they denote and connote?

4   Do they contribute to the story, mood, and theme?

5   Which of these codes are filmic and which are cultural?

Examples of films that construct meaning through codes are *Bringing Up Baby* (Howard Hawks, 1938), *Pleasantville* (Gary Ross, 1998), and *Chinatown* (Roman Polanski, 1974).

Another of de Saussure's ideas to be taken up within the field of cultural and film theory is that of binary oppositions. According to de Saussure, within the field of language, signs are also accorded value not in and of themselves (positively), but in terms of what they are not (negatively): 'Concepts are purely differential and defined not by their positive characteristics but negatively by their relations with the other terms of the system' (1916: 117). So, for de Saussure, nothing has significance on its own, only in relation to other elements or concepts within the system. Difference, then, is a fundamental principle of language. Signs, then, are not positively determined through the relation to a referent. In fact, de Saussure suggests that the connection between signifier and signified, the sign, is arbitrary.

For example, the letters F-I-L-M have no obvious relation to the concept of film. An outsider or a person unfamiliar with the English language would not understand the sign (the meaning of the word). One needs to be familiar with the system of language in order to understand it. And one understands a particular utterance of a specific unit of language or a sign, through its difference to other units and signs. This becomes very important when we begin to think of certain binary opposites as they function: man/woman, black/white, good/evil. As we shall go on to see throughout the chapter, these are particularly relevant to filmmaking and film studies.

Claude Lévi-Strauss (1962, 1976), an anthropologist also associated with structuralism, was greatly influenced by the work of de Saussure. Lévi-Strauss was concerned with the rituals, customs, and habits of particular groups, as he saw that such practices could reveal a great deal about the organisation, social hierarchies, and internal contradictions or conflicts within the group (Lévi-Strauss, 1962). In the context of film, however, Lévi-Strauss's greatest influence in the field of film is his study of myth. Where de Saussure studied the structure of language, Lévi-Strauss looked towards social groups and the production myths, which he saw as part of language, since myths were passed on through speech. Myths, for him, could be understood as an effort to make sense of the world, to cope or deal with uncertainties and contradictions (Lévi-Strauss, 1976). Myths functioned as explanations for our being, for certain phenomena not yet fully understood, for coping with death, and so on. Like de Saussure in relation to parole and langue, Lévi-Strauss suggested that individual myths only take on meaning as part of an overall deeper system of beliefs. For example, Lévi-Strauss contradicts Jung's interpretation of the archetype as possessing meaning. For Lévi-Strauss, such signs only have meaning within the totality of the system. Thus, Lévi-Strauss breaks down myth into its various and multiple components, in essence tracing the 'grammar' of the language of myth (ibid.). The components can be combined to create meaning, and these myths shape the thinking and practices of individuals within the group.

These myths may alter in terms of the content, but generally the structure and message remains the same. The myths can be adapted to suit particular societal needs, reflecting newer contradictions and tensions that the social group must contend with. For example, creation myths are found in many cultures. Although each myth may differ in terms of how it tells the story of creation, all are concerned with origins. Within myths, binary oppositions are found. So, like de Saussure, Lévi-Strauss recognised the way in which signs are not inherently meaning-'ful' but take meaning from what they are not, or their opposite. For Lévi-Strauss, binary oppositions are fundamental principles of myth. The function of such binary opposites is to determine the group's identity and values against its opposition. Here we find the most common forms of myths, which define 'us' in terms of 'them': nature/culture, good/evil, man/woman, hero/villain. As you can see, these binary oppositions are thematised extensively within film. In fact, as we shall go on to see in the section on genre, these theories have shaped the development and analysis of certain genre films, such as the western, as well as film narrative more generally.

EXERCISE FILM MEANING THROUGH BINARY OPPOSITIONS

Make a short film of between one and three minutes that is structured around binary oppositions. Think about how you can produce meaning through these oppositions. Examples of such oppositions might be nature/culture, man/woman, hero/villain, urban/rural, young/old, good/evil, and black/white. Remember that binary oppositions are generally hierarchical and one is privileged over the other. Consider:

1   what meaning you want to generate through these oppositions;

2   how your chosen oppositions are usually presented in film;

3   who is privileged and why; and

4   what ways you will produce binary oppositions (through characters, location, theme, or filmic devices such as framing, lighting, and so on).

See *Star Wars Episode IV: A New Hope* (George Lucas, 1977), *The Searchers* (John Ford, 1956), *The English Patient* (Anthony Minghella, 1996), and *Blue Velvet* (David Lynch, 1986).

SEMIOTICS AND CULTURE

As we can see, the original work of de Saussure and other semiotic theorists (or structuralists) points to the way in which meaning is created at the level of language and culture more broadly. Their work was to become very significant in a number of disciplines in the following years. These theories formed the basis of Roland Barthes's (1915–80) seminal text, *Mythologies* (2009; first published in 1957 in French, and first English translation in 1972), which used the concepts of language and myth in the analysis of topical everyday images, films and other popular cultural products. For Barthes, everyday cultural items and products are akin to de Saussure's parole, in the sense that they are signs belonging to a larger system of social values and conventions. For Barthes, the perpetual circulation of these signs or myths through media and cultural practice served to uphold the ideologies of those in power. Thus, hegemonic society prevails through these individual 'texts', which range from the world of wrestling to children's toys. In order to demonstrate this, Barthes develops de Saussure's notion of the sign as the relationship between signifier and signified by suggesting that there are two levels of signification, that of denotation and connotation. In other words, a sign can denote one thing and connote another, something beyond the denoted meaning.

Barthes uses the example of an image from a French magazine, *Paris Match* (ibid.). The picture shows a young black soldier saluting. The immediate interpretation at the level of primary signification (denotation) involves reading the codes in their most basic, obvious, and literal form. A young black soldier is saluting the French flag. Yet, Barthes wants to move beyond the first level of signification and into ideology. So, what else can we read from the image? Here, we move into the field of myth, the secondary meaning that can be interpreted from the image. For Barthes, the connoted meaning might suggests France's imperial superiority, which is served happily by the black colonial subjects. The image might thus be read as supportive of French imperialism by implying that colonial subjects support their rulers. Evident in Barthes work is a concern about the way in which mass culture is encouraged to subscribe to the values and ideology of those in power. This encouragement functions through texts, through the combination of their denotative and connotative meanings, which tell us stories about family, society, values, history, and so on.

It was Barthes's later book *S/Z* (1974) that was to prove influential for film studies. In *S/Z*, he offers a close analysis and systematic breakdown of the Balzac book *Sarrasine* into over 500 units of meaning. Barthes then organises the books through a set of five codes of discourse, all of which have the propensity to produce meaning, but none being prioritised. For Barthes, meaning is produced through the interaction and oscillation between the various codes. All of the codes relate generally to how the narrative produces meaning (for example, the hermeneutic code that drives the narrative forward through obstacles and the setting up of questions and answers), yet draws from outside narrative through cultural codes and codes of the body (Mayne, 2002: 15). As Mayne suggests, 'Barthes's analysis defines an approach to the study of textuality that "reads" in a "writerly" fashion, attentive not to any single determination but rather to how textuality is formed by the interplay of different discourses – political, narrative, psychoanalytic' (ibid.). Here, Mayne introduces another key concept adopted by film academics, that of discourse. So far, we have traced the connection between language as a series of codes and structures and film as a series of codes and structures like that of language. Semiotic theorists such as Barthes worked hard to make sense of these codes and to understand how these codes function in society, and what purpose (or whose) they serve.

DISCOURSE

The term 'discourse' was originally associated with language, and particularly in the content of speech and the way in which it communicates. In other words, in the field of linguistics, discourse referred to 'language in use'. Those analysing discourse in this sense focus on the way in which texts, whether spoken words or written, are used in particular ways and produce particular meanings. These accepted meanings form the ideological underpinning of society, whereby what is discursive becomes naturalised. So, an analysis of discourse allows for an understanding of how ideology functions. Extending upon this, those such as Barthes and especially Michel Foucault recognise discourse beyond language. For them, discourse refers to the meanings through which people, cultures, or societies communicate. Foucault refers to discourses of power (1969/2007). For Foucault, the subject (the hypothetical person) is created through discourse. In other words, we are the sum of our experiences. And since everything that we come to understand about ourselves and the world occurs through our experiences with others, we are essentially products of those experiences and that knowledge. Hence, if a person grows up in a Catholic family, that person is likely to take on and reflect those values and beliefs. If one grows up in a racist family, one will also come to understand society as such (even if racism itself is rejected). In other words, and as Foucault suggested, our sense of values, our beliefs, morality, what we believe to be true are all produced discursively. They are not, however, real, natural, or obvious. So, like the semiotic analysis discussed previously, discourse is concerned with questioning what is culturally 'taken for granted'. However, as Stam *et al.* suggest:

> Rather than analyse culture in semiological terms of 'systems of signs', Foucault sees culture as a social constellation of sites of power. Thus Foucault grounds discourse in relations of power, and specifically in the forms of power embodies in specializes and institutionalized language.
>
> (1992: 211)

In addition, Foucault stressed that discourses are not the same as ideology (another term used frequently within film studies). Where discussion of ideology is often concerned with the way in which the values of the dominant social groups come to shape society, and the way in which power struggles emerge within this (for example, between classes or genders), Foucault argues that discourses operate at every level, and are not just produced by power groups: 'Discourse transmits and produces power; it reinforces it, but also undermines and exposes it, renders it fragile and makes it possible to thwart' (1998: 100–1).

There are multiple and conflicting discourses in operation at any given time. Although we might think of speech as the most common form of discourse, Foucault suggests that 'whenever, between objects, types of statement, concepts, or thematic choices, one can define a regularity (an order, correlations, positions and functionings, transformations), we will say that we are dealing with a discursive formation' (2007: 41). Among some of the discourses that Foucault studied were medical discourses, discourses of sexuality, and discourses of incarceration. Foucault analyses the way in which discourses produce 'truths'. For example, he suggests that madness or insanity was not something that was 'discovered' by medical practitioners; rather, madness emerged as a concept within particular social circumstances. Whereas madness was once thought to be a product of the supernatural (the mad person as blessed by God or cursed by the devil), as the medical sciences turned to it, it became a mental and/or physical condition. The shift in the language of madness then produces social change. Where the mad person might have been attacked or feared previously, under the guise of medical knowledge madness becomes something to be treated. However, this does not suggest that medicine is progressive. After all, the mad person is now relegated to the asylum and is separated from the sane. As we can see, such discourse analysis, as it is called:

> is not concerned with language alone. It also examines the context of communication: who is communicating with whom and why; in what kind of society and situation, through what medium; how different types of communication evolved, and their relationship to each other.
>
> (Cook, 1992: 1)

Such an understanding of discourse and knowledge/power has proven attractive to those interested in film, primarily because of the way in which it allows for a questioning of film and cinema. If we return to Cook's statement, we can ask: Within film (singular) and cinema (plural), who is communicating with whom and why? In what kind of society and situation are these films communicating? What different types of film communication have evolved, and what is their relationship to each other? There are various ways of approaching discourse through film. First, we can think about discourse outside the text, which works its way in.

FILM AND DISCOURSE

We might think about the kinds of ideological discourses of masculinity or femininity in film and how they speak to our prior cultural experience of gender. Take the film *Pretty Woman* (Gary Marshall, 1990), which offers an interesting example of how competing discourses are managed. In what way do we make meaning of this film by drawing upon sociocultural gender discourses? The protagonist, Vivian, is a prostitute who is eventually saved through her relationship with a well-to-do man. Among the discourses of femininity operating here are that of the woman as object of male sexual gratification and that of the fairy tale. These are only two of the discourses that allow the audience to make sense of the representation of woman on screen. In terms of the discourse of prostitution, we can return to Foucault who, in his *History of Sexuality: The Will to Knowledge* (1998) discusses how various institutions and disciplines (such as police, state, religion, medicine) produced a discourse of sexuality. This discourse shaped the way in which people understood sex not simply as an act, but as an aspect of identity. Proper sexuality was defined in relation to improper or deviant sexuality. Thus, those who operated outside of the repressive morality of normative sexuality were rejected from society, either as outlaws, criminals, or mentally ill or diseased. The prostitute entered the discourse of sexuality as the deviant other. Here, we can see how discourse is related to knowledge and power. In terms of *Pretty Woman*, the film draws upon this discourse of prostitution in a number of interesting ways. The prostitute is, of course, figured as deviant and as socially marginalised. This discourse is not challenged or undermined by the film. Vivian's narrative goal is to reject a life of prostitution and become sexually 'normative'. This goal is relayed through the prism of another discourse, that of the fairy tale, and primarily that of Cinderella. The fairy tale produces a discourse of female sexuality generally centred on passivity and domesticity. For example, in the fairy tale, the rescue of the woman by the 'prince' generally functions to position woman as disempowered and passive. Similarly, the tradition of the woman climbing the social ladder through her relationship with a man continues in *Pretty Woman*. However, while we might understand the film as speaking to sexist notions of womanhood, we might also recognise the feminist discourse in the film. At certain points in the film, Vivian rejects the offer of 'salvation' from her lover/prince Edward and challenges him on his perception of her as a prostitute. The final scene of the film re-negotiates the Rapunzel fairy tale, where instead of the prince climbing up the tower to save the princess, Vivian literally meets Edward halfway down. While this might seem like token feminism, it demonstrates that there is no singular discourse that produces meaning within a text.

EXERCISE SELF-REFLEXIVE FILMMAKING AND DISCOURSE

Make a short fiction film that engages with discourses of family. The film can challenge or reproduce such discourses. You might consider the way in which discourses of the family intersect with other broader discourses of state, religion, gender, nationality, and so on. Consider:

1   how the film produces a collection of ideas, concepts, and 'truths' about family;

2   how the visual elements and *mise en scène* can contribute to the development of this filmic discourse;

3   how the film points towards external cultural discourses and from where these discourses emerge (what groups, communities, power actions);

4   yourself as somebody embedded in the discourse and how that might frame your film (are there any competing discourses that you don't give voice to, and why?); and

5   if the film attempts to propose a 'truth' of the family or make any claims about 'real' families or the reality of family.

See *Ordinary People* (Robert Redford, 1980), *The Parent Trap* (David Swift, 1961), *The Grapes of Wrath* (John Ford, 1940), *It's a Wonderful Life* (Frank Capra, 1946), and *The Hills Have Eyes* (Wes Craven, 1977).

NARRATIVE

Narrative discourse is precisely the text itself – the actual arrangement of signifiers that communicate the story – words in literature, moving images and written titles in silent films. It is only through this means of expression that we come into contact with either the story or the act of narrating. The story is an imaginary construction that the spectator or reader creates while reading the narrative discourse of the actual text.

Tom Gunning, 'Narrative discourse and the narrator system'

The above example of *Pretty Woman* relates to the exterior discursive elements of film. Here, we can see how discourses outside of the film text shape the audience's understanding of the text. Yet, the same strands of thought (semiotics and discourse) have been taken up within the field of film studies in order to shed light on the structure and form of film narrative. Studies of film narrative attempt to organise and categorise the systems and conventions at work within a film text. In other words, these studies attempt to identify the visual strategies that are specific to film as an aesthetic medium. Although narrative is often used as a blanket term for elements of a text such as plot, story, and sequence, in order to understand the relationship between theories of narrative and semiotics, we must distinguish between the specific components of narrative: namely story, narrative (or narrative discourse, as Gunning (2009) has renamed for clarification), and, sometimes, narration. As a practitioner, you might think of the story as your initial pitch of a script, which outlines the series of events that the audience can make some sense of. So, the story can be thought of as the events as they are represented. We might think of narrative discourse as the way in which the events are represented. This would include the camera movement, the editing, and the construction of time and space. All of these can be understood as narrative strategies. An understanding of narratology is useful, as it enables the filmmaker to be inventive with the storytelling process.

As an example, think about the way in which you might describe the film *Memento* (Christopher Nolan, 2000) to a friend. You might loosely recount the story of an amnesiac man who attempts to find out about the murder of his wife. Ordinarily, this story might seem uninspired. However, if we think about the way in which the story unfolds, it becomes rather more exciting. Similarly, we might describe *Requiem for a Dream* (Darren Aronofksy, 2000) as the story of the character's descent into drug addiction, but, again, this would not really account for the particular filmic methods and narrative style that make the film so memorable. What we can see, then, is that there are various ways in which narrative operates. Narratology is the study of systems of narrative. Your understanding of this can contribute towards the development of your own narrative style. Once you have become comfortable with the basic skills of filmmaking, you can begin to think about modes of narration.

At the most basic level, we can think about how story is transformed through plot. As mentioned, the story can be understood as the way in which we recount the events of a film, or the way in which we order the events chronologically (even if the film is not ordered chronologically). In film terminology, the story is often referred to as the *fabula*. So, for example, your initial concept or idea for a film might take the form of a *fabula*/story. To use the example of another group of filmmakers who developed a simple story into one of the most successful films of all time, *The Blair Witch Project* (Daniel Myrick and Eduardo Sanchez, 1999) tells the story of a group of students who go to the woods in search of a legendary witch. The plot of a film, or the *syuzhet*, orders the story in a particular way. This ordering can shift the temporal occurrence of events, play with chronology, and restrict or reveal knowledge and information at particular junctures in the film. To return to the case of *The Blair Witch Project*, we can note the way in which information is withheld from the audience, the way in which details of the witch are revealed through the characters' dialogue rather than shown, and the way in which the film creates confusion about the organisation of space in the woods.

Each of these elements are plot devices that shape the way the story is told. The plot/*syuzhet* includes all of the necessary events that will enable the viewer to make sense of the story/*fabula*. But the plot/*syuzhet* needs to organise these events in a particular way in order to shape how the audience will come to understand the story/*fabula*. During the scripting process, you will transform your initial story/*fabula* concept into a plot/*syuzhet*. The plot is what will make your film interesting. For example, we can think about the general story of a slasher film or a romantic comedy. Both are very common, yet some are far more popular than others. While there are numerous reasons why one might succeed where another fails, we can look towards the plot to account for the difference in reception. In the case of the slasher film, the general story might be that a killer begins to hunt and kill a group of youths, culminating in a battle between the killer and a survivor. The slasher film depends upon a certain amount of tension and violence; however, the plot can increase the pace of violent events or withhold such events. In the case of the romantic comedy, the romance often depends upon the stalling of the eventual union between the two lovers. While these might seem like generic plot devices, or plot devices pertaining to genre, it is only through such strategies that the audience will understand the film.

Audiences familiar with film narratives (and narratives more generally) have expectations about what will happen and how it will happen. The audience also expects that most or all of the information presented through film will have some bearing on the overall meaning of the text. In any narrative, enough information should be present in order that the story can be extracted from the plot. On the other hand, too much information dilutes the story, as it does not move on and seems to stall on unnecessary information and events. We can use two examples to illustrate this. The first is an example of plot devices that shape the telling of the story. The second is an example of a film that contains far too much extraneous plot that it renders the narrative relatively unintelligible at points, discussed further below. In the first example, we will focus on temporality. Films very rarely occur in real time outside of a few exceptions such as *Cleo From 5 to 7* (Agnes Varda, 1962), *Timecode* (Mike Figgis, 2000), and *Rope* (Alfred Hitchcock, 1948). In most cases, films will condense time or re-arrange the temporal order of events in order to shape the story into an interesting plot. At times, a few days might be condensed into a few hours, as in the case of *Lost in Translation* (Sofia Coppola, 2003), and in other cases centuries might take place over the span of a film, as in the case of *Intolerance* (D.W. Griffith, 1914) or *Orlando* (Sally Potter, 1992). In each case, enough information is needed to ensure that the audience understands the temporal structure and span of the film. In the case of *Intolerance*, titles were used to make the temporal transitions comprehensible. Today, film audiences have enough familiarity with the structure and organisations of film to make sense of the temporal transitions. For example, in a hypothetical film scene, a character might say, 'I am going home'. The following scene will show them in the process of going home, and the following shot will show them entering the door of their home. The audience can fill in the blanks between the shots. They can imagine that the person took much longer to go home than the film represented. Films might be arranged chronologically, as in the case of *Psycho* (Alfred Hitchcock, 1960) or may be in non-chronological order, as in the case of *Pulp Fiction* (Quentin Tarantino, 1994) or *Irreversible* (Gasper Noe, 2002).

The way in which the story is structured through plot will have implications for what and how the film 'means'. In the case of *Irreversible*, the story is plotted in reverse chronological order. When the story's beginning, which occurs at the film's end, is revealed, it is far more profound and allows the audience to reflect upon the film's violence. There are various techniques that can be used to serve the plot's temporal arrangement (for example, flashbacks, flash-forwards, narrator recollection, and on-screen titles). When a film's plot manipulates the story action and the temporal order, it is often done to create a sense of anticipation. In the case of *Fight Club* (David Fincher, 1999), and particularly the opening and closing scenes, the film plays with temporal order by beginning the narrative with the story's end.

Fight Club opens with 'Jack', the protagonist, held at gunpoint by Tyler. Jack's narration refers to Tyler's 'controlled demolition thing' and as he details the efforts of Project Mayhem to cause a series of large explosions, the camera visually traces the location and arrangement of said explosives. Thus, the plot begins at the end of the story. Within this short sequence, enough information is revealed about the characters, their status, and the setting and mode of the story. Notice that 'Jack', although unnamed within the film, is established as the primary character here. We can, of course, gauge this from his narration. Yet this is also represented visually. There are numerous close and mid shots of Jack; however, there are none of the other character present, Tyler. The camera reveals only the hands or the torso of Tyler in close-up (Figures 7.1 and 7.2).

Therefore, in a short sequence, a huge amount of information is revealed about the characters and their relationship with each other, the general story about the origins of the explosives and the intent of Tyler, and the role of Marla in these events. Based on a select number of details (Jack is held captive, Tyler is intending to set off a series of big explosives in a city, and the current situation can be traced back to a woman named Marla), the film establishes the general terrain of the action, including what is logical, rational, and possible in the world (also known as the diegesis). Guns, explosions, and assumed kidnapping are all included in the opening sequence, so it would be reasonable to assume that this theme of violence will continue throughout the film. In addition, other themes are included by way of the non-diegetic material of the film. Both diegetic (within the world of the film) and non-diegetic (coming from outside the world of the film) material form the plot. In the case of *Fight Club*'s opening sequence, the electro music is paced in quite a frenzied way. This, of course, supports the visual images as well as the narration.

FIGURE 7.1
Close-up on Jack

FIGURE 7.2
Tyler's arms

So, the opening scene of *Fight Club* organises the story into plot in the following way: the plot manipulates the event order of the story, with the opening scene being the culmination of events; the *mise en scène* contributes to the construction of mood and theme through the dark, empty setting and the sombre performance of the character, as well as the framing of the characters; the primary character acts as narrator of the events, thus setting up a point of identification for the audience; the narrator makes reference to current and past events and characters, thus propelling the narrative into an extended flashback. We can think about other ways in which the plot might have been organised. The opening few scenes are organised in reverse chronological order, beginning with Jack being held by Tyler, moving back into the past to Jack's group counselling sessions, and again moving back to Jack's experience of insomnia and his work and home life. If we consider alternative plot structures, we can consider how the film might have progressed in chronological order. In this case the film would begin with Jack's miserable work and home life. Following this, he would attend the group sessions, where he meets Marla, and finally he would begin his association with Tyler.

While this plotting of the story would make sense, the audience would not have any sense of a trajectory. Part of the satisfaction gained from watching films is not attained from finding out what happens at the end of the story; rather, satisfaction is gained through experiencing how the film arrives at the story's end. By having access to the final events of the story, the audience can frame all preceding events from this perspective. Thus, we know that the road that Jack will take will lead to his own downfall. This gives further meaning to his group counselling sessions and his relationship with Marla. There is a sense of foreboding for the audience upon the introduction to Tyler on the aeroplane, since it has already been inferred that this association will not work out well. As we can see in the case of *Fight Club*, the plot's manipulation of the story creates certain effects and meanings.

EXERCISE CREATING NEW STORIES FROM OLD THEMES

Make a short film based on one of the following generic topics below. These themes are often used as the basis for many films and, as a result, some of the narrative structures of these stories have become quite clichéd. For this exercise, you will use narrative strategies as a way of re-telling these common stories. Pick from:

1   The hero or heroine must save the day.
2   Dysfunctional relationships between parents and children.
3   Getting revenge.
4   The road movie.

Think about:

1   What is your basic story?
2   What theme or mood will the film evoke?
3   How can plot devices, such as withholding information, revealing information, flashback/forwards, condensing time/space, and revealing backstory without showing, be used? How will these contribute to theme or mood?
4   What effect does the plot have on the audience (tension, fear, anticipation, mystery)?

See *Memento* (Christopher Nolan, 2000), *Eternal Sunshine of the Spotless Mind* (Michel Gondry, 2004), and *Rashomon* (Akira Kurosawa, 1950).

It may also be useful to consider films that organise plot less effectively. We are all familiar with the feeling, upon viewing a film, that there is something that we missed or did not understand. At times, this can be the result of particularly intricate plots that require a great deal of recall and interpretation (such as the detective or thriller). Yet, there are plenty of films with relatively unintelligible plots, or plots that contain too many events or scenarios that are unnecessary to the overall film. Similarly, many student films tend to suffer from the poor organisation of plot. Far too often, student films contain lengthy scenes of dialogue that contribute little to the overall theme or story. Another common issue is the failure to develop plots effectively. For example, a scene might make reference to a character or situation that never materialises (it may have been cut from the final film). Each plot device or subplot device should form part of a cohesive and comprehensible totality. Generally, a film needs events and exposition as much as it needs pace. If the pace suffers due to far too much exposition, consider revising the exposition. Let's use the example of a film that contains extraneous plot material that has no place within the overall narrative. *The Room* (Tommy Wiseau, 2003) is now considered to have cult status, in part due to its often nonsensical narrative exposition.

The storyline of the film is rather straightforward. A couple, Johnny and Lisa, live together in an apartment. Lisa begins to have doubts about the relationship and has an affair with Johnny's best friend, Mark. Upon finding out, Johnny kills himself. The film is set largely within the apartment, and most scenes occur within the living room. There are a number of other characters who act as causal agents (who propel the narrative through actions), or who enable exposition (of past events, of characters' dispositions, and so on). However, there are a number of plot issues that result in an over-lengthy film and a great deal of confusion for the audience (although this confusion is now what makes the film rather endearing). Many of the problems relate to cause and effect and plotlines that are never resolved. Typically, films contain a number of plotlines rather than just one. For example, the film *Avatar* (James Cameron, 2009) has a main plotline about the threat to a non-human civilisation and a subplot of a romance between a human and a non-human. These plotlines do not develop separately from each other; rather, at many points they converge. For example, the non-human romantic interest is part of the warrior group who resist the attacks by the humans. The human's role in the conflict is determined by his relationship with the non-human. Thus, the subplot of romance is a cause that produces an effect. The human joins the non-human struggle and attacks the humans' machinery, which in turn provokes violent retaliation from the humans. Equally, in *The Room*, there are a number of plotlines operating at any given time.

However, many of these have little causal function and produce no effects. For example, the character of Denny, a teenager from the apartment block adopted by Johnny, at times provides backstory and emotional context, which reveals Johnny to be a caring, responsible person. In this sense, Denny's place within the narrative is justified. Such minor characters can be used to reveal more about major characters and can act as causal agents at points within the narrative. However, a subplot involving Denny's use of drugs stalls rather than propels the narrative. In it, Denny is attacked by a drug dealer; Johnny saves Denny; and he, Lisa, and a few other characters present attempt to find out more about Denny's drug use. Denny refuses to reveal any more, which suggests that this issue will return at another stage. However, the film never reveals why the confrontation took place and this story never develops or contributes to the overall plot.

Similarly, other scenes seem to operate as plot devices only to be abandoned quickly. For example, at one point, Johnny and his friends congregate in his apartment all dressed in tuxedos (Figure 7.3). Their reason for this is not explained. Denny and the others want to play football outside (Figure 7.4). One friend does not want to since they are in tuxedos. They coax him into playing outside and he falls over. The film then cuts to a later day, with Johnny and Mark now in a café dressed in casual clothes (Figure 7.5). While the transition from the football scene to the café scene suggests the passing of time (a shot of the city, a shot of Johnny walking in a park, and then the shot of Mark and Johnny in the café), there is nothing to suggest how much time has passed, nor to suggest what the outcome of the previous scene's action was. In this sense, there is no causal link between the scene in which the characters play football in tuxedos and the later scene in the café, or any further scenes. In fact, the scene seems not only redundant in terms of narrative, but also causes some confusion, since it might imply that the characters are attending Johnny's wedding, which they are not.

So why are the scenes (and so many others that seem to either repeat material or information, or establish potential plot devices that are never followed up) there?

FIGURE 7.3
Group in tuxedos in apartment

FIGURE 7.4
Group plays football

FIGURE 7.5
Mark and Johnny in café

First, it must be stressed that scenes that have no immediate causal function do not necessarily make for a poor narrative. Such scenes are often integral to understanding the lifestyles and motivations of characters, even if they don't seem obviously causal. Likewise, such momentary pauses from narrative action might also serve to emphasise theme and mood. For example, the films of Terrence Malick often contain lengthy scenes or cutaway shots that have no direct bearing on the immediate action. *The Thin Red Line* (Terrence Malick, 1998), for example, uses shots of the natural environment (animals, birds, trees, rivers, and so on) to manipulate the pace of the action, slowing down the usual pace of the war film. These lingering shots are supported by the reflections of a narrator who establishes the mood of the scene. Yet, *The Room* does not establish any guiding principles that would allow the audience to make sense of such scenes. What might be learned from *The Room* is the extent to which each event, whether a singular cutaway shot of the surrounding environment or a conversation between characters, must contribute to the overall plot, theme, or mood of the film. While it might make sense to the filmmaker or the scriptwriter, it also needs to make sense to the audience.

EXERCISE NARRATIVE, PLOT, AND CAUSE AND EFFECT

Organise these elements into a coherent narrative. Make sure that each individual event clearly contributes to the overall narrative through plot, theme, or mood. You need to create a pattern or cause and effect, whereby each causal element (for example, a fight) produces an effect elsewhere. This is a simple exercise that can take the form of a film treatment or a short film. The purpose of this exercise is to practice restriction and frugality in terms of narrative information, plot exposition, and dialogue. The following are short snippets of story information for you to work with:

1 Person A is at work.
2 Person A has a conversation with Person B in a car.
3 There is a shift in the overall landscape/environment.
4 Persons A and B are in an old building.
5 Person B makes a phone call.

As you can see, there is little sense of cause and effect here. Neither is there a coherent narrative. There are many ways in which you might produce a story and a plot out of these occurrences. Think about creating a clear causal chain without any extraneous or redundant information.

See *Se7en* (David Fincher, 1995), *All the President's Men* (Alan J. Pakula, 1976), and *Citizen Kane* (Orson Welles, 1941).

SUTURE

Not only does film narrative create meaning at the level of the broader organisation of events through cause and effect, or narration, it also creates meaning at the level of narrative space. We can understand narrative space in a number of ways. Obviously, narrative space may refer to the film story's location and setting. In some films, the story space is limited to a small number of locations (if not just one). For example, *12 Angry Men* (Sidney Lumet, 1957), *Night of the Living Dead* (George A. Romero, 1968), and *The Birthday Party* (William Friedkin, 1968) are all set largely within one key space. Plot space refers to space that may not be visually represented but that the audience must imagine in order to make sense of the story. In *Thelma and Louise* (Ridley Scott, 1991), two spaces are evoked through reference to past and future events. Louise at one point refuses to travel through Texas, inferring that she has had some bad experiences in the state. Both women are escaping to Mexico, which represents freedom from the domestic or legal constraints they are faced with in their current lives. Thus, the two spaces are mirrored with the women's desires and fears, even though neither space is directly represented. In addition, we can consider screen space, which refers to the actual space represented on film. This element of narrative space is worth elaborating on further here, as it is precisely this form of space that has been widely discussed by film theorists (specifically in terms of the ideological function of film narrative) but is quite often neglected to an extent within the filmmaking process, particularly by students. We might think of it this way: film seems more realistic than other media arts such as painting, sculpture, and photography.

The process of narrative turns image representation into a 'realistic' form through the use of narrative techniques (such as shot/reverse shot, camera framing, and continuity editing). These tools form a grammar that, in some sense, correlates with human perspective. For example, the process of continuity editing avoids sudden jumps, ruptures, and shifts that would draw attention to the grammar at work. Thus, the space constructed and represented through narrative allows the spectator to be immersed within the illusionary 'reality' of the text. However, as filmmakers, you already know that this space is manipulated. The project of the filmmaker (in the case of the realist or classical Hollywood text) is to make the narrative space seem 'natural' to the spectator. Despite how much time or space may be manipulated, the filmmaker must be able to express some spatio-temporal logic. The spectator is placed within the narrative space and, as Stephen Heath (1976, 1981) suggests, the subject is produced through narrative discourse. By this, Heath suggests that the narrative produces a perspective that folds in the spectator's gaze or look. Imagine that the narrative space is not organised in such a way. Let's use the example of a filmic moment of pathos. Our scene has a person crying as they watch a friend leave. The intent of the scene is to evoke sympathy for the person crying. How do you shoot this? How do you construct the narrative space? A master shot that examines all of the action from afar? This will certainly make visible some of the narrative action, but something is missing. What would make this scene achieve its project of pathos? A close-up? A point-of-view shot? A reverse shot of the friends exchanging goodbyes? What we really want here is to fix meaning or fix the subject/spectator into a fixed sense of meaning.* This is referred to as suture.

The process of suturing, as the word suggests, weaves the spectator into the filmic text and, in doing so, closes or limits the relationship between the subject and the signifying chain (in the case of film, the signifying chain refers to the film text). The term originated in psychoanalytic theory through Lacan, was revisited by Jacques-Alain Miller (1977), and was later adapted by film theorists. In the psychoanalytic sense, suturing refers to subject formation through Lacan's 'mirror stage' in which the child, at first, revels in the shifts from the realm of the maternal through to the paternal. The maternal realm (the imaginary) is perceived as fulfilling and symbiotic and, here, the child imagines itself as whole, or as complete. However, with the acquisition of language (through the encounter with the paternal realm), the child comes to recognise the illusionary nature of its self-image as whole. This shift is necessary for the child to become a social being capable of communication, but it also produces the sense of loss in the child. So the subject is formed through the experience of lack, which contributes towards its position within the symbolic. Jean-Pierre Oudart considered this process in relation to film. Like Christian Metz, Oudart compared the cinematic operations to that of the mirror stage. Oudart suggested that like the child's initial relation to the mirror, the screen spectator is momentarily caught in a moment of illusionary misrecognition (like the child's initial understanding of itself as within the realm of the imaginary).

However, this is threatened by the recognition of the frame of the film in a similar way to which the language of the symbolic undermines the child's sense of completeness. So, the spectator, according to Oudart, experiences a sense of loss, an anxiety at becoming aware of a space outside of the frame that it cannot recognise. In other words, it becomes aware of an absence. The absence is the articulation of the subject's anxiety about where it is in the enunciation of cinema (just as Lacan questions how the subject can be represented through language): 'The revelation of this absence is the key moment in the fate of the image, since it introduces the image into the order of the signifier and the cinema into the order of discourse' (Oudart, 1977: 42). In other words, the sudden awareness of the frame of the film field, or of the 'absence', draws attention to the very production as signifier (Heath, 1976: 91). At this moment, when the spectator experiences displeasure in the revelation of the production of the signifier, the absence is again

---

* The term 'spectator' refers to the hypothetical figure who watches the film. In contrast, the audience, or the viewer, refers to actual people who can be counted, analysed, and monitored. You can think of it this way: the spectator is the hypothetical subject that the film constructs. Variations in the shots of a film sequence position the imagined spectator. However, the viewer is the very real person who actually does the watching. This person may or may not take up the position offered by the film text. For example, a film might construct a subject position that aligns the spectator with a character who expresses racist views. The viewer, however, may reject these views.

hidden. Oudart (1977) identifies the shot/reverse shot mechanism as that which makes the absent present. The shot initially holds the spectator. However, this hold does not last as the spectator comes to realise all that is not articulated within the frame (the absence). The reverse shot shows what is absent, thus making the filmic experience pleasurable/imaginary again. This is the process of suturing at work, as the spectator is sutured or interpolated back into the filmic field, into a pleasurable experience and into cinematic discourse. In this sense, Oudart suggests that film is ideological, as it hides the production of cinematic discourse through codes and techniques.

The process of suturing hides the mechanisms of production and situates the spectator in in an ideological relation to the film. The shot/reverse shot process, based as it is on the 180° rule, masks the technical operations at work since it does not expose its artifice. The initial shot is an eye that sees, and the corresponding reverse shot locates that eye in another character. So, it is not the camera that directs the 'seeing', but the characters or action within the scene. For Oudart, the result of this is that the imaginary is understood as real or as 'truth'. Stephen Heath takes some issue with the way in which Oudart draws upon the mirror stage as analogous to the relationship between spectator and screen. For Heath, Oudart's distinction between pleasure/imaginary and anxiety/symbolic/absence is too simplistic. Heath essentially develops and expands Oudart's work, rather than dismissing it. For Heath, the subject is sutured into the film text not only through shot/reverse shot, but through a variety of mechanisms. Following Barry Salt's (1992) reassessment of the shot/reverse shot principle (which he maintains is not as common in cinema as might be thought), Heath maintains that suture is one of many ways that film creates meaning (Heath uses the examples of music, narration, and particularly editing practices).

Like Heath, Kaja Silverman (1983) proposed that the process of suturing was not simply limited to the narrow process of shot/reverse shot. Silverman offers a reading of *Psycho* whereby suturing is evident throughout the various processes of narration. Silverman suggests that every cut, pan, and moment of disjuncture and fragmentation alludes to an absence or a lack, which is then negated by the presentation of fiction:

> It is not merely that the camera is incapable of showing us everything at once, but that it does not wish to do so. We must be shown only enough to know that there is more, and to want that 'more' to be disclosed. A prime agency of disclosure is the cut, which divides one shot from the next. The cut guarantees that both the preceding and the subsequent shots will function as structuring absences to the present shot. These absences make possible a signifying ensemble, convert one shot into a signifier of the next one, and the signified of the preceding one.
>
> (1983: 222)

Suture, then, refers to the means by which the spectator is positioned within the film text. The filmmaker can create meaning within a text by using techniques that will encourage the spectator to take up a particular position in relation to characters and the narrative. In other words, the vision of the spectator is framed using film techniques that are based on perspective. In the case of shot and reverse shot, the spectator accesses two perspectives rather than just one. The cut, shot/reverse shot, and tracking shots all 'stitch' the gaps or absence left within the field of vision and knowledge. For example, the filmmaker could use a master shot of a scene in order to convey all of the spatial information required for the spectator to understand the space and duration of the scene. However, a large amount of other information would be left out of this, and, for the filmmaker, there would be little opportunity to create drama. So, the filmmaker employs tools that will maintain spatial and temporal continuity and encourages the spectator to have particular types of relationships with characters and the narrative. The filmmaker will cut into action if it is important within the scene. They may also cut to characters so that the spectator will identify more closely with them.

EXERCISE SUTURING THE SCENE

Shoot a one-minute film that considers the process of suturing in making absent the fragmentation of space. Consider the ways in which suturing acts as a means of encouraging identification with characters and narration. The scene should represent two characters having a conversation. The scene should be emotive and identification with one character should be encouraged. You may use the following techniques:

1   master/establishing shot;
2   closer shot to characters;
3   shot/reverse shot; and
4   180° rule.

See *Stagecoach* (John Ford, 1939), *Mildred Pierce* (Michael Curtiz, 1945), and *Tape* (Richard Linklater, 2001).

CHAPTER 8

Spectatorship and audience

As you can see, the issue of spectatorship is central to film theory. While such academic work seems to stem from purely theoretical concerns, an understanding of spectatorship can also enable you, the filmmaker, to either produce films that appeal to the conscious or unconscious desires of spectators, or to challenge those 'safe' positions of spectatorship. Think of it as follows: every filmmaker, regardless of the nature of his or her film, wants people to watch his or her films. Thus, the filmmaker, whether intentionally or not, makes films that will mean something to other people. Even the most obscure or avant-garde films use cultural or filmic codes that will somehow make sense to the spectator, even if they are wrapped in a difficult formal or aesthetic system. Therefore, the spectator has a particular relationship with the screen image that will allow him or her to decipher, identify with, decode, and understand the screen image and its representations. This is, in fact, the contract between filmmaker and spectator. The filmmaker will produce a certain filmic experience that the spectator can enter into a relationship with. Judith Mayne summarises the experience of spectatorship as follows:

> Spectatorship is not only the act of watching a film, but also the ways one takes pleasure in the experience, or not; the means by which watching movies becomes a passion, or a leisure-time activity like any other. Spectatorship refers to how film-going and the consumption of movies and their myths are symbolic activities, culturally significant events.
>
> (2002: 1)

If we are to think films as myths, the consumption of which are symbolic activities, then the filmmaker is equally active in this process. The filmmaker, as such, becomes the myth-maker who produces films that are part of the culturally significant event of the film screening and film viewing. Important to remember, however, is the fact that the filmmaker does not produce these myths in a vacuum; rather, the filmmaker enters into a pre-existing cultural system. The filmmaker is aware of how he or she constructs these myths in some ways and unaware in others. To use a simple example in the context of speech or writing, when we refer to an object, or even person, of unknown gender, we often presume masculinity. I might refer to an animal as 'he' despite my lack of knowledge about its sex, I might presume an author of a newspaper is male, or I might refer to a genderless object in the masculine. These are some examples of the way in which I unconsciously recirculate certain 'myths' about gender and sex. Many filmmaking manuals and academic studies of films tend to do this. I engage in gender discourse unconsciously. Similarly, the filmmaker uses similar gender representations that presume the masculine, perhaps without realising it (regardless of whether they are male or female). So, even if I make a film with the intention of representing strong women, I might still use a cinematic language that is 'masculine' in form. This demonstrates the extent to which filmmaking occurs at a conscious and unconscious level, and equally takes on meaning for the spectator at a conscious and unconscious level.

However, as much as academics have been concerned with the conscious and unconscious operations of the film text, many filmmakers share this concern. We need only think of the films of Kathryn Bigelow, David Cronenberg, Brian De Palma, Betty Gordon, Michael Haneke, Alfred Hitchcock, Gasper Noe, Sally Potter, and Michael Powell, among many others, who are either concerned with the responsibility of filmmaking in terms of how it positions the spectator, or whose films thematise the process of looking or spectatorship itself (a prime example would be Powell's 1960 film *Peeping Tom*). Filmmakers, of any school or background, more often than not utilise sets of codes and conventions drawn from cinema or culture more broadly. While using these codes and conventions is not in itself an unconscious process on the part of the filmmaker, it is useful to keep in mind that the filmmaker is as much a reflection of these codes and conventions as an active producer of them. In this sense, the filmmaker consciously produces meaning at the level of narrative and form, but often this meaning is already prescribed through discourse.

Spectatorship theory (or screen theory) emerged in the 1970s as an attempt to account for these issues. Aligned with semiotics and psychoanalysis, theories of spectatorship foregrounded not only the film text, but also the spectator who entered into a relationship with the film text. Among the questions were: What happens to the spectator in the cinema? What do films do? How does the whole experience of spectatorship have meaning? The spectator here must be differentiated from the viewer. We can think of it as such: the spectator is a hypothetical person who is constructed by the film text and the cinematic experience. Any discussion of the spectator tends to focus on who the film text is speaking to. We will begin with the study of the 'immobile spectator' in the cinema, and end with the later considerations of sexuality and spectatorship, which formed much of spectatorship studies. This section will be divided into three sections: (1) apparatus theory; (2) Mulvey and feminist film theory; and (3) 1980s feminist theory.

APPARATUS THEORY

Apparatus theory developed in the 1970s and used psychoanalysis as a way of accounting for the cinematic experience. Among the key theorists here was Jean-Louis Baudry, who wrote the seminal text, 'Ideological effects of the basic cinematographic apparatus' (originally published in 1975). Here, he argues that screen theorists should not only be concerned with the individual film text, but with the institution of cinema. He notes that cinema is ideological since it is based on an illusion (of movement). The spectator is situated by the cinematic apparatus 'as the active centre and origin of meaning' (Baudry, 1985: 533). The technical nature of cinema may conceal the capacity for cinema to be ideological at an institutional level. Baudry notes that transformations take place between 'objective reality', the camera that records, and between recording and projection. The means by which this is recorded and projected discourages the spectator from being conscious of these transformations. Baudry notes how the monocular vision of art and film produces a perspective that constructs an all-seeing, all-knowing spectator, who is the source of all meaning (this is the illusion). Such perspectivism is, as a result, ideological. Baudry goes on to suggest that the moving image, while seeming to offer multiple rather than singular unifying images, is equally complicit in this, as it denies differences between images. The projection of the moving images enables them to be seen as whole and continuous rather than separate and discontinuous. Thus, the movement allows for cinema to engage in illusion. As Baudry argues, cinema 'lives on the denial of difference' (ibid.: 536).

In order to account for why the spectator engages in this, Baudry turns to psychoanalysis. He seeks to understand why and how the spectator identifies with the screen image and finds answers in psychoanalytic accounts of infantile development, which examines scenarios of identification and recognition (of images outside of ourselves). Drawing from Jacques Lacan and his theory of the 'mirror stage' of infantile development, Baudry notes the comparison between this and the screen–spectator relationship. For him, it was not simply a case of similarity; rather, the process of spectatorship reflected and evoked in the spectator the same processes as experienced in the mirror stage. Lacan has argued that the 'mirror stage' was a pivotal point in which the child recognises itself as separate and complete (individuality), although this is a false recognition. In the cinema, the spectator experiences the same sensation when watching the screen. The mirror stage forms one important aspect of the developmental system characterised by three stages: the imaginary, the symbolic, and the real. The imaginary stage is defined through the infant's close association with the mother. Here, the infant experiences symbiosis with the mother. The mirror stage acts as a key point within the imaginary. The later symbolic stage (the point at which the child enters language and becomes 'socialised') is governed by the father. So, the mirror stage acts as a point in which the infant is still immersed in an imaginary identification with the 'self'.

It is called the mirror stage because it describes a moment in which the child sees an image (a reflection, for example), which it perceives as 'I', as though it had looked in the mirror. Here, the infant forms an identificatory relationship with the image and this instigates a sense of selfhood (ego formation) since it can now conceive of a self. However, this is not a realistic or actual sense of self, since it perceives itself to be whole and complete when in fact it is an uncoordinated, dependant infant. Therefore, the image is an 'ideal I', which the infant (and later, the adult) aspires towards, rather than an actual self. It is perhaps not difficult to see the similarities between the infant of the mirror stage and the spectator looking at the image on the screen. As Baudry suggests, 'just as the mirror assembles the fragmented body in a sort of imaginary integration of the self, the transcendental self-unites the discontinuous fragments of phenomena, of lived experience, into unifying meaning' (1985: 540). So, the cinema carries out the ideological effect of constituting the subject since the spectator only experiences the effect of unity. The apparatus creates this, not the subject. The spectator simply has the impression that it is transcendental.

Christian Metz (1986) extends this position, and while there are some differences between their articulations of the 'look' (Metz is critical of Baudry's application of the mirror stage), both draw from similar psychoanalytic positions. Where Baudry emphasises the imaginary stage and its relationship to screen spectatorship, Metz draws equally from the imaginary and symbolic states. Whereas Baudry suggests that the mirror stage is re-enacted through the spectator's identification with on-screen characters (as reflections of themselves), Metz suggests that the spectator identifies with perception, and with the experience of the controlled position of spectatorship. This difference led to some further theoretical developments by Metz. First, Metz argues that unlike theatre, which is a fictive form taking place in 'real' time and space, the film performance in the cinema takes place elsewhere/prior to the spectator seeing the performance. It is therefore absent because it has already been recorded (Metz, 1986: 56). It is not the actual performance/props/objects/ spaces that the spectator sees, but their shadows. Here, Metz then terms the cinema the 'imaginary signifier'. This refers to the way in which cinema achieves signification through this absence – presence is only imaginary. The spectator is somewhat aware of this and experiences a sense of absence or lacking in relation to the screen image.

Metz suggests, then, that cinematic spectatorship is a voyeuristic activity, since the screen image is distant from the spectator (already absent). The spectator looks at something that, because of its absence, cannot return the look. As Metz (who always presumes male spectatorship) suggests:

> The voyeur is very careful to maintain a gulf, an empty space, between the object and the eye, at the object and his own body: his look fastens the object at the right distance, as with those cinema spectators who take care to avoid being too close or too far from the screen.
>
> (1986: 60)

Metz goes on to suggest that this voyeurism is associated with the control of the look: the spectator's control of the screen image, which is again an illusion. Cinema is complicit in this. While the cinema is more closely aligned with public voyeurism (which is sanctioned), it gives the impression of private voyeurism (unsanctioned, 'peeping tom'). Metz sees in this an element of sadism, since such a mechanism of viewing is dependent upon the spectator perceiving their mastery over the 'unknowing' screen objects or characters. This point was taken by Laura Mulvey (1975) and other screen theorists who, noting Metz's insistence of the male spectator, analysed the gendered components of cinema in terms of both spectatorship and film practice.

Metz's other focal point was the fetishistic elements of film spectatorship. In order to explain this more fully, it is useful to outline Freud's analysis of infantile development and later fetishistic behaviour in order to draw parallels with cinema. Metz (like Freud and Lacan) referred primarily to the male child. Metz, like Baudry, used psychoanalytic theory to understand cinema. He specifically referred to the Oedipal scenario of the male child. As Freud postulated, during the male infant's early years, the infant does not perceive sexual difference (between him and the mother). Later, the infant recognises itself as different from the mother and, according to Freud, recognises sexual difference in the sense that the boy has a penis and the mother does not (which comes to define women in terms of 'lack'). In order to avoid being like the mother, the child turns towards the father and gives up his desire for the mother (desire is formed at that moment when the child turns away from her). The child sacrifices the symbiotic relationship with the mother and enters the law of the father (we might name it patriarchy). This loss brings forth desire. So, in order to become a social, individual 'self', the child must give something up. This produces a conflicted 'self'.

To return to Metz, he uses this Freudian notion of the fear of sexual desire (and the castration that it threatens) in order to explain the fetishistic elements of cinema spectatorship. For the infant, once the mother is understood to be sexually different (because she lacks a penis), he fears that he 'might be subjected to a similar fate' (Metz, 1986: 69). In other words, he fears that as punishment for being too close to the mother or of not giving her up, he might become castrated like her (disempowered). In order to cope with this, the child must 'double-up' its belief and hold two contradictory positions: first, that the mother is castrated; second, that she is not. So, the child thinks of her lack of a penis as castration, but he also disavows this too (knows that it is not the case). More broadly, this means that the male fears woman because of her subordinated position within society (which he understands as relating to her female sexuality) and, yet, at the same time he knows that her sexuality is not really a subordinate one (which is threatening to the male). Both socially and within cinema, there are methods of coping with this contradictory position of woman as threat. Another form of disavowal is available through fetishisation. The fetishist will deny or cover up the 'lack' through over-investment in another object, a kind of substitution for what is lacking. Of course, this also draws attention to the lack, since the fetish always evokes what is lacking. We need only think of the iconic images of female, starting with an emphasis on fetish objects – high heels, cigarettes, guns – in order to see the correlation between the psychoanalytic explanations for the fetish and its representation in cinema. For Metz, cinema is the fetish to the spectator's fetishist. Since the spectator knows that the screen image is not real (it represents lack/absence), but is able to take it as such, the spectator is able to disavow that knowledge of absence and replace it with presence (taking the screen image to be real, suspension of disbelief).

This model of apparatus theory offered scope for understanding what cinema is and how it functions at the level of industry, apparatus, and spectatorship. As Susan Hayward notes:

> it is in these investigations into cinema's relation to voyeurism and fetishism and its relation to the Imaginary and Symbolic Orders that these early years of psychoanalytic film theory made their greatest inroads into the advancing of film theory. Cinema was seen as to embody psychic desire. The screen became the site for the projection of our fantasies and desires.
>
> (2006: 285)

MULVEY AND FEMINIST FILM THEORY

As has already been made clear, such a theory was reductive in terms of gendered spectatorship and made no effort to reflect upon the phallocentric nature of film, film studies, and even psychoanalysis. Laura Mulvey's (1975) seminal text, 'Visual pleasure and narrative cinema', attempted to account for the gendered dynamics of cinema and cinema spectatorship by analysing the film text and form through a similar psychoanalytic model. This model of psychoanalytic theory, while both popular and controversial within film academia, certainly offered scope for a more reflective filmmaking practice that would avoid the derivative model of representation found in popular cinema. Mulvey went on to practise film using these theories and insights.

For Mulvey, cinema functioned to reinforce 'patterns of fascination' already existing within wider society and culture. So, the study of cinema offered a way of under-standing the gender dynamics evident within film and wider society. Mulvey states that her paper examines 'the way film repeats, reveals and even plays on the straight, socially established interpretation of sexual difference which controls images, erotic ways of looking and spectacle' (2009: 711). Mulvey's project is to take cinema to task for its conservative and suppressive representational strategies, and she uses psychoanalytic theory as a 'political weapon' because 'it demonstrates the way the unconscious of patriarchal society has structured film form' (ibid.). Central to Mulvey's argument was the perpetuation of a cinematic mode that constructed the male spectator and filmic characters (male) as active and the woman as passive and in terms of castration (in the way that their presence caused anxiety for the male, and in the way did she not have agency). According to Mulvey, phallocentrism depends upon the image of the castrated woman in order to give patriarchy meaning. It is only through her subordination as an image signifying 'lack' that patriarchy can insist on the phallus as a signifier of power. So, woman first comes to symbolise castration or she comes to have meaning only through motherhood (for Freud, this demonstrates her desire to have the phallus, through having a child as a substitute for the phallus she cannot have): 'Woman is bearer of meaning, not maker of it' (ibid.: 712). It is important to remember here that Mulvey is attempting to account for the way in which the unconscious gender mechanisms born of the nuclear family structure lead to a society (and a cinema) in which woman does not have the same access to power as man. She is advocating an understanding of these processes in order that we might challenge it. She turns to cinema both as a way of drawing attention to gender imbalances and also as a potential tool against it (through experimental cinema).

First, she notes that cinema promotes pleasure through 'looking' (at other people) – scopophilia. Freud had discussed scopophilia in terms of how children developed sexually through taking pleasure in looking at people and turning them into the object of the gaze. Voyeurism for Freud was a perversion of this pleasure in looking whereby the 'looker' can only gain pleasure from 'peeping'. For Mulvey, the cinema (darkened auditorium, screen image cannot return the look) creates the conditions for voyeuristic activity. It positions the spectator as voyeur. Mulvey adds that this is a narcissistic voyeurism since there is pleasure in looking at the performances on screen, but in addition (and here Mulvey, like Metz, uses the mirror stage model) the spectator identifies with the performances as ideal egos (the image the spectator wishes to emulate or aspire to). This is a contradictory and conflicting position: to look at the screen object (sexual desire) but also to identify with it, and to see oneself in its place (ego identification). For Mulvey, cinema reinforces this dichotomy. Since, in Hollywood cinema, for the most part, the spectator is constructed as male and the object of the look female, this also poses a threat to the male because the woman evokes castration. In Mulvey's account of the sexual imbalance of cinematic gender representation, she notes that 'pleasure in looking has been split between active/male and passive/female' (2009: 715), and women are constructed in exhibitionist terms, displayed for erotic desire, connoting what she refers to as 'to-be-looked-at-ness' (ibid.). She points to the tendency to represent women, especially in classical Hollywood cinema, as show girls, pin-ups, and so on. The presence of the woman also tends to work against the narrative, particularly in those moments of erotic contemplation where the woman is simply 'on show'.

Narrative is the realm of masculine agency because men take steps that lead to narrative progression. Women have no agency and are simply objects of the look for the most part. While Mulvey's theory seems like an indictment against the way in which men and women are structured and represented, any overview of a large body of popular film will find that this is the tendency. Women in film function as objects of desire for the male characters within the diegesis, as well as objects of desire for the male spectator.

Because the heterosexual dynamics of cinema insist that the (male) spectator cannot gaze at another male, the on-screen male character is constructed as a point of identification (ideal ego). The narrative is situated around the male character's actions, allowing the spectator access to agency and power through him. In addition, the on-screen male character also employs the conventions of the 'look', by looking at other female characters. This offers not only a point of identification, but also the power of the look in terms of sexual agency and desire. However, as Mulvey suggests, the woman as an object of the look also poses a problem, for she also threatens castration, thereby threatening unpleasure. Since woman connotes sexual difference and points back to male 'entry into the symbolic order and the law of the father' (ibid.: 718), she also provokes anxiety, since she signifies the 'lack' so threatening to masculine power. The male unconscious can deal with this in two ways: voyeurism or fetishism. The first, voyeurism, focuses on the woman's sexual difference, and returns the man to the original trauma (ibid.). In this scenario the woman is investigated and the man seeks to understand woman's mystery. Here, sadism features, as the woman is often punished or rendered guilty. Often, this guilt is connected to her sexuality. This is typical of the film noir, in which man is confirmed as being on the correct side of morality and woman is confirmed as deviant. The sadistic component of the film involves the battle with and punishment of the woman. Mulvey uses the example of Hitchcock's films *Rear Window* (1954) and *Vertigo* (1958), in which the (male) spectator is closely aligned with the identificatory position of the male protagonists, and in which the woman is punished or ultimately controlled by the male. The second way in which the male unconscious can cope with the female is through fetishistic scopophilia. This involves the male investing in the beauty of the object as a means of compensating for or disavowing woman's lack and the threat of castration brought about by her presence. The woman is turned into a fetish or fetish objects are suggested/evoked within her sphere in order to deny the threat of castration posed by her. The fetish acts as a sort of phallus substitute (minus phallic power, of course), which renders woman safe for erotic contemplation. In its most basic or obvious form, this might take the form of long, lingering shots of female body parts such as legs, ankles, breast, and outstretched arms. This also extends to inanimate objects such as cigarettes and jewellery, as mentioned already. These draw attention away from the absence of the phallus by invoking them through such objects and shots. The male is then safe from the anxiety of castration and woman can remain the object of sexual desire. The threat of female sexuality has been offset by the introduction of the fetish.

EXERCISE **SELF-REFLEXIVE FILMMAKING**

Make a two-minute film that considers the means by which the spectator is invited to identify with male figures and look at female figures. You may employ either males or females, or both. The film should attempt to subvert or undermine the typical modes of representation that construct power relations through the mechanisms of the gaze. The film, therefore, should be centred on strategies of 'looking' and 'looked at'. Think about the ways in which such representations might seem naturalised or inevitable.

See *Peeping Tom* (Michael Powell, 1960), *Rear Window* (Alfred Hitchcock, 1954), and *Psycho* (Alfred Hitchcock, 1960).

FEMINIST FILM THEORY OF THE 1980S

While Mulvey's paper contributed towards the understanding of how cinematic mechanisms perpetuate sexual subordination and imbalance, it was sometimes questioned as being too totalising. In the wake of her contribution, other theorists attempted to open up avenues of exploration and interpretation that would point to alternative means of understanding the cinematic unconscious. Others determined that the psychoanalytic approach was too text-based, and they turned instead to cultural studies and, more specifically, audience studies in order to determine if and how audiences negotiated meaning. Within psychoanalytic film studies, theorists questioned Mulvey's account of gender identification (Mulvey even did this in a later revision of her position). Mary Ann Doane (1987), for example, argued that female spectatorship could be accounted for though an examination of the woman's film. Doane argues that, unlike the male spectator who maintains distance from the female screen image through disavowal, the female spectator did not maintain such distance. Instead, there is over-identification with the female screen image. In other words, female spectators identify with lack. This lack of distance explained for Doane and like-minded feminist film theorists the tendency towards pathos and extreme sentimentality in the woman's film, and the responses to the films by female audiences. Similarly, she notes that this lack of distance from the image inhibits desire. Women do not desire or have a problem relating to desire. Not only are the characters often victimised, but the female spectator identifies with this victimisation. Later feminist film theorists interrogated the universalising of the gaze as inherently male. E. Ann Kaplan (1994) countered that films evidenced a female look. Yet, often the female look, as in the case of 1970s male stars, was stripped of its affection and kindness (its femininity). When the woman did look, she was represented negatively. She had a deviant sexuality; her ability to look was symptomatic of her personal and emotional defects. Kaplan notes that while films might allow for a female look and a reversal of the typical male/active/dominant, female/passive/submissive binary, the female look did not challenge the binary of masculine and feminine. As she argues, 'recently, women have been permitted in representations to assume (step into) the position defined as "masculine", so long as the man then steps into his position, thus keeping the whole structure intact' (Kaplan, 1994: 29). In other words, in this scenario, the woman takes on a masculine position and masculinity is still represented as dominant. So, as Kaplan summarises, 'the gaze is not necessarily male (literally), but to own and activate the gaze, given our language and the structure of the unconscious, is to be in the "masculine" position' (ibid.).

Other theorists questioned Mulvey's claim that only the female body could be constructed as the object of the look. For Richard Dyer, it was not the case that men are not represented as objects for erotic contemplation (in film or other popular imagery), but that different photographic strategies were employed in order to deal with this violation of the typical codes of looking (men who look/women who are looked at). Whereas the represented, 'looked at' woman will avert her eyes, noted Dyer (2002), while still maintaining the contract of looker and looked at, the male image stares elsewhere, as if concentrating on something else, entirely disinterested in the looker. Often, the male looked above and out, which contrasted with the downward look of the woman. Dyer examined images from erotic magazines, particularly the male pin-up, in which the act of being objectified is countered by an over-expression of masculine and phallic connotations: muscles, sporting symbolism, and so on. His analysis pointed towards the tensions of representation and to the ways in which the phallic signifier is just that: a signifier equally unattainable for man as for woman. If man had access to it, why overemphasise it? Similarly, Steve Neale, in his article 'Masculinity as spectacle', suggests that the thesis proposed by Mulvey paid little attention to the complexities of male representation and spectatorial identification. Neale argued that while the male character might act as a point of identification, he 'may also be a source of further images and feelings of castration, inasmuch as that ideal is something to which the subject is never adequate' (1993: 15). So, even the narcissistic identification so readily assumed by Mulvey and others is not necessarily established unproblematically. Using the same concepts and terminology as Mulvey, Neale suggested that voyeurism is not necessarily bound to gender binaries, and that men are subject to the sadistic mechanisms of voyeurism, especially in the case of war films, actions films, and westerns. He noted that masculinity as spectacle is de-eroticised and instead represented though violence and action scenes whereby the 'male struggle becomes pure spectacle' (ibid.: 16). He used the example of Leone's westerns, whereby the spectacles of violence, through freeze-framing and extreme close-ups, evidence both voyeurism and fetishism. In the place of desire (the look) is fear and aggression (ibid.). Important within Neale's works was the insistence that the male look is not a simple manifestation of desire in relation to the female. Rather, the male gaze is more complex and, in addition, the on-screen male is as much subject to the gaze as the female, and that the 'spectacularised' male body disavowed eroticism through representational strategies that emphasised masculinity and agency.

EXERCISE **LOOKING AT THE MALE BODY**

Produce a short film that visualises a female looker and a male 'looked at'. You may consider using shot/reverse shot, long shots, and close-ups, but the film must construct a position of identification with the on-screen woman. Consider Kaplan's and Neale's discussions of how the woman looks and how the man is looked at. Following the film, consider your film in relation to their arguments. Did your film demonstrate their claims or undermine them? Does the reversal of the look pose problems for the film, and you as filmmaker? Does it seem realistic? Why?

See *American Gigolo* (Paul Schrader, 1980), *Saturday Night Fever* (John Badham, 1977), and *Variety* (Bette Gordon, 1983).

CHAPTER 9

Contemporary cinema

FROM CLASSICAL TO POST-CLASSICAL HOLLYWOOD

Our discussion of contemporary cinema will begin with Hollywood, and trace the transformations within the Hollywood system outwards. This is not to suggest that Hollywood is central to an understanding of contemporary cinema, simply that such transformations are more recognisable through Hollywood and American cinema more generally. As a dominant mode of film (industry and form), we can see how institutional and cultural shifts slowly changed the American film both in terms of practice and in terms of the films themselves. The Hollywood system was, in fact, always transformative, and the classical Hollywood film was anything but stable. If we are to attempt to identify the 'beginning of the end' of the classical Hollywood period, we could end up going back to the early days of cinema. However, there are key moments within classical Hollywood's later years that act as significant markers of change. The post-war years, in particular, saw a number of scandals, legal cases, and social crises and ideological shifts that are now considered to be part of the move from the classical to the post-classical era.

Institutionally, the monopolistic practices of the Hollywood studios were being challenged legally. Between 1938 and 1948, the US Justice Department had been investigating the film industry's practice of block booking, monopoly of production and distribution, and even its practice of censorship. The antitrust suit was filed against the eight companies of Paramount (which formed a kind of test case about vertical integration and monopolisation), Loew-MGM, RKO, Warner Bros, Twentieth Century Fox, Columbia, Universal, and United Artists. The final decision of 1948, and upheld in 1949, banned unfair distribution practices, limited vertical integration, and demanded that studios were divested of their theatre pools (Balio, 1985: 403). But, as we know, this did not lead to the collapse of the studios altogether; rather, it led to a restructuring of them. The studio system did decline but the studios themselves found alternative ways to maintain dominance over the industry. They focused on distribution, rather than production and exhibition. After the boom year of 1946, then, the studios witnessed a complete overhaul of the system. In the next 15 years, the film industry would see a 43 per cent decline in box office receipts. Not only did the studios have to contend with the Supreme Court's Paramount ruling, changing their relatively efficient system of standardisation, but there were other issues that complicated matters further.

Maltby connects the decline of the film industry with the growing prosperity of the average American during the war years. At the time, wages and savings increased, leading to a comfortable leisure class in the post-war years (Maltby, 2003). People had far more disposal income, which was in turn disposed on the growing amount of consumer products made available through advertising and marketing. People were working less and spending more time on entertainment. In addition, the post-war years saw an increase in the birth rate, hence the term 'baby boom' (baby boomers being the generation born between 1945 and 1964). This was also a society scarred by the effects of World War II, and far more liberal than the pre-war generation. The old values that had defined the pre-war society were shifting. In the 1950s, civil rights movements began to emerge. The middle classes increasingly moved to the suburbs, since they could now afford homes of their own in neighbourhoods outside of the cities.

As Maltby notes, by 1960, a quarter of the American population had moved to the suburbs. Of course, this, coupled with the growth of TV culture, led to a huge decline in city cinema attendance, as more people began to stay within their local areas. Newer forms of exhibition became popular, including the drive-in, which Balio (1985) links to the growth of car ownership during the 1950s. The drive-ins catered for this new mobile audience, and demonstrated a shift in the nature of cinema exhibition not only in terms of the way that people saw the films, but also in terms of a more casual film viewing experience. Because these drive-in theatres generally only had access to second-rate films, they tended to show the exploitation teenpix, double bills or low-budget horrors. But even the themes of these drive-in movies suggest the shifting within the film industry – they were largely targeted at youth markets, they were often relatively explicit for the time, and they actually shifted the film industry's big season from winter to summer.

In addition, the system of censorship in Hollywood during the studio years, the Production Code, or Hays Code (named after William Hays), was increasingly challenged and undermined in the later years of the classical Hollywood period. Hollywood had enacted a system similar to self-regulation, whereby each film was subject to approval by the Production Code Authority. This code was initiated due to the pressure from certain groups within the public, who saw cinema as a potentially immoral influence on the general public. The Production Code had initially been quite strict, forbidding graphic sex, interracial relationships, crime, and the positive representation of anything that could be considered immoral. However, in the post-war years, and increasingly throughout the 1950s, the moral codes that seemed to structure and determine the Production Code were becoming disregarded. Given the social climate of change (in terms of gender, civil rights, and so on), the Production Code seemed to belong to a bygone era.

Frank Caso suggests that the challenge to the Production Code was influenced by and part of the overall shift in the industry, audiences, and films of the time. He notes:

> The decline of the Code's censorship power actually began in the 1950s, as the studios' control of the American entertainment business came under attack. The antitrust suit forced the studios to sell of the movie theatres they owned, opening the doors for foreign films that did not have to adhere to the Pro-duction Code. However, cultural historians agree that the mass introduction of television . . . was the single most important factor in the decline of the Hollywood studio system.
>
> (Caso, 2008: 30)

This suggests that the shift to post-classical cinema must be contextualised. Not only was the industry transforming internally, but the media landscape was providing threats and opportunities for film. Among the consequences of the decline of classical Hollywood (as an institution and, in some ways, as a mode of practice), was the rise of independent film. However, it must be noted, as Maltby (2003) suggests, that the rise of 'independent' film did not necessary represent freedom from the studios. Rather, where studios had stepped back from the production of film, they now benefited from the new system, which afforded them less risk. Studios did not need to commit themselves to productions; rather, they would contract smaller independent companies on a short-term basis. Instead, independents were still dependent upon the studios for distribution.

POST-CLASSICAL

Nevertheless, in terms of the 'independent spirit' of films, there was certainly an ideological shift evident in some sense. This is perhaps unsurprising, given the broader socio-political era of post-classical Hollywood: the1960s (Ryan and Kellner, 1990; Monaco, 2003; Shiel, 2006). Remember that this is a period marked by both turmoil and progressive social liberalism. On the one hand, the Vietnam War produced a charge of anti-war sentiment, all of which questioned the morality of US imperialism. Counter-hegemonic movements arose in response to this and extended to national interests. Rejection of American ideological norms was manifested in the counter-cultural movement, in the student protest groups, in radicalism, and the general rise of the left. The civil rights movement highlighted a long legacy of American prejudice and social inequality, and the feminist movement questioned dominant patriarchal discourse and practices. In addition, key events, marked by tragedy, indicated the extent to which the calls for progressive reform were resisted. In 1963, John F. Kennedy, a symbol for progressive liberal transformation, was assassinated. In 1967, the civil rights activist Malcolm X was assassinated, followed by Martin Luther King and Robert Kennedy in 1968 (Ryan and Kellner, 1990).

The 'independent spirit', part of the broader New Hollywood era (Elsaesser, 2004), which reflected the social turmoil of the period, was not manifested throughout the post-classical period, but in a selection of films that became popularised at the time: *Bonnie and Clyde* (Arthur Penn, 1967), *Midnight Cowboy* (John Schlesinger, 1969), *Night of the Living Dead* (George A. Romero, 1968), *Easy Rider* (Denis Hopper, 1969), and *Medium Cool* (Haskell Wexler, 1969). In fact, many films retained the formal mode of the classical Hollywood film. Similarly, the general tendency of popular cinema was to maintain the status quo, rather than reflect the social reality for some (not all) of the time. Finally, many of the films that are now considered key examples of the alternative or counter-cultural trend in cinema were studio films, either partly or wholly. Thus, these 'art' films, as they are sometimes referred to, formed one minor aspect of a re-arrangement in Hollywood practice. Horwath refers to the ways in which the film industry responded to the social climate:

> The great (and adaptable) majority of those employed in the film industry experienced this period as one phase among many, as a stage which allowed them to behave in a more 'radical' or 'independent' manner but which didn't adversely affect their ability to survive the more conservative climate that lay ahead. A none too small minority, however, identified more deeply and concretely with the new opportunities of art and life; they exhausted their energies more rapidly . . . and had difficulty making the transition when all the 'fun' was over.
>
> (2004: 13–14)

The 'independent spirit' of the alternative, social realist, and/or radical films of the late 1960s seemed to have a limited life span. In fact, in retrospect, the movement was particularly brief, and its emphasis, both socially and within academia, is somewhat disproportionate to the output of films. However, in terms of the influence of the films of this period, Shiel notes that:

> The new topicality of film as a medium and its reinvigorated popularity with youth also led to its growth as a widespread pursuit in film schools and universities across the country, by virtue of which film carried a new intellectual, artistic and political legitimacy.
>
> (2006: 20)

This independence, institutionally at least, later manifested itself in another trend of New Hollywood cinema: 'Hollywood's reorientation' (Kramer, 2005: 174). This 'reorientation' is more clearly marked with the film *Jaws* (Steven Spielberg, 1975) and the rise of the 'movie brats': the young generation of filmmakers, influenced by the European films and movements of the 1950s and 1960s, yet accepting of mainstream cinema and the re-aligned studio conglomerates. Many of these New Hollywood directors were film school graduates (Martin Scorsese, Brian De Palma, George Lucas, Paul Schrader, and Francis Ford Coppola) whose work was informed by film criticism (King, 2004: 20). Their independence, therefore, stems not from their political or institutional opposition, but more in the form of their directorial authorship within the reformed post-classical film industry. After all, both *Jaws* and later *Star Wars Episode IV: A New Hope* were blockbuster films that, in contrast to earlier socio-political films, were generally ideologically conservative and sought not to challenge or alienate audiences, but to please. Such films are indicative of an industry that is responding to the entertainment and media market. The blockbuster functions not as an isolated film text, but as part of the broader commercialisation of the film industry, in which synergised conglomerates come to use film as one element of a larger commodity.

Thomas Schatz notes that the end result of this commercialisation process is that is it impossible to extrapolate the 'text' from the commercial process (Schatz, 1993: 10). Schatz notes that this commercialisation of film texts coincides with a shift in emphasis from character to plot. For him, in films such as *Star Wars Episode IV: A New Hope*, 'characters are essentially plot functions' and such films focus more on pace, spectacle, and special effects (ibid.: 23). Instead, a film such as *Star Wars Episode IV: A New Hope* (and perhaps *Raiders of the Lost Ark*, Steven Spielberg, 1981) plays upon generic codes and evokes nostalgia for past genres. The potential danger here, for Schatz, is that films are, consequently, depoliticised. This point is perhaps reflected in the recent film *Avatar* (James Cameron, 2009), in which the colonialist and imperialist subtext is negated by the focus on spectacle, action, and special effects. Indeed, the film's narrative plays a secondary role to the display of a futuristic world, and complex characterisation is replaced with the spectacularisation of narrative. Problematically, this world reflects stereotypes of indigenous and ethnic groups. The veil of political correctness and the seeming call for indigenous rights and sovereignty belie the association between non-white racial groups and primitiveness. It is, therefore, possible to read New Hollywood and the post-classical period more generally, as reflective of the era's identity politics. The early post-classical period, with its relative investment in ideological and political debate, was followed by a perceived return to right-wing conservatism (Ryan and Kellner, 1990).

IDENTITY POLITICS

As we have seen, in tandem with the institutional re-organisation of American film, 1960s society was equally in flux. The movements towards liberalism and equality were politically motivated and emphasised the centrality of identity in oppressive social and cultural structures. The civil rights movement, the feminist movement, and gay liberation, as well as counter-cultural movements, sought to question the hegemonic structures that organised and perpetuated social imbalance. Identity politics was (and is) the process of raising awareness about the systems and structures (whether political, religious, familial) that maintain this imbalance, and recognising the means by which such discourses of identity function (ibid.). Thus, identity politics is reflective but also actively seeks to challenge the status quo through the politicisation of identities, in the sense that the concept of identity is caught up in politics (for example, the politics of race, or of gender and sexuality). If identity is interconnected with, and formed through, discourses of power (and equally disempowerment), then film is implicated in this. After all, film shapes the ways in which identity is represented; film represents and identifies. Thus, we can examine how films represented identity in 'normative' or 'conservative' ways, as well as how film challenged hegemonic notions and constructions of identity. Film can be complicit with, or resistant to, dominant ideologies (Wood, 1986), representing those with socially 'normative' forms of identity yet marginalising or misrepresenting those considered outside of 'normative', or using transcoding strategies to undermine or subvert negative representations of identities (Hall, 1997).

During the 1960s and 1970s, identity politics, organised through the various movements above, challenged the notion of 'normative' identity, since normative was generally understood as white, male, middle class, and heterosexual. During the classical Hollywood period, films generally maintained a system of representation that reflected the ideologically normative formulations of identity. While the post-classical period by no means marked a fundamental break from this tradition, the institutional transformations, coupled with the wider social call for change, meant that some re-articulation of identity, and therefore a re-figuring of discursive formations of power, was evident to some degree. Such identity politics can be identified both through readings of films, and thus a reading of how the films construct identities, and through the films themselves and their representations of the politics of identity. We can use two examples to illustrate this: race and racial politics, and gender and gender politics. We will limit ourselves to a discussion of the New Hollywood era, as an in-depth review of the post-classical period is beyond the scope of this project.

As Hall (ibid.: 256) notes, classical Hollywood cinematic representations of race tended to perpetuate hegemonic discourses of white superiority. For example, Hall (ibid.) outlines the various manifestations of racial representation, which functioned largely to alleviate white guilt and dispel any form of racial politics. Where some mainstream films in the later classical Hollywood period encouraged 'integration' between blacks and whites, this was later challenged within oppositional or alternative films of the New Hollywood period. The problem with representations of integration was that films (such as *Guess Who's Coming to Dinner*, Stanley Kramer, 1967) tended to view integration as black integration into white society.

Later films about and/or by black people rejected such calls for assimilation, echoing the wider sentiment among black radicals during the period. As Ryan and Kellner (1990: 31) suggest, revolutionary blacks resisted engaging with whites in order to reform the system. Equally, filmmaking needed to come from the source, rather than through the oppressor. Where liberal films had sought to represent black people more fairly, the issue was that white people, and the largely white Hollywood industry, controlled production. Films such as *Shaft* (Gordon Parks, 1971) and *Sweet Sweetback's Baadasss Song* (Melvin Van Peebles, 1971) attempted to re-frame popular film within a black context. The blaxploitation film, as it became known, was situated within the urban social reality of contemporary America. *Sweet Sweetback's Baadasss Song*, in particular, employed a practice of resistance by abandoning many of the conventions of dominant cinema. In the film, a young man, Sweetback, is positioned against the police, and the film traces his ultimately successful attempts to evade them. Throughout the film, Sweetback becomes more politicised, and thus the film acts as a potential message for black spectators. Thus, this film uses transcoding strategies to subvert negative stereotypes of blacks by re-appropriating them as positive.

The feminist movements of the 1960s and 1970s were part of the overall cultural shift that was taking place in the US. Feminists recognised the subordinated position they held under patriarchy and attempted to challenge this in a number of ways. While early second-wave feminists sought to distance themselves from the perceived source of their oppression (men), a later, less radical form of feminism emerged. However, while feminism and feminist practice entered the mainstream, feminist film practice did not (for example, in the same way as black filmmakers and the blaxploitation film). So, New Hollywood feminist film of the period was, for the most part, made by men. Female feminist filmmakers operated from the margins or sporadically within the industry, and female filmmakers noted the lack of access for aspirational women filmmakers into the film industry (Kearney, 2006). So, while there were many female film directors practicing at the time, their films did not receive the same backing or exposure as male-directed film. A number of women filmmakers successfully entered the mainstream, with films such as *The Heartbreak Kid* (Elaine May, 1971), *Wanda* (Barbara Loden, 1970), *Between the Lines* (Joan Micklin, 1977), and *Girlfriends* (Claudia Weill, 1978). Kuhn (1994) terms the films 'New Women's Cinema' (which includes films by men about women), although this term was not widely adopted by the filmmakers at the time. This is not to suggest that such films did not evoke the subversive and oppositional voice of the 'other'. *Girlfriends*, for example, uses a similar strategy to *Sweetback*, in terms of adopting a formalist mode that negates the patriarchal form of classical Hollywood narrative. The film uses an episodic structure and uses what we might today term 'guerrilla' practices.

The centrality of women within the narrative demonstrates the differences in representational strategies and thematic concerns between male and female directors, and especially between male and female directors thematising feminist concerns. Where films such as *Alice Doesn't Live Here Anymore* (Martin Scorsese, 1974) and *Klute* (Alan J. Pakula, 1971) have a tendency to reproduce the very patriarchal gender stereotypes they seek to question (both films end in the suggestion of the re-establishment of the heterosexual romance), in both *Klute* and *Alice Doesn't Live Here Anymore*, male figures are represented as villains or protectors. Each woman is initially confronted by a 'bad' male figure that does not fulfil the 'normal' role of protector of woman, and each encounters a 'good' male figure with which they form an attachment. However, in *Girlfriends*, women's most important relationships are with each other, and the film is primarily concerned with how women might overcome disempowerment, oppression, and/or marginalisation through communities of help and support. Instead, the film denies the traditional happy ending, and therefore refuses to close off meaning. Identity, here, is not fixed or something that is resolved through partnership or the attainment of goals; rather, identity is in flux, is not stable, and is never 'normative'.

GLOBAL INDUSTRIES AND GLOBALISATION

So far, we have discussed US, or more specifically Hollywood, cinema. However, Hollywood has never been at the centre of film production, distribution, and consumption. It is only from a particular Anglo-European perspective that this may seem the case. More recently, and because of the development of communications and entertainment technologies, scholars and consumers alike have recognised the globalisation of the film industry and film consumption as one of the defining features of cinema today (Jenkins, 2006; Zaniello, 2007; Acland, 2003). The globalisation of film can be understood in terms of the film industry, filmmaking, and the film products. In the book *Transnational Cinema: A Film Reader*, the section 'Global Cinema in the Digital Age' suggests how globalisation in filmic terms is interlinked with the rise of digital technologies (Erza and Rowden, 2006). Similarly, the globalisation of the film industry is often associated with the rise of media conglomerates. First, we will outline a definition of globalisation before considering these issues in relation to current cinematic practice.

Globalisation refers to the way that economic, cultural, political, and communicative activity is freed from the constraints of national borders. For example, where lack of infrastructure, poor communications, or trade barriers might have previously limited the free flow of products across national boundaries, today such barriers are far less apparent. Giddens defines globalisation as the 'intensification of worldwide social relations which link distant localities in such a way that local happenings are shaped by events occurring many miles away and vice versa' (Giddens, 1990: 64). To use a clichéd example, the fast food chain McDonald's demonstrates both economic and cultural globalisation, in which the company can trade in areas outside of its own nation and also exert soft power over other nations. Such cultural influence is often read as a negative element of globalisation (Ritzer, 1993; Stiglitz, 2002). In some ways, globalisation represents a progressive shift that encourages communication and interaction, and eradicates cultural barriers. Yet, in others, globalisation is interconnected with power. Here, powerful nations (or corporations) exert influence over less powerful nations, challenge national sovereignty (as argued by anti-globalisation organisations), and have the capacity to eradicate local cultures through cultural imperialism. The media industry is at the centre of debates about globalisation since the last few decades have seen the rise of transnational media empires that own and run a huge range of entertainment media companies, many of which are synergised and converged. Newer film and entertainment technologies both act as transnational bridges for film communication and are often one subset of the media conglomerates' distribution channels. Acland notes that 'since the 1980s there has been the parallel evolution of multiple windows of exhibition and distribution for filmed entertainment and the globalization of both markets and ownership structures of the corporations involved' (Acland, 2003: 24).

Concerns about the rise of globalised conglomeration usually refer to the ways in which such global flow is typically one-way. For example, the internationalisation of the film market has meant that smaller national cinemas have little chance to compete against the marketing and distribution power of the larger globalized conglomerates and, without national film protection policies, national cinemas may fall into decline. A brief look at the UK box office ratings paints a slightly less damning picture; however, UK cinema screens seem to mainly exhibit US films. In the week of 16–18 December 2011, the top 10 films were (Film Council, 2011):

1. *Sherlock Holmes: A Game of Shadows* (Guy Ritchie, 2011, UK/USA, Warner Bros).

2. *Alvin and the Chipmunks: Chipwrecked* (Mike Mitchell, 2011, USA, Twentieth Century Fox).

3. *Arthur Christmas* (Sarah Smith, 2011, UK/USA, Sony Pictures).

4. *Puss in Boots* (Chris Miller, 2011, USA, Paramount).

5. *New Year's Eve* (Gary Marshall, 2011, USA, Warner Bros).

6. *Hugo* (Martin Scorsese, 2011, UK/USA/France, Entertainment).

7. *Happy Feet 2* (George Miller, 2011, Australia, Warner Bros).

8. *The Twilight Saga: Breaking Dawn – Part 1* (Bill Condon, 2011, USA, eOne Films).

9. *A Very Harold and Kumar 3D Christmas* (Todd Strauss-Schulson, 2011, USA, Warner Bros).

10. *My Week With Marilyn* (Simon Curtis, 2011, UK/USA, Entertainment).

What we can see is that even within a localised market, local film is secondary to foreign (US) imports. Similarly, those films with UK productions are generally US–European co-productions, and, for the most part, all film companies are attached (either through production or distribution) to larger globalised media conglomerates.

This is by no means a recent phenomenon, but it demonstrates the challenges of globalisation for those film industries that operate outside of the major players. There are of, course examples, of largely UK-funded and -produced films (*The Kings' Speech*, Tom Hooper, 2010), but the point is, perhaps, that the concept of national cinema is somewhat at odds with the globalisation of the film industry. International co-productions allow filmmakers to combine financial, creative, and practical resources. Often, co-productions operate under treaties between nations, whereby in order to participate, a certain financial commitment may be required. In Europe, funding is available for co-productions through a number of European initiatives such as the Council of Europe's Eurimages (2011), which supported *Enter the Void* (Gasper Noe, 2007) and the European Commission's MEDIA (2011), which supported *Melancholia* (Lars von Trier, 2011), since co-productions have access to more markets than a single national production. The expansion of markets is one of the driving forces of the contemporary globalised film industry. Such co-productions occur at the level of financing, production, and distribution. While there is concern that the integration and interdependence between national film markets puts non-US cinema in a vulnerable position (Real, 1996; Miller *et al.*, 2001), the relationship is perhaps more complex than this. While it may be the case that non-US films have less penetration in the US market and that US films have far more exposure in non-US markets (Miller *et al.*, 2001), it must be acknowledged that films take on a more transnational dimension.

NATIONAL/INTERNATIONAL/TRANSNATIONAL

The concept of national cinema has been much debated due to its slipperiness (Higson, 2000; Vitali and Willemen, 2006). National cinema might be defined in economic terms, thematic or representational terms, aesthetic or stylistic terms, and/or production terms. Where Hollywood is assumed to have transnational reach in the sense that it does not really exist or function as a national cinema (Crofts, 2002: 26), other cinemas are considered national in the sense that they are pitted against and struggle to compete with external (primarily US) cinema, both in industry and cultural terms (ibid.). It may even be problematic to refer to a national cinema beyond the influence of dominant US cinema. As O'Regan (1996) suggests, many national cinemas draw from the traditions of US film. This does not necessarily suggest that US cinema is simply mapped onto national cinematic strategies, rather national cinemas appropriate and localise US film forms, styles, genres and aesthetics (ibid.: 115). While this might suggest that national cinemas (and national identities) are formed in relation to outside forces, at times this cultural flow and appropriation comes to define particular national cinemas. As Higson (2000: 61) notes, 'cinemas established in nation-states are rarely autonomous cultural industries and the film business has long operated on a regional, national and transnational basis'. Higson identifies two levels of transnational film. First, transnational film operates at the level of production, where productions are formed across nations.

This has happened since the early years of film, where cast and crew would migrate to places for the purposes of film production. Similarly, we might note that *The Lord of the Rings: The Fellowship of the Ring* (Peter Jackson, 2001) was funded by Hollywood, filmed in New Zealand, and had a largely English cast. Second, we can understand transnationalism in the context of the distribution and the reception of film. Films are rarely distributed only to the country of origin; thus, the experience of watching a foreign film is a transnational one (Higson, 2000). And as Higson adds, 'when films do travel, there is no certainty that audiences will receive them in the same way in different cultural contexts' (ibid.). Often, when films are distributed to other countries, they undergo a process of localisation, whereby they will be dubbed, subtitled, or edited in order to appeal to the local audience. This might involve the translation of particular cultural references or codes, or the elimination of details that would not be appropriate for particular markets (for example, through censorship).

A useful example that demonstrates the complexities of transnationalism is that of anime. An analysis of anime reveals that cultural flow operates, not just from West to East, but back and forth between nations. As a transnational cultural force, anime also undermines arguments about Hollywood's dominance over local markets, as well as the US resistance to foreign film products. Anime reflects both the globalisation of the film industry and the relationship between cinema, nation, and the international. Anime, the term given to Japanese animation outside of Japan, is a general term for animation within Japan. The term has come to represent, in the West, not only the national origins of particular animations, but also a stylistic and aesthetic mode. While anime might be thought of as 'culturally fragrant' (Iwabuchi, 2002), it has more transnational origins. Anime obviously has its origins in the Japanese arts, and stems from the tradition of Japanese woodblock printing and later manga cartoon books (Brenner, 2007: 3). However, the Japanese arts were also influenced by (and influenced) Western artistic traditions, particularly in the Meiji Period (1868–1912). Brenner notes that 'in . . . adoptions of Western style . . . Japanese artists immediately incorporated their own styles and traditions to create a hybrid art form' (ibid.: 4). Brenner goes on to note how Japanese cartoons constructed Westerners as stereotypical caricatures, indicating how they did not simply reproduce Western representational strategies. Similarly, the manga and anime characteristic of large, expressive eyes has its origins in US cartoons such as Mickey Mouse and Betty Boop. Disney animation also influenced Japanese artists. Films such as *Snow White and the Seven Dwarfs* (David Hand, 1937) were well regarded by Japan's top manga and anime artist, Osamu Tezuka, whose artistic style inspired anime aesthetics (Gray, 2010). Today, we can also assess anime in terms of its flow from East to West. In the 1960s, Japanese anime became popularised on US television through the TV show *Astro Boy* (Osamu Tezuka, 1963–1975). Later, anime became more widely available on Western television, and, during the 1980s, anime had a key success with the film *Akira* (Katsuhiro Otomo, 1988). At first, anime was distributed in the West rather sporadically, and fan groups acted as underground distributors and, at times, translators of anime. However, in the 1990s, one of the main anime studios, Studio Ghibli, formed a distribution deal with Disney, allowing Disney the rights to distribute Ghibli-produced films on the world market outside of Asia (Cavallaro, 2010: 43). What is particularly interesting about this deal is the contractual obligation by Disney not to cut the films in any way (ibid.). Thus, Disney relies on careful dialogue adaptation in order to localise the film and explain or contextualise any culturally specific references that non-Japanese audiences might struggle with. Films such as *Princess Mononoke* (Hayao Miyazaki, 1997), *My Neighbour Totoro* (Hayao Miyazaki, 1988), and *Spirited Away* (Hayao Miyazaki, 2001) were all released by Disney for Studio Ghibli and were extremely successful in global markets. This suggests that industry cooperation and symbiosis has more positive outcomes, and undermines the argument that cultural influence only sways from West to rest.

POSTMODERNISM

Terms such as 'globalisation', 'transnationalism', and 'hybridity' are often accompanied by the term 'postmodernism'. Postmodernism is both a concept and a theory that aims to account for and explain the conditions of late capitalism and the effects of globalisation on culture, communications, and identity. The postmodern refers to the era or period of post-war capitalism, and postmodernism refers to the critical thinking about this particular period. Denzin outlines four strands: '(1) a movement called postmodernism in the arts; (2) a new form of theorizing the contemporary historical moment . . .; (3) historical transformations that have followed World War II; and (4) social, cultural, and economic life under late capitalism'(Denzin, 1991: 3). During the 1960s, French intellectuals began to reflect upon the postmodern era (although it was not necessarily identified as such at the time). As we discussed in terms of post-Classicism, the 1960s saw a paradigmatic shift towards the left, encapsulated in civil rights and liberation movements, anti-war protests, and the counter-cultural. In France, these sentiments were also apparent, and culminated in a year of particular socialist struggle in 1968. However, the failure of such movements and protests to enact any real change caused many of the intellectuals to reconsider the validity of many of the defining 'narratives' that had structured their social and political outlook. This questioning of worldviews and universal political positions framed the later philosophical thought that emerged from France at the time. We will go on to discuss some of these theories in relation to film shortly. At the same time, capitalism had developed a broad consumer culture, where identity was structured no longer only around previous markers such as family, community, religion, and gender. As Featherstone notes:

> The term consumer culture points not only to the increasing production and salience of cultural goods as commodities, but also to the way in which the majority of cultural activities and signifying practices become mediated through

consumption, and consumption progressively involves the consumption of signs and images.

(1995: 75)

Similarly, media establishes itself as a significant cultural mode. Communication takes place as much via communication technologies and information is circulated through media rather than through human interaction. Such thinking has been used to read contemporary film, and has, indeed, informed certain contemporary film practices. We'll use two key examples to illustrate this: Frederic Jameson's account of film in *Postmodernism and Consumer Society* (Jameson, 1998) and Jean Baudrillard's theorisation of the 'real', the 'hyperreal', and the 'simulacra' in *Simulacra and Simulation* (Baudrillard, 1983).

In his account of postmodernism, Jameson (1998) notes how those artists and works that are often identified as postmodern (Jameson makes reference to Andy Warhol, Talking Heads, Jean-Luc Godard, and William Burroughs) commonly break down the borders between high and low culture. He argues that 'the line between high-art and commercial forms is increasingly difficult to draw'. Jameson traces this to the concept and practice of individuality. In the past, artist creativity stemmed from the individual. Thus, originality and uniqueness were strived for by artists who sought to represent an individual perspective of the world, of reality, of experience, and so on. However, in the era of postmodernism, this concept of the individual no longer holds sway. Jameson is not interested in whether the individual once existed only to be lost in the era of late capitalism, or whether identity was only ever a myth (the poststructuralist position). He instead argues that the loss of the concept of individuality results in a lack of creativity in the artistic domain. As he says:

> If the experience and the ideology of the unique self, an experience and ideology which informed the stylistic practices of classical modernism, is over and done with, then it is no longer clear what the artists and writers of the present period are supposed to be doing.
>
> (Jameson, 1998: 6)

So, if individuality can no longer be imagined, and all that could be said or represented in the world is felt to have already passed, then artists turn towards pastiche.

Pastiche thus represents the exhaustion of creative innovation, where newer forms, modes, or subjects cannot be discovered – what Jameson terms 'the failure of the new, the imprisonment in the past'. For him, the nostalgia film exemplifies this trend, evident in films such as *Star Wars Episode IV: A New Hope* (George Lucas, 1977), *Blade Runner* (Ridley Scott, 1982), and *Chinatown* (Roman Polanski, 1974). These films either attempt to recreate or reflect the past in nostalgic celebration and stylisation, or, in the case of *Star Wars Episode IV: A New Hope*, try to recreate a particular viewing experience (1950s film matinees in the US). Pastiche films, then, demonstrate an over-investment in the past, or searching back for it, or the representation of it as more authentic, more real, more satisfying, and more interesting. It also demonstrates the stylistic block of filmmakers, who, instead of searching for new forms, borrow heavily from the past. Individually, a nostalgia film tells us nothing about film and the postmodern; however, as a body of films, or a trend in film practice and representation, these films are telling. As Jameson surmises, it is 'as though we have become incapable of achieving aesthetic representation of our current experience' (Jameson, 1998: 9). Interestingly, the recent film *The Artist* (Michel Hazanavicius, 2011) functions on a similar level. A beautiful silent film that centres on 1920s Hollywood, the film nevertheless evokes nostalgia for a glamorous past that is outside of the experience of most using a form that has long been abandoned. As Jameson continues, 'we seem condemned to seek the historical past through our own pop images and stereotypes about that past, which itself remains forever out of reach'.

A second concern of postmodernism is the notion of the real and the hyperreal (Baudrillard, 1983). In a social environment dominated by media, theorists such as Jean Baudrillard question whether we have access to the 'real' anymore. For Baudrillard, in the postmodern era, representations come to take the place of real things themselves. It is not that the real does not exist (although this is also questioned), but that the real becomes lost in an era of simulation. For example, we might note the ways in which the 'real' self is replaced by a virtual self, who might share few characteristics with the 'real' self. Social networking sites and massively multiplayer online role-playing games (MMORPGs) all transform modes of communication and allow for alternative identities. Similarly, consumer signs and symbols come to shape social reality. A particular car is not only representative of identity (for example, as a status symbol), but, in fact, constitutes that identity (in the sense that the desire for such objects structures our identity, life goals, aspirations, and so on). Baudrillard explains this with the example of Hollywood film:

> It is pointless to laboriously interpret these films by their relationship with an 'objective' social crisis . . . It is in the other direction that we must say it is the social itself which, in contemporary discourse, is organized according to a script for a disaster film.
>
> (1983: 75–6)

Rather than film reflecting upon an external social reality, film comes to participate in the construction of social reality. There is, therefore, no border between media as representation and social reality as authentic 'real' experience. This is simulation, and this blurring of the boundaries between real and hyperreal is evident in a number of films that thematise simulation (*eXistenZ*, David Cronenberg, 1999; *The Matrix*, Larry and Andy Wachowski, 1999), or where the very film itself takes on characteristics of hyperreality (*Catfish*, Henry Joost and Ariel Schulman, 2010;

I'm Still Here, Casey Affleck, 2010). Baudrillard defines the simulacrum through the various stages of the sign, where the sign begins as representing an external reality, and culminates in the postmodern era in the complete eradication of the real, where the sign 'is its own pure simulacrum', making reference to nothing but itself (Baudrillard, 1983: 11).

For example, Quentin Tarantino's *Inglourious Basterds* (2009) can be understood in terms of hyperreality and the simulacrum. The film disrupts the distinction between history or historical record and filmic representation. However, the film is self-reflexive and comments upon the nature of and problems with representation. Here, World War II and the events that take place within it are reduced to pure signs that represent nothing but representation itself. The film makes reference not to history itself (which is equally as problematic since history is discursive), but to filmic representations of World War II. In the film, loose historical record is interwoven with purely fictional events to construct an alternative war outcome. The film addresses the problems with war films that claim to speak a truth about the war. However, whether the comment upon simulacrum can be differentiated from the simulacrum is debatable.

QUEER CINEMA

Questions of identity that had circulated in 1960s cinema included not just feminism and race, but sexuality. The climate of liberalism meant that hetero-normative identity was problematised. For example, *Midnight Cowboy* had a subtle homosexual undercurrent and represented the 1960s counter-cultural scene as sexually liberated. Yet, Benshoff and Griffin suggest that, for the most part, 'sexuality itself was still mostly understood as an either/or binary, reducing the diversity of human sexuality to simplified concepts of "gay" and/or "straight"' (Benshoff and Griffin, 2009: 328). Shortly after the release of *Midnight Cowboy*, the Stonewall Riots led to the emergence of the gay liberation movement (Davies, 2008: 51). The movement was characterised by social initiatives, protests, and the raising of awareness about homosexuality. The gay liberation movement was crucial to providing positive discourses of homosexuality, particularly in a largely conservative environment that tended to associate it with sexual deviancy and perversion. The term 'queer' was later appropriated by people who considered the terms heterosexual or homosexual restrictive and reductive. It encapsulates a much broader range of diverse and non-conformist identities, such as transgender, transsexual, bisexual, interracial relationships, sadomasochistic, and in some cases heterosexuals who don't identity with the dominant mode of heterosexual practice or expression (Benshoff and Griffin, 2009: 329). Discussions and debates about hetero-normativity and sexual identities in academia became known as Queer Theory. As an academic discipline, it sought to reframe and broaden discussions about sexuality, and challenge and destabilise dominant hegemonic discourses of sexuality. Theorists began to discuss the ways in which sexuality was socially constituted and inscribed onto identity. Hayward goes on to suggest that, 'As a politics, it seeks to confuse the binary essentialisms around gender and sexual identity, expose their limitations and suggest that things are far more blurred' (Hayward, 2006: 291).

Thus, Queer Theory focuses not as much on marginalisation and oppression as on the ways in which sexuality is generally constructed, practiced, and performed in society. For example, Judith Butler argues that gender is not natural or inevitable, but is the means by which identity is performed. For her, gender performativity serves hegemonic regimes and is not an inherent human quality. Gender is, therefore, unknowingly learned and performed through repeated rituals and rites that begin with the gendered classification of children. Butler writes that such rituals and acts are 'performative in the sense that the essence or identity that they otherwise purport to express are fabrications manufactured and sustained through corporeal signs and discursive means' (Butler, 1990: 136). Accordingly, there is no authentic or original gender outside of its performativity. Butler uses the example of drag performance to illustrate the ways in which gender can be exposed as fluid and disassociated with sex. Butler argues that:

> If the inner truth of gender is a fabrication and if a true gender is a fantasy instituted and inscribed on the surfaces of bodies, then it seems that genders can neither be true nor false, but are only produced as the truth effects of a discourse of primary and stable identity.
>
> (Ibid.)

If gender can be consciously performed by anyone regardless of sex, this would seem to suggest that gender is not stable, but simply practiced, and can be assumed by anyone regardless of sex.

The film *Paris is Burning* (Jennie Livingston, 1991) both demonstrated and problematised some of these issues. The film came out at around the same time as Queer Theory entered academic discourse. *Paris is Burning* was part of a cinematic trend that became known as New Queer Cinema. The documentary film follows a group of black and Latino male-to-female drag artists who participate in drag balls, aimed as showcasing the participants' performance of particular identities, often, though not always, feminine. While the drag performances may point to how gender is imitative, Butler is keen to stress that this is not necessarily subversive in and of itself. In fact, in the film, the drag performers as much idolise icons and markers of white heterosexuality as they subvert or undermine them. It is clear from the competition titles such as 'Ivy League' and the feminine styles that they draw upon for their acts that the performances (of gender and in the balls) perpetuate hegemonic norms as much as they challenge them. However, elsewhere in New Queer Cinema, films were equally, if not more, oppositional and political. Among the films associated with the movement are *My Own Private Idaho* (Gus Van Sant, 1991), *Edward II* (Derek Jarman, 1991), *Poison* (Todd Haynes, 1991), *The Living End* (Derek Akari, 1992), and *Go Fish* (Rose Troche, 1994).

As Benshoff and Griffin note, New Queer Cinema was also referred to as 'Homo Pomo' because of its postmodern concern with 'permeable boundaries, the crossing of styles and genres, and more generalized border crossings – whether those borders be sexual, regional, national, ethic, or racial' (Benshoff and Griffin, 2009: 330). For Aaron, the films display defiance against societal norms and the celebration of deviancy, whether sexual or social. This defiance stretches to a disregard of dominant discourses of history, as well as a disregard for mainstream cinematic practices (Aaron, 2006: 399). Hayward similarly claims that 'New Queer Cinema is unconcerned with positive images of queerness, gayness or lesbianism, but is very clearly assertive about its politics' (Hayward, 2006: 291). Many of the films disregard the typical tropes of moralistic mainstream film and position the text and the characters on the margins (rather than as assimilating into hetero-normative society). For example, *My Own Private Idaho* is about a group of male prostitutes and street kids who form a community outside of the 'ordinary' social reality of Portland. Throughout the film, sexual identity is continually ambiguous, both flexible and fixed. The hustlers have both male and female clients, but also express either fixed sexual desire outside of their hustling. Similarly, in one scene, the street kids talk directly and explicitly about their first sexual experiences and/or prostitution. These are largely negative, and so the film seems to refuse to gloss over the negative aspects of sexual identity and expression. New Queer Cinema, therefore, offered more complex and ambiguous representations of sexuality, mirroring the Queer Theory of academic study.

C@SE STUDY

CLOVERFIELD (Matt Reeves, 2008)
Reality horror and the postmodern

In the exhausted landscape of contemporary horror cinema, a particular mode has emerged that attempts to resituate the spectator as a viewer of the 'authentic' rather than of the fictional text. Reality horror relies upon the spectator's ability to navigate and recall a wide body of media aesthetics and forms. The horror of these reality texts is found in the immediacy of the documentary mode (including video diary, amateur recording, news footage, and so on), which implies the 'really did happen' of reality television, news television, and the world of factual television and the Internet. However, the 'really happened-ness' of factual media is an issue worth dwelling on. If reality horror situates its very project in the supposedly authentic mode of factual media, then does it not negate the very inauthenticity of media itself? Does reality horror not present us with a double fiction (the fiction of the horror text as well as the fiction of the original media text) while denying any fiction at all?

Cloverfield (shot in the pseudo-amateur format) has a scene that emulates the handheld footage taken of the Twin Towers collapse in the wake of the 9/11 attacks.

While this film may be understood as a form of mourning through memory and re-visitation, the consequences of this particular mode of filmmaking are multifaceted. The spectator may experience the scene (in both this film and others similar) as 'realistic', since it recalls both a historical event and the specific experience of viewing the news footage in the aftermath of the attacks (after all, most people experienced 9/11 as a global media event). However, the scene exists as pure simulacrum (Baudrillard, 1983). Not only does it stage the 'event' (re-presenting it), but it stages the staging of the 'event' (re-re-presenting it). The 'real', therefore, does not exist for the spectator; only the mediated visualisation of it. The scene mimics not the 'real'-some *actual* event that people *really* experienced, but media itself. In other words, the fictional scenes in *Cloverfield* make the spectator feel that the media footage of 9/11 was 'real'. Of course, I am not suggesting that the events of 9/11 did not happen. The attacks were real, people really died, and the trauma experienced as a consequence was real. But the spectator's access to the event is always regulated, manipulated, and framed by these very media images.

Jean Baudrillard offers a useful analogy in his analysis of Disneyland in America. Like *Cloverfield*, Disneyland appears to be an obvious fiction. It is fantastic, over-the-top, and 'magical'. While this may allude to its falsehood, Baudrillard suggests that in contrast to the rest of America and, in particular, Los Angeles, Disneyland is merely presented as a fiction. As a result, the remainder of America seems real by comparison:

> Disneyland is presented as imaginary in order to make us believe that the rest is real, when in fact all of Los Angeles and the America surrounding it are no longer real . . . It is no longer a question of a false representation of reality (ideology), but of concealing the fact that the real is no longer real, and thus of saving the reality principle.
>
> (Ibid.: 25)

We can see something similar at work in *Cloverfield*. Its co-option of 9/11 news media proposes that the media footage is the real event itself. *Cloverfield* does not present us with the narrative point of view of a character caught up in the crisis of attacks. Rather, it utilises a camera point of view (a film within a film) – the very frames that we are all undoubtedly familiar with. The fictional shaky amateur footage of *Cloverfield* alludes to the supposed 'realness' of the shaky amateur footage taken during the World Trade Center

C@SE STUDY

attacks. And so, we momentarily forget that the camera footage is not a stand-in for truth. It cannot be taken for the real itself. In fact, in the background of some of the footage taken on 9/11, we hear people urging others to record the events for the media. Like Daniel Boorstin's analysis of the pseudo-event (where those partaking in the event have a distinctly less significant experience than those watching the same media event), this indicates that even those most directly confronted with the event perceive it as a media event or narrative (Boorstin, 1992). Indeed, *Cloverfield* counts on this.

CHAPTER 10

Eisenstein and Bazin

Formalism and realism, two modes of practice

From the earliest years of cinema, practitioners and critics alike have questioned, debated, and considered what film is or should be. When cinema began to break from the traditions of the theatrical mode, there were opportunities to reconstitute film as a separate, unique form, with its own organising principles. Our inclination might be to view the history of cinema, cinematic and technological experimentation, and modes of representation as teleological, culminating in the narrative tradition. Yet, equally, we might also recognise the formal differences between individual films and might make value judgements based upon such differences. For example, there is a recent trend in horror and science fiction film, which we might refer to as 'news-realism', mockumentary, 'found footage', or the amateur aesthetic. Films such as *The Blair Witch Project* (Daniel Myrick and Eduardo Sánchez, 1999), *Cloverfield* (Matt Reeves, 2008), *Children of Men* (Alfonso Cuaron, 2006), and many others use an aesthetic strategy that evokes media realism, in the sense that it presents itself as uncontrived, authentic, and spontaneous. Equally, we might note that the films of David Lynch or mainstream MTV music videos emphasise and play with the form itself through the foregrounding of editing or style. The differences between these two modes can be traced back to the early days of film and the often-noted distinction between the films of the Lumière brothers and the films of George Méliès (Figures 10.1 and 10.2). Theorists often claim that the Lumière brothers' films correspond to the realist tradition, which aspires towards the outward, 'really lived' world. In opposition are the films of George Méliès, which use early special effects techniques to create fantasy worlds and speak little of real experiences. While such comparisons are not absolute, we can note that the realist films treat film as a window upon the world, and the formalists treat film as a canvas. This distinction points to the contrasting motivations of film practitioners from cinema's earliest days. On the one hand, film has the special capacity of showing and representing the reality of the world that we perceive. On the other hand, film is itself a special medium that allows the practitioner to manipulate reality and to produce alternative subjective realities. While we might understand formalism and realism as distinct traditions, in your own practice you might oscillate between them. There are certain moments and movements in which each tradition is insular and separate from the other, but, equally, the forms interact with each other. Thus, we might understand realism proper and formalism proper as lying on each end of a spectrum.

FIGURE 10.1
Lumière's *Workers Leaving the Factory* (1895)

FIGURE 10.2
Méliès's *A Trip to the Moon* (1902)

However, while we might note that, in practice, films can have both a realist and formalist aesthetic, the realist and formalist modes have, at times, been at odds with each other. The primary issue at stake is the political effect of film as a mode of expression. These are essentially questions about film's status and nature; namely, again, what it is and what it does. As filmmakers, these are questions you can ask yourself. What kind of formal system will be best suited to your needs? What effect will this formal system produce in your film? Often, filmmakers rely on diegetic events, actions, and dialogue for filmic meaning; however, the filmic mode itself is just as responsible for meaning. For example, David Lynch's *Eraserhead* (1977) (Figures 10.3 and 10.4) uses a formalist mode in order to produce the nightmarish effect of the nuclear family on the male protagonist, Henry. The formalist elements, such as the use of overt metaphor and the dreamlike spatio-temporal order, are used in an anti-naturalistic way. This has the effect of destabilising the family so that the family become the sources of horror and the grotesque. However, such a nightmarish aesthetic, dominated as it is by a dreamlike logic, source the horror not in the 'really lived' world, but in Henry's subjective reality.

We can compare the subjective experience evident in *Eraserhead*'s formalism with realist films also preoccupied with the family. For example, Gary Oldman's *Nil By Mouth* (1997) (Figures 10.5 and 10.6), which similarly thematises paternal angst and dysfunction, follows in the tradition of social realism. Here, the violence and disorder of the family is clearly linked to the 'really lived' world, whereby the family's troubles are representative of wider concerns with poverty and domestic unrest. This is done not through symbolism, surrealism, or dream logic, but through the use of loose narratives (which are representative of 'real life'), location shoots, and natural rather than stylised lighting, among other realist techniques discussed later in this chapter. For example, in Figure 10.5, the lighting of the scene is both natural and symbolic of the character's inner world. Similarly, in Figure 10.6, the contrast between the darkness of characters is juxtaposed with the harsh lighting in the background.

As you can see, then, similar themes or subjects can be treated using different modes. If you are following in the formalist tradition, you might think about how the form itself can be used to evoke themes, moods, and feelings through the manipulation of temporal and spatial order, and the control of the *mise en scène*. If, on the other hand, you are making a film in the realist tradition, you might consider using a chronological temporal order that aspires more towards 'really lived' experiences of time and space. Here, you could use natural lighting and place less emphasis on controlled *mise en scène*.

Before you begin using either mode, it is worth examining the techniques and ideas developed within each mode. Each technique and aesthetic mode was borne out of a desire to produce intense, and often political, meanings and effects. The filmmakers at the forefront of these traditions, within both formalism and realism, were often passionate about the social value of film and believed that film was a

FIGURE 10.3
Eraserhead – torment in Henry's nightmarish world

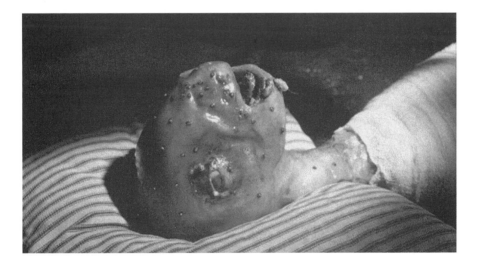

FIGURE 10.4
Eraserhead – Henry's nightmare of fatherhood

radical medium that could empower and engage audiences. At times, these filmmakers also produced critical work on filmmaking. While much has been written about these filmmakers within the context of academic film criticism and theory, their work, innovations, and writings prove fruitful for filmmakers, too. The following sections will be based upon two case studies within the formalist and realist traditions: Eisenstein (filmmaker and theorist) and Bazin (critic). Important in the following

FIGURE 10.5
Nil By Mouth – an aesthetics of discontent

FIGURE 10.6
Nil By Mouth – framing discontent

examination of their film modes is not simply *how* films were made in the formalist or realist tradition, and what this entailed, but also *why*. Understanding why a particular mode is useful to your own practice allows you to develop and expand your own personal stylistic and aesthetic signature. Ultimately, film theory is about films. Since you are the filmmaker, film theory is only enabled by, and in service to, the films that you make.

SOVIET MONTAGE AND EISENSTEIN

Montage editing was not only revolutionary in the context of film practice, but also grew out of the social revolutionary moment in Russia. The purpose of montage editing, as practised by Sergei Eisenstein, was to shock the audience into understanding the significance of the political statement made within the montage edit. It is, therefore, unsurprising that such a practice had its foundations in the Russian Revolution of 1917 that heralded the era of Soviet communism. The Soviet leader, Lenin, recognised that cinema could be used for the purposes of propaganda and to educate the people about the new socialist system now in place. Following World War I and the revolution, many of the filmmakers and private film companies either fled the USSR or were unhappy with the new socialist system or limited their film production and distribution. As a result, there was a decline in filmmaking and a shortage in film equipment and stock. In response to this, the film industry was nationalised and a State Film School was established in Moscow with the purpose of training socialist filmmakers (Nelmes, 2003). Soviet montage emerged from this investment in film. Many of the films made during this time were distinctly political in tone, with many articulating the experience of revolution and post-revolution life. The films drew upon the stylistic mode of the *agitka* films (agitational films that functioned as propaganda films during the civil war). Often filmed on the battlefront, the shorts 'had a documentary quality which distinguished them from more studio-bound, pre-revolutionary forms of filmmaking; while the imperative to complete films quickly led to the development of innovative editing, acting and other stylistic practices' (Aitken, 2002: 57). Such innovations, coupled with a political objective, led to a particular mode of filmmaking that reflected the times.

While montage is often referred to in relation to Eisenstein, the experimentation with editing pre-dates his work. Lev Kuleshov, who had been an *agitka* filmmaker, began developing editing practices when he began holding workshops at the State Film School. His resulting method of editing, which is referred to as the Kuleshov Effect, was the end product of much experimentation with film editing. The story of Kuleshov's experiment has, perhaps, become somewhat tired over the years. Essentially, he used one static image and paired it with alternate images in order to transform the meaning of the initial shot. Thus, if a picture of a face is coupled with a picture of food, the first image of the face evokes hunger. Likewise, if the image of the face is coupled with that of a small coffin, the actor's face evoked sorrow. Although the anecdote is often circulated on film courses, what is important to note is the way in which the editing of frames rather than the frame itself determined meaning. In other words, the filmmaker could control meaning through the careful organisation and manipulation of shots through the edit. These experiments revealed, for Kuleshov, the way in which montage or assemblage (editing) was paramount to real time and space (Cook, 2004: 120). As Cook goes on to note, 'Kuleshov and his pupils conceived of montage as an expressive or symbolic process whereby logically or empirically dissimilar images could be linked

together synthetically to produce metaphors (to produce, that is, nonliteral meaning)'
(ibid.). The metaphor was found in the difference between the shots. This was a
crucial element of montage editing. Unlike conventional narratives, which subordinate
editing to narrative, montage foregrounded it.

We will situate the discussion of montage in practice within the films of Eisenstein
before setting a number of editing exercises that utilise this technique. Eisenstein
is perhaps most noted for his appropriation of the techniques of montage editing.
He began his career in theatre, later working under the tutorship of Kuleshov.
Eisenstein's interest in film extended to its theorisation, and his articles on montage
were published in literature of the day. In practice, his use of montage differed
somewhat from that of Kuleshov. Where Kuleshov saw montage as the bringing
together of two shots, Eisenstein regarded it as a collision. It was this idea of the
edit as a collision that informed many of his films. He wanted cinema to be just
as revolutionary as the political movement that had preceded it, and he used montage
editing to fulfil this. Eisenstein used intellectual montage (montage that forces thought
and consideration) in order to shock the audience into interpretation. His films were
often about revolution, radical changes, and uprisings. In order to emphasise the
plight of the proletariat and the ordinary people (often against the state, the bourgeoisie, or capitalists), Eisenstein would create textual metaphors in the edit. He
would also juxtapose a variety of contrasting shots to produce the effect of shock
in the audience. Close-ups were followed by long shots, nature by industry, darkness
by light, and so on. Such a collision of shots was intended to force the audience
into a deeper contemplation of meaning.

Eisenstein used the term 'dialectical montage' to refer to the way that the collision
of shots produces change (either political change or change in the audience). Thinking
scientifically about the relationship between frame and edit, Eisenstein proposed
the equation *thesis + antithesis = synthesis*. Here, the first shot functions as the
thesis, the second as the antithesis, and the meaning is produced out of the montage
of shots, the synthesis. In other words, the dialectic relationship between each
shot, particularly when the shots might be contrasting (in terms of different
composition, lighting, or subject matter), is conceptual and, according to Eisenstein,
intellectual. His films were, therefore, agitational, with the purpose of forcing the
audience to be awakened and politicised, since they were active in producing
meaning through the interpretation of the montage.

For example, Eisenstein's film *Strike!* (1925) demonstrates the means by which the
editing technique of montage could produce a political effect, simply through collision,
juxtaposition, and contrast. *Strike!* was Eisenstein's first feature-length film and
showcases many of the techniques he developed and theorised about. The film is
about a strike held by dissatisfied factory workers who are being exploited by
the capitalist factory owners. Thus, thematically, it follows in the tradition of the
propaganda film, which illustrates the nature of class struggle and the limits of
capitalism. By the end of the film, the capitalists disband and slaughter the strikers,

arguably a more powerful and provocative film as a result. Some (including Eisenstein himself) have criticised the overwhelming range of cinematic techniques used in the film; nevertheless, the film showcases many of the elements of montage that can be put into practice in various ways. Eisenstein was producing theory as he was filming, so his films, and *Strike!* in particular, can be understood as experiments in form. One method both written about and practiced in *Strike!* was what Eisenstein referred to as the 'montage of attractions'. This terminology can be attributed to his theatrical background. Attractions in this context refer to 'aggressive aspects' that 'subject the spectator to a sensual or psychological impact', such as the circus acts or over-the-top performances and behaviour of the performers (Eisenstein, 1974: 78). The 'attraction' is a singular element that can produce a profound effect in the spectator – it has autonomous meaning and can shock the audience on its own. By producing a 'montage of attractions', the intention was to organise attractions in such a way (through montage) as to provoke a particular response in the audience.

In Eisenstein's case, this was often to agitate the audience into action through propaganda pieces based upon the revolution or strikes by the proletariat. In *Strike!*, he used a range of montage 'types' in order to produce the effect of collision and juxtaposition that would deny the audience the illusionary capacity of standard narrative film. The audience would have to actively participate in the construction of meaning with the guidance of the 'author'/director. This is perhaps most clearly demonstrated in one of the final sequences of *Strike!*, in which the strikers are gunned down by the military. In the scene, the strikers are separated from the military; instead, the concept is illustrated by intercutting between the military firing and the strikers running and falling. Thus, the contrast between the oppositional forces is maintained, while the effect of the slaughter is clear. In addition, the sequence is also intercut with a sequence that bears no temporal or causal relationship to the action. Here, a bull is being killed in a slaughterhouse. These shots function to evoke a concept rather than as part of the overall action. The purpose is for the audience to draw comparisons between the 'slaughter' of the strikers and the slaughter of the bull.

Such conceptual filmmaking extends to the nature of performance and characterisation, too. Like he did later in *Battleship Potemkin* (1926), Eisenstein uses character types rather than psychological elements in order to make broader political statements. Thus, collision and juxtaposition extends to the means by which characters are represented. Just as the slaughter of the strikers is compared with the bull slaughter, similarly the villainous characters are compared with other animals. For example, the spies are associated with animals in order to, again, evoke concepts rather than forward narrative. For Eisenstein, montage offered one way of escaping the limitations of plot-centred narrative. In *Strike!*, Eisenstein was eager to represent the political situation rather than individual situations, and 'typage' was one means by which he achieved this. Thus, the characters' association with animals functions to dehumanise them. Shots of the spies are superimposed with shots of the animals, which first obscures the faces of the informants, but also evokes the concept of animal-like behaviour (Figure 10.7). Similarly, the strikers are de-personalised in order to emphasise class struggle through the collective force of the strikers rather than through individual struggle of a 'hero'. Thus, the shots of the strikers' collective are contrasted with shots of individual factory owners, spies, and police, their individuality closely aligned with greed.

Within Eisenstein's montage of attractions, there are specific forms of montage that he identified as having certain uses. Each of the five montage types, outlined below, had the purpose of creating conflict rather than cohesiveness, so that the audience would be forced into interpretation, instead of having meaning neatly determined already. By fragmenting, rather than fusing, shots, through contrast in size, shape, light, or colour, Eisenstein believed that the audience would be shocked or provoked into producing meaning from such disparity of shots. The types of montage that follow can be used interchangeably within a film, or in isolation. Eisenstein often oscillated between them, although he is most remembered for the last – intellectual montage. An understanding of montage is especially useful for both directors and editors, as it offers the potential to add further layers of emotion, meaning, and aesthetic power to a film.

- *Metric montage.* This refers to the length of shots or frames, the timing of which produces an emotional effect. While the overall length of the piece remains the same, the pace of the shots creates a base reaction

FIGURE 10.7
Strike! – spies as birds

in the audience. This type of montage foregrounds the cut rather than the content of the frame, as the cut allows less time for the audience to take in the content of the frame. The juxtaposition is found in the cutting between different lengths of shots, which is not determined by the content of the shot.

- *Rhythmic montage*. This type of montage occurs when contrast is created through the movement or direction within the frame. Thus, content determines the cut to another shot. Rhythmic montage, nowadays, may also refer to the length of the shot, but here the length is determined by the content within the frame. This type of montage is particularly effective in creating tension between shots such as through comparison of movement. A classic example occurs in Eisenstein's *Battleship Potemkin* (1926), in which shots of the Cossacks marching down from one corner of the frame are juxtaposed with shots of people moving in the opposite direction.

- *Tonal montage*. Here, the tone of the scene determines the edit. So, where the length and movement within the frame determine the edits in the previous two types of montage, here the emotional impetus, often centred on characters and their situations, determines the edit. Thus, tonal montage can be used to heighten the emotion of a scene. For example, a person lying on the street might be juxtaposed with a shot of the sun going down, indicating the death of the person and adding emotional depth and poignancy to the scene.

- *Overtonal montage.* This can be understood as the synthesis of the previous forms of montage mentioned above, whereby there is no dominant motivating montage, but instead each form interacts and works with other forms of montage, which are the 'overtones'. We can think of this at the level of the film rather than at the level of the scene.

- *Intellectual montage*. This is the final and most important stage of montage. Where the previous forms of montage are intended to frame emotion and direct the audience's attention and perspective, intellectual montage goes much further in its degree of juxtaposition. Here, we can note the difference between Eisenstein's concepts of representation and image. The representation is the meaning within an individual shot. He uses the example of the shot of a woman crying, and another shot of a grave. Each shot carries its own representable meaning. However, put together, the representations produce a new meaning, that of a widow. This is the image. In intellectual montage, two shots/representations that don't necessarily have any spatial or temporal relationship with each other combine to produce an image that is not available in any of the single shots. This is most apparent in the defeat of the strikers in *Strike!* (Figure 10.8), whereby the slaughtered cow is compared with the defeated strikers, now dead.

a

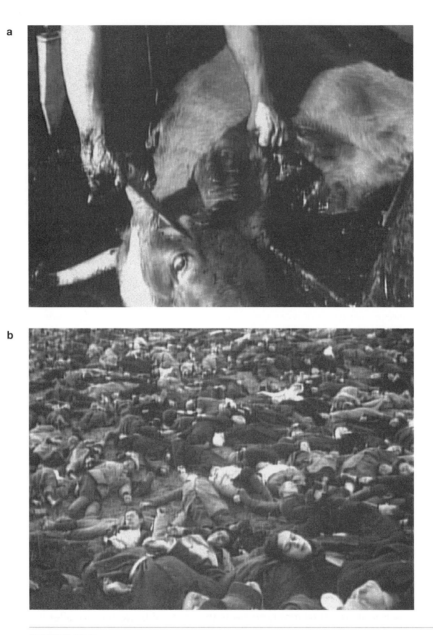

b

FIGURE 10.8
Strike! (a) The bull is slaughtered. (b) The next shot shows the strikers also slaughtered. The slaughter of the bull has no temporal or spatial relationship to the narrative. It is used as a way of commenting upon the defeat of the strikers

EXERCISE MONTAGE

This exercise is designed to enable you to learn alternative forms of editing. In undertaking this task, you should become more aware of the power of the edit and the way in which editing can be used creatively and for social or political ends.

Following the practice of Eisenstein, use montage editing to create socially and politically engaged short film pieces that demonstrate each of the montage types outlined above. In order to emphasise your social or political statement and film thesis (for each piece), you should first outline in writing your overall point. You may also use this as an opening intertitle for each film piece. Remember that montage, as Eisenstein notes, 'is not an idea composed of successive shots stuck together but an idea that derives from the *collision* between two shots that are independent of one another' (Eisenstein, 2009: 27, emphasis added). You may base your film on any of the following ideas, which, like Eisenstein's films, represent particular issues that are socially significant at the moment:

- contemporary strikes/strikers;
- protest and resistance;
- the nature of poverty today;
- consumer society;
- nationality and patriotism; and
- the environment.

Remember that each of these themes must be used to demonstrate montage editing in practice. So, each of your short film pieces (or you may choose a longer piece that uses a variety of montage types) should be formally precise. Think about the length of your shots, the content and composition of each frame, and the relationship between each shot. This exercise would benefit from being carefully storyboarded prior to shooting. Montage, in this respect, is about collision and conflict created within the edit, so you might experiment with direction, performance, framing, colour, light, and also sound. For example, you might choose a lighting model that represents the contrast between two different characters, or locations, or subjects. Similarly, you could use sound in contrast with the image (a scene of nature with a frenetic, industrial soundtrack). Essentially, you are creating meaning through the edit, so consider the point that you wish to make and then base your shot decisions and arrangements on this.

See *October* (Sergei Eisenstein, 1928) and *Mother* (Vsevolod Pudovkin, 1926).

MONTAGE TODAY

While Soviet montage faded during the 1930s, the legacy of montage is evident in a range of visual media, from film and television to advertisements and music videos. Soviet montage was criticised for its intellectualism, which was seen as alienating for the ordinary people to whom it was addressed. So, while montage in its intellectualism is not particularly evident in mainstream film, it has had an influence on the development of avant-garde cinema, particularly in the art cinema of the 1960s. There are also a number of directors and famous film sequences that have their origins in Soviet montage, either as a homage to Eisenstein or particular films of the era, or as a result of the film school education many of the 'movie brats' underwent in the US in the 1970s. However, as noted by Bordwell (1985), the practice of montage outside of Soviet montage and particularly in Hollywood mainstream cinema is bereft of the social and ideological context of the Soviet montage films. Where Eisenstein's films produce a political aesthetic, the use of montage in the post-Soviet montage era is sometimes political, yet, more often than not, stylistic. Nevertheless, montage remains in use, albeit sporadically.

The term 'montage' today is often used broadly to define any form of editing that stresses discontinuity (in contrast to Hollywood continuity editing). It may also be used to define sequences where time is condensed through rapid cuts that indicate different periods of time, hence time passing, such as in the case of a calendar moving combined with a person at various stages of his or her life. An example of this type of montage can be found in the film *Rocky* (John A. Avildsen, 1976), where there is a montage sequence of Rocky's training, culminating in his rise up the steps to the Philadelphia Museum of Art, indicating the hours of practice that have prepared him for the fight. Unlike the films of Eisenstein, these montage sequences are not representative of any political or ideological project and are typically interpolated into an overall convention narrative. Below are some examples where aspects of Soviet montage have been used.

Koyaanisqatsi (Godfrey Reggio, 1983)

This documentary abandons conventional narrative in favour of a contemporary form of Soviet montage. The film uses a broad range of images, stretching from representations of the natural environment to technology and urban life. The film uses a variety of montage types (metric, rhythmic, tonal, overtonal, and intellectual) and techniques, ranging from the juxtaposition of music and image (Philip Glass's score was written as the film was shot, and the shots were determined as much according to the music as vice versa). Sombre music accompanies images of urban life, indicating the extent to which modern civilisation is 'out of balance' (which is the translation of the Hobi word *koyaanisqatsi*). As in the practices of Eisenstein, in *Koyaanisqatsi*, the pace of editing alternates throughout and film speed moves faster and slower, accelerating at the pace of modern urban existence.

The Godfather (Francis Ford Coppola, 1972)

While *The Godfather* uses conventional formal devices for the most part, there are a number of moments when the style of Soviet montage is used. However, this use of montage, while echoing intellectual montage, can be understood more as a revised version of it. The scene in question has the new leader of a mafia gang, Michael Corleone, attend his godchild's baptism, while in another place, which is represented through parallel editing, members of Corleone's gang murder opponents. As the scene develops, the contrast between Michael's commitment to his family and religious duty and his burgeoning life of crime produces a conflict not apparent in either of the shots alone. In a shot in the church, Michael is asked if he renounces Satan, and the next shot shows one murder take place at another location, followed by a return shot to the church where Michael says that he 'renounces Satan', which is again accompanied by a shot of another murder. The scene produces a conflict between the commitment to God and the disregard for the teachings of the church or the responsibilities of faith. Thus, the third meaning that emerges from the montage is that, first, Michael has been 'baptised' into a life of crime, but, more importantly, the criminal organisation that Michael now leads is hypocritical, untrustworthy, and lacks the loyalty it is supposedly built upon.

My Winnipeg (Guy Maddin, 2006)

Maddin's film reproduces a history of the director's city from an entirely subjective perspective, blending factual detail about the city with accounts of fictional events that occurred or did not occur within the city. Within the broader treatment of Winnipeg as a home is an examination of Maddin's own (or not) family history. In telling his story of Winnipeg, Maddin utilises a range of formal practices, ranging from film noir to German expressionism and Soviet montage. There are specific references to the films of Eisenstein, most notably the reference to the stylistic representations of the strikers in *Strike!* (there is also reference to a 1919 strike in *My Winnipeg*). In addition to intertexual references to early Soviet montage films, Maddin also employs its aesthetic mode in a number of scenes that resemble the Eisenstein-like practice of metric, rhythmic, and tonal montage. For example, in the recounting of a fire at a stable, the pace of the editing intensifies erratically to evoke the scene of chaos; animated shots of horses are intercut with intertitles, which are so short that they can barely be understood. Likewise, in the scene of the strike, the staff and students of St Mary's Academy for girls are shown left of frame with minimal movement. This is juxtaposed with the strikers who march rapidly from right of frame. The pace of editing continues at a frantic pace as the two sides come to clash. Although Maddin does not use montage for the same political effect of the Soviet montage filmmakers, *My Winnipeg* does, to an extent, use montage to challenge or shock the audience into reconsidering the history and memory of Winnipeg, and, more generally, the way in which history is mythologised. If classical realism denies the illusionary nature of cinema (and its myth-making capacity), then *My Winnipeg* uses formal devices such as Soviet montage precisely to undermine this illusion.

Requiem for a Dream (Darren Aronofsky, 2000)

Again, like many of the recent practices of montage, *Requiem for a Dream* lacks the political scope of Soviet montage. Where the films of Eisenstein were dramatic attempts to jolt the audience into politicisation, Aronofsky uses montage to provoke emotional jolts in the audience. The film uses what Aronofsky refers to as 'hip hop montage', a reference to the rapid editing pace accompanied by exaggerated sound effects, which condenses time and produces a disorientating and fragmented experience. Aronofsky uses the term 'hip hop' in reference to hip hop's tendency towards sampling and collage. This is apparent in the scene in which each character hits rock bottom. The four characters of the film are show in succession, each experiencing a personal hell. The diegetic sound of one scene, in which a prison guard calls out to prisoners, 'can you hear me, can you see me, okay for work', provides the rhythm for the scene. Successive shots of drug taking are cut with shots of the four characters, with the movement of one scene echoing the other. For example, the light of the torch in the prison scene is cut with the torch on the face of a character about to be sexually humiliated by a group of men. Similarly, the crowds of men gathered around Marion are mirrored with the crowds of medical staff gathered around Sara. Here, montage is used to isolate the once close characters and draw parallels between the experience and final outcome for each. The pace of the disjointed editing produces the sense of being overwhelmed and, as montage often does, denies the audience the capacity to view passively. And here, again, the meaning is created through the relationship between the shots rather than in any independent shot. Moving from the formalist practices of Eisenstein and the Soviet montage films, we will now move to the traditions of realism in cinema.

REALISM

We might, in an unsophisticated sense, interpret film realism or film reality as the capacity to imitate or record reality. Coupled with the way in which film is a mechanical reproduction of a pro-filmic reality (let's leave out CGI and special effects for the moment), then this crude definition might suggest that film has the potential to make 'truth' claims about its recorded events. The capacity for film realism became a point of debate throughout the 1950s and beyond. This debate raised many questions as to whether film as a mechanical recording did have the capacity to represent reality, and, later, whether film actively shaped or transformed reality. If we consider that reality itself is not static, but rather it is in flux and transformative, then we must question what reality is being represented. Even if a film accurately represents reality, this reality might just as easily transform (for example, if one were to make a film about a historical event, and shortly after new information about that historical event changed its 'reality' or our understanding of it, then what reality does the film speak to?). Equally, reality is as much shaped, constructed, and manipulated by other forces such as the state, religious or educational institutions, and culture, so we can note that reality is transformative across national, social, and cultural boundaries. In addition, film is rarely the 'lens upon the world', as even most realist films involve some form of narrative, use cuts, and frame in particular ways for particular effects. All of this shapes the external reality that the realist films seek to represent. Therefore, film realism does not and cannot refer to a pre-existing social reality that is captured unawares. Rather, film realism demands an alternative definition. Instead of conceptualising film realism as a representation of objective reality (which, we have noted, is not static) or as an objective representation of reality (since it is always constructed and uses devices, techniques, and conventions as much as 'illusionary' film), we can think of film realism as an aesthetic, stylistic, and political mode of filmmaking. Thus, in the most general sense, we can think of film's capacity to record a pro-filmic space or event as realist, since the image represented can be close to the spectator's perception. A representation of a chair has a likeness to a 'real' chair. Yet, the way in which film realism tends to be practiced and understood is more political than that. The realist filmmakers strive to not just represent objects and events that are perceptually real, but also experiences and social situations.

Both Siegfried Kracauer and André Bazin took note of the films of the Italian neo-realists, which abandoned many of the tropes of classical or conventional narrative film by using episodic narratives, on-location shooting, available lighting, long shots, and many other devices and conventions that undermined the illusion of cohesiveness offered by classical cinema. For Kracauer, film had as its primary function the ability to record 'nature in the raw' (Kracauer, 1960: 30), and he rejected the traditions of formalism and the stylisation of film: 'films come into their own when they record and reveal physical reality' (ibid.). Kracauer asks us to:

> imagine a film which, in keeping with the basic properties, records interesting aspects of physical reality but does so in a technically imperfect manner; perhaps the lighting is awkward or the editing uninspired. Nevertheless, such a film is more specifically a film than one which utilises brilliantly all the cinematic devices and tricks to produce a statement disregarding camera-reality.
>
> (Ibid.)

Although Kracauer acknowledges that cinema techniques can be used to great effect, he was keen to promote and 'redeem' films that were neither in the tradition of theatre nor of the experimental, surrealist tradition. If film had the capacity to record a pro-filmic reality, then it should do so, rather than pander to the other art traditions.

Within the many traditions of realism, which range from the poetic realism of 1930s French cinema, the neo-realism of 1950s Italian cinema, the British social realism of the past 50 to 60 years, and the Dogme realist movement of the 1990s, there are a number of similar codes and conventions that evoke realism through aesthetics, style, and politics. Below are some of the key practices of two movements.

FRENCH POETIC REALISM

This form of realism emerged in France in the 1930s in the wake of fantasy, surrealist, and expensive and lavish studio productions that were popular at the time. The poetic realist films were so called because they represented ordinary social life lyrically and through aesthetics of mundane beauty. As was a tendency among later realist movements, the French poetic realists focused on characters usually excluded or marginalised within popular filmic representation (for example, the working classes, the poor, and criminals). The films are often negative in tone, and illustrate the hopelessness of such characters' lives. While this, in and of itself, is not necessarily a characteristic of realism – we equally find hopelessness in films of German expressionism and Soviet montage – the difference between French poetic realism and the latter movements was the way in which it employed an aesthetic that tried to imitate the social reality, rather than use formal devices that foregrounded the cinematic apparatus. While the films were often made in studios, the studios were carefully constructed to appear like real streets, not ideal versions of the outside world, or entirely subjective representations of the world. Thus, poetic realism offered a representational mode that was at odds with the illusionary practices of theatrical or studio films of the day, while still not operating in a documentary mode. Among its thematic and stylistic characteristics were:

- disillusionment and disappointment;
- the brief opportunity for hope or romance, often lost by the end of the film;
- contesting the illusionary happiness of popular film, especially Hollywood film;
- attacking the bourgeoisie (for example, in the films of Jean Renoir);
- stylistic sophistication (use of studios, lighting, set design); and
- *mise en scène* evoking fatalism of character (Hayward, 2006: 151).

Key films are *Pépé le Moko* (Julien Duvivier, 1937), *Le Grande Illusion* (Jean Renoir, 1937), and *Hôtel du Nord* (Marcel Carné, 1938).

ITALIAN NEO-REALISM

Italian neo-realism emerged in the wake of World War II, whereby the decline of the film industry, coupled with the uncertain future of the country, led to the development of the neo-realist film movement. Limitations in equipment and funding led to the use of such techniques as location shooting and cinematography more akin to documentary. The lack of investment in filmmaking resulted in the use of basic-quality film stock and equipment that resulted in the grainy, 'realist' visual aesthetic. This actually served the movement well, as it matched the post-war terrain, which was the subject of many of the neo-realist films. Like French poetic realism, the neo-realists were dissatisfied with the illusionary style of the pre-war fascist films and sought to represent the new social reality of war-torn Italy. Thus, Italian neo-realism was the synthesis between production techniques and a political thesis. They were deeply sceptical of and resistant to the illusionary popular cinema of the Fascist years, which denied the extreme political tensions of the era. The neo-realists often brutally exposed not only the consequences of Fascism and war, but also the cultural and economic divide between northern and southern Italy, the devastating poverty usually absent within popular film, and the social and political tensions that were a product of the times.

Italian neo-realism was not simply a matter of style, but, as Rossellini (one of the key filmmakers of the movement) noted, it was a 'moral position' (Brunette, 1996: 257). This moral position rejected the codes and conventions of popular entertainment film, favouring fractured and episodic narratives over cohesive plot and narrative. In place of grand and extravagant settings and characters were ordinary and everyday settings and characters: a man struggling through poverty in his later years (*Umberto D*, Vittorio De Sica, 1952), a man searching for his stolen bike, so necessary for his employment (*Bicycle Thieves*, Vittorio De Sica, 1948), life under German occupation (*Rome, Open City*, Roberto Rossellini, 1945), and the exploitation of poor fishermen (*La Terra Trema*, Luchino Visconti, 1948). In place of highly stylised cinematography, Italian neo-realism generally lent towards an aesthetic subtlety of observation evident in the static camera, functional rather than symbolic lighting, long shots, and deep-focus photography. For example, the film *Umberto D* (Vittorio De Sica, 1952) demonstrates a number of these techniques. Many of the scenes are shot in real locations rather than in studios. There are also scenes that have little relationship to an overall plot, such as an extended scene in which a woman prepares coffee in the kitchen of Umberto's lodgings. Plot details are not resolved; the maid never decides what to do about her pregnancy. The protagonist drifts aimlessly through his life with little motivation or no clear goal. The cinematography mirrors this through its long shots and deep-focus photography, which equally do not draw the spectator into a fixed meaning (as does popular cinema). Such deep-focus photography allows for ambiguity and self-reflection. As with many other neo-realist films, *Umberto D*'s realism stems from its exploration of themes and issues rejected within popular films, using an aesthetic strategy that refuses the illusionism of popular films. Among some of the themes and stylistic characteristics of Italian neo-realism were:

- rejection of neat plots and happy resolutions;
- emphasis on consequences of war and Fascism, particularly on the poor;
- socialist in tone – emphasis on need for equality and welfare;

- use of non-professional actors instead of stars;
- location filming, accompanied by post-synched sound; and
- rejection of stylistic editing and cinematography in favour of documentary style.

As you can see, realism is not to be confused with filming 'reality'. Instead, film realism, particularly in the modes and movements outlined above, usually emerges as a response to dominant cinema, and as a response to a particular social and political environment.

BAZIN AND REALISM

Although not a filmmaker, André Bazin was a key film theorist and critic who founded seminal film journals and whose theories were crucial to the development of the French New Wave cinema. In *Cahiers du Cinéma*, one of the film periodicals that would prove to have a lasting influence on film critics and filmmakers alike, Bazin championed a realist cinema with an emphasis on *mise en scène*, and particularly deep-focus photography and the long take (Braudy and Cohen, 2009: 41). Like Kracauer, Bazin regarded realism as the fundamental principle of film. He did not consider film as 'objective'; rather, he proposed that the capacity to mechanically record a pro-filmic reality meant that film was closer to realism than other arts. He compared the painter, whose panting of the canvas was far more subjective than the filmmaker operating a camera (Bazin, 2009). Sometimes, this has been misinterpreted as naïve by critics who argue that cinema is as ideological and manipulative or constructed as the other arts (Carroll, 1998). What Bazin means is that film has the potential to more closely represent reality when compared with other arts that do not mechanically record. Consequently, Bazin feels that cinema should exploit this closeness to realism. In his writings on film realism, Bazin notes that, historically, people have strived towards realism in representation through artistic or creative practice – what he refers to as the 'myth of total cinema'. Likewise, he suggests that cinema has evolved or moved further towards realism through its history, and reads the technological and stylistic developments of sound, colour, deep-focus photography, and widescreen as shifting closer to a cinema of realism than formalism. Bazin notes how the imagists foreground formal elements through montage (editing) and 'plastics' (lighting, set design, performance). For him, the era of the imagists ended with the development of technology that allowed for more realism. For him, *mise en scène* emerged as a realist style in the years 1940–1950, indicative not only in Italian neo-realism, but in a shift away from montage to depth of field; he uses *Citizen Kane* (Orson Welles, 1941) as a prime example of this. Bazin justified his emphasis on realism through depth of field and the long take by arguing that 'in addition to affecting the structures of the of the film language, it also affects the relationships of the minds of the spectators to the image, and in consequence it influences the interpretations of the spectacle' (Braudy and Cohen, 2009: 50). So, for him, depth of focus, in which everything from the foreground to the background was clearly in focus, is much closer to what the spectator experiences in reality and, thus, more realistic. In addition, depth of focus allows the spectator more scope for interpretation and analysis of the screen image. For example, a scene with everything in focus allows the spectator to shift his or her view to different aspects of the frame without being led or manipulated into viewing only a certain portion of the screen action. Finally, the result of this is ambiguity, since stylistic devices do not narrow or limit meaning through an edit that might clarify the preceding image.

Bazin acknowledged that films ultimately necessitated an edit at certain points, and notes that *Citizen Kane* oscillates between moments of montage and superimposition. However, he suggests that where montage was previously the dominant practice, *Citizen Kane* introduces an alternative and realist practice. In those moments of deep focus in the film, there is a wealth of detail available to the spectator. For example, in the scene where young Kane's adoption is arranged by his parents and Mr Thatcher, the shot is orchestrated in such a way as to keep young Charles Foster Kane in the background of the frame while his parents, distanced from him, negotiate with Mr Thatcher. The scene opens in what appears to be a static omniscient shot of Charles playing in the snow. The camera pulls back to reveal that the shot is positioned inside the house at the window with Charles's mother. Mrs Kane and Mr Thatcher move towards the foreground and discuss the terms of the adoption, while Mr Kane remains in the mid-ground, demonstrating his resistance to the adoption. In the background through the window, Charles continues to play in the snow. Charles remains visible throughout the shot, his father stands to the right of him in the frame, and Mrs Kane and Mr Thatcher are seated towards the front and left of the frame. Thus, Charles is caught between a father who has a weaker position within the frame and the mother and Mr Thatcher who retain a more powerful position within the frame.

Bazin often discussed deep focus along with the long take, which, for him, pro-duced the effect of deep space, whereby continuity of time and space is achieved and the action unfolds across all planes of the shot. Thus, depth of focus is often accompanied by the long take, as it complements the staging of action within and across the frame. The long take, for Bazin, achieved one of the fundamental elements of the experience of reality – temporal and spatial continuity. The long take can represent the passing of time realistically where montage can only hint at it, since the cut disrupts the temporal flow, even where temporal unity is implied. Bazin championed the work of Jean Renoir for his rejection of montage and use of mobile camera and the long take, as well as deep focus. For Bazin, Renoir:

> forced himself to look back beyond the resources provided by montage and so uncovered the secret of a film form that would permit everything to be said

without chopping the world up into little fragments, that would reveal the hidden meaning in people and things without disturbing the unity natural to them.

(Braudy and Cohen, 2009: 54)

Thus, the long take was one element in a process that is, according to Bazin, the true nature of cinema. Bazin refers to the scene in *The Rules of the Game* (Jean Renoir, 1939) in which the camera lingers in spaces and hallways, and at one point almost gets stuck in a corner from which it cannot move without disturbing the performances of the actors. As Bazin says, 'this sort of personification of the camera accounts for the extraordinary quality of this long sequence' (Bazin in Branigan, 2006: 59). The power of the scene lies in the way that the camera observes the actions. A similar scene occurs at the start of *Touch of Evil* (Orson Welles, 1958), where the first scene is shot entirely in one take, tracking along the main characters as they navigate the border town between Mexico and the US. Bazin's preference for deep focus and the long take stem from his understanding of cinema as inherently photographic. In this sense, the image itself is paramount.

Thus, deep-focus and long-take photography work creatively with the image to produce a 'realistic scenario' (Figures 10.9 and 10.10). In contrast, the edit disrupted the photo image because it fragmented it and disturbed temporal and spatial unity. In addition, deep-focus and long-take photography, simply due to the complexity and richness of detail in the shot, provided much more scope for ambiguity. This allowed for much more participation on the part of the spectator. In contrast, editing, and montage in particular, refused ambiguity and fixed meaning. Meaning was not found within the shot, but within the edit.

REALISM TODAY

While the Bazinian notion of cinematic realism did not come to dominate film as he predicted, the legacy of realism is apparent in a range of movements and filmmaking modes. The tendency towards realism today is evident in parallel cinema of India, British social realism, and the Dogme 95 movement, to name a few. Today, it still operates as a response to, or turn against, entertainment cinema. In these other manifestations of film realism, there remains a political overtone that emphasises social issues relating to class, race, and equality. As Hallam and Marshment suggest of British Social Realism, it 'was constructed as an aesthetics of responsibility with a mission to incorporate its citizen subjects within the public sphere by addressing the social issues of the times' (Hallam and Marshment, 2000: 34). It is not simply that the British social realist film speaks the truth or is ultimately 'authentic'. Rather, it is still representational, but in the sense that it seeks to represent experiences that reflect the social reality of many citizens. It also values those lives and experiences ordinarily deemed inconsequential within entertainment cinema: the working classes, industrial and post-industrial life, youth culture, and so on.

FIGURE 10.9
The Rules of the Game (Jean Renoir, 1939) – deep-focus and long-shot photography
create three fields of action

FIGURE 10.10
The Rules of the Game (Jean Renoir, 1939) – deep-focus and long-shot photography
establish two points of narrative interest (foreground and background)

The political scope of realist film is similarly evident in the Danish Dogme 95 movement, which called for a 'pure' cinema that refuses the manipulative and illusionary techniques of entertainment cinema. Dogme 95, so called because of its sudden and deliberate emergence in 1995, was a conscious attempt to develop a realist film movement that abandoned many of the practices of popular film. Its founders, Lars von Trier and Thomas Vinterberg, articulated their mission in a 'manifesto' that consisted of a 'vow of chastity', outlining a set of rules or formal practices for filmmakers. Like the realist traditions before it, Dogme 95 sought to strip away technical devices that were felt to interfere with the truth capacity of film. The rules of the movement included:

- location shooting, with no foreign props or sets;
- only diegetic sound and music;
- handheld camera;
- colour film with no artificial lighting (apart from one bulb where necessary);
- no superficial action; and
- no temporal or spatial alienation.

There are traces of Bazin's ideas here, particularly in the way that formal techniques are figured as counter to realism. The Dogme films strived for realism in two ways. First, the films have raw handheld camera work that evokes the documentary aesthetic (a more 'realist' style). Second, and what is sometimes understood as a contradiction, the raw and amateurish aesthetic also draws attention to the artifice of the films. Although the 'vow of chastity' calls for the filmmaker to force the 'truth' out of the characters and scenarios, the rules also ensure that the viewer will not invest in the image as reality itself, but always representation. This form of aesthetic realism has provoked much debate about the extent to which it is possible to produce an authentic cinema (Jerslev, 2002). For example, the 'vow of chastity' discourages genre filmmaking, yet in many instances the Dogme films draw upon the conventions of the melodrama. In any case, we might think of Dogme 95, as well as the other realist traditions, as seeking out truth rather than producing it.

FESTEN (Thomas Vinterberg, 1998)

Festen (released under the title *The Celebration* in the USA), like other Dogme films, uses a set of rules aimed at producing a purer form of film. The film is shot in handheld, uses existing exterior and interior lighting, uses improvised performance, and uses few post-production effects outside of conventional editing. Unlike traditional realist movements, however, 'the Dogme filmmakers are not concerned with the film as it will appear on the screen, but the manner in which the film will be produced: they are production rules' (De Valck and Hagener, 2005: 184). De Valck and Hagener note that the Dogme movement is different than the Bazinian approach to film realism. Bazin was concerned with perceptual realism at the level of spectatorship such that the spectator would recognise the resemblance between a 'real-life' scenario and its filmic representation. In contrast, the Dogme filmmakers are not concerned with ensuring that the screen image looks like reality. Rather, they insist upon the foregrounding of the recording mechanism. In *Festen*, the camera takes on the characteristic of spontaneity, clumsily navigating the space even as characters get in the way. In this sense, the camera gives the impression of being suddenly caught in the action. In the film, a family gathers in a hotel to celebrate the birthday of the patriarch. Throughout the film, it becomes clear that the family is quite dysfunctional, as revealed by son Christian who announces to all that his father had sexually abused both him and his now dead sister. The claustrophobic atmosphere of the hotel is accentuated by the use of close-ups and rapid, disjointed editing. For example, in the dinner scene, as each person makes their successive speeches, the camera cuts across the table to reveal the expression of each family member.

The Bazinian tradition would call for a deep-focus shot along with a long take. *Festen* seems to do the opposite, leading to accusations that the movement's commitment to 'purity' is ill-conceived, if not naïve. Yet, *Festen* refers to an alternative form of realism not dependent upon the perceptual similarity to 'real life'. The film's use of an amateur, home-movie aesthetic evokes another form of reality, which spectators will no doubt be familiar with. The film resembles a home video of a birthday celebration rather than a birthday celebration, and this form of 'realism' demands a different aesthetic strategy than that which Bazin called for. The home-movie aesthetic allows for edits, since it is not unrealistic for home movies to be roughly edited, shaky, and framed erratically. This form of home-movie realism also accentuates the sensation of 'live-ness' that other realist traditions strive for.

C@SE STUDY

EXERCISE **REALISM THROUGH DEEP FOCUS, LONG TAKE, AND CAMERA MOVEMENT**

Although today there seems to be an over-indulgence in shallow-focus photography, especially given that many students use digital SLRs in filmmaking, it is extremely important to learn to shoot in different ways. Film realism does not refer to poorly shot material that appears flat and 'spontaneous', although many contemporary realist films give the impression of this. Filmmaking according to the principles of realism is potentially far more complex, since it requires the careful organisation of space, forward planning in terms of camera movement, and the deliberate and controlled construction of *mise en scène*. It is also perhaps a deeply rewarding mode of filmmaking, as one shot can represent much more visual detail than in an edited sequence. The following exercise is designed to prepare you for such complex shots. In keeping with the theme of realism, you should also prepare a short narrative that encompasses some of the characteristics of realism (for example, situations or groups of people normally excluded from film representation, marginalised people, difficult personal circumstances, and ambiguity, perhaps in the ending).

Shoot a one-minute shot without an edit. The shot should use deep-focus photography and include at least two planes of action (for example, foreground and background). The shot should also include an element of camera movement such as tracking, panning, or tilting. Remember that this scene will need to be very carefully rehearsed. Using deep-focus photography means that you should control the stage and space rigidly. Every detail from foreground to background will be visible and noticeable to the audience, so make sure that it has a purpose. The background props and cues can be used to support the realist tone of the piece or can also be used to reflect on the characters. If your performers are moving within the space, you should practice this with them and the camera operator. Likewise, you will need to practice any camera movement with the performers. As you can see, this can be far more complicated than setting up a new shot. So, your task is as follows:

1   Pick a theme that evokes one or more aspects of film realism.

2   Use one deep-focus, long take that incorporates camera movement.

3   Storyboard the shot (you can trace movement and performance).

4   Stage the scene carefully, paying attention to the background detail and how it supports the overall theme.

5   Rehearse the movement of camera and actors a number of times.

See *The Idiots* (Lars von Trier, 1998), *Sweet Sixteen* (Ken Loach, 2002), and *Fish Tank* (Andrea Arnold, 2009).

CHAPTER 11

Genre

In his chapter 'Genre and Hollywood' in the book of the same name, Steve Neale suggests that genre theory is often limited in scope (Neale, 2000). He notes that in certain instances, the discussion of genre is limited to a narrow range of films and textual structures, and is often understood outside of much institutional and economic consideration. So, while we will consider a few key debates in terms of the canon of film genres, we will also pay attention to the wider social and economic conditions that produced such genres in the studio period. As we will see, genres are not absolute in terms of function, history, mode, or style. In fact, during the classical era, the industry did not prioritise genre films; instead, it focused on producing bankable, risk-free film themes that were most likely to produce returns. So, in order to understand the function of genre, we must reflect upon the origins of genre as a concept, the possible reasons for and consequences of the development of genre, particularly in the early years of the Hollywood studio system, and finally we must reflect upon the alternative and sometimes conflicting methods of approaching genre.

WHAT IS GENRE?

One of the key ways in which films are identified and categorised is by genre. We might go to the cinema to see a horror or an action film. We might identify our taste in terms of genre ('I like musicals'). Film libraries often arrange catalogues in terms of genre. In the earliest years of commercial cinema, films were made and marketed by 'type'. Later, Hollywood studios were associated with certain genres (for example, Warner Bros and the gangster film). Yet, analysis of genre in film studies only really emerged (as a discipline within the field) in the 1960s (Hutchings, 1995: 60). While there was some debate about how to theorise genre, it became clear that genre study revealed a great deal about the intersections between text, industry, and audience. As Peter Hutchings argues:

> [Genres] offer a means by which the industry can seek to repeat and capitalise upon previous box-office successes. This connects with the way in which genres also provide audiences with particular sets of knowledge which they can use to organise their own viewing.
>
> (Ibid.: 61)

For film practitioners, a study of genre indicates the ways in which it draws from and contributes to a set of codes and conventions that create meaning for the audience. In addition, and as Barry Langford suggests, 'For film-makers, organising production around genres and cycles holds out the promise of attracting and retaining audiences in a reliable way, so reducing commercial risk' (Langford, 2005: 1). Part of the appeal of the genre film is the way in which it produces expectations (for example, in the case of an action film: suspense, dramatic explosions, fights, fast-paced editing) and delivers on those expectations (with some variation). Steve Neale writes that:

> Genres do not consist solely of films. They consist also of specific systems of expectation and hypothesis which spectators bring with them to the cinema and which interact with films themselves during the course of the viewing process. These systems provide spectators with means of recognition and understanding. They help render individual films, and the elements within them, intelligibly and, therefore, explicable.
>
> (2000: 31)

So, audiences read the genre film in relation to other codes and conventions with which they are familiar. These codes and conventions represent a contract with the audience.

Conventions are the accepted norms of the genre film. For example, in the horror film, empty screen space serves to indicate that there will be a fright. Often, the character is placed to the front and side of the frame, with the remainder of the frame in the background left empty of action. The conventions of the genre point to the potential filling of this space by an antagonist. The empty space creates suspense, as the audience anticipates the generic convention of the horror: the arrival of the monster. *Halloween* (John Carpenter, 1978) uses this convention a number of times. Many films intentionally undermine these conventions in order to be innovative or as a reflection or comment upon genre. For example, *Scream* (Wes Craven, 1995) is a self-reflexive recycling of the slasher film. In the film, a serial killer (eventually revealed to be two killers) is killing high school students. One of the characters is a horror film fan and outlines the conventions of the slasher film in order to ensure their survival. In addition, iconography is central to discussions about genre. Iconography refers to the pattern of iconic representation across a number of texts. Genres contain icons that carry symbolic weight and meaning through their repeated use across a number of films. For example, *mise en scène* is often iconographic. Genres might have particular ways of representing a scene through lighting, staging, scenery, and costume. For example, in film noir, low-key lighting often conveys the dangerous underworld in which the characters find themselves. In the western, the large expansive scenery symbolises the mythology of the American frontier and the potential of the country. Similarly, costume is not only functional, but symbolic. In the western, the hero wears lighter clothing that is neater and more formal. The antagonists might be dressed in darker, scruffy clothes. This binary distinguishes not only the hero from the villains, but law against order, and good against evil. These are not absolutely fixed. Genres tend to shift and change over time. Some genres can be understood as historically specific (film noir) and others are more stable (western). Genres may also be cyclical. Once the codes and conventions of a genre become overfamiliar, they can become tired and the genre will decline in popularity. Genres can be revisited, as in the case of the western and the gangster film, where the codes and conventions are refreshed or considered.

THE ORIGINS OF GENRE

In *Film Genre: From Iconography to Ideology*, Barry Keith Grant (2007) traces the origins of film genres back to the early myths that circulated within primitive societies. He draws comparisons between the ritualisation and practice of myths in earlier societies (for example, sitting around a campfire), and the modern ritualization and practice of film viewing, collectively in a cinema. Just as certain patterns emerged in the nature and type of stories about heroes, villains, and quests among various cultures and societies, Grant suggests that film genres circulate similar stories in a fashion akin to myths. While this might seem a simplistic comparison, it does point to the fact that film genres did not appear out of the blue in the early years of the studio system. In fact, genre theory, as a method of classification and identification, did not begin in modern times. As far back as Aristotle's *Poetics*, we can see an effort to distinguish the characteristics of certain modes of literature. In fact, many of the terms we use to classify a genre come not from the world of cinema, but from a tradition in literature or the arts – the melodrama, the horror, and even the western all have their basis in literary trends that pre-date cinema. In fact, the debates about whether and how melodrama is defined as genre serve as interesting examples of how genre is, in fact, constantly under revision. For example, we might locate the western firmly within the paradigms of classical Hollywood. Yet, a film such as *The Great Train Robbery* (Edwin S. Porter, 1903) pre-dates this era, while containing some of the genre features we might identify with the classical Hollywood western. As Neale (2000) also notes, it was not classified as a western, but as a chase or crime film. Similarly, when we look to the terms used to identify films of the pre-Hollywood years, we can see some overlaps with the genre method of classification. For example, Richard Maltby notes that in 1905, film companies were categorising their films according to type, which included comedic, mysterious, scenic, and so on (Maltby, 2003: 78). So, how did the film industry during the studio era move from making films by theme (in which a basic storyline was apparent across a range of films) to genre (in which basic conventions, film techniques, motifs, and iconography are apparent)?

GENRE AND HOLLYWOOD

In order to understand how genre manifested in classical Hollywood, we can look at the text itself, and how the genre film differed from the thematic film, and we can look at how and why the industry came to involve itself in the production, distribution, and exhibition of genre films. We cannot think of the development of genre in Hollywood without considering the means in which production took place.

So, theme films do exactly what they say on the tin. They are visual stories that share thematic elements. The chase film will involve somebody chasing, somebody being chased, there may be a to and fro between geographically different but temporally similar events. The primary meaning of the film is found in the narrative – in other words, in the way that the story unfolds. Film companies certainly invested in familiarity and responded to the audience's preference for certain film types. So, these film types were the beginnings of what we later came to know as film genres.

That prompts the question: Why is a genre a genre, and not a type film or theme film? We can begin to think about the institutional transformation of the early studio years. Each studio built particular stages and sets, and each contracted particular stars, directors, and scriptwriters. In doing so, the studios were able to implement a number of cost-cutting measures by attaching particular stars and directors to projects. In addition, the studios were able to work to efficient schedules and production plans because they had contracted so many producers, directors, and stars. Finally, the studios had developed a system of vertical integration, which meant that they had control over exhibition and distribution. All of this together made for a finely tuned production system, which produced formula films, with regular cast and crew, in a tightly controlled schedule. As Neale goes on to argue:

> The routines and formula of genre complemented the routines and formulas of factory production. They enabled the studios to plan, to produce and to market their films in predictable ways and to dovetail their output with the expertise of their production staff . . . and with the plant, the costumes, the props and the other facilities in which they had each invested.
>
> (2000: 227)

So, we can think of genre as closely tied to the rise of the studio system, as well as the star system, and so on.

Hollywood industry

The move to Hollywood in the early years of cinema was accompanied by a continued rise in the demand for film product. Before the studio system, production, exhibition, and distribution were treated as relatively separate ventures. More to the point, the studio system refers to the way in which film companies began to 'integrate' these in order to produce the most profits (and thus cut out the middlemen). The studios engaged in year-round production in order to meet the demand of audiences. As Grant and others have suggested, the studio system resembled (somewhat) the Fordist model of production (Grant, 2007). Production schedules ensured that film production was standardised (in terms of the way in which films were made, distributed, and exhibited). In terms of the films themselves, they also became relatively standardised. Since many of those involved in the production of films were under contract to studios (including casts, directors, and writers), they had little scope for great innovation. Studios preferred low-risk endeavours and selected projects that reflected this. As Maltby notes, vertical integration and the increase in production was not necessarily economically viable (Maltby, 2003). Films still cost a lot to make, distribute, and exhibit. So, studios wanted to make films that would be safe with audiences (as opposed to making films that would be hard to market). Films that were formulaic and contained already-popular themes, stars, and conventions would allow for this. While Hollywood never employed the term 'genre' itself, many films produced in this way later came to be referred to as genre films. In other words, groups of films that we later came to understand as genre films (such as the gangster, the musical, and the screwball) were products of film cycles that emerged when a particular type of film was commercially successful. Andrew Tudor states that 'financially successful films encourage variations on their proven themes, thus generating a broadly cyclical pattern of successes which then decline into variously unsuccessful repetitions of the initial formula' (1989: 23). While this critique of film cycles seems damning, it serves as a useful way of understanding the genre film as a marketable commodity, which was subject to the interests of audiences.

Maltby goes on to suggest that these film cycles are often understood as genres in and of themselves, even though they could be read more as production trends (the prime example being the gangster film, which lasted only one cycle). Other film trends only lasted a brief season and so never came to be understood as genres because they never developed enough films to read them as such. Ultimately, producers were able to recognise how audiences responded to particular categories and types of films. In turn, they were able to market these films easily, since audiences would recognise some of the generic aspects prior to the film's exhibition: theme, star, which studio produced it, and so on. This is not to suggest that genre films were purely a product of commercial interests (as we shall go on to see), but that any consideration of genre must take into account these kinds of economic imperatives. After all, these genre films had initially been thought of as low-culture products. It was only later that theorists began to reflect upon the meaning and potential value of studying genre film.

Genre and the Production Code

The Production Code played a part in the form of these genres. Up until 1934, the Production Code was not enforced to any great degree. Yet, following pressure from lobby groups and amid threats of boycotts, the Production Code came up with a Seal of Approval that would be necessary for films to carry (there was an agreement with the studios). As certain genres were emerging (in particular, the gangster, the horror, and the romantic comedy), there was an effort to bring in a more rigid form of censorship. Not only did some of these genres have instances of violence, sexual 'corruption' (in the eyes of the moral guardians), and other potentially immoral activities, but they had these themes at their very core. When Joseph Breen took over the PCA in the early 1930s, he paid particular attention to horror films, cutting dialogue and scenes he deemed too terrible for mainstream audiences. Similarly, the gangster genre came into decline, as the Production Code influenced the shift from gangster-centred crime films to police-/authority-centred ones. As such, earlier genre cycles, such as the horror and the gangster, were forced to amend their forms, while later genres such as the screwball emerged in the wake of the PCA; in other words, the kind of comedy and humour we find in the screwball is a result of the limit placed on sexual comedies by the Hays Code. So, parts of these genres' aesthetic projects are due to the regulatory constraints of censorship.

Tod Browning's *Dracula* (1931), for example, was later re-cut to conform to the post-Code regulations. Similarly, James Whale worried that *Bride of Frankenstein* (1935) had suffered so much editing and re-cutting that all the horror had been removed. For example, the censors were concerned about Dr Frankenstein's continual reference to 'God'. Universal were additionally worried about the level of censorship abroad – Britain had a habit of constantly cutting or banning the Universal horrors, as did a good many other countries.

THE MONSTER FILM

Since the horror film is so expansive, encompassing various subgenres and types (the monster film, the supernatural film, the gothic tale), which often overlap, for the sake of clarity we will limit our discussion of horror to the monster film. The horror film had enjoyed success during the silent era, with Universal releasing films such as *The Hunchback of Notre Dame* (Wallace Worsley, 1923); however, at this stage none of the studios had managed to garner consistent success with the genre. Popularised in 1931 with the release of *Dracula* (James Whale, 1931) and *Frankenstein* (James Whale, 1931) by Universal Studios, the horror film, and more specifically the monster film, enjoyed a sudden and unexpected peak in success. In fact, this success was almost accidental. Universal Pictures was, during the late 1920s, a struggling company that had no theatres of its own, renting them instead from the majors. The Great Depression proved a difficult time for Universal, so when *Dracula* was commercially successful, the studio aimed at repeating this success. They followed with *Frankenstein* and when this, again, proved popular, Universal began to invest in the formula of exotic, distant locations, monster figures, and often mad scientists that were often drawn from literature or existing mythologies. While other studios briefly dabbled in horror films at this time, the profits were too small for the bigger studios, and so Universal became synonymous with the horror film during this period.

In fact, the genre's success was partly found in the fact that horror was cheap to make. As a struggling studio, Universal saw the benefit in using the cheapest sources available. This included adapting copyright-free literature, using existing sets (rather than investing in their own) and using 'cheaper' stars, who were popular but were not yet at the career stage of other established film actors. Familiar names such as Bela Lugosi and Boris Karloff became stars from horror films, but were paid very little while they were making these films. So, part of our understanding of Universal's monster genre, again, must come from the economic climate and the industry at the time.

The monster film later years

Other monster films included *The Mummy* (Karl Freund, 1932), *The Invisible Man* (James Whale, 1933), *The Black Cat* (Edgar G. Ulmer, 1934), *The Bride of Frankenstein* (James Whale, 1935), *The Wolf Man* (George Waggner, 1941), *The Phantom of the Opera* (Arthur Lubin, 1943), and *The Creature from the Black Lagoon* (Jack Arnold, 1954), which signalled the end of Universal's monster cycle. In between, there were a whole series of monsters' 'sons', 'daughters', and 'she-wolves', which drew from the popularity of the originals. As Andrew Tudor sum-marises, the years after the 1930s were characterised by a lack of innovation (Tudor, 1989). Films such as *House of Frankenstein* (Erle C. Kenton, 1944) signalled the end of the initial monster cycle, since they relied on genre traits that were becoming over-familiar with audiences. The only other studio to have consistent success with the horror genre was RKO, which, again due to financial difficulties, began a series of horror films that utilised existing sets and props (hence, we find that many of the films are set in contemporary towns and cities) and gave relative autonomy to independent production units (like the one headed by director Val Lewton). With this system, RKO was able to produce inexpensive, modestly successful horror films such as *Cat People* (Jacques Tourneur, 1942), *I Walked With a Zombie* (Jacques Tourneur, 1943), and

Body Snatchers (Robert Wise, 1945). In contrast to the Universal monster films, the RKO horror films, perhaps reflecting the times, blur the distinctions between monster and hero/human. Monstrosity in these films is largely from within. This pre-dates the social anxieties later reflected in RKO's films noirs.

CONVENTIONS OF THE MONSTER FILM

Gothic horror

These early horrors drew from the Gothic tradition – gothic writers such as Shelly (*Frankenstein*, 1818), Stoker (*Dracula*, 1897), and Poe (*The Black Cat*, 1843). So, each film's architecture, *mise en scène*, and cinematography all reflect this. Similarly, we find gothic locations – non-American locations, foreigners, the supernatural, the castle/haunted house/crypt, and so on. In contrast to other genres, such as the gangster, the screwball, and the western, these films are either set within, or evoke the past. There are a number of ways in which we can draw meaning from this. If we think about the period in which these films were made, we might read them as escapist fantasies – since there was so much 'horror' at home, in the wake of World War I, as well as the Great Depression, it may have been more reassuring that these monsters were located in far-away countries. In addition, the supernatural (in literature) had not yet been incorporated into the modern twentieth-century period. Although many of the films may have been set in the present, they were symbolically in the past, which was more associated with superstition. Even many of those films that presented modern science (the mad scientist) did so in the context of the nineteenth century (for example, *Frankenstein*'s old Europe as a location). Likewise, it is possible to understand the marked and maimed bodies of some of these films as responding to the horrors of World War I.

German expressionism and the European influence

We can see influences of German expressionism in the use of lighting and shadow in opposition to the naturalistic, evenly lit sets of most other films of the time. Like German expressionism, the claustrophobic sets and dark images were as much to do with limited budgets as they were to do with style. Some of the directors from Germany went on to make horrors and psychological thrillers, but we can see the influence in the monster film, particularly in the films of James Whale. For example, the film *The Black Cat*, based upon American author Edgar Allen Poe's story of the same name, is the most expressionist and European in form and content. The director, Edgar G. Ulmer, was from Austria (or the old Austro-Hungarian Empire), the story is set in old Europe in an ageing castle (although with modernist inclinations), the cast were largely Europeans, and the soundtrack composed of

European classical music. But this film was made for an American audience. The male and female leads are an American couple who arrive at this European destination on their honeymoon, and so the film is framed by their experiences. In fact, the director wanted to bring the experience of World War I to America (in the film, the landscape is filled with reminders of the wars that took place there and even the story weaves in the war). So, the American couple, a stand-in for the audience, is confronted with the devastation of the war, as well as the trauma experienced by those who are left with its legacy.

The monster

In the most obvious reading of the monster, it stands for the other, or it represents 'otherness'. As we know, the other is constituted through difference. It is different from me. I form my very identity through the marking of a boundary between what I am – my culture, society, and so on – and the other, which does not belong, which is rejected. In dominant Western culture, the self is embodied in the WASP (white Anglo-Saxon Protestant) and patriarchy. The monster is often marked as other. The monster, therefore, poses a threat to the self (in the films, usually a hero) because it threatens to dominate the self. It seeks to take over the position of the on-screen self. We see this manifested in a number of ways. The monster may be an ethnic other, such as Dracula or the Mummy, or may be represented as such (*King Kong*, Merian C. Cooper and Ernest B. Schoedsack, 1933). Such films have been charged with covert racism. For example, Dracula has been read as a representation of the eastern European Jew, and King Kong as representative of 'blackness' (Wartenberg, 2001). Otherness is likewise manifested as other in the form of the woman (*Cat People*, Jacques Tourneur, 1942) or of 'degenerate' or 'primitive' people (*Island of Lost Souls*, Erle C. Kenton, 1932).

Similarly, the monster has been understood as 'sexually' other – the monster possesses a deviant or confused sexuality. Dracula is clearly a sexual aggressor – the bite of the vampire signalling both sexual desire and violence. Frankenstein, as in *The Bride of Frankenstein* (James Whale, 1935), is sexually juvenile. This otherness is often contained within the same person. In *The Invisible Man* (James Whale, 1933), *The Wolf Man* (George Waggner, 1941), and *Cat People* (Jacques Tourneur, 1942), monstrosity invades the self and the line between self and other is blurred even further. In both cases, the monster as distinct other, or as internalised, questions of identity abound: What it is to be American in contrast to non-American? To be civilised as opposed to primitive? To be sexually normative as opposed to deviant? In other words, and as Robin Wood (1985) suggests, the classical horror film brings on an encounter with the other only to render it safe or annihilate it, thus re-establishing the normal self, and the normal social world. While this is not an exhaustive list, it should point the way to understanding some of the elements of the monster genre at this time.

Stars and directors in the horror film – Karloff and Lugosi

As Thomas Schatz notes, 'at the heart of the classical Hollywood and of each studio's house style were those star-genre formulations, the Davis melodramas and Karloff horror pictures' (Schatz, 1988: 492). A number of key people were central to the monster genre both behind and in front of the camera. The horror stars that emerged in the genre were specific to the horror film, and rarely worked outside of it, two of the most popular being Bela Lugosi and Boris Karloff. What was particularly unique about the stars of the horror film during this time was that the star was not connected to the heroic, nor do they represent the aspirations of the audience – as Dyer (2001) has argued about the star in other genres. Like the gangster, the monster is not intended to be a character of positive identification for the audience, although some might argue that the sexual appeal of the vampire may have played a role in the appeal of these monsters. Under normal circumstances, and in most cases of stardom, the star functioned as an ideal ego for the audience. While the name 'star' assumes that they were somehow elevated above the rest of society, at the same time they represented convention. They formed a template of normative sexuality, gender, race, and class.

However, the stardom of Lugosi and Karloff, and its associations with the monstrous, problematise this concept of stardom. The hero, representative of white, middle-class, heterosexual masculinity, is not the star of the horror film; rather, it is the monster – the non-white or non-American, sexually ambiguous or deviant, and the physically other. Both actors were non-American – Karloff was British (but with Indian ancestry), and Lugosi Hungarian. Thus, their real-life personas were reflected in their on-screen characters. Similarly, their real life personas were understood in terms of their monster characters. Lugosi's reputation reflected that of the villain Dracula – news stories played upon his history in Hungary, where rumours circulated about his involvement in duals and his aristocratic background (Cashill, 2003). Karloff, who played a sympathetic Frankenstein, became known for his philanthropic work for children's charities and so on. However, both actors, consequently, became typecast as monsters and villains. Lugosi, in particular, never achieved any success outside of the horror film, because his fame was so closely connected to the Dracula character. Effectively, what Lugosi and Karloff demonstrate is the interconnectedness of genre and stardom.

James Whale in Universal Studios

Similarly, it is clear to see that genre is also closely tied to the concept of authorship. By authorship, I am not necessarily simply referring to the auteur or the director, but to the system that enabled (or forced) particular studios, producers, directors, and stars to work with one another on a continual basis, and often within the same genre. In reference to Universal, and Whale's horror films *Frankenstein* (1931), *The*

Old Dark House (1932), and *The Bride of Frankenstein* (1935), Thomas Schatz has noted:

> The quality and artistry of all these films were the product not simply of individual human expression, but of a melding of institutional forces . . . The 'style' of a writer, director or star – or even a cinematographer, art director or costume designer – fused with the studio's production operations and management structures, its resources and talent pool, its narrative traditions and market strategy. And ultimately any individual's style was no more than an inflection on an established studio style.
>
> (1988: 6)

So, if we are to consider genre and authorship during the studio years, in the case of the monster film we might consider Universal as the studio, Carl Lamelle Jr. as the producer, James Whale as the director, and Boris Karloff and Bela Lugosi as the stars. In addition, many of the other cast and crew were regular contributors to the monster film output. So, for example, we could consider one member of this team and reflect on his role as author within the whole system. James Whale has only recently become a figure of interest in discussions of authorship, genre, and the studio system. Having been neglected from previous authorship studies, precisely because of his position within the system as of his quick decline as an 'author', he poses a number of difficulties for researchers. In his early career (1931–6), he was certainly a studio director; in many ways, he was a genre director (even though he did work outside of the horror film) but at the same time his films display a concern with the outsider, and present a unique theatricality through expansive staging and dark comedy. Even within the confines of the studio and in the few horror films he produced, and as David Lugowski suggests:

> so many aspects of Whale's fascinating life, and so many compelling themes and moods, are to be found in his films: his Englishness; his sensitivity to regional and class differences and to many types of outsiders; his early background in sketch art and cartooning; his service during WWI and his period of capture, during which he savoured male companionship and discovered theatre in shows that the prisoners staged; his deep friendships with women, beginning with his theatre days (he was even briefly engaged to costume designer Doris Zinkeisen in the '20s); and yes, his homosexuality. All of these factors, plus his use of a campy gallows humour, and a resistance to and critique of heterosexuality, are filtered through a style I would call 'theatrical'.
>
> (2005)

We can therefore read the monster genre of the early 1930s as an intersection between: (1) the standardisation of production under the studio system; (2) the development of a star system where genre vehicles produced and retained particular stars; (3) the reaction to and engagement with world politics and scepticism about economic, social, and political developments in the early part of the twentieth century; (4) the horror film's troubled relationship to censorship; and (5) the development of a particular aesthetic and stylistic strategies across a body of films.

So, we can see that when we use the term 'genre', we are not simply referring here to particular textual devices or iconography, but to the entire system that produces the text. We can, of course, look within the text in search of answers about what genre is, but unless we situate these answers within the institutional and social surroundings, then they are limited. These genres respond to particular needs of studios and audiences. The genres also help us understand stars and the meaning of performance; they help us understand directors not only as auteurs, but also as working within a particular set of rules; and they help us understand the larger project of the studios – to produce films through a standardised model.

EXERCISE MAKING THE GENRE FILM

There are a number of genres that would be practical to make for a short film. Among them would be a horror film (and perhaps a subgenre of the horror), a gangster film, a sci-fi film, or a film noir. You may choose any genre but first you must think about the codes and conventions that structure the genre, as well as the iconography. The genre film is not a singular film text. It refers to a body of films that exist outside of it. Be sure to watch a range of the genre films first and do further research on writings about the genre. Then, make a short film that uses a range of generic characteristics, motifs, and traits, including:

1   narrative (what form do the narratives usually take);

2   *mise en scène*;

3   character types; and

4   iconography (props, costumes, and objects).

See *The Godfather* (Francis Ford Coppola, 1972), *The Haunting* (Robert Wise, 1963), *Double Indemnity* (Billy Wilder, 1944), and *Alphaville* (Jean Luc Godard, 1965).

Part III

Guerrilla filmmaking
Practice as subversion

CHAPTER 12

Experimentation and the short film format

As a student, you will clearly be working within the boundaries and means of the short film format for your university projects (and, hopefully, beyond). This distinct format has been a mainstay of the creative filmmaking process since images were first committed to celluloid in the late nineteenth century and onward through the decades of the twentieth century right up to today, where even the most successful of current-day studio filmmakers have, in the early part of their careers, produced and directed short films. Today, an abundance of short films, professional and amateur, current and historical, can be found on YouTube and throughout the Internet. Are they successful and satisfying in terms of narrative and insight into world around us? Are they just 'time wasters' or fully formed vignettes that pack a thematic and aesthetic 'punch'? Whether 'real life', drama, documentary, pastiche, or parody, a wide range of short product is available to view and study. Now, how to separate the wheat from the chaff? This, of course, is purely subjective in terms of what constitutes a 'good' or gratifying short film. For our purposes, at university level, we'll focus on how to work to develop your *personal signature* by considering how experimenting with film aesthetics, narrative convention, and the use of *simplicity* are effective and cohesive means to form an original and dynamic short story for the screen. An excellent example highlighting these notions is Christopher Nolan's (*Memento*, *Batman Begins*, *Inception*) three-minute 16 mm black and white short *Doodlebug* (1997) (Figure 12.1).

Here, Nolan's short film demonstrates and exemplifies *simplicity* and economy of narrative as it follows one man in one room who is 'haunted' by and pursues a small insect. The film has a clever twist ending whose thematic, arguably, explores the notions of 'just who is watching who' and 'I am my own worst enemy'. From

FIGURE 12.1
Nolan's protagonist realises who is watching who!

these humble short film beginnings, Nolan has fashioned a very successful and creative film career as a director whose films are known for their 'psychological' thematic and bent. At this point, it would be wise to view the short films of some your favourite directors. Pay particular attention to how they tell a story both through their use of visuals and sound. You will see that many early short film works don't make use of character dialogue, or, at the least, it is kept to a minimum. Focus on how they structure the narrative or, if they are more avant-garde or experimental, the use of imagery and *mise en scène*. Can their *personal signatures* be witnessed to be emerging and developing in their early short works? The use of minimal dialogue can serve you well on your short productions. This is so on two counts: (1) by demonstrating your ability to tell a story through imagery and *mise en scène*, which not only hones and challenges your imaginative use of the frame, but shows (as an artefact on your demo reel) prospective film and media industry employers that you are developing a personal and unique cinematic *signature*; and (2) as a student filmmaker, you will likely be working with an absolute minimum budget and thus unable to secure highly seasoned and professional actors that have the acting craft experience to deliver dialogue in a believable and 'non-forced' way, so to speak, particularly if the written dialogue is trite and clichéd due to an inexperience of script-craft. However, you should not worry on this account, as at this point in your creative development you are 'learning the ropes' of cinematic storytelling and navigating your way through to figuring out what best works for you in terms of how to most competently express your storyline and thematic through imagery and character. By keeping dialogue to a minimum, you can cast the most interesting looking of up-and-coming or less seasoned actors to populate your production. An interesting filmmaker to consider on this account is Guy Maddin.

Canadian director Maddin is a good example of an independent filmmaker who has forged a 'personal identity' within his film works, both feature and short, who, in most cases, works with non-professional actors. Maddin argues that they give a more 'uninhibited' performance, less constrained and formulated. A notable exception to Maddin's utilisation of unseasoned film performers is his working relationship with the actress Isabella Rossellini who appears in his low-budget feature *The Saddest Music In The World* (2005) (Figure 12.2) and the short film *My Dad Is 100 Years Old* (2006), which is an homage to her director father, Roberto Rossellini (*Open City, Rome*, 1945; *Germany, Year Zero*, 1948).

Italian director Rossellini (married to the actress Ingrid Bergman, mother of Isabella) was a pioneer of neo-realism, employing on many occasions the use of non-professional actors and shooting on actual locations (as opposed to the mostly interior, set-constructed form of European and Hollywood studio filmmaking conventions of those times). After sending her samples of his early film work and pitching to her, Isabella Rossellini was impressed enough that she agreed to be in a number of Maddin's film productions.

At this point, it will make for a good case study for you to review both Maddin's short and feature-length films, such as *Sissy Boy Slap Party* (1995), *The Heart Of The World* (2000), *Cowards Bend The Knee* (2003) (composed of 10 six-minute chapters that are constructed as 10 linked short films to comprise an overall narrative thread), *Sombra Dolorosa* (2004), and *Send Me to the 'lectric Chair* (2009). You will experience in his short film work, and in much of his feature work, a sparing use or non-use of dialogue. In fact, Maddin draws from the silent era of filmmaking as a structural and aesthetic device to create his personal visions and to explore

FIGURE 12.2
Isabella Rossellini as Lady Port-Huntly, beer Baroness

family histories, time, place, and dreams. He works with minimal budgets but has gained a solid reputation, both within film art circles and mainstream film circles, for his experimental notions of narrative, use of black and white imagery, and non-traditional sound and music to create dynamic atmospheres and the idiosyncratic worlds where his characters reside and the spaces they populate. All of these films are available on DVD compilations and YouTube, and need to be seriously studied, discussed, and debated. You should also seek out a range of filmmakers and film artists that you may not have considered before. In particular, I would recommend you view a series of European and Russian directors and their short material (for example, Andrei Tarkovsky, Lars von Trier, and Jean-Luc Godard). Additionally, the short documentaries of Krzysztof Kieslowski are instructive, as they informed his developing personal style later in his fiction work, in particular his excellent film-series *Dekalog* (1988), which consists of 10 one-hour episodes set within a low-income, high-rise apartment block. For the purposes of this chapter, it will be of benefit for us to consider the short film form in terms of its ability to encompass a unique approach to aesthetics, *mise en scène*, and editing – a form that is fundamentally dissimilar and resistive to generic studio film conventions. These notions are encapsulated in what is often referred to as 'underground' or avant-garde film. Here, a cinema that can be 'transgressive' and non-conformist, one that pushes boundaries and, perhaps, societal tastes and social mores. By adopting these experimental concepts, you can truly begin to develop your own personal visual field to tell a story.

David Lynch is another good example of how an early short film he directed constructed a personal 'surreal' vision of the world around us. *Eraserhead* (1977) (Figure 12.3) was developed over a five-year period as it was re-worked from a short film to its eventual feature-length time. Lynch's current creative feature-film

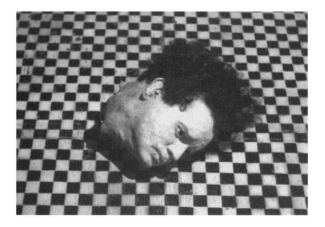

FIGURE 12.3
Henry Spencer (John Nance) 'loses' his head

work draws from his early filmic short film roots, in particular his surreal and experimental treatment of narrative, *mise en scène*, and character as found in *The Grandmother* (1970). Lynch is one of the few filmmakers working at this 'experimental' level who is able to garner financial support and distribution deals from mainstream Hollywood studios.

What also distinguishes the film is its use of an original sound design as created by Lynch from recording various industrial and nature sounds and re-working them to create a dynamic sense of atmosphere, unease, and foreboding. As student filmmakers, this form of auditory experience for your short films can be obtained through this cost-effective manner of self-recording original sounds at various exterior and interior locations.

EXERCISE **SOUND**

Break down your script in terms of how you 'see' the film's soundtrack and envision what sounds and/or effects would/could enhance the imagery, narrative flow, and thematic. Make a list of potential sounds that you could use to create the atmosphere you want for a particular scene or sequence in your film. Using a digital sound recorder and good-quality microphone (bring both omnidirectional and unidirectional microphones if possible for varying effect), spend a day travelling about your city or town, traversing industrial, residential, and countryside spaces, and record a series of particular interesting sounds, both natural and mechanised. Keep a written record of the location, time of day, microphone used, and what object or source produced the sound. Now, work them into your edit timeline, either in their original form of by creating an effect through combinations, and experiment with pitch, tone, and speed. You'll be amazed at the results and the endless combinations that you can create. (This is also a great way to begin to compile a sound library that you can access for future productions).

The short film format is unique unto itself, as it requires the skill and acumen to tell a distinct and succinct story, either through a conventional narrative or as a means to adopt and invoke an experimental approach that resists customary and traditional techniques. This experimental methodology is particularly useful for emerging filmmakers, as it provides an impetus for you to develop and hone a cinematic *personal signature*. Here, you can work at a level (that is, within budgetary and logistical constraints) that challenges you to find and develop a storyline that can be told from a personal context; one that is personified by utilising abstract practices and a non-linear plot. As we discussed earlier, it may be silent, it certainly can be a radicalised and distorted *mise en scène*, one that pushes boundaries and taboos. The short film has a unique history of contesting orthodox culture and challenging audience expectation, one that baits the spectator to draw active meaning from the imagery, theme, and scenario. As you have likely come across in your previous studies, experimental short cinema has been sectioned into various delineations that comprise the notion of *underground* cinema; these include: 'transgressive', 'exploitation', 'cult', and 'alternative' as sub-forms of 'independent' filmmaking practices. These sub-strata of experimentation defy and confront conformist and moderate forms of the big studio production practices in terms of their portrayal of character, plot, *mise en scène*, sexuality, and cultural subject matter.

In the early era of cinema's rise to cultural prominence (from the late 1910s to the 1930s), both aesthetically and economically, the short film format was employed by a vast confluence of artists who wanted to push cinematic limits to forge new frontiers of moving image expression. Here, notions of the *avant-garde* and its artistic principles of abstraction, lyricism, and iconoclasm were applied to a series of cinematic 'movements' that included *surrealism*, *Dadaism*, *expressionism*, and *futurism*. Look further into these radical film movements and study a range of filmmakers and their creative and aesthetic rationales for their imagery and themes. The goal of these 'experimental' filmmakers was to transform or reinvigorate the public's consciousness from the slumber of orthodox perceptions and viewpoints. From the post-World War I period to today, avant-garde film practices continued to push boundaries, experimenting with form and content. In particular, the work of Maya Deren (*Meshes in the Afternoon*, 1943) led the way into this new era of experimentation, as she raised questions of female identity, suppression, and anxiety within our patriarchal society.

As students, you are encouraged, and should take the opportunity, to use the short film format to subvert established aesthetic conventions and focus on creating an 'out-front' work, one which may challenge hegemony, social mores, ideologies, and economics through a personalised, ground-breaking, and questioning form of film production techniques and practices. Additionally, drawing from your theoretical practice to date can serve as a wealth of inspiration and idea generation. Review the cinema and cultural theory units you have studied over the tenure of your scholarship. Consider the set and additional readings you have reviewed and written or presented on. Are there particular notions, concepts, and philosophies that you can draw upon for story, theme, and/or image ideas? Review the writings and authors that pique your interest and consider carefully if any of their academic analyses and views can underpin and inform your practice.

By way of an example, let's consider how a theoretical essay explores notions of 'cult filmmaking' practice. Here, consider how the analysis can/could contribute to your own personal filmmaking style and approach. The concept of 'cult' has had a dynamic output both in feature and short form, so this case model can be applied to your current university productions. Review the case study and make notations on how this written work can/could provoke and generate story inspiration and ideas. How would you approach/consider such theorisations (in particular, those academic works that are of most interest to you) as a way to meaningfully contribute to your creative practice? While reading the excerpted article, be reflective and ask yourself:

1   Is the deliberation on 'cult filmmaking' useful in terms of your current filmmaking practice and/or project(s) that you are developing?

2   Is the article useful in terms of contributing to and developing a deeper understanding intellectually, politically, and aesthetically of your current filmmaking practice and/or project(s)?

3   How can you apply and utilise the essay's notions in a way that can underpin a filmmaker's *personal signature* in terms of creating a non-traditional storyline, the *mise en scène*, and thematic approach?

Keep these questions in mind as you read through the material and take note of any ideas you have that arise from the reading that might infuse your own filmmaking practice. You will derive great benefit and use in applying these questions and thoughts to particular cultural theorisations as a means to draw thematic and image inspiration.

C@SE STUDY

CULT FILM – THEORY UNDERPINNING PRACTICE

Edited excerpts from *Notes Toward a Masochizing of Cult Cinema: The Painful Pleasure of the Cult Film Fan*, by David Church (used by permission of the author and *Offscreen* online journal).

The phenomenon of cult cinema is most often generated by the dual combination of a) textual peculiarities and b) specific audience reading/consumption strategies. Violence and sexuality of a deviant or perverse variety are generally the key motifs in most cult films, as are other forms of taboo breaking and transgression that somehow set these films apart as "less accessible" to all tastes (typically through opposition to bourgeois social norms). Often situated both within and against low/mainstream/mass and high/elite/art tastes, cult films are also marked by "formal bizarreness and stylistic eccentricity" denoting a predilection for considerable excess (Sconce 1995, p. 386).[1] Excessiveness and eccentricity are also traits commonly attributed to cult movie buffs, and it is the particular devotion of the cultist that will be my primary focus in this essay.

My starting point will be an understanding of all film spectatorship as masochistic, a theory most usefully advanced by Gaylyn Studlar and Steven Shaviro. Following Deleuze's early work, Studlar (1988) posits that the cinematic apparatus serves as a "dream screen" that causes regressive spectatorial pleasures hearkening back to the infant's experience of perceived union with the pre-oedipal (or oral) mother representing plenitude. As a form of (un)pleasure open to male and female spectators alike, cinema unleashes these repressed desires for symbiotic re-union with the mother's body as the spectator's ego boundaries are temporarily dissolved and he/she is fixed in a submissive position of inability to control the dreamlike images being projected, while identification with on-screen characters remains bisexually fluid and constantly shifting.

Barry Keith Grant (2000) argues that cult films "share an ability to be at once transgressive and recuperative" (p. 19) because the excessive and taboo-breaking qualities of the text are merely temporary, for social order is eventually restored at narrative's end. As an example, he notes that *Rocky Horror*'s campy, bisexual excesses are finally ended once Dr. Frank-N-Furter is destroyed at the conclusion, leaving the heterosexual couple Brad and Janet reunited. Grant explains that cult films also encourage viewers to "laugh at the normal, tame the Other, but nowhere see themselves" (p. 27), because typically caricatured representations of the Other serve to cast all characters along solid binary oppositions (e.g., normal/abnormal, establishment/anti-establishment, straight/gay, male/female, etc.), allowing viewers no solid points of identification in between.

Sconce (1995) describes how "paracinema" (exploitation film) cultists define their tastes as a sort of "counter-cinema" (e.g., through violations of continuity editing, suturing, etc.) opposed to both mainstream Hollywood cinema and elite art cinema—so perhaps we can see the ironic excesses of cult films as a repudiation of normative cinema's patriarchal imperative toward Oedipal resolution in heterosexual family formation. In place of normative cinema's identification with a male heterosexual protagonist in an Oedipally-based narrative arc, cult cinema is more prone to ironic (and/or camp) readings of such narratives, instead focusing on spectacle and excess—particularly when marked by alternative sexualities. Cultists typically refuse patriarchal imperatives, engaging in a (bisexual) polymorphous perversity by finding a plethora of unconventional and downright bizarre sources of fetishistic pleasure within the text—pleasures which can masochistically shatter a viewer's pre-existing schema for interpreting films. This is not to say that all cult films are politically progressive (nor do they all feature counter-cinematic elements), especially because, as Grant (2000) says, many end with a recuperation of the [superego] norms that have been previously transgressed.

C@SE STUDY

However, the fetishistic repetition of cult viewing makes it quite obvious that the transgression offered throughout these films is far more attractive than any recuperation at the end of a given narrative; it is not narrative closure that cultists are after, but the radical indiscretions leading up to that point. The myriad perverse pleasures of the text seem to exceed the ability of the narrative to contain them, ultimately leaving binary oppositions and generic tensions unresolved, thus encouraging repeat viewings *ad infinitum*.

On a textual level, many cult films often appear excessively sadistic, sexual, and exploitative (especially towards women)—notably in films that fall under horror, sexploitation, action, and other male-oriented genres. Mendik and Harper (2000b) argue that the cult audience for a horror film like *From Dusk 'Til Dawn* (Robert Rodriguez, 1996) operates much like the diegetic audience within the works of the Marquis de Sade (specifically *The 120 Days of Sodom*), being "both enticed into its celebrations of evil and perversity before being shocked, misled, or violently forced to reflect on their gratifications from the narrative proceedings" (p. 238). This takes place through a process that positions the film-savvy target audience as "captive" spectators to a text which is overloaded with difficult and non-traditional information (in this case, originating from screenwriter Quentin Tarantino's penchant for self-referential postmodern pastiche), moral ambiguity, and "sadistic" excess (simultaneously referencing creation and destruction). The viewer is free to seek pleasure from multiple sources (not just one aspect of the text) by drawing upon a compendium of filmic and extra-filmic (or more appropriately, intertextual) knowledge (i.e., trivia) with which to retrospectively interpret the narrative's unexpected generic shifts and transgressive hedonism. Mendik and Harper conclude that when these sorts of individualistic reading pleasures coalesce at a communal level, a "cultifying" of the film occurs, and thus a new film cult is born from pleasures at a textual level.

While certainly not all cult films contain the degree of intertextual information and trivia as *From Dusk 'Til Dawn* and other Tarantino-spawned cult items, the basic concept of "cultification" and its link to individuals' varied pleasures in a cult text deserves more discussion. As noted earlier, knowledge is not used to establish ownership (as in Sade's works) over the cult film, but rather to establish loyalty and achieve a closeness to the powerful text. As Studlar (1988) points out, masochism is an entirely different perversion than sadism, not the opposite end of a spectrum (p. 13-14). The ostensibly sadistic fantasies found in many cult films can actually be read as projections of masochistic fantasies about destruction, abandonment, and even Oedipal rivalry, for fantasies from other developmental stages can co-exist with pre-oedipal ones, but are constantly undergirded by masochistic desires (p. 57). Shaviro's (1993) analysis seems closer to the mark when he explains that . . . the aggressive

C@SE STUDY

act of filming is only a detour en route to the passivity and self-abandonment of spectatorship. And violence against the Other is finally just an inadequate substitute for the dispossession of oneself. The reflections of masochistic spectacle create a space of superfluity, of violently heightened ambivalence, in which every exercise of power gets lost (p. 62).

He uses cult horror films like *Peeping Tom* (Michael Powell, 1960), *Opera* (Dario Argento, 1987), and George Romero's zombie series to conclude that viewers empathize with both the victim's subjection *and* with the monster/antagonist's passive compulsion toward violence (p. 61). Viewers may be "overtly appalled by the violence they are compelled to see, yet there's a latent—secretly desirable—erotic thrill in the way these gory spectacles are being produced for *them*" (p. 50), held captive by the flow of images because "Violent and pornographic films literally anchor desire and perception in the agitated and fragmented body" (p. 55). Of course, Shaviro does not just apply this argument to horror films, but rather uses horror as a particularly explicit example of how spectatorship in general is masochistic.

Paul Watson (1997) and Eric Schaefer (1999) each observe how all cinema is historically predicated upon an aesthetic of exploitation, both using Tom Gunning's formulation of the early "cinema of attractions" as kindred to the exploitation film's more direct address to the spectator (who is fully aware that the spectacle is being made for him/her) and its emphasis on spectacle over narrative and character identification. The concept of *photogénie* (an automatism, intentional or not, whereby the camera turns otherwise ordinary things into captivating spectacles) can potentially be applied to the extreme fetishism inherent in the spectacular excesses of cult films, especially due to the surrealists' interest in the *photogénie* of "bad" movies and the experience of *photogénie* as "intermittent intensities . . . that break free from the sometimes indifferent narratives that contain them" (Ray, 1998, p. 69). This is linked to the notion that *photogénie*, like masochism, is a fetish for the pre-oedipal mother, given that *photogénie* entails a pleasurably automatic submission to (and fantasy of fusion with) powerful images in the absence of words or language (Willemen, qtd. in Gorfinkel, 2000, p. 163). Because "every exercise of power gets lost" during the masochistic viewing experience, such a position exists above the logic of political correctness that so many cult films deliberately violate.[2] This begs the question of whether films that knowingly defy social norms can really be appreciated apolitically since they seem to be premised upon transgression. However, just as cult films do not appeal to all audiences and do indeed contain multiple textual sources of pleasure, there exist many ways to interpret these films by sidestepping issues of political correctness and instead focusing on the visceral affects of images upon bodies divorced from political considerations. For example,

C@SE STUDY

Tanya Krzywinska (2000) observes how disgust (a common response to various violent and sexual elements of cult films) blurs "the distinction between authenticity and artifice," transcending traditional forms of representation because disgusting images evoke the same visceral response when viewed on-screen as when viewed in real life (p. 33, 38)—and therefore it seems obvious to me that wilfully and (un)pleasurably submitting oneself to the often disgusting and otherwise transgressive content of cult films is a profoundly masochistic act.

As Carol J. Clover (1992) and others have argued, spectatorial identification often entails a bisexual, transgender fluidity, masochistically shifting from one character to another with little regard to biological sex—even in the most ostensibly gender-biased films, such as horror and rape-revenge pictures (many of which are also cult objects). Our empathies flow from one character to another, perhaps even more fluidly and liberatingly than Clover and many other theorists are willing to admit (due to the particular political concerns underlying their respective analyses). This masochistic bisexual impulse is not just restricted to character identification, however. Hawkins (2000) observes that cult films are generally dominated by the visceral affect associated with "body genres" (horror, pornography, and melodrama) (p. 4). Linda Williams (1999) explains how the spectacle of body genres manipulates the viewer into involuntarily imitating the pain, fear, or pleasure of the on-screen female body, becoming masochistically "feminized" in the process. While the homosexual connotations of camp readings (which often overlap with cult readings) and the theatrical performativity of spectacle tend to destabilize traditional masculinity, Moya Luckett (2003) analyzes Doris Wishman's sexploitation films in order to argue in favor of a more radical take on gender in the cult film. "Often latent or found in inopportune places, femininity emerges as arguably *the* structuring force in cult films" (p. 142), she explains, additionally noting that the (male-to-female) sex change is "Perhaps the cult film's central trope," presenting "the ultimate correction of the pathological male body, the dominance of femininity, and the breast's pre-eminent role in defining and revealing sexual difference" in its symbolizing of female power (p. 151). The breast attracts the gaze while the sex change repels it, and this tension between attraction and repulsion is "the core pleasure of many cult film genres, particularly horror, the educational film, the sex hygiene film, the vice and atrocity films" (p. 154). This tension would appear to be a particularly masochistic one, drawing upon various sorts of body genre affects, repeatedly engendering pleasure only to then destroy it. Elena Gorfinkel (2000) also examines Wishman's work (focusing on 1974's *Double Agent* 73), specifically utilizing Studlar's theories to discuss exploitation films as a form of masochistic heterocosm that exists both within and beyond

C@SE STUDY

historical (and political) representation, using the masochistic aspects of *photogénie* as a potential key to "the space of cult film's affective investment" (p. 169).

Studlar (1989) herself discusses cult films in an essay not devoted to masochism, arguing that "feminine" (but not necessarily female) figures typically unite revulsion and fascination in the cult film (thus arguing directly contrary to Luckett, 2003). Although sexual perversion (e.g., taboo breaking, inversion of gender/sex roles) is playfully celebrated as an "outlaw sexuality" in cult films, Studlar argues that it is done so in a "de-eroticized" way, temporarily disorienting gender lines but not actually powerful enough to break down patriarchal law. Femininity instead becomes equated with a grotesquely perverse sexual difference, merely reinforcing gendered power relations. For example, she argues that in *Pink Flamingos* (John Waters, 1972), Divine parodies femininity to the point of inviting the audience's ridicule, using disgust and grotesquerie to distance (heterosexual) viewers from the subversive potential of bisexual desire. However, I would argue that the disgust created by Divine's grotesque appearance and actions is part of the masochistic process of submitting oneself to the visceral affects of cult films. Furthermore, the idea that Divine is not the film's (anti-) heroine but rather the object of mocking scorn seems more of an "outsider's view" of the film, not necessarily that of most cultists; fans of the film are more likely to laugh *with* Divine's campy appearance and aggressively "proto-punk" mentality, not *at* them. The film's pleasure derives not just from the character of Divine, but also from the liberatingly bisexual (not just "feminine") and polymorphously perverse "transparent subculture heterocosm" that Waters creates, "where sexual perversity as social deviance shows up everywhere" (Studlar, 1989, p. 5).

Chuck Kleinhans (1994) notes of films like *Pink Flamingos* that camp "operates within the larger boundaries of a racist, patriarchal, bourgeois culture. That it defines itself in difference from the dominant culture does not automatically construct Camp as radically oppositional. Only an audience and the work's exhibition context can complete that subversion" (p. 195). This statement seems also quite applicable to the overlapping concept of "cult," for the (politically incorrect) cult text acquires so much of its meaning from the diverse, perverse, and often contradictory readings that spring from its audience, constructing a cult reputation as readings cannibalistically feed back into one another.

If, as Studlar (1989) says, cult films seem to denigrate femininity, it may be due to the aggressive symbolic return of the previously (but never permanently) dispelled superego/father within the masochistic scenario, an attempt to spoil the fantasy by reasserting patriarchal norms toward masculine privilege and phallic sexuality (Studlar, 1988, p. 25). This defense against feminization is evidenced in some cultists' stance toward the object of their desire. Joanne Hollows (2003) and Jacinda Read (2003) observe how "cult" is a male-dominated phenomenon, self-differentiated from the supposedly "feminine" (passive) aspects of mass/mainstream culture through the active ("masculine") process of selecting texts. High culture and academicism are also a source of contention for the cultist, for academicism is often linked to a political correctness (i.e., feminism) that would reject the disreputable pleasures of many cult films, while high culture is often viewed as more "effete" and unable to stomach the more visceral affects of cult films. Cultists therefore find themselves trapped between the supposedly feminizing effects of both high and low culture, typically resorting to a "laddish" (playfully over-masculine) opposition to femininity to dispel such threats.

As with camp and the Bakhtinian carnival, there are material and temporal limits to the transgressions of the cult film, but the recuperation of social norms (including patriarchal law) at film's end is severely undercut by the spectator's repeated pleasurable submission to transgressive excess upon subsequent viewings; the film's preferred ideological reading is only one potential point of indulgence, but is often confounded by the (ironic) excesses of the text and experienced in dramatically different ways through the body. Following Shaviro (1993), we can see how the wild visceral spectacle endemic to cult films bypasses processes of solid character identification and aesthetic distance, making the film's only exercise of power into that of the powerful text over the spectator. The cultist can potentially be socially and sexually liberated within the context of total submission to the masochistic fantasies perpetuated indefinitely by the cult film. Although masochism in the cult film experience deserves more in-depth analysis than the scope of this essay will allow, looking at the peculiar qualities of cultism has the potential to enrich our understanding of just what cinematic spectatorship can mean. By repeatedly uniting the viewer with both the film and a select subculture of fellow travellers, this particularly fetishistic mode of spectatorship offers a picture of viewers submissively offering themselves to pleasurable extremes again and again, temporarily pacifying strange desires that cannot be filled elsewhere in cinema.

NOTES

1   Sconce's discussion centers around what he terms "paracinema," which can more broadly be described as exploitation film. However, it is important to remember that exploitation film is but a subset of cult cinema in general.

C@SE STUDY

2   Many cult film theorists attempt to maintain some sort of critical and aesthetic
     distance from the object of their study, and so it has become almost a
     convention for theorists to explain their personal stake in such disreputable
     pleasures before going into a more "objective" analysis. In contrast, Shaviro
     (1993) champions looking at film without this clinical distance, instead fully
     embracing the visceral pleasures of spectatorship experienced through the
     body itself.

BIBLIOGRAPHY OF WORKS CITED

Clover, C.J. (1992). *Men, women, and chainsaws: Gender in the modern horror
     film*. Princeton, NJ: Princeton University Press.
Gorfinkel, E. (2000). "The body as apparatus: Chesty Morgan takes on the
     academy." In X. Mendik and G. Harper (Eds.), *Unruly pleasures: The cult film
     and its critics* (pp. 156–169). Guildford, UK: FAB Press.
Grant, B.K. (2000). "Second thoughts on double features: Revisiting the cult film."
     In X. Mendik and G. Harper (Eds.), *Unruly pleasures: The cult film and its
     critics* (pp. 14–27). Guildford, UK: FAB Press.
Hawkins, J. (2000). *Cutting-edge: Art-horror and the horrific avant-garde*.
     Minneapolis: University of Minnesota Press.
Kleinhans, C. (1994). "Taking out the trash: Camp and the politics of parody." In
     M. Meyer (Ed.), *The politics and poetics of camp* (pp. 182–201). London and
     New York: Routledge.
Krzywinska, T. (2000). "The dynamics of squirting: Female ejaculation and lactation
     in hardcore film." In X. Mendik and G. Harper (Eds.), *Unruly pleasures: The
     cult film and its critics* (pp. 30–43). Guildford, UK: FAB Press.
Luckett, M. (2003). "Sexploitation as feminine territory: The films of Doris
     Wishman." In M. Jancovich, A.L. Reboll, J. Stringer, and A. Willis (eds),
     Defining cult movies: The cultural politics of oppositional taste (pp. 142–156).
     Manchester: Manchester University Press.
Mendik, X. and Harper, G. (2000a). "Introduction: Several theorists ask 'How was it
     for you, honey?' Or why the academy needs cult cinema and its fans."
     In X. Mendik and G. Harper (Eds.), *Unruly pleasures: The cult film and its
     critics* (pp. 7–11). Guildford, UK: FAB Press.
Mendik, X. and Harper, G. (2000b). "The chaotic text and the Sadean audience:
     Narrative transgressions of a contemporary cult film." In X. Mendik and
     G. Harper (Eds.), *Unruly pleasures: The cult film and its critics* (pp. 236–249).
     Guildford, UK: FAB Press.
Read, J. (2003). "The cult of masculinity: From fan-boys to academic bad-boys."
     In M. Jancovich, A.L. Reboll, J. Stringer, and A. Willis (Eds.), *Defining cult
     movies: The cultural politics of oppositional taste* (pp. 54–70). Manchester:
     Manchester University Press.
Schaefer, E. (1999). "Bold! Daring! Shocking! True! A history of exploitation films,
     1919–1959. Durham, NC and London: Duke University Press.
Sconce, J. (1995). " 'Trashing' the academy: Taste, excess, and an emerging
     politics of cinematic style." *Screen*, 36(4), Winter 1995, 371–393.
Shaviro, S. (1993). *The Cinematic Body*. Minneapolis and London: University of
     Minnesota Press.

C@SE STUDY

Studlar, G. (1988). *In the realm of pleasure: Von Sternberg, Dietrich, and the masochistic aesthetic*. Urbana and Chicago: University of Illinois Press.

Studlar, G. (1989). "Midnight s/excess: Cult configurations of "femininity" and the perverse." *Journal of popular film and television*, 17(1), Spring 1989, 2–14.

Watson, P. (1997). "There's no accounting for taste: Exploitation cinema and the limits of film theory." In D. Cartmell, I.Q. Hunter, H. Kaye, and I. Whelehan (eds), *Trash aesthetics: Popular culture and its audience* (pp. 66–83). London and Chicago: Pluto Press.

Williams, L. (1999). "Film bodies: Gender, genre, and excess." In S. Thornham (ed.), *Feminist film theory: A reader* (pp. 267–281). New York: New York University Press.

Published with the permission of the author and editor of *Offscreen* online journal, Vol 11, Issue 4, April, 2007.

As you have now just read, and no doubt considered, David Church's examination and analysis of cult filmmaking practice is both dense and demanding in terms of digesting his theorised concepts and critical formulations. Understanding and writing theory (in our study, cinematic/cultural) is a demanding form of language that takes effort and focus to see its 'light'. Re-reading, taking notes, and pondering the use of language and formulation of concepts is essential to grasping modes of theoretical expression and the form it takes to construct an argument. When reading and studying academic text, I find it useful to note down particular referenced theorists within the essay whose ideas interest me. Then, I go to the original sourced material and read through the referenced work in its entirety, jotting down notes from the text that interest me in furtherance of its potential to underpin or inspire thematic ideas. Essential to understand here, for our purposes, is the potential to consider and discover which, and how, theoretical lines of inquiry can be manifested conceptually to underpin our creative film practice.

For example, an experimental film that I produced and directed, *The Body as Montage: A Spectacle of Punishment* (Mark de Valk, 2010) (Figures 12.4a and 12.4b), draws from the theoretical work of Michel Foucault and Elizabeth Grosz as a means to inspire and infuse my storyline and visuals in terms of the thematic I was exploring: that being notions and critique of how the body (in particular, the female body) has been subjugated, surveilled, and punished by 'sovereign' factions (that is, the state, the military industrial complex, and the corporation).

Foucault and Grosz's notions (among others) examining the effect of 'sovereign' power and subjugation of the corporeal body and human psyche contributed to underpinning and developing my creative and personal film signature in furtherance of creating a 90-minute experimental docu-narrative.

FIGURE 12.4a
The 'subjugated' female body

FIGURE 12.4b
The 'compartmentalised' body

CHAPTER 13

Working with non-professional actors

Many young filmmakers ignore, or do not bestow enough credence upon, working with their actors to obtain an optimal performance in front of the camera. This may be due to lack of organisation or focus on the exigencies that less-seasoned actors bring to the set. Or, perhaps, too much time is being spent on preparing the lights, props, costumes, and camera positions. However, first-rate settings, composition, and lighting will have little or no weight if the acting is sub-standard, weak, or sloppy. Nothing sinks a good script faster than inadequate or amateur performers, particularly those with minimal acting craft skills and experience in front of the camera. Conversely, a solid or riveting performance can raise a soft or mediocre script to a dynamic level. So, how to remedy potential casting limitations and varying acting performance abilities? As a filmmaker, it is your duty and responsibility to draw out distinct, judicious, and discriminating performances from limited-experienced actors. You are required to educate and impart the craft knowledge of acting to your performers in a clear, coherent, and uncomplicated manner.

DIRECTING THE NOVICE ACTOR

First, let's consider the standard series of main approaches a filmmaker can take when directing professional actors. An initial considered approach asserts that the performer will be left to his or her own devices to allow him or her to create a personal interpretation of a character's emotional state and physicality. Here, the filmmaker draws together the performers, outlines and describes the scene at hand, then allows the actors to interpret their characters' emotional context and physical responses, only interjecting if one performer interferes with another performer's own translation. The rationale, here, is that this tactic affords the actors a more plausible construction through their own 'sculpting' of character nuance rather than allowing the malleable notions of the director to intercede. The second approach allows for the actor to embrace a particular creative autonomy to articulate his or her character and with the director not as appraiser and witness, but as an architect who defines the strategy and decrees that no deviation from his or her design will be accepted. Here, the performer keeps to the director's expression of the desired emotional temperament, tone, and context of the scene to be filmed. Hence, the actor must fashion or craft the character's emotion and mood within the margins as charted by the director and not outside these set parameters. The third approach forces the performer to subjugate to the complete determination and control of character by the director. The actor becomes more of an 'object' that the filmmaker works with, with minimal or non-existent participation as to movement and creation of character. Here, the director is the architect and builder who allows the performer no self-determination or choice of interpretation. The rationale, on this account, is that the director's vision has been pre-carved in stone and that input and augmentation by the actors cannot be envisioned, in any manner, as a means to enhance the blueprint of the scene at hand or the characterisations. It has been argued that this particular 'harsh' methodology can be effective for the overall film; however, it does so to the detriment of the performers who may personally feel dejected, on some level, due to the 'robotic' construction of how they must apply their acting craft. But such is life within the acting world.

WORKING WITH THE 'UP-AND-COMING' FILM ACTOR

Let's now consider the amateur performer in relation to the above listed three approaches. As such, we need to contemplate what type and ability the actor has. Is he or she malleable enough to take on instruction or is he or she rigid and uncomfortable in front of the camera? It is one thing to have a grand personality among friends and colleagues, but it is quite another to reproduce that charm and effervescence when a camera, lights, and other crew are bearing down on him or her. This is when an amateur's self-consciousness can kick in and render him or her 'cardboard' or appear 'wooden' on screen. Hence, before any shooting begins, the adoption and planning out of an audition session is crucial for the low-budget filmmaker, both at university level and beyond. Generally, most of the non-professional actors to be found are of student age. You will find that as actors increase in age, so too will their relative experience. It will always to be your advantage if your cast is older than the required chronological age of the characters to be portrayed on screen. A good rule to follow is that an actor can be up to 10 years or so older than what the character's age calls for in the script. Good studio film examples of this can be found in the casting of *The Graduate* (Mike Nichols, 1967) (Figure 13.1) and *Apocalypse Now* (Francis Ford Coppola, 1979).

FIGURE 13.1
College grad Benjamin Braddock (Dustin Hoffman) 'assists' Mrs Robinson (Anne
Bancroft) while daughter Elaine (Katherine Ross) 'gazes' on (far left)

In *The Graduate*, Dustin Hoffman, who turned 30 during the time of filming, plays
a 20-year-old college graduate, as the script called for (Anne Bancroft was 36). In
Apocalypse Now, Martin Sheen plays the lead character of Willard, a 26-year-old
army captain; his actual age was 36 (Sheen also suffered an on-set heart attack
while filming in the Philippines). What other examples of good casting can you think
of, particularly in low-budget independent film projects? Many directors started their
careers with a keen eye for an unknown actor and on no-budget film scripts they
penned themselves. Consider the work of director John Cassavetes, in particular
his first film *Shadows* (1959); Jean-Luc Godard's first film *Breathless* (1959), with
an unknown Jean-Paul Belmondo; and the first films of Brian De Palma (*The Wedding
Party*, 1969) (Figure 13.2) and Martin Scorsese (*Mean Streets*, 1973), both of whom
cast a young Robert De Niro in his early 'unknown' years as an aspiring film actor.
There are many examples of current-day filmmakers who had the temerity to seek,
find, and cast these dynamic 'up and comers'.

Please keep this consideration of casting practice in mind when searching for actors
to be in your current student production and beyond. An actor's maturation will
serve to give 'weight' to most amateur performances, particularly if he or she is
playing a character years younger than his or her own chronological age relative
to, say, using one of your friends or a family member who is the exact age of the
character, again, in particular to script that has characters in their late teens
or early/mid-twenties. At this developing stage of your creative development,
experienced and seasoned acting professionals will most likely be out of your budget
and access range. However, there are exceptions, as there are those young
filmmakers who have connections into the film industry through friends, family, or
a fortuitous meeting at a film festival. Can you think of any relatives or friends of
relatives or acquaintances who are in the film industry? This certainly can be a
route or avenue to be developed if it so appears for you. In terms of developing

FIGURE 13.2
Robert De Niro (far right) debuts in Brian De Palma's first film *The Wedding Party*

industry contacts, one can make the case for attending a festival beyond just to watch the line-up of good films on hand, as many 'up-and-coming' actors attend festivals to network and meet 'up-and-coming' filmmakers. Even as a director at the sunrise of your career, these actors are willing, and wanting, to be cast in short films and low-budget indie features as a means to advance not only their experience, but their demo reels and perhaps come across the next 'Tarantino' in the making.

Another good tip, here, is to mine and seek out agents of actors who have only performed previously in television commercials or corporate promotional videos in their careers to date. In many instances, you can find real 'gems' in terms of finding an 'unknown' actor who has either natural and/or studied craft skills, and technique in terms of character projection, 'look', and performance on set and on camera. Start to form relationships with talent agencies and the agents themselves who cater to advertising and commercials. They are generally quite approachable and understand that their less-experienced clients would jump at the chance to be in your short film or first 'guerrilla-type' feature. An excellent example of how these casting notions all came together to an extraordinary level (albeit, perhaps, a one-in-a-million chance in terms of the economic return that resulted) is the film *The Blair Witch Project* (Daniel Myrick and Eduardo Sánchez, 1999). Here, the filmmakers had an open casting call that drew in close to 2,000 people who were then vetted through a series of improvisational scenarios that the directors had planned. The filmmakers self-constructed an effective manner of working to advance the drawing out, and culling, of on-camera performance potential from those amateur actors who showed up for the open auditions. This is a good technique for you to emulate (albeit on a smaller scale).

TECHNIQUES TO ENGAGE AMATEURS

You, as filmmaker, will be privileged if your actor brings what you have instilled in him or her during your rehearsal time to the set. This involves not allowing inexperienced actors too much autonomy or independence of choice. I would suggest drawing up a set of action verbs as a means to sculpt performance. Instead of 'telling' your actor what to do, give him or her particular language cues that he or she can respond to. Instead of over-explaining a particular movement or exact emotion that the actor 'must' reproduce for a scene, ply him or her with verbs that advocate a particular action. This technique works well for the less-experienced actor and allows him or her to implore a physical act, which is much less complicated a task, rather than getting him or her 'worked up' or over-wrought trying to somehow figure out in his or her head how to 'portray' what it is you, as the filmmaker, want from him or her in front of the camera. Compounding his or her inexperience with 'over-direction' is a sure way for your actor to start 'forcing' a performance, one which will ultimately end up coming across as wooden, awkward, or rigid on screen. I would recommend that you compile a list of potential action verbs in advance of your shoot and for particular shots and scenes. You can try some of these out during the audition and rehearsal period, as well, to fine tune them for when the actual shooting takes place. Amateur actors have great intentions, but you will need more than their good graces to get a vibrant and believable performance. A good starting point is to consider yourself as both director and teacher, and convey to your 'new' actors that there is a prodigious divide between performing for the camera and being an exhibitionist (that is, projecting internal emotion rather than preening the external body). Modesty and unpretentiousness is the model of invention here, inhabiting the character as opposed to 'pretending' to 'be' the character.

One of the important paths to travel in your relationship with the amateur is to build rapport and confidence by complimenting his or her brave faculty for the challenge at hand and the intelligence he or she must possess to traverse the undertaking ahead. Actors, both amateur and seasoned professional, want to please their director, so infuse encouragement and acknowledge accomplishment throughout the rehearsal period and on set. Additionally, you must also demonstrate the notion of discipline (that is, the focus on the production and all its requirements must be uninterrupted with no squandering of precious time). This starts at the initial engagement with your performers and the concentration required during rehearsal and on set. Time-keeping enforcement on scheduled pre-production and production days is indispensable to maintaining such discipline. An inattentive or lax approach by you, the filmmaker, will trickle down to both cast and crew; in particular, the inexperienced or young actor may lose attention and effort may drift without a strong hand to guide and navigate the production. If one of your cast members is late or not motivated to be on time, it will contribute to a ripple effect through to the other performers.

This is a situation you must avoid, especially if time at a specific location is tight and you have limited time to shoot, particularly on a location that you may be 'borrowing', such as a shop or public space, where your scene has been planned to take place. Your success as a filmmaker inter-depends on implementing and administering punctual comportment and a committed dedication to the production. Another step for you to take is to manifest an affable demeanour, which will create for your cast an atmosphere without apprehension or trepidation. It creates a milieu where your actors sense an openness to demonstrate emotion – a space devoid of anxiety, one which fosters expression about character portrayal, uncertainties, or construction. Keeping performers relaxed nurtures a creative environment that tolerates missteps or gaffes as the actor works to perform and shape the scripted character. As a developing filmmaker, these skills of interpersonal conduct afford you the opportunity to then critique performance minus the spectre of coming across as insensitive or callous. Directing requires an engagement rather than a remoteness or standoffishness with your cast. This may sound common sense (and it is), but without due diligence and a concerted consciousness to acknowledge these working-with-actors points, you may not obtain the desired and strong performance you need for your film. Building sureness with the amateur allows you, as filmmaker, to push performance in the direction that you need to be captured on screen. But what if you're not getting the performance you require? Lines forgotten, attitude lethargic, perhaps the actor is 'just not into it'. Here, a good technique encompasses your ability to bring calmness to the situation, and not heat it up by becoming exasperated or doing a lot of head shaking in front of other cast and crew.

It is imperative to maintain decorum and work to illicit your actor's viewpoint or feelings of what it is that is 'blocking' his or her abilities. Diagnose the situation and the information. A means to this end requires that you must have knowledge of an actor's process and craft; here, a working knowledge of various acting 'schools' is, at a minimum, essential. You must read and study the written work by, and on, the renowned acting teacher and theatre director Constantin Stanislavsky (1863–1938) regarding his development and approach to a particular system of acting protocols and character craft development for actors. Stanislavsky, a Russian theatre director, pioneered the notion of having performers draw upon (and project) emotion through a series of bodily actions in order to manifest an authentic representation of human response, interaction, and communication when portraying their characters. Stanislavsky's technique was further revised, up through the mid-part of the twentieth century, into various tributaries of approach as developed by other acting teachers into what we refer to, today, as 'method acting'. The various schools of method acting are mandatory to study and get up to speed with. Understanding these various concepts will enrich your approach to working with both amateurs and those more experienced in the craft of acting. These include seminal texts by Stella Adler, Lee Strasberg, Sanford Meisner, and Uta Hagen. It is indispensable for you to have knowledge of an actor's process and craft development and the stages that a performer puts himself or herself through to internally create and physically express an unaffected emotive interpretation of his or her character on the page. These acting techniques and concepts will help inform, guide, and inspire if you are working with any minimally experienced actors that you have cast in your current student production and projects beyond. Developing empathy, attentiveness, and tone of expression skills will serve you well to keep actors unruffled and get them to relax in front of the camera.

A good tip, here, is to keep your amateur from over-analysing how he or she is physically functioning before and after each scene take. Reducing his or her focus on 'judging' one's performance and bodily appearance assists an actor to relax; this is accomplished by keeping his or her attention on your sincere supportiveness. This will help halt any 'bad habits' the actor might be repeating. Again, draw from your list of action verbs for your actor to interpret as a means to cease repetitive unwanted behaviour. In getting your amateurs to act you, will need to highlight and provide the fundamentals of acting technique, the concept of pause and rhythm, gesture, and the value of voice both as speaker and as listener to the other characters. There are a myriad of varying personalities that you could end up with as your actors.

Generally, you will find that working with inexperienced actors requires the following tactics and methodology, depending on their individual personality: (1) You, as filmmaker, will have to expound and clarify on a rash of questions about a character's motivation and rationale for his or her emotional responses, then he or she will take whatever information he or she has gleaned and physicalise it. (2) For others, you elucidate on a particular scene and the actor stoically remains silent, thoughtfully ingesting what approach he or she will take to play out the action and characterisation. (3) Some actors cannot create a visual picture in their mind of their character and will require you to physically 'act-out' what it is they have to do and from there they will work to mimic the actions as displayed to them. This is not an optimal method and should be used more as a last resort if all else fails to provide inspiration for a performance. (4) The novice performer may also be one who requires stimulation of his or her mind's eye or imagination. Here, logical explanation or a director's physical manoeuvrings will not suffice or serve to tempt out characterisation. In these cases, stimuli can be generated through filmmaking devices such as make-up, props, set pieces, lighting, exterior location, and costume. By immersing the actor in a particular setting, affording a particular fashion, or giving him or her a prop, you can rouse and motivate his or her character into action or elicit an emotional response.

To sum up, you can employ these methods individually or as a mishmash of technique when working with the amateur or novice actor. The filmmaker takes on the role of mentor, counsellor, and psychologist in the quest to capture a believable and 'honest' performance. Although it may be a grind, it will all be worth the effort when you elicit the conviction of character that you require from your actors on screen.

CHAPTER 14

The avant-garde, subtext, and symbolism

WHAT IS AVANT-GARDE?

> We can use the term 'avant-garde' for any film whose technique, employed with a view to a renewed expressiveness of image and sound, breaks with established traditions to search out, in the strictly visual and auditory realm, new emotional chords . . . The sincere avant-garde film has this fundamental quality of containing, behind a sometimes inaccessible surface, the seeds of the discoveries which are capable of advancing film toward the cinematic form of the future. The avant-garde is born of both the criticism of the present and the foreknowledge of the future.
>
> Germaine Dulac, 'The essence of cinema'

Germaine Dulac, the French avant-garde filmmaker and critic, recognised the potential of the film medium for the 'abstract exploration of pure thought and technique' (1987: 48). Dulac worked within both commercial and avant-garde film traditions (around the 1920s) and was conscious of the way in which film was both an artistic and a commercial medium. For her, avant-garde filmmaking worked to progress the medium, and was 'essential to the evolution of the film' (ibid.: 44), yet the commercial cinema and the public were against. The purpose of avant-garde, she noted, was to 'free the cinema from the hold of existing arts' and emphasise 'movement, rhythm, life' (ibid.). Yet, while the artistic tradition of avant-garde was rejected within mainstream or commercial cinema, many of the developments of the avant-garde were later utilised within commercial cinema (with less revolutionary or political aims). So, we might think of avant-garde and commercial cinema not as completely separate modes; rather, they exist on a continuum of film practice, and, at times, intersect with and speak to each other, although this might not be a happy conversation.

The avant-garde, at times, rejects and opposes the practices of the mainstream and, unlike the avant-garde of other artistic traditions, has remained on the margins of cinema (O'Pray, 2003: 1). Unlike mainstream cinema, which tends to be governed by relatively limited techniques, devices, and tropes, the avant-garde is much more open and free of definitive form. While there have been movements (surrealist, new American cinema, underground cinema) that might be understood as belonging to the traditions of the avant-garde, these terms are, at best, slippery. Pramaggiore and Wallis attempt a broad overview of some of the characteristics of avant-garde film. They note that:

> Some avant-garde films tell bizarre stories, others focus on abstract qualities of the film images, while still others may choose to explore one particular technical aspect of film, such as slow motion, and to exploit its effects to the full . . . Avant-garde films rarely present straightforward stories of characters. Instead, they approach the film medium as an aesthetic, philosophical, and/or political means of expression. They often isolate elements of film art – including cinematography, sound, and editing – and subject them to intense scrutiny.
>
> (2005: 258)

Avant-garde film might seem, for those unfamiliar with such an experimental form, alienating and confusing. To watch Luis Buñuel's *Un Chien Andalou* (1929), Kenneth Anger's *Fireworks* (1947), Maya Deren's *Meshes of the Afternoon* (1943), or Michael Snow's *Wavelength* (1967) might be a challenge initially for those already familiar with the language and form of commercial cinema. As Scott MacDonald notes, our first experience of 'avant-garde films . . . can catalyse . . . our first fully *critical* response to a set of experiences our culture has trained us to enjoy, primarily as a process of unquestioning consumption' (MacDonald, 1993: 2). In other words, because it is the dominant mode of filmmaking (in terms of production, distribution, and consumption), it might come to be understood as the correct or proper mode of film. Yet, as we know, the particular mode of mainstream practice serves to conceal its ideological operations. Even when the tools and techniques of the avant-garde are used within mainstream film (as in the case of the films of David Lynch, Darren Aronofsky, John Waters, and Michel Gondry – the style of music videos often borrows from the avant-garde), they are not necessarily as oppositional, radical, or political in motivation not only in form, but also in practice. Verrone identifies the project of avant-garde filmmakers as follows:

> Avant-garde filmmakers tend to work in a particular and highly personal way, making films that are consciously anti-mainstream, deliberately aesthetically challenging, and purposefully intellectually and emotionally demanding. Inasmuch as they are making a film, they are also provoking the spectator . . . Even more importantly, 'avant-garde' is an attitude-one that stirs, instigates, irritates, and incites.
>
> (2011: 7)

So, there is a tension or difficulty in reading mainstream film with avant-garde tendencies and avant-garde films on the margins in the same terms. While crossover is certainly apparent, the difference lies not only in the avant-garde's oppositional formal and aesthetic mode, but also in its relation to institutional practices. As Verrone notes, avant-garde filmmaking is highly personal and subjective. There are usually fewer people involved in the production of the films. However, this offers many opportunities for filmmakers. Such a practice is accessible for student filmmakers, who often work in smaller groups and prefer such autonomy. Similarly, avant-garde film practice allows the filmmaker much more scope for experimentation than mainstream practice allows for. In addition, it allows the filmmaker to consider his or her practice in relation to dominant film practices and to reflect upon the range of available practices outside of the mainstream. For example, William Wees outlines some of the techniques used in avant-garde practice:

> superimposition, prismatic and kaleidoscopic images, soft focus, unusual camera angles, disorienting camera movements, extreme close-ups, negative image, distorted and totally abstract images, extreme variable in lighting and exposure, scratching and painting on the film, slow motion, reverse motion . . . intricate patterns of montage, single-frame editing, and flicker effects . . . these techniques pose questions about seeing and are . . . more complex and dynamic than normal film viewing.
>
> (1992: 55)

While all of these are rarely employed in the same film, we can note that there is far more scope for such experimentation within avant-garde practice than within commercial film, which rejects many of these (unless they are safely embedded in normative and conventional film practices). You might also note that these are techniques that you might rarely use precisely because, as Wees suggests, they draw attention to the very practice of filmmaking. However, the avant-garde does not seek, like mainstream cinema, to make invisible the practice itself. If the foregrounding of practice serves to distance the spectator from the image or from interpolation into the screen text (as we discussed in the section on apparatus theory in Chapter 8), this also ensures that the spectator is not positioned ideologically in relation to the text, or at least not in the same way as with mainstream film. This points to the function of such experimentation – to explore the film medium itself (as an artist form rather than a form of popular entertainment) and to question and oppose through experimental and anti-mainstream techniques such as the above.

WHAT DOES AVANT-GARDE DO?

The term 'avant-garde' is originally a French military term meaning 'advanced guard'. The advanced guard were those soldiers who pushed ahead and led the army. It was adopted by artists to refer to those artists whose practices equally pushed ahead, tested the terrain, and took risks. Using this analogy, this places mainstream cinema in the position of the army and the avant-garde filmmakers in the position of those brave soldiers who are willing to take risks. In other words, mainstream cinema is 'safe' and behind, and avant-garde is 'dangerous' and ahead. This notion of mainstream being behind the avant-garde seems to make sense when we consider the way in which avant-garde practices are subsumed by the mainstream (Verrone, 2011: 10). However, it is not simply the case that the avant-garde pushes ahead and the mainstream follows. As we have already noted, the avant-garde often operates in opposition to the mainstream and in opposition to the dominant ideologies or social practices of the day. For example, the Dadaists emerged at the same time as World War I, and responded to the social institutions that had produced such a war by creating an art form that reflected the anxieties and uncertainties about faith in logic, reason, and order. Equally, the Dadaists saw that art (artistic practices of the time) had become the art of the bourgeoisie. Duncan Reekie describes the situation that the Dadaists were faced with:

> After Art for Art's Sake, after Modernism, after the carnage of the Great War of 1914–18, art had developed its institutional autonomy to the degree that its political irrelevance was irrevocably revealed. More than that, the Dadaists realised that this autonomy was in fact the complicity of art with the bourgeois war machine and a means to enervate radical dissent.
>
> (2007: 120)

The anti-art project adopted by the Dadaists was intended to end this autonomy and to re-situate art within the everyday. It was not art for art's sake, but art for revolutionary ends. The Dadaists, such as Marcel Duchamp, Man Ray, Viking Eggeling, and Hans Richter, did this through transgression and subversion. Spanning Western Europe, the movement functioned in slightly different ways across France, Germany, Italy and Switzerland, but shared the characteristics of subverting the traditions of art and using techniques intended to shock and offend. For example, many of the films foreground and experiment with movement, rhythm, and shapes, as well as form. The films often used both natural, everyday imagery and objects and subverted or undermined them using techniques such as negative exposure, frame scratching, or tinting and abstract imagery. Man Ray's *Return to Reason* (1923) begins with a series of images of contrasting shapes, ranging from salt on a dark background to dark nails on a white background, with the images being shown first in positive and then negative photography. The object itself is unimportant; it is the shape and the relation between the shapes that is foregrounded. Following these frames, a shot of a fairground ride appears. The fairground ride itself is represented equally in terms of shapes and movement, the lights of the ride mirroring the rhythm of the previous images. Thus, the film is structured in terms of a consistent pattern of shapes rather than as a narrative system. Such a formal system develops alternative modes of film practice and film form that are reactionary in terms of the politicisation of the movement (anti-art) but also in the rejection of conventional filmic modes. As Verrone notes, 'avant-garde films are pedagogical interventions that allow us to see cinema from an entirely different perspective' (2011: 14).

The counter-cinema practices of Godard function in a similar way, but are more directly related to the practices of the mainstream than the Dadaist films were. Counter-cinema practices were often taken up by those who were already working in or close to the commercial industry (Godard) or theorising and writing about it (Peter Wollen). Wollen coined the term in relation to the practices of Godard (Butler, 2007: 92) and it was used to distinguish from the avant-garde, which 'led' or was ahead of the mainstream. Godard's work functioned in relation to the mainstream. Counter-cinema refers to the practice whereby the film denies or challenges many of the codes and functions of the mainstream – narrative closure, temporal continuity, and spatial continuity. As Butler suggests:

> Counter-cinema starts from the assertion that the illusionist conventions of mainstream cinema function to obscure the real conditions of its production. Ideology, by this analysis, is ingrained in mainstream cinema at the level of form and it is the task of radical cinema to break with that form as well as with its political content.
>
> (Ibid.)

Counter-cinema sets out to attack mainstream cinema by using and then undermining many of its practices. Godard, for example, undermines the processes of identification by breaking the fourth wall where characters speak directly to camera (for example, in *Breathless*, 1960). As we noted in the section on spectatorship, such practices deny voyeuristic pleasures so necessary for mainstream cinema. Similarly, in Godard's *Weekend* (1968), there is no single strand of action or story and the main characters enter into a number of different actions. Equally, the narrative is interrupted by intertitles that comment upon the action. This practice did not utterly reject the formal conventions of the mainstream. Part of the project of counter-cinema was to use the tools of the mainstream to critique dominant cinema. Godard's *Breathless*, for example, pays homage to Hollywood iconography and form, most evident in its repeated reference to 'Bogie' in the character of Michel, and the use of the genre iconography of the road movie and crime film. Such a conflictory relationship with the mainstream was also evident in the avant-garde and experimental practices in the US in the post-war years.

AVANT-GARDE AND POPULAR CULTURE

In the US post-war period, avant-garde filmmakers were benefiting from the availability of cheaper film technology, which allowed them to work independently or with intimate groups and collectives outside of the mainstream. Unlike their European counterparts, the American avant-garde filmmakers did not have the same tense relationship with the arts. Their intent was not to destroy or undermine the arts, but to revitalise the arts. The American avant-garde filmmakers, while operating outside of the mainstream and the popular, often engaged with it in terms of content and theme. The films of Kenneth Anger, Jack Smith, and later Andy Warhol, for example, all evoke and reference Hollywood and popular culture, even while they do so using experimental techniques and styles. These filmmakers were part of the underground film movement of the 1940s to the 1960s. Their relationship to the popular was ambivalent with the films celebrating and condemning Hollywood and popular culture in equal measure. Reekie accounts for this mode of artistic expression by comparing the European and American artistic traditions:

> The cultural context and ultimate trajectory of post-war US experimental film was critically different to the European avant-garde film culture. Firstly, the role of art as the official, sacred, elite and autonomous culture of the ruling class was contested in the nineteenth-century American and was not secured in the first half of the twentieth century . . . Secondly, American popular culture was more socially mobile, traditionally valued and commercially dynamic than in Europe, and the border between the popular and American art was more interactive.
>
> (2007: 134–5)

Benshoff and Griffin note that all three filmmakers use camp iconography in their films. The notion of camp functions as a way for gay and lesbians to decode Hollywood and Hollywood film as 'an appreciation of Hollywood style and artifice and at the same time as a critique of it. Camp reception is always a "double reading" in which the form and content of Hollywood film are both passionately embraced and simultaneously mocked' (Benshoff and Griffin, 2009: 324). As they go on to note, the camp appeal of Hollywood stars and films could be understood as related to performance (of gender, heterosexuality) whereby the excessive performances of stars and within films demonstrated the performativity of socially prescribed identity. For these gay filmmakers, camp strategies served as a critique of dominant strategies of representation and performance, and also offered ways of securing pleasures in texts that, in ideological terms, excluded them. For example, Anger's film *Scorpio Rising* (1964) is both a critique of and homage to the youth rock and roll culture of the 1950s and 1960s. The film, a documentary of sorts, uses archival footage and popular music to detail the motorcycle groups and their destructive behaviour. The film uses shots from *The Wild One* (Laslo Benedek, 1953), with the iconic image of Marlon Brando in his motorcycle gear, and images of motorcycle crashes in order to demonstrate both the appeal and danger of the subculture. The film also constructs the biker image in terms of camp. As Suarez suggests, 'the hyper-masculine images of bikers implied an ironic detachment characteristic of camp' (2002: 122). The overt focus on signifiers of masculinity, rather than securing masculinity, problematise it. That the bikers invest so heavily in the masculine suggests that masculinity is not inevitable, but performative. This is also evident in the scene in which Scorpio lies on his bed before going to a party. In his room are posters of Hollywood 'outsiders' such as James Dean.

These images, along with the Marlon Brando image on the television screen, indicate the extent to which masculinity is constructed through Hollywood. Throughout the film, shots and frames of Hollywood films are intercut with shots of the bikers, demonstrating the cult and iconic status of the biker. Similarly, Jack Smith's *Flaming Creatures* (1963) evokes Hollywood glamour through the over-stylisation and camp representation in an evocation of figures such as Marilyn Monroe. Andy Warhol (sometimes with Smith) went on to film parodies of Hollywood films such as *Tarzan and Jane Regained . . . Sort of* (1963) and *Batman Dracula* (1964). The performers of his films, often friends, were titled 'superstars', and his film *Camp* (1965) equally parodies and celebrates the performative aspects of popular culture and Hollywood. Each of the filmmakers evoked the mainstream thematically while undermining it formally. Operating outside of the mainstream (in terms of financing, production, and exhibition) offered relative freedom from the industry, even while reflecting upon it.

C@SE STUDY

LA JETÉE (Chris Marker, 1962)

Chris Marker's time-travel short film uses still photographic images woven together to create a relatively continuous narrative maintained through a voice-over narration that describes the relationship between the images and the action. The film is set in a post-apocalyptic France, where the survivors of a nuclear war live underground. Scientific experiments are carried out to try to send a person into the future to seek help for the present. The protagonist subject to the experiments is initially sent into the past, where he meets and falls in love with a woman. The film is presented in a photographic montage of past and present. As with many experimental films, sound and voice-over serve to create continuity between the images. The impression of movement is rendered through zooms in and out of the static photographic images and changes in photograph duration. For example, the opening shot of the airport begins with a close shot of a photograph of the terminal and runway, and tracks out to reveal the scale of the location. The accompanying soundtrack uses wild track of engine jets. This has the effect of rhythm, pace, movement, and liveness. Shortly after the inter-tiles, which explain the events, multiple shots of planes, the control tower, and travellers increase the pace of movement. Audible along with the photos are sounds of airport announcements, which contribute to the dynamic movement of the film. The closing shots of the scene increase in pace as the narrator recounts the memory of the protagonist. As a child, he saw a man die at this airport.

C@SE STUDY

Here, the rhythm of the photos shifts and is accompanied by loud sounds of plane engines. The shot cuts between images of the airport and of onlookers who witness the scene, all of which develops a sense of dramatic action. Similarly, in the underground scenes, the impression of diegetic sound is created through the use of whispers, which sound over the scene in which one of the operations takes place. The cut from photo to photo, along with the soundtrack of whispers, infers that the characters within the scene are whispering about the operation. In other places, dissolves are used to transition between shots. Thus, the film uses a range of traditional techniques, from transition shots to conventional framing techniques such as the close-up, while at the same time the unconventional technique of static frames. In many ways, the film conforms to the mode of dominant cinema; however, it does so within an unconventional temporality. As a film about time and the past, such experimentation through the photographic image works well. The protagonist is transferred back to a time within his memory and so the static images work as snippets of his memory, much in the same way as the photograph captures a moment in our past.

EXERCISE **EXPERIMENTING WITH FORM**

Experimental and avant-garde film allows you freedom from the conventions of mainstream and dominant cinema. It can also act in opposition to dominant cinema. For this exercise, you should make a film that foregrounds the use of technique. For the moment, then, there is no need to consider story or narrative in the traditional sense. Think instead about the possibilities of film as a medium and as a technology.

You can consider experimenting with the following:

- film as counter-cinema;
- film as formally subversive;
- film as textures and layers; and
- film as movement, rhythm, pace.

See *L'Age d'Or* (Luis Buñuel, 1930), *Dog Star Man* (Stan Brakhage, 1961), and *Nitrate Kisses* (Barbara Hammer, 1992).

CHAPTER 15

Documentary as resistance

FORMING A DOCUMENTARY OF RESISTANCE

> Documentaries *represent* the historical world by shaping its photographic record of some aspect of the world *from a distinct perspective or point of view. As such they become one voice among the many voices in an arena of social debate and contestation.*
>
> Bill Nichols, *Introduction to Documentary*

As Nichols suggests, the documentary inevitably takes a position and has a point of view. The documentary enters social debate and acts as a comment upon a particular issue or subject. In this chapter, we will address some of the issues regarding documentary as a political tool, as an aesthetics of the social, and of counter-hegemonic modes. Here, we will read the documentary as a mode of resistance (of societal norm, of hegemonic structures, of representational strategies). There are a number of documentary modes, not all of which 'resist'. Documentary was, after all, not always politically motivated. The early Lumière brothers films certainly documented the social reality of the day. However, it would be hard to note any form of resistance. The actualities demonstrated the filmmakers' fascination and wonder at the social reality. 'Documentary as resistance' functions differently. There may be fascination with the subject or scene, but such documentaries question and interrogate the social reality. From the 1930s, documentary filmmakers began to use the form in order to provoke or promote social or political engagement, as evident in the British documentary films of John Grierson and others (e.g. *Housing Problems*, E.H. Anstey and Arthur Elton, 1935), or the US government-sponsored films of Pare Lorentz (e.g. *The Plow that Broke the Plains*, Pare Lorentz, 1936). Such films, while not framed within a discourse of resistance, demonstrated the extent to which documentary was used not only to reflect upon social reality, but to investigate and consider it beyond indifferent representation. Grierson, in particular, emphasised how a subject could not be removed from its socio-political context. For him, films that romanticised through formal and artistic expression neglected some of the more important political dimensions of the documentary form (Benson and Snee, 2008). Paul Rotha, a contemporary of Grierson's, was perhaps more excited by the socio-political potentials of documentary. Rotha was both a writer and a filmmaker, who was, as Petrie notes, 'politically motivated' and socially aware (Petrie, 2000: 27). Rotha's political outlook leaned towards the left, and he was conscious of the consequences of austerity and poverty in 1930s and 1940s Britain. He was also concerned about the way in which dominant fictional film could potentially serve as a tool of the dominant ideological system. In his writings, he criticised the dominant social structures that attempted to maintain the status quo regardless of the needs of others, and he was concerned about the role that cinema played in perpetuating this. For example, he writes that:

> All institutions, whether political, sociological or aesthetic, fundamentally reflect and assist in the maintenance of the predominating interests in control of the productive forces of their particular era. To this the cinema is no exception.

> Hence it is clear that, under present policies of production, we cannot expect any film do deal impartially with such vital subjects of contemporary interest as unemployment, the problem of the machine, slum clearance, the relation of the white man to the native, or the manufacture of armaments. To do so would be to lay open to criticism some of the fundamental principles upon which modern society stands and for which the cinema, consciously or unconsciously, must act as a sort of deodorant.
>
> (Rotha, quoted in Petrie, 2000: 56)

Rotha's film *Shipyard* (Paul Rotha, 1935) demonstrates the means by which he sought to find a formal mode of documentary that would acknowledge social inequalities and question dominant social discourses. The film traced the process of shipbuilding in Barrow-in-Furness in the UK. It followed the building of the *Orion*, and, more than this, represented the impact of the shipbuilding industry on the local economy. The dominant image of the ship's construction pointed towards productivity, industriousness, and the mechanical and technological achievements of the workers and the British more generally. This image of growth and development is juxtaposed with the difficult social realities for those dependent upon work. Rotha draws from the traditions of Soviet montage, whereby conflicting shots, frames, and narrations produce additional meanings. Shots of labourers hammering and building the ship are superimposed with images of guests relaxing on the decks, indicating social imbalance. The film uses a dual-narrative technique whereby one voice (spoken in the Queen's English) accounts for the technical process of building the ship and other contrasting voices come from the labourers themselves, who wonder if anyone ever gives a thought to their efforts. Towards the end of the film, following the launch of the *Orion*, well-dressed passengers are shown disembarking from the ship from back-left to front-right of frame. The following shot shows the labourers moving from front left to back right away from the dock, indicating that they are leaving the shipyard now that they once again have no work. Rotha's film was certainly not an overt attack on the shipping industry. In fact, his film was financed by the *Orion*'s parent company, the Orient Shipping Company. However, his subtle acknowledgment of the way in which the town was left dependent upon the shipping companies offered some form of critique.

PRACTICES OF RESISTANCE

Further documentary movements and traditions took a far more resistant or anti-establishment position. The British documentary tradition that had expanded its influence and aesthetic across the water to North America developed into a more consensual form following the war years. The films, particularly those sponsored and supported by government and state agencies, were less oppositional. Other films, as Nichols notes, 'took up positions that opposed the policies of governments and industries. These filmmakers constituted the political avant-garde of documentary filmmaking' (Nichols, 2001: 148). Documentary filmmakers working outside of the mainstream had much more scope to be oppositional, since they were not bound to funding agreements or supervision of their projects. Benson and Snee suggest that:

> Documentary filmmakers have not always supported those in power. Since the inception of the medium, a 'political avant-garde' has worked mostly on the margins of both society and the film industry to challenge the social structures that seem to oppress the many for the benefit of the few. Filmmakers working within nearly every political system used documentary to question authority and promote change.
>
> (2008: 7)

Resistance and opposition can take many forms. Resistance can act as the subject or theme of the documentary film. For example, a documentary film may follow a protest or resistance to state or dominant power, as in the case of *Harlan County, USA* (Barbara Kopple, 1976), *The Pipe* (Risteard O' Domhnaill, 2009), *Las Madres de La Plaza de Mayo* (Susana Munoz and Lourdes Portillo, 1985), *Winter Soldier* (Winterfilm Collective, 1972), and *Underground* (Emile De Antonio, 1976). Films that document resistance, however, do not necessarily support it. In both *The Pipe* and *Underground*, for example, the films question *those resisting* corporate power and the state as much as they do corporate power and the state. Films may also take a perspective of resistance in the sense that they are politicised or activist films.

For example, the films of Michael Moore (*Roger & Me*, 1989; *Bowling for Columbine*, 2002; *Fahrenheit 9/11*, 2004) situate wider social, political, and cultural issues within a personal narrative. In *Roger & Me*, Moore films his attempts to trace the CEO of General Motors, Roger Smith, in order to interview him about redundancies at its Flint, Michigan plant. A comical personal tone frames an otherwise grim account of the effect of the redundancies and plant closer on various locals. The film shifts between the personal and comical, and the communal and serious, which functions to endear the spectator to the documentarian, and thus identity with his perspective. This form of personalisation has been criticised for 'enlisting the support' of the audience (Spence and Narvarro, 2011: 233), even while he revitalises the documentary form through informal narrational and interview techniques. This form of documentary practice lies somewhere between the participatory and performative modes, as outlined by Nichols (2001).

The participatory mode of documentary practice refers to the placing of the filmmaker within the narrative and the scene (ibid.). Interaction between the filmmaker and other subjects takes place through interviews, or conversation between a visually absent or behind-the-camera filmmaker and the participants. As Nichols notes, 'participatory documentary gives us a sense of what it is like for the filmmaker to be in a given situation and how that situation alters as a result' (ibid.: 116). The filmmaker, here, transforms the film and the events through his or her active role within the structure and direction of the narrative. For example, in his films, Michael Moore determines the organisation, if not the outcome, of particular scenarios. In *Roger & Me*, his attempts to visit the CEO of General Motors are intended to fail. Thus, the filmmaker actively scripts scenarios for which he knows the outcome. On the one hand, his encounters with the hostile and nervous members of General Motors reveals the extent to which they refuse to acknowledge the damage enacted upon the locality. However, this also raises questions about the potential for objectivity within such a documentary mode. The power of Moore's films lies in his personal investment in the films through voice-over narration, informal interview technique, and the centring of himself within the stories and events. However, such a subjective approach risks becoming a documentary polemic equally as insular and non-negotiating as those he seeks to interrogate. As a practitioner, a balance must be found between the personalisation of the social (framing the documentary from a specific and, possibly, narrow perspective) and allowing the subject or issues to speak for themselves. For example, it might be useful to consider whether events would have unfolded in a similar way had the documentary filmmaker not organised them as such. While the filmmaker can promote positive change through his or her participation (as is sometimes the case with Moore's films), he or she may also produce less positive effects that would otherwise not have occurred without the filmmaker's intervention. For example, the intervention of the filmmakers in *Catfish* (Henry Joost and Ariel Schulman, 2010) reveals much about the problems of social networking but, in doing so, scrutinises the behaviour of its subject, a woman who creates multiple identities online. While this may seem justifiable, it becomes clear that the wider point about social media is projected onto a woman who is perhaps unaware of the full implications of her actions. Therefore, in the practice of resistance, the filmmaker must also consider how his or her actions of resistance impact on the subjects of the documentary. This will be considered further in the section on ethics and responsibility below.

Nichols outlines another form of documentary practice in his description of the 'performative mode' (2001: 130), which also involves the adoption of strategies of resistance. While such specific categorisations are perhaps less useful for practitioners (who are free to incorporate many different modes and practices as required), an understanding of them can reveal how they function. Therefore, the practitioner would benefit from remaining conscious of its functions (without limiting himself or herself to any one mode). The performative mode, for Nichols, refers to documentaries that seek to question knowledge and set out to 'demonstrate how embodied knowledge provides entry into and understanding of the more general processes at work in society' (ibid.: 131). The performative documentary often is situated on the filmmaker, and explores, celebrates, and foregrounds the subjective experience of the world. So, in contrast to documentaries that find meaning in the external, social world, the performative documentary often looks inward, and finds that knowledge is subjective, as much as it is objective. This mode of documentary tends to represent those whose subjectivity might be marginalised (either socially or within filmic representations). As Nichols goes on, 'recent performative documentaries try to give representation to a social subjectivity that joins the general to the particular, the individual to the collective, and the political to the personal' (ibid.: 133). As such, these documentaries evoke the political through the personal. Their mode of resistance can be found in the testimonial methods of reflection and articulation. For example, the films of Sadie Benning (*Me and Rubyfruit*, 1989; *Girl Power*, 1992), Marlon Riggis (*Tongues Untied*, 1989; *Anthem*, 1991), and Jonathan Caouette (*Tarnation*, 2003) all situate questions and examinations of sexuality, particularly lesbian and gay sexuality, within personal narratives. In doing so, the films abandon the observational mode and distance and objectivity, as well as the traditional formal structures of narration. In telling such personal stories about coming out, about the experience of sexuality, of ethnicity, or race and sexuality, the films employ non-mainstream techniques. Benning, for example, uses the autobiographic mode of video diary, with personal, reflective voice-over narration, interspersed with archival footage. In *Girl Power* (1992), she demonstrates her resistance to dominant conformist notions of sexuality. Television, archival, and historical footage of homophobic constructions of and reactions to homosexuality are juxtaposed with her defiant celebration of her own sexuality.

Benning's personalisation of experience is pitted against a society that seems to demonise and deny it. For example, archival footage of an American Nazi claiming that 'queers' should be gassed is framed within Benning's own account of her oppositional identity. Inter-tiles express her reaction to such expressions of homophobia: 'Fuck you, man'; 'Violent Youth Fierce and Furious'. Such personalisation is an alternative way in which to express resistance to societal norms or expectations. It does not need to, nor is it concerned to, speak any broader truth about the external world though facts and information. Truth and, as Nichols argues, knowledge are produced through the subject.

The performative and participatory modes involve the filmmaker's entry into the text, either visually, or through his or her 'own engagement with the subject' through a rejection of aspirations towards objectivity (Nichols, 2001: 34). These modes contrast with the observational mode of documentary, which distances the filmmaker and his or her authorial voice from the subject. This distance, however, is not 'true' distance, as the filmmaker must still make decisions about what to record, when to record, and what to edit. This mode of documentary practices emphasises the capacity to observe the subject without the noticeable presence of the filmmaker. This practice of documentary was popularised in the 1960s, when cheaper, lighter 16 mm cameras became more widely available. In addition, lighter, more portable sound recording equipment allowed sound to be recorded on location and synched in the edit. Such technology enabled filmmakers to be more mobile and spontaneous, which then produced an aesthetic of immediacy. Scenes did not need to be carefully planned and rehearsed, and required less staging. The light, portable cameras enabled filmmakers to move freely among the locations. The lighter cameras were also more discreet and allowed filmmakers to remain relatively removed from the subject. Direct cinema and *cinéma-vérité* are two movements that are observational in some ways, both of which benefited from the technology and both of which aspired towards representing 'reality' as much as could be possible with the presence of a camera. There are various degrees of observation within both. *Cinéma-vérité* films, for example, were more inclined to allow some kind of participation by the filmmaker while still maintaining the spontaneity and observational stance of being 'suddenly present within the scene'. Direct cinema preferred authorial absence from the scene. Here, the filmmakers hoped to capture events as they were, as they would unfold, regardless of the presence of the camera. This, of course, became a questionable goal, since it was impossible to determine how events were shaped simply by the presence of the camera (Bruzzi, 2006; Röhl, 2009). However, the intention was to evoke and refer to 'reality' by employing the realist aesthetics of film movements before it.

Direct cinema documentaries included those of Albert and David Maysles (*Salesman*, 1969; *Gimme Shelter*, 1970), Frederick Wiseman (*Titicut Follies*, 1967; *High School*, 1968; *Welfare*, 1975), and Richard Leacock (*Primary*, 1960; *Crisis*, 1963). Although the films were not overtly political (in the same way as *cinéma-vérité* films, for example), they tended to represent a concern about pressing contemporary issues, such as unemployment, power and government, and public institutions. For example, *Salesman* observes the stress experienced by a group of door-to-door bible salesmen who struggle with the threat of unemployment, the isolation of the road, and the indifference of resistant customers. One of the salesmen, Paul, suffers most throughout the film. His inability to secure sales frames the narrative and is accentuated through intimate shots of him expressing his anxieties, followed by near-uncomfortable shots of him desperately pitching to potential clients. Prior to filming, the Maysles brothers had not identified Paul as a clear central character. This was a result of the 'chance' of such observations, where Paul happened to be having a dry sales period. The focus on Paul, then, indicates the extent to which direct cinema finds its story in the process of filming, rather than starting out with a specific story in mind. Wiseman's *Titicut Follies* moves slightly beyond the tradition of direct cinema but remains clearly within the observational mode. Wiseman terms his films 'reality fictions', which suggests an acknowledgment of the interpretive function of documentary (Röhl, 2009: 51). The film uses the observational mode of documentary practice in order to represent the experiences of patients at the Bridgewater State Hospital for the criminally insane in Massachusetts. The film provoked controversy due to both the cruel and unethical treatment of the patients by the staff at the hospital and the potentially unethical treatment of the patients by the filmmaker. While the observational mode might create distance from the subject, questions might also be raised about the participant's understanding of the implications of their representation. In the case of *Titicut Follies*, the subjects were not in a position to make informed decisions. On the other hand, if duty of care was being neglected by those in command, the film identifies some crucial failings of the institution. In addition, Wiseman presents the film not as an objective lens upon the institution. The opening and ending scenes are framed by a theatrical show performed by the patients. This reference to performance indicates the constructed-ness of the documentary. In between these framing scenes, the film presents a much starker image of the institution through a number of moments, events, and practices within the institution. There is no central character or a particular story strand that binds each event together. Instead, each scene represents an instance of dehumanisation by the guards, prison staff, or medical staff of the patients. Yet, because focus does not fall on any patient or member of staff, the film avoids situating blame on any one individual and, instead, points to institutional failures. Here, the observational mode still offers the potential of resistance, even though the filmmaker remains silent within the text.

Each of these modes of documentary practice raises issues about the potential for objectivity, the capacity for resistance through representation, and the ethical implications of the documentary itself. In the following section, we will examine some of the latter concerns in an examination of ethics and responsibility.

ETHICS AND RESPONSIBILITY

> Developing a sense of ethical regard becomes a vital part of the documentary filmmaker's professionalism.
>
> Bill Nichols, *Introduction to Documentary*

> The act of photographing . . . is a way of . . . encouraging whatever is going on keep happening. To take a picture is to have an interest in things as they are . . .

> to be in complicity with whatever makes the subject interesting, including . . . a person's pain and misfortune.
>
> Susan Sontag, *On Photography*

To have a sense of ethical regard means that the filmmaker considers the implications of representation. The filmmaker must consider what meaning his or her representations of social actors will produce. Does the filmmaker become too close to the subject, therefore compromising the subject's ability to remain guarded? Does the filmmaker remain at a distance, resulting in the social actor forgetting that he or she is being recorded? How much can the filmmaker manipulate scenes in the edit before he or she strays from truthful? Does the filmmaker have a responsibility to intervene in situations (a crime, a violent act)? Filmmaking is inherently exploitative, and this is why the filmmaker should have ethical regard.

Nichols claims that all films are inherently documentaries. For him, there are documents of wish fulfilment and documents of social representation. Both arrange visual material into stories (Nichols, 2001: 1). Where the documentaries of wish fulfilment are dependent upon the suspension of disbelief in order to encourage believability in the filmic world, documentaries of social responsibility are dependent upon belief in the actual world, or that the documentary refers to an actual social reality (ibid.: 2). Nichols then identifies three ways in which the documentary represents the world. First, we might consider documentary as indexical. It literally documents a scene for which there is, or has been, an actual occurrence. There is a correlation between the represented image and the real world as it exists. However, we must keep in mind that, in practice, the documentary filmmaker shapes this social reality through the use of technology (mechanical or digital). The image corresponds to social reality and the story shapes that into a particular perspective on that social reality. The second characteristic of documentary is that it 'stands for or represents the interests of others' (ibid.: 3). Here, filmmakers take on the task of representing the interests, cultures, and lives of others. The filmmaker represents his or her own interests (in the way that he or she chooses to represent others) but, more importantly, gives voice or expression to others too. And finally, documentary 'may represent the world in the same way a lawyer may represent a client's interests' (ibid.: 4). Here, documentaries make specific cases or arguments for or against something in order to sway public opinion. For example, the films of Michael Moore are often critical of the government, the military, or capitalism. The films build a case against them in the same way a lawyer would build a case. In all three scenarios, the filmmaker takes on the responsibility of representation. This is a responsibility towards the subject (of the documentary) and the audience. If the filmmaker ignores these responsibilities, then the documentary has, in some ways, failed. For example, Michael Moore faced such criticism with his film *Roger & Me*. In it, Moore intentionally makes the corporate people look idiotic in order to discredit their behaviour. Such a tactic raises questions about the responsibility of the documentary filmmaker to the social actors who are the subject of the film. Similarly, Moore manipulates the order of events to support his overall case against

General Motors. Plantinga suggests there are two ways of approaching this ethical dilemma (2009: 502). On the one hand, since Moore's overall argument is convincing, such manipulation is reasonable. On the other hand, the re-ordering of events creates a comic layer not apparent in the events themselves. While documentary practice always involves some level of manipulation, in this case it might be more problematic. It deceives both the subjects of the documentary and the audience. As Plantinga goes on to suggest, 'the documentary filmmaker's obligations to the audience are varied, but chief among them is the obligation not to deceive or mislead, or in other words, to strive for accuracy and truth' (ibid.). This is equally the case for the social actors of the documentary.

Social actors are those who participate as the subjects of the documentary. In most cases, they volunteer their participation (or are even paid for it) and, in others, they are reluctant participants. In either case, the filmmaker must consider the ethical implications of the representation of these social actors. If, for example, the documentary argues one case above another, does it provide the other side a chance to voice their views? For example, in the documentary series *The Staircase* (Jean-Xavier De LeStrade, 2004), the filmmaker allows the defendant and his lawyers, as well as the prosecution, to state their views on a murder that took place. In it, Michael Peterson stands trial for the murder of his wife. The series follows Michael's lawyers as they build their defence case, but also has a number of interviews with the prosecution. The film refuses to foreground any one perspective and avoids pointing towards any truth about the killings. Despite the verdict, the film creates uncertainty about both sides of the story. The film, instead, questions the integrity of the judicial system. A poorer documentary might have sought to produce a definite answer and end to the film. So, responsibility for the representation of social actors is not simply a matter of taking sides, but of representing everyone fairly and accurately. This does not deny the possibility of critique, but means that this critique cannot simply involve the denial or ridicule of one perspective.

Documentaries employ many of the devices of fictional film, including voice-over narration, the staging of events (reconstruction), musical scores for emotional effect, and the shaping of space and time. If the documentary uses the same tools as the fiction film, we may then ask what the difference ultimately is. While Nichols's reference to documentary as wish fulfilment and documentary as social responsibility might account for some differences, we might also note the degree to which they are similar. All of the above devices are used to shape reality, not to re-present it. Renov notes that 'non-fiction contains any number of moments of "fictive" elements, moments at which a presumably objective representation of the world encounters the necessity of creative intervention' (1993: 2). An ethical regard ensures that the use of fictive elements does not produce a piece of fiction. For example, *King of Kong: A Fistful of Quarters* (Seth Gordon, 2007) uses a binary structure in order to represent the struggle between two Donkey Kong competitors. In order to encourage emotional investment in the film and in the players, the film represents the players as polar opposites. Steve Wiebe is constructed as the underdog and the eventual hero, in contrast to Billy Mitchell, who is represented as his evil nemesis. Although the players only meet briefly in the film, their characteristics are often placed in opposition to each other. Steve is a shy teacher and family man. He is unassuming and modest. Billy is presented as arrogant, selfish, confident, and egotistical. Thus, the film uses the strategies of drama in order to create a story out of events that might otherwise be less interesting.

Other fictive devices such as dramatic reconstruction move further away from the indexical nature of documentary. Here, events are not recorded live or as they unfolded; rather, they are staged and performed by actors. Dramatic reconstructions are often used in cases where the original event has already passed. If documentary is already interpretive, then reconstruction is even more so. Where belief might be assumed because the filmmaker has acted as witness, the reconstruction scene has no such claims of authority. Its only claim can be that 'this may have happened like this'. However, dramatic reconstruction might be used in an ethical way when it makes no claims to truth. Errol Morris's *The Thin Blue Line* (1988) uses dramatic reconstruction (as well as film noir style) in order to recreate the shooting and murder of a police officer. The film investigates the justifications for imprisonment of Randall Adams, who was convicted of the murder. The documentary uses interviews with Randall and another suspect in the case, David Harris, as well as with those leading the police investigation. Since the events remain beyond direct representation, Morris uses the information collected from the interviews and police reports in order to recreate alternative versions of the events than the police version. The re-enactments do not provide a final version of the events; rather, the multiple versions represent the testimony of witnesses that contradicts the police version. Like *The Staircase* (Jean-Xavier De LeStrade, 2004), *The Thin Blue Line* does not attempt to extract a truth from the interviews and accounts of the night. Instead, it poses questions about the nature of memory and reliability.

The authorial voice may also be used to frame a sequence of events that might otherwise make little sense. This may take the form of the voice-over narration of the filmmaker or maybe the voice of another person. The voice-over also offers a perspective on events. For example, a news story might be narrated by a newscaster who explains and contextualises an accompanying visual image. As Annette Kuhn notes:

> The documentary voice-over is typically marked as authoritative, as a metadiscourse which orders the potentially erratic signifiers of image and diegetic sound. In this case, the guarantee of the 'truth' of the film lies in the relationship between voice-over and image, in that the latter may be read as 'illustrating' the former.
>
> (1994: 129)

The relationship between voice-over and image is often less clear. As Kuhn indicates, the image suggests that it refers to or illustrates the voice-over. However, the voice-over also imprints the image with a meaning that may not be found in the image alone. For example, Werner Herzog frequently uses voice-over narration in such a personally reflective way that the image seems to function as a visual footnote to his own internal musings. In *Grizzly Man* (2006), Herzog narrates the story of Timothy Treadwell, who was killed by the bears with which he lived alongside in an Alaskan national park. However, Herzog's interpretations and analyses of Treadwell often veer into personal self-reflection.

For example, he often uses Treadwell's role as a filmmaker of sorts as a means of reflecting on his own experience as a filmmaker: 'Having myself filmed in the wilderness of jungle, I found that beyond a wildlife film, in his material, lay a dormant story of astonishing depth and beauty'; 'The actor in his film has taken over from the filmmaker. I have seen this madness before on a film set'. Similarly, *March of the Penguins* (Luc Jacquet, 2005) offers a voice-over that creates a story frame around its subject. The film details the migration of emperor penguins during breeding season. The French documentary was adapted with an English-speaking voice-over narration by Morgan Freeman. In both versions of the film, the penguins are anthropomorphised, no more exemplified than in the poster tagline: 'In the harshest place on earth love finds a way'. The reference to the love between the penguins and, in particular, the use of the term 'child' for the young penguins, humanises the penguins in a way that might seem at odds with scientific discourse. More problematically, the voice-over projects human emotions on to the penguins. In a scene in which a penguin's chick dies, the narrator claims that this 'loss is unbearable'. Such references to family, love, and loss not only anthropomorphise, but also infuse the film with an ideological tone about these themes and emotions while presenting them as objective and natural.

In this respect, then, we can see that documentary has an ideological position. A documentary does not represent truth or fact any more than the fiction film. The documentary may situate itself within social reality and represent events that 'really happened' and characters that are 'real people', but the documentary is always framed from an ideological perspective. This may be more overt, as in the case of the propaganda documentary, or more subtle, as in the case of the voice-over of *March of the Penguins*, which can be understood as speaking from the position of patriarchal ideology. A 'documentary of resistance' considers such issues. The filmmaker who resists does not simply challenge the dominant ideology or reflect upon hegemonic power; rather, the filmmaker reflects upon his or her position. Here, the filmmaker considers the ethical implications of his or her practice and takes responsibility for his or her representations.

HEARTS AND MINDS (Peter Davis, 1974)

The Vietnam War documentary film *Hearts and Minds* was released in 1974, only a year after the US had officially exited from Vietnam. Attention had turned away from the war, and was more focused on internal national events and crises such as Watergate. Compared with the huge attention the war had been given in the previous years, the post-Vietnam War years saw it largely drift from public consciousness (Hillstrom and Collier Hillstrom, 1998: 153). As Hillstrom and Collier Hillstrom note (ibid.: 154), the documentary had begun production in 1972 and the filmmakers unsuccessfully attempted to secure interviews with some of the key political and military figures, such as Richard Nixon, then president of the US, Henry Kissinger, the Secretary of State, and Robert McNamara, the Secretary of Defence (who since took part in the Errol Morris documentary *The Fog of War*, 2003). In the place of such interviews, the documentary uses a range of archival material, interviews with war veterans, and interviews obtained via other media. The resulting documentary was criticised by those on both the right and the left. For some, it was anti-American in its condemnation of both soldiers and policymakers, and, for others, it offered too much voice to those very people. It is clearly intended as a criticism of the war, in particular the US government and military. While it employs some of the techniques of the observational mode, this is not intended to offer an unbiased overview of the war. The film attempts to dispel the notion at the time (perpetuated by US policymakers) that the Vietnamese were violent, chaotic people. The documentary does not simply reflect on the US military, but juxtaposes interviews with state representatives and government and military officials, with images of the Vietnamese countryside and daily life. This is done through the editing of conflicting images that compare the patriotic claims and calls of US officials with that of the Vietnamese (and the implications of such US dominance on the landscape and people).

For example, the opening shot shows life in a Vietnamese village north of Saigon. Accompanied by Vietnamese music, the images show schoolchildren walking across fields, labourers working on the land, and women sitting in the shade. In one shot, soldiers walk by, but are ignored by the women in the background. As the opening sequence of the film, it establishes the ordinariness of existence. The scenes are quite unremarkable, beyond the brief appearance of the soldiers. Following this short sequence, the film cuts to an interview with Clark Clifford, aide to President Truman (an archival interview). Here, Clifford explains how the US began to consider itself a superpower, where it could 'possibly control the future of the world'. This then cuts to archival footage of a Hollywood war film, with soldiers marching with rifles and singing about how they 'won't stop winning until the world is free'.

C@SE STUDY

C@SE STUDY

The order of these sequences is key to the meaning of the film. By opening with the Vietnamese, the subsequent commentary by Clifford is understood in relation to this first sequence. US military dominance, the film suggests, needs to be understood by an examination of the effect on those who are subjected to it. Clifford is celebratory in the delivery of his historical overview, and, when considered in relation to Vietnam, this is intended to be treated with suspicion. Similarly, the inclusion of a Hollywood war film indicates the means by which such wars and hostile actions towards other films are framed as just within dominant cinema, and how cinema serves as a tool for dominant hegemonic power. This process of juxtaposition is later reversed, where US pilots discuss the skill needed to fly a bomber and the excitement of seeing the bombs drop. This is then followed by interviews with Vietnamese who talk frankly about the cost to them. One man stands beside his pig pen that was destroyed and another two women talk about the death of their sister from the bombs. The contrast between the US pilots' discussion of the superiority and magnificence of the bombers is undermined and subverted by the realisation of what these bombs do to the Vietnamese. This is then intercut with a pilot who says that he does not think about the consequences, again followed by an interview with a woman who can clearly think of nothing else. This form of editing, reminiscent of montage, exposes the contradictions and hypocrisies of the US position. Each justification of the war, and of actions committed within it, is undermined by an image or a sequence that shows the opposite.

EXERCISE **FIVE-MINUTE DOCUMENTARY –**
AN OPPOSITIONAL PERSPECTIVE

Think about a dominant or common idea, concept, or point of view that you disagree with or that you would like to challenge. You will need to represent this idea in order to oppose it. You may use archival footage (permissions may be needed), stock footage, or interviews. You will then need to formulate a way of indicating your resistance to this point of view. This may be done with voice-over narration, a musical score or sound effects, through montage editing, or through interviews. You will need to research your topic (through the study of the subject, through reading newspapers, through discussion with a range of subjects) in order to provide evidence for your opposing point of view. You will also need to consider your responsibility as a filmmaker. Each point of view must be treated fairly and represented accurately. You must not deceive the viewer through the use of techniques (for example, using a sinister-sounding score over an interview).

Among the subjects might be:

1   politics
2   education
3   media
4   history
5   the 'local'.

See *Night and Fog* (Alain Resnais, 1955), *Dark Days* (Marc Singer, 2000), and *Bus 174* (Jose Padilha and Felipe Lacerda, 2002).

Part IV

Persistence of vision

CHAPTER 16

Screenwriting
From script to screen

John Brice

HOW TO WRITE A COMPELLING STORY—IN TWO EASY STEPS (REALLY!)

Step One: your story's got to be crucial to you

All the intellectual kit that spews from workshops and books by screenwriting gurus boils down to just one thing: how to write a gripping story. "Good" structure, characters, dialogue, and action are important, but, even if they are brilliant, they are, nonetheless, just tools in the service of the essential thing that moves us most—"theme," what stories are about. Because the word "theme" is interpreted so broadly, to be precise (which is always useful), I mean the writer's *personal point of view about how best to live* in regard to a particular topic. It is a "truth" that the writer has discovered about life, large or small, and cares ardently about.

When a writer taps into his or her own truth, the writer reveals an understanding that elucidates some mystery of human life and, chances are, this "revelation" of insight or wisdom will just as deeply affect an audience. This is the key to writing a gripping story. Movies and TV shows can be successful for a lot of reasons— but none is more vital than having something powerful to say . . . and saying it articulately. The adage I use for myself as a writer, that I tell other writers when I work with them as a producer, and that I tell my students is, *"writing compelling stories begins by making sure they are imperative to the storyteller."*

Is this true of all stories in all genres? I believe it is. We generally expect small, dramatic films to explore some "truth" about our lives, but even the biggest Hollywood action movies will do so, too—if they are going to be compelling and memorable. The first *Star Wars* trilogy is an excellent example. It has all the bits of a mythic action movie that we've come to expect—a young man's separation from his society, his venturing out into a fantastic world where he faces superhuman tests, then his return to his society having accomplished his hero's mission of "saving the world" as he knows it. But what sets this trilogy apart from the other *Star Wars* instalments that followed and from most other mythic movies is the truth about life at its core.

Star Wars Episode IV: A New Hope begins with the protagonist, Luke Skywalker, encountering the mystery about his roots: who his father was, his "death" at the hands of Darth Vader and about his being a Jedi Knight. In *Star Wars Episode VI: Return of the Jedi*, the last of the first three released *Star Wars* movies, Luke confronts Darth Vader—who he has discovered is his father. Luke's real confrontation, though, is with the revelation of his father's weakness, which has made him a monster. As Darth Vader's son, Luke must wrestle with his own sense of identity and with his need to find love and compassion for his father in the face of his father's betrayal while he fights Vader in a life-and-death showdown on the Death Star. In their confrontation, Luke battles against his pain and hate and to stop himself from falling into the dark side—that is, Luke must avoid becoming consumed by anger or he will wind up just like the monster he is fighting.

This allegory is primordial and it reveals an elemental truth. We must all grow up by growing past our idealization of our parents, by passing our resentments for their weaknesses, which we begin to discover in our teen years, and by finally coming to understand that our parents are flawed human beings just like everyone else, including ourselves. To fully grow up, we must come to accept and love them, despite their flaws, or else we will carry inside of us resentment and a false sense of superiority that will sabotage our chance for other intimate relationships and for our successes in the world. These three *Star Wars* films illuminate this subject in a simple but powerful manner. Their theme, that there is great power in hate, but that it will destroy us in the end, is an important pearl of wisdom.

Myths are allegories for our rite of passage to adulthood and to becoming a person in our own right. They demonstrate the path to gaining our outer identity—our identity in society (as opposed to gaining our inner identity, our relationship to our self, which is what fairy tales are about). By the time the mythic hero has returned 'home' after achieving his hero's mission, he does so as an 'equal' and as someone who has obtained clear gifts to offer his world. The first three *Star Wars* movies deliver all this and more. The thematic truth at the heart of them is as profound and sophisticated as in any movie, in any genre, from around the world. It is why this mythic story is at the top of the all-time box office charts and why *Tron*, another big, Hollywood special effects movie of the time is nowhere to be found on the charts. When I talk to my students, they all remember vividly and still love these first *Star Wars* films—which they vastly prefer to the more recent and more technologically advanced ones.

Why exactly is theme so important, so central, to making stories compelling? There are three reasons, and they go to the core of how audiences' minds work, what art is, and what the purpose of stories is.

AUDIENCES

We are creatures who "make meaning," full stop. We continually make meaning of our physical, emotional, and intellectual environment—*in order to survive*. Every second of the day, every one of us takes in new information and revises what we previously understood. This can be in regard to objects and people around us as we drive a car, or it can be in regard to the intonation in our lover's voice-over the phone, the events of our life recounted to a friend or a therapist, or in understanding the sounds that make up music—or it can be in regard to the structure, dialogue, actions, music, and film grammar of a movie we are watching. It's the way our brains work.

The way we make meaning is through taking in this information and discovering the patterns in these worlds (i.e., through the patterns in life's events, mathematics, music, words and language, psychology, I.Q. tests, and so on). From patterns, we're able to derive *concepts*—the big ideas—that help us make sense of our world and anticipate future events in it in order to become successful in it and avoid calamity. So, we, the audience, are constantly and actively looking for the big idea in everything around us. Audiences are active participants in constructing the story and its meaning.

ART VERSUS REALITY

Reality is everything that occurs in the universe and, so far as we know, it is random and chaotic. No one has yet proven any core, guiding principle or theory behind it. There may be a God, but the point of faith is we don't "know" it. Reality simply is (or is not, as some believe). However, individuals and groups can find whatever meanings they want in reality if they choose, and most of us do.

Art, on the other hand, is not reality—and it is not random. It is expected to make sense on some level, no matter how abstract or subtle. Whereas science investigates the measurable aspects of reality, art explores the ethereal aspects of human life: morality (how people treat each other) emotion, perception, and beliefs. It does so by isolating a given aspect of life and putting a "frame" around it in order to probe that part's "meaning" or to advocate a certain interpretation of it. Every effective work of art is, therefore, organized around and is an expression of a single, central idea (a concept, theme, or big idea). Even works that have been termed "avant-garde," such as John Cage's *4'33"*, Picasso's invention of simultaneous multi-views of subjects, and Fellini's *8½* (1963), express some central, thematic idea. It is the thematic, big idea that defines any work of art. Without one, there is no expression and no work of art.

THE PURPOSE OF STORIES

We know that from the beginning of time, cultures have used the story form to convey their received wisdom about life and their core values to future generations. Since our Western culture believes in, and is predicated on, "free will" and the belief that our choices make a difference, our stories demonstrate what are "good" and "bad" choices and show their outcomes. They advocate what their authors believe are the best ways to live by showing the result of these healthy and unhealthy choices.

Alternatively, another kind of story deals with this fundamental belief of Western civilization by questioning if, in fact, choice and meaning truly exist, among other queries. For lack of a better word, one might refer to this latter type of story as "concept stories" rather than as "thematic stories." These don't "advocate" the best way to live in any regard, but rather question whether things such as love, morality, or meaning exist. Examples are films such as the under-acknowledged, classic Ealing comedy, *The Man in The White Suit* (1951), which ultimately examines the concepts of progress and the belief in technology, leaving the moral choice of their benefit or danger to the audience. The Coen Brothers' movie, *No Country for Old Men* (2007), is another example. It looks at the concept of morality in society and asks whether there is any point to fighting evil and to standing up for the moral code. Either way, thematically or conceptually, our stories, like all art, are organized around some central "big" idea.

Incidentally, our need to explore the truth of our lives is the main reason for the development of story genres; they aren't merely a marking ploy. Genres are story "templates" that exist because we find it valuable to investigate, repeatedly, the central issues each addresses—because we all struggle with these issues. The fundamental story genres illuminate the key aspects of our lives:

1 *Drama and tragedy* (stories that uncover the lies and discover the truths of our relations to others, to our institutions or to ourselves)—the development of our healthy and moral relationship to society or to ourselves.

2 *Detective/mystery*—the development of our self-control. To use Freudian terms, the detective protagonist in mysteries functions like the superego, "the inner policeman." He or she is coolly rational. The crime perpetrated always involves one of the seven deadly sins and is usually committed in a fit of passion—by a character who could be seen to have been taken over by his or her id (our impulsive or instinctual drives).

3 *Relationship stories* (including love stories, buddy stories, and team stories)—the development of our relationships to others.

4   *Fairy tale and horror*—the development of our inner identity. Fairy tales are ultimately allegorical and, thus, represent an "inner journey" to enlightenment. Similarly, horror stories are allegorical tales, whose monsters connote repressed sexual urges and/or angers and fears that lurk in the shadows of our psyches.

5   *Mythic stories*—the development of our outer identity in society.

If one looks closely at these genres, it's clear that all stories explore our relationships to people and society by advocating some truth about how we should live with others or by questioning if it's possible to live with others and ourselves in relationship to some aspect of human experience. Inherently, therefore, stories deal, on some level, with issues of morality—simply, how people treat each other.

When a writer conveys some personal truth about life and that truth resonates with us, we learn more about our own lives and how to live with others—and, therefore, we care about the story and its characters, with whom we develop powerful empathy. In this sense, writers are philosophers, at least to some degree, and always have been. It's no accident that Plato used allegory to express his insights or that profound "truth" is attributed to Shakespeare. As St. Augustine said, "Of all human pursuits, the pursuit of wisdom is the most perfect because in so far as a man gives himself up to the pursuit of wisdom, to that extent he enjoys some portion of true happiness."

DISCOVERING THEMES WITHIN OURSELVES THAT ARE IMPORTANT TO OTHERS

Everybody has a piece of the truth in them—a unique perspective on life—because of their individual personalities and experiences. The problem is that, to one extent or another, our themes remain largely out of our reach, submerged in the sea of our unconscious. We must use methods to snare the bits of our themes that float up and bob on the surface of our consciousness—then pull on them to hoist up the rest of our submerged themes.

But before talking about these methods, it is important to briefly mention the snags in which writers can become tangled when they try to do this. You might have heard of Frank Capra's remark, "if you want to send a message, try Western Union." The thing is, writers don't have to be overt or fear that the mere thought of writing to a theme or concept will automatically equal a cloying story. The most memorable films articulate themes, but they do so subtly in a way that feels organic.

Another snag is feeling self-conscious about what you believe and the fear that you don't know enough to have a valid opinion. This is particularly an affliction of younger writers, who aren't sure that they've lived enough to be "convinced" that what they think is "right." This feeling isn't justifiable for two reasons, though. Even if you are "young," your perspective on any a topic is just as valid and useful as anyone who has lived longer and is more experienced because it articulates what people of your particular age, from your particular part of the world, position in society, and socio-economic level experience, feel, and think. Yours is a vital and unique voice that greatly adds to the broad social conversation. Second, everyone's opinions change as they grow older—it's natural. What you believe at any given point of your life is not set in stone—you won't be held accountable for it 10 years from now if it changes . . . as it will. Yet, every phase of life is important and brings with it unique perspectives. All opinions, if they are thought out a bit, are good and interesting, and we all learn from listening to others of different ages and experiences.

As mentioned above, an additional obstacle is that writers often confuse their "topic," such as love, for theme. When this happens, writers never get past their general topic, which results in work that is blunt and generic.

The last impediment is the oft-misunderstood difference between plot and theme. Plot is what happens in a story, its central conflict, but it is just another important tool, like character and dialogue, to help articulate theme. It's interesting when one asks someone what a film was about; they'll most likely tell you what happened in it—but not what its theme was. Plot is one of the most obvious elements of story, while theme is harder to discern, particularly when it is subtly handled.

Hence, a lot of writers race to construct their plots, mistaking plot for story and theme rather than just a part of them. Especially students but even many professional writers do this—because not "knowing" your story is unsettling, since you fear you may well be wasting your time and making an ass out of yourself. Writers want to feel secure as soon as possible that the tale they're developing is good, and getting one's plot down feels like *it*. And writers can get pretty far down the road with just plot. They may even have an enticing and vivid opening, as well as many colourful and clever scenes through the middle of their story. But then they remark about things like not quite knowing how to end their story: should the protagonist live or die at the end? Or maybe they just tack on some resolution after 90 or 120 pages that gives the feeling of "The End."

When these things happen in story development, it should signal to a writer that he or she is in trouble. Confusion over opposite story outcomes or tacking on "so what" endings confirms that your story is random because it is missing a central, organizing "big idea." When a writer has a theme/concept clearly in his or her head, then he or she knows precisely the ending that is needed to articulate it. In fact, he or she will know what the right choice is for everything else that happens in his or her story, down to what words to use in every piece of dialogue. In stories, beginnings and ends are the same thing: one sets up the other and together they articulate a story's theme. So, if your story doesn't have a powerful ending, it doesn't have a good beginning, no matter how enticing its pyrotechnics may seem. Plot without theme makes for stories that are mechanistic, pointless, and boring— the opposite of compelling.

TWO TECHNIQUES TO A POWERFUL THEME

There are two simple exercises that can help writers discover the themes inside of them that will make their stories compelling to others. Both are based on the observation from above that stories inherently involve "morals."

The first exercise is simple. Think for a moment about the kinds of story themes that you are drawn to in movies, novels, comic books, and so on, and then write them down. For instance, do you like stories about the underdog or about characters that get their comeuppance or about characters that get away with "murder," and so on? Once you jot these down, forget about it/them, but put your list away for safe keeping. When the bits and pieces of a story you're developing begin to coalesce, fish out that short list of themes and see if the elements of what you're developing don't somehow begin to fall into the thematic categories that you're drawn to. It usually does. If so, knowing this can help you get a clearer idea of the heretofore-unconscious themes at work in your nascent story. Once you are aware of this relationship, you will be more able to understand the themes suggested in your story and can then consciously explore and shape them through the entire writing process.

The second exercise is just about as simple, if it involves a few more steps. It is to listen for the moral "value" words that you use to describe your situations and characters (particularly the antagonist—whether it's another character, the protagonist against himself or the environment, God, nature, and so on) and the words you use to characterize your plot as you think through these or talk about them to others. If you throw out an adjective to describe a crooked cop, such as "corrupt"—stop for a moment. Write it down and brainstorm the word in all its forms. The same thing goes for the story genre you are working in. If it's a drama, think about what lies and truths about society or individuals your story might be dealing with and then brainstorm those. If it's a fairy tale, think about what elemental wisdom the characters need to learn in the story to be truly happy.

As you brainstorm these "value" words and core elements of the story genre you're writing in, you will pull up from your unconscious a myriad of forgotten feelings and experiences in relationship to them. Say one of the value words is "corrupt." If so, think about what you've read about corruption, look the word up in a dictionary and think about its ramifications in all the aspects of its definition, think about what you've seen of it in the world, in your society, in institutions, in businesses, personal relationships, and in individuals. Most importantly, think about how you've experienced corruption personally—in work or school, in love, in any fiduciary relationship, in relationship to spiritually, and so on.

By the end of this short process, you will be surprised by how deep your feelings are about "value" words such as "corruption" and how much you have to say about them. You will further see how aspects of your characters and plot might be adjusted to support your "new" ideas about them and so unite disparate aspects of your story in interesting and often surprising ways. This will likely be so not just in regards to your central plot involving the "crooked cop," but in the possibility, perhaps, of a subplot that illustrates another side of corruption, such as a love story that becomes poisoned by some kind of intimate "corruption." Suddenly, you will be excited by what your story is *about*—not just what happens in it. You will suddenly know a lot of things about your story that you didn't before, like how to end it powerfully. And your story will be compelling to both yourself and to an audience.

There is one final reason to develop themes in your stories. Scripts can take years of struggle to write, only to suffer through heaps of rejections until they get made . . . if the writer is lucky. Returning to the *Star Wars* example, it was rejected by every major studio in Hollywood before it was green lit. Writing and getting scripts produced often feels like a game of "the last man standing." They don't call it "development hell" for nothing. However, if your story and its theme are vital to you, you will more likely have the drive and tenacity to make it through the gauntlet. And even if you don't get it made, you will have had the reward of spending time with something that you care about.

Like the holy trilogy, stories stand on three legs: the theme, the protagonist, and the antagonist. As for the protagonist, ideas and advice abounds for developing them (some helpful and some less so). However, the antagonist is far less explored— which is extraordinary since it is he or she (or the thing) that is equally needed to articulate a story's theme even if he or she (or it) nearly always occupies less screen time than the protagonist.

WHY WE NEED THE DEVIL IN OUR STORIES—THE ROLE OF THE ANTAGONIST

Step Two: of how to write compelling stories

In the beginning—the Old Testament—God was the god of love *and* the god of judgment (i.e., retribution, suffering, pestilence, famine, and so on), observed Carl Jung, one of the founders of modern psychology, along with Freud. He pointed out that when Jesus became God the Son, the embodiment of God's love, in the New Testament, then the Devil needed to be invented to represent God's retributive side. Thus, Jesus and Satan became the personifications of this dualistic Christian concept. Since then, Christianity has told its story through their opposition—and through the conflict of their values. Christian duality forms a closed system—a yin-yang relationship that, taken together, presents one whole idea. Without the Devil, the Christian message could not be articulated any more than you can clap with one hand.

Dualism is also at the core of our secular stories. Make no mistake about it—compelling stories need the Devil every bit as much as the "good guy" if they are to be compelling and to articulate themes effectively. Creating brilliant antagonists makes all the difference at the box office and to TV ratings as well. From time immemorial, the great storytellers have known how vital the role of the antagonist is.

Yet, today, so many story gurus, books, and classes treat the antagonist as merely an afterthought, if this essential character is mentioned at all. One otherwise extremely savvy and sought-after Hollywood story consultant listed the antagonist as one of the secondary characters, along with foils and helpers, in her latest book.

Many student writers, and even lots of veteran writers, focus their attention nearly exclusively on their protagonists, who are often unconscious versions of themselves or of who they would like to be. The result? Vaguely and generically developed antagonists, emblematic protagonists who don't confront grave challenges (and so cannot grow), and stories that offer minimum jeopardy, energy, and meaning. The writing experience itself bogs down since it is the antagonist that drives most of the story—and most of its development. This is especially so in the first two thirds of traditional stories, during which time the protagonist is reactive to the antagonist's force and plan.

Stories start in one of two ways for the protagonist: he or she either inhabits a paradisiacal or a dystopian world. His or her world, though, will go through a sea change by the end of the story because of the antagonist's intervention. If the protagonist begins in a dystrophic world, by the end he or she will live in a healthy and free way. If he or she begins in a paradisiacal world, then by having to fight to protect it, he or she will come to appreciate it instead of taking it for granted, or, in the case of tragedy, he or she loses it due to his or her own inner weakness.

Whichever world the protagonist is seen in at the story's beginning, the antagonist invades from the "outside" and "attacks" the protagonist (at the end of the first act in traditional stories), forcing the protagonist to desperately seek the core of the antagonist's plan and power if the protagonist is to survive while he or she fights off waves of attacks from the antagonist throughout the second act (by far the longest part of the traditional story). It's not until the end of the second act that the protagonist finally discovers the essence of the antagonist's power and plan (the event that marks the end of the second act). It is with this discovery that the protagonist moves on to a more equal footing with the antagonist, thus giving the protagonist his or her first real chance to "win." The protagonist's choice to continue fighting the antagonist at this point is an "informed choice" (a choice that neither the writer nor his protagonist should take for granted—it should be filled with horrifying challenges). It's not until this moment in the story that the protagonist becomes truly proactive and becomes the main driving force for the story and its conflict.

Taking the 10,000-foot view of the antagonist's workings, one must understand that in effective stories, the protagonist is *forced* into massive change of some sort by the antagonist. The protagonist may gain some crucial power, learn something vital, or vastly grow in stature. Thus, by the end of the story, he or she will be free of the dystrophic world he or she had been slave to, or he or she will be grateful for the boons of the paradisiacal world he or she started in.

This change, often referred to as "the protagonist's journey," is what articulates the theme. And in stories, just as in life, change is hard. Nobody, but nobody wants to "change"—in fact, we hate it and will do everything we can to avoid it. Only crises force us to change. In stories, "the crisis" is brought about by the antagonist's "attack." One of my favorite fortune cookie messages put it so well: "A change for the better will be made against you." This is a good way to think about what happens to the protagonist by the end of the story. When we—or a protagonist—manage adversity correctly, we and he or she come out the other end a better, stronger, and wiser person. So, as in life, a central conflict that makes a protagonist strong and whole can be viewed as a "necessary" crisis or conflict and the person or thing that initiated the crisis as the "necessary" antagonist. Thus, breakdowns become breakthroughs. Or as another aphorism puts it, what doesn't kill you makes you stronger. This is how thematic stories, which advocate "the best way to live," work.

Thus, one of the great "secrets" of writing compelling stories is to develop powerful antagonists. It is a fundamental axiom that the protagonist and meaning of his or her character journey can only be as strong and great as the antagonist is powerful.

THREE KINDS OF ANTAGONISTIC FORCES— THREE KINDS OF STORY CONFLICTS

Man against man

These are externalized battles between men/women in which the antagonistic force is personified. Compared to the other two types of opposition below, "man-against-man" conflicts are relatively the easiest to write and to understand. That is not at all to suggest they're simple or easy to write successfully. Creating effective external antagonists takes considerable craft and imagination. And in the most interesting stories, these adversaries exist on the metaphorical as well as the literal level. This is the most common variety of opponents in mainstream cinema and television.

Man against himself

These are relatively more complex stories. They are about some "internal conflict" within the protagonist between how he or she lives at the beginning of the story and how they should live. The adversary is solely a wrong or disturbing belief within the protagonist about life and how to treat others and with which he or she struggles. In the beginning, the protagonist is living immorally in some aspect of his or her life because of some crucial misunderstanding about life—the story's antagonist.

Therefore, these are dramas of self-discovery that end in the protagonist's deep and profound self-enlightenment.

However, these "man-against-himself" stories must have a parallel, external conflict ("man against man") to force the protagonist to face the untruth of his or her life and so to open the door to self-enlightenment. The thing that makes these primarily "man-against-himself" conflicts and only secondarily "man-against-man" conflicts are two things. First, the major character change is internal, not external. Second, and most importantly, is that "what's at stake" in these stories hinges primarily on whether the protagonist discovers the lie about how he or she has been living and reaches self-enlightenment in time to do the right thing in the outer world before it's too late to effect a positive outcome in it. Incidentally, when the protagonist achieves self-enlightenment too late to change himself or herself and affect a positive story outcome, then these stories of self-discovery become tragedies. Examples are *American History X* (Tony Kaye, 1998) and *Casablanca* (Michael Curtiz, 1942).

Man against God/nature/his environment

These are stories about conflicts between man's awareness of himself, including his finiteness, and his environment, whether it is a natural or God-made world or a man-made world such as the "city." In these stories, the protagonist is living out of harmony with his or her world at the beginning on some level and must reconcile his or her inner world or nature with the outer one. These stories call into question the protagonist's nature, belief, or courage to face life truthfully, which he or she must come to terms with if he or she is to survive and integrate fully with his or her world. An example is the 1984 Oscar-winning film for Best Screenplay, *Tender Mercies* (Bruce Beresford, 1983). Occasionally, these stories do the opposite. They call into question the external world, especially the man-made world. Fascinating examples are *Taxi Driver* (Martin Scorsese, 1976) or *Jeder für sich und Gott gegen alle* (*Every Man for Himself and God Against All*) (Werner Herzog, 1974).

THE SPECIAL CASE OF ANTAGONISTS IN RELATIONSHIP STORIES

In love stories, buddy stories, and team stories, the lovers, buddies, or team members are the antagonists of each other. No matter what external threats the protagonists have, the real conflict—who the protagonists argue with about the best way to live—is each other. In other words, the protagonists and antagonists are the same characters. Unique to these stories, the central conflict ends with the protagonists/ antagonists coming to appreciate each other and finally to forming a union rather than having one defeat the other, as is the case in every other kind of story. Examples are *When Harry Met Sally* (Rob Reiner, 1989), *Twins* (Ivan Reitman, 1988), and *The Guns of Navarone* (J. Lee Thompson, 1961).

Incidentally, relationship stories shouldn't be confused with "twin protagonists" or "multiple protagonists" stories, in which two or more main characters share the same goal and work together from the beginning of the story to achieve it against the antagonist. For examples of this kind of story, see *Butch Cassidy and The Sundance Kid* (George Roy Hill, 1969), *The Italian Job* (Peter Collinson, 1969), and *Ocean's Eleven* (Lewis Milestone, 1960).

SEVEN SUGGESTIONS ON HOW TO CREATE GREAT AND POWERFUL ANTAGONISTS

Create the "necessary opponent" in the antagonist

Exciting and terrifying antagonists don't just block the protagonist from his or her goal. They must be the best person in the world to attack the protagonist's flaws and so expose him or her and make him or her utterly vulnerable—they must be the protagonist's "necessary opponent." And if the protagonist doesn't get on top of his or her weaknesses, he or she will perish. Understanding this is vital not only to producing prodigious amounts of jeopardy and thrills, but, more importantly, to creating deep and dynamic character change in the protagonist, and hence compelling stories and themes.

Developing an antagonist that is treacherous enough to expose the protagonist's deep vulnerability is straightforward in theory. He or she must be powerful in exactly the areas that the protagonist is weak. Simple examples are *On the Waterfront* (Elia Kazan, 1954) and *The Lord of the Rings: The Fellowship of the Ring* (Peter Jackson, 2001). In *On the Waterfront*, the protagonist, Terry Malloy (Marlon Brando), is the lowest of the low flunky, a "bum," who works for the antagonist, Johnny Friendly (Lee J. Cobb) who is a mob boss and the king of the waterfront. In *The Lord of the Rings: The Fellowship of the Ring*, the protagonist is Frodo Baggins (Elijah Wood), a Hobbit (more or less a small human), who has to fight supreme evil with no more than his pure heart.

Develop a principle of the antagonist just like one might for the protagonist

Create a clear and simply defined concept for the antagonist by asking yourself what epitomizes him or her. Try to boil this concept down to its essence. Doing this will create a clear, powerful, and unique antagonist rather than a generic mustache twirler. As with the protagonist, the core of the antagonist's concept will define his or her internal logic (i.e., his or her motives, beliefs, predilections for *specific* behaviors, and, most importantly, the *precise* choices he or she makes). With main characters, as with stories in general, it is the core of them that is simple—while the expression of that core becomes complex. Incidentally, the principle of the antagonist is best developed with consideration for what the principle of the protagonist is.

Give the antagonist a strong moral point of view and clear values that are antithetical to the protagonist's

This idea has never been more vividly expressed than in the creation of Harry Lime, one of the unsurpassed film villains of all time, in *The Third Man* (Carol Reed, 1949), a story set in the ruins of post-war Vienna. Through the movie's protagonist, Holly Martins (Joseph Cotton), we come to find out that his one-time hero, Lime (Orson Welles), is actually an unscrupulous manipulator and black marketer, who has profited from the mass sale to hospitals of tainted drugs that have killed scores of sick children in hospitals. Graham Greene, author of the novel and screenplay, along with Welles, who played Lime to the hilt and added significant improvised speeches, created possibly the most renowned piece of antagonist rhetoric in the confrontation between Harry and Holly in the famous Ferris wheel scene. This is because Greene and Welles understood so extremely well the vital importance of values in developing powerful and terrifying antagonists.

At the beginning of the story, Holly arrives in Vienna believing that his old pal Harry has a job waiting for him only to find out that Harry has died and he has no job. Holly sticks around, though, because the police want him to, he's got nowhere else to go, and because he begins to fall in love with the girlfriend Harry left behind, Anna. Then, one night, deep into the story after Holly has been shown the devastation that Harry caused, he leaves Anna's place and catches a glimpse of Harry in a dark doorway. He's alive!

Arrangements between Harry and Holly are surreptitiously made to meet "safely" at a mostly empty fairground. Harry leads Holly into a gondola of a big Ferris wheel—where Harry offers his devastating reasoning behind his moral views and choices in three parts.

As the gondola rises up high above the tarmac, Harry chides Holly for going to the police, to which Holly asks if Harry has ever seen any of his victims. Harry banters evasively for a moment, and then tells Holly to look down to the ground. Well below, crossing the tarmac, are people—who, from the gondola's elevation, appear like mere dots. Harry opens the gondola door to a full view of the ground and the dots while the action simultaneously hints at a threat to Holly's life—he could be easily pushed out.

With the door wide open, Harry delivers the first part of his moral point of view as he blithely asks if Holly would truly feel any pity if any of those dots below stopped moving forever; if he offered Holly £20,000 for every dot that stopped, would Holly tell him keep his money? Or, would he think about how many he could afford to give up?

What good will his money be when Harry's in jail, goads Holly in response. Harry's reaction is a thinly veiled threat, as only Holly knows Harry is alive, which leads to a discussion of Harry's true intention for meeting up with Holly: killing him and pushing his body out of the gondola to make him unrecognizable. Holly plays his trump card. He tells Harry the police have dug up "his" coffin and found another man's body in it—they know Harry is alive. Harry laughs, dismissing any idea that he'd ever hurt Holly. Instead, he begins to co-opt him.

The scene, thus, turns to the second part of Harry's moral justification for his actions so that Holly can see things Harry's way and so join with Harry, not turn him in. He suggests that Holly is morally out of step with the realities of the post-war world, telling him that nobody thinks in terms of human beings anymore. Governments don't do it, so why should they? Governments talk about the people, the suckers, and the dupes—they have their "five year plans" and Harry has his. He ends by "observing" that the deceased are happier dead and don't miss much. The scene carries on a little longer until the gondola reaches the ground and Harry steps out.

Harry's parting words to Holly are the third part of his moral self-justification. Don't be sad, he tells Holly, and points out that under the Borgias, Italians lived for 30 years with war, terror, and slaughter, but the Borgia reign also brought the glories of Michelangelo, Leonardo Da Vinci, and the Renaissance, one of the great high points of human achievement. Then, Harry mentions the Swiss, who enjoyed 500 years of democracy, peace, and brotherly love, then rhetorically asks what did they achieve—the cuckoo clock. He bids Holly a jaunty farewell and skips away down the tarmac.

In this wickedly twisted scene, Lime's nearly unassailable—yet perverted—logic for profiting from the deaths of innocent children (his moral values and beliefs) is what makes the scene so chilling and this antagonist so memorable. His evil is so "reasonable."

Make sure that the protagonist and antagonist are fighting over the same main goal

While the simple definition of the antagonist in "man-against-man" stories is that he or she is the character that competes against the protagonist for the story's goal, identifying the story's goal isn't always simple in every story. In a Hollywood action movie such as *Raiders of the Lost Ark* (Steven Spielberg, 1981), the story goal is absolutely clear and straightforward: Indiana Jones and the Nazis are competing for control of the Ark of the Covenant. However, in movies such as *The Servant* (Joseph Losey, 1963), *Sunset Boulevard* (Billy Wilder, 1950), and *One Flew Over the Cuckoo's Nest* (Miloš Forman, 1975), the goal is subtle. In these three films, the protagonist and antagonist compete for control of the protagonist's mind, a far subtler thing than an object that will give its possessor the power to control the world.

Make the antagonist human

In a way, the antagonist should be the protagonist's darker double—someone who is as complex and vulnerable and wants to attain his or her goal just as much as the protagonist does. At some point or points in the story, discover where the antagonist may begin to feel strain and frustration from the protagonist's continued survival and small victories despite all his or her and his or her henchmen's attempts to squash the protagonist. Consider where and how you might allow him or her to bubble up or explode.

Further, there are a few exercises that may be useful in to helping you understand your antagonist better and more deeply.

- Ask what made the antagonist the "monster" that he or she has become— what was the catalyst for this in his or her life?
- Find the credibility in his or her values about how to best to live and in their goals.
- Try spending a little time telling the story from the antagonist's point of view as if he or she were the protagonist. Also, try linking to the first points above and putting them in a backstory or even into the script. There is no reason to include this in your script unless it becomes useful to the story.
- Investigate the antagonist's thoughts and emotions by writing an inner monologue scene for him or her. It could be a monologue in parallel with one of the key scenes of your script or a scene in which the antagonist awakes in the morning as his or her mind begins to spin, or an imaginary scene just before the antagonist's planned attack against the protagonist as he or she waits to carry it out, and so on.

Make the antagonist powerful

The antagonist should be someone or something of great power and ability, whether it is overt and physical or psychological, so that the protagonist has to be just that much stronger to win. The more pressure the antagonist puts on the protagonist, the better the middle of the story will be and the more suspense will be built up for the decisive battle (climax). Note that "more is not better" when it comes to antagonists in stories. Having too many antagonists splinters the power of the antagonist and so also the conflict and, ipso facto, the protagonist's force. Too many antagonists make stories episodic and disconnected. This is especially a potential problem in mythic stories (myths, action, adventure, westerns, and gangster stories), where a writer can easy fall into the trap of developing multiple opponents.

A prime example of this kind of antagonist problem is *Road to Perdition* (Sam Mendes, 2002), a mythic/gangster story. This movie offered four antagonists: Connor Rooney, a gangster and perpetrator of the initial attack against Michael Sullivan, the protagonist; John Rooney, Connor's gangster father and protector; Nitti, the head gangster and protector of both Rooneys; and, finally, Maguire, a contract killer who the three gangster heads hire to murder Sullivan. To make matters worse, Maguire doesn't enter the story until the second act, when the main antagonists completely drop out of the story. It is then that Maguire becomes the protagonist's sole pursuer and ultimately his murderer, even though Maguire is just a hireling and has no personal animosity against Michael Sullivan whatsoever!

If a writer begins to realize that he or she has fragmented the antagonist force, the force can be unified by developing one main antagonist and making him or her ultimately responsible for all the challenges that the protagonist faces.

Keep the danger high and close

Since they define and motivate each other, try to create a plausible way to keep the protagonist and antagonist in the same place. It may be useful to keep the old movie western saying in mind, "This town ain't big enough for both of us." One of the other weaknesses in *Road to Perdition*'s line of antagonism is that the three key antagonists disappear to three separate locations, far removed from each other and from the protagonist throughout the vast majority of the story. Thus, the suspense and threat that they might have posed are non-existent. On the other hand, the mythic *The Lord of the Rings* trilogy smartly keeps its danger constantly close at hand—by keeping the evil ring actually on Frodo's hand and allowing it to relentlessly wear him down, raising the story's danger ever higher. Dramas such as *On the Waterfront* (Elia Kazan, 1954) and *One Flew Over the Cuckoo's Nest* (Miloš Forman, 1975) place and keep their protagonists in a den of snakes. In these stories, there is no other world but the antagonist's world.

For writers, then, the Devil is your great friend. He or she is *the* character who forces the protagonist into action and onto his character journey that will change him or her—against his or her initial will—for the better. He or she is *the* rocket that propels the conflict forward at light speed. He or she is *the* character who gives the protagonist's values definition and distinction in the story by his or her personification of the opposite values so that together these two main characters articulate a story's theme or raise its vital question about life.

It takes more than just fascinating protagonists to make stories compelling. Writers must also develop powerful themes and antagonists if their stories are to be gripping and moving to audiences.

CHAPTER 17

Soundtracks
Using music in film
Paul Rutter

INTRODUCTION

The aim of this chapter is to explore the creative aspects and considerations for the filmmaker in respect of soundtrack production. Whether in film, TV, or video production, the inclusion of music and an appropriate audio palette has become a fundamental norm. This may be a daunting prospect for the new filmmaker – knowing where to start and how to provide solutions to problems that surround the legitimate use and exploitation of music, sound effects, or audio accompaniment. Filmmakers new to the idea of construction of an appropriate soundtrack, working on a low or non-existent budget should find appropriate information, music production ideas, and guidance here in support of their work. It should be noted that from the very earliest moments of silent film creation, and the following screening to audience, the 'soundtrack' became a crucial component in the film-going experience:

> Indeed, when the Lumière brothers first screened a selection of their films at the Grand Café, located on the Boulevard des Capucines in Paris, 28 December 1895, they did so with piano accompaniment.
>
> (Redner, 2011: 6)

Alongside creation of the soundtrack, due consideration must also be given to the legal intellectual property issues that surround the use of music, whether the soundtrack is supplied by a composer, or perhaps even created by the filmmaker himself or herself. Sourcing music for TV or film may seem like a relatively straightforward operation; music can be found online in abundance and there are rafts of musicians and composers who would be willing to create music for film, given the opportunity. Profits and revenues returned to music recording companies for sales of their product have fallen from the 2000s onwards, due to the acceleration in illegal music download culture and *à la carte* music download purchasing, and falling revenues from CD sales have also contributed to this. Partly due to this monetary evolution, many composers and musicians have moved towards making music for film and gaming media, diversifying their composition output, in order to get their music heard and exploited. Many musicians and composers who are involved in the creation of sound recordings are increasingly aware that 'diversification' is the key to future income streams derived from music. Given this shift in the reasoning behind composers making commercial music, there has probably never been a better time for the grass-roots filmmaker to source a music producer or composer willing to contribute to his or her work. Many filmmakers may already know of a person making music, playing in a band or composing music in a home studio. Even if on a low budget, the filmmaker could call upon such a person to compose a bespoke soundtrack to accompany his or her visual art. Digital recording technology and advanced music production software has provided music makers with home studios, the opportunity to produce high-quality music in a much smaller setting; music that could be good enough to accompany film – *if* the ideas and musicianship carry high production values. Quite simply, today, one does *not* necessarily need a huge budget for soundtrack music and audio; music technology and equipment is cheaper, large studios are not necessarily required, and infinite libraries of high-quality commercial sound samples have been amassed and are within easy reach. The young budding filmmaker can be confident that he or she may also easily source musicians and composers through online searches and social networking associations, in his or her quest to piece together a credible, viable soundtrack.

SYNCHRONISING MUSIC TO FILM

Synchronising music, sound effects, noises, or any audio accompaniment to film is an art form in itself; done well, it will enhance the film beyond measure – done badly, and the film could easily be consigned to failure. An intriguing chemistry exists in the through processes of synchronisation; it is often hugely time consuming and painstaking, the 'soundtrack' may be a work of art in itself – sometimes a complete 'stand-alone' creation that may take on a life of its own and become equally successful in commercial terms. The layering of music, sounds, and accompanying audio over film and TV must be 'appropriate' – and deciding what is appropriate is a collective task. In bigger-budget films, the film producer, the composer, the music finder, and production supervisors will often have a stake in sourcing what is appropriate and what will enhance the film. In a low-budget film venture, it could simply be the film producer and composer or soundtrack recordist that may make key decisions that would affect the final output; in any of these scenarios, quality control is of utmost importance. Music *and* sound in film is crucially import-ant; to realise just how important, one could experiment simply by muting the volume on a TV or film production; what would that same programme or film actually convey in terms of meaning without audio, or, without an appropriate soundtrack? If one were to imagine re-modelling a soundtrack to fit those moving images from scratch, it would be difficult to calculate how long this may take, what equip-ment would be needed, and, more importantly, how much human effort and time would be needed to create such a soundtrack. It is therefore worth investing in the thinking surrounding the film soundtrack and how this should be approached, in order to maximise the quality of the final film output and the resultant production values.

SYNCHRONISATION: A BRIEF HISTORY

In the beginning, silent filmmakers had little or no control over the music used and played in accompaniment to their films in the theatre. Solo piano players were employed to accompany silent movies, with musical scores placed in front of them in theatres, and, often, there were inconsistencies concerning whether or not the music actually fitted the on-screen narrative:

> In the 1900s, a trip to the cinema might mean crowding on to a bench to watch a film projected on to a 6ft by 6ft sheet. Admission was cheap (children got in for halfpence if they sat behind the screen) and music would be courtesy of a solo pianist and the audience's enthusiasm for a sing-along.
>
> (Hutchinson, n.d.)

Competent piano players learned to adapt their playing styles to fit certain scenes (for example, crashing chords in accompaniment to 'slapstick' movies, featuring comedy actors such as Buster Keaton or Charlie Chaplin in execution of exaggerated physical comedy movement, from the 1910s to 1930s). The piano accompaniment also assisted in masking the clattering sound of early cinema technologies, such as the film projector. Classical music scores were also later used and adapted in the cinema, improvised and elongated by the piano player. Early in the 1900s, piano players were replaced by small orchestras (sometimes just a few musi-cians); with a greater range of instruments to hand, more authentic sounds and effects could be generated from the instruments. A percussionist in the orchestra would have various 'toys' to punctuate the narrative, such as a washboard to make a clattering sound, or a snare drum 'crack' to emulate a gunshot; the violin player could emulate on-screen 'wailing' with a screeching bow across the strings. When bigger-budget movies were launched at this early time, an orchestra would be hired for premier performances. Erno Rapee, respected US silent movie orchestra conductor, claimed that 'there were 52 different moods of music required to accompany a silent movie'; styles such as 'lament', 'humorous', 'chasing' and

49 others that were developed (www.silentmovieshows.com). Further developments did not occur until the 1930s, when bespoke music was then scored specifically for film; previously, mainly existing classical scores were used in accompaniment to film. Synchronisation concerns the timing of the music 'matched' with the film, so the orchestra conductor would be watching the film in order to synchronise the playing exactly. The conductor's job was also to 'punctuate' the film with orchestral sounds and special effects by physically cueing and conducting musicians at key points in the film, indicating exactly when they must play or add certain sounds. The first original film score was commissioned in 1933 when Max Steinar created the soundtrack for *King Kong* (an RKO Radio picture). From this moment on, film became a creative playground for the composer and a place for experimentation. In the 1940s, the art of soundtrack-making gained momentum; then, in the 1950s, jazz music was used in films, often making music production cheaper, as fewer musicians may be required to play in that particular stylistic accompaniment. From the 1960s to the present day, the mix of orchestra, new music technologies, and sound samples has set high standards of expectation concerning the film-going audience; big budget movies are very often about 'wow factor', and that often includes a bold soundtrack. Today, music used in major film comes from a huge range of sources (for example, scored music designed for specific purpose, and, in many cases, established successful popular music songs that are well known and already hold a strong resonance with potential cinema audiences is commissioned for use, off-the-shelf). The decision to use this music is often made on commercial grounds and, in the past, pop songs used in films have produced and perpetuated enduring hit recordings as a result. In the 1970s and 1980s, films such as *Saturday Night Fever* (RSO), *Grease* (Paramount), and *Dirty Dancing* (GAFLP) evidences the way in which films can help to create global popular music hits, then subsequently the films become noted for those very same songs, creating an enhanced value and anticipation for returning film audiences and fans. Film music that resonates strongly with its audience, and then also proceeds to become successful on radio and in mainstream media, will often immortalise the movie further. Therefore, the relationship between the film company and the music recording company becomes highly valuable on a commercial level. There is often a close working relationship between the recording company and movie mogul when the whole package is put together, especially when at a multinational level and their aims are common. In the case of *Saturday Night Fever* (John Badham, 1977), Robert Stigwood, producer of this movie, managed the band the Bee Gees in the 1960s and later commissioned the group to provide songs for the film. The film soundtrack, supervised by Bill Oakes, revived the fortunes of the band and enhanced the cultural impact of the film worldwide by perpetuating the 'disco' music scene.

The film text and use of media sound has given way to advancing theoretical and critical debate; in Tim Crook's chapter on 'Sound Philosophies', Crook asks: 'How is the sound construction and texture being used to communicate meaning and precipitate an emotional and imaginative reaction from the audience?' (Crook, 2012: 11). It could be argued that this question may be answered, in part, through the art of synchronisation. The term 'synchronisation' is still used today in consideration of matching the soundtrack to the film, accurately making the right things happen at the right time. Through this, appropriate moods and sounds can be matched to scenes where they have the right impact and appropriateness – an ever-advancing art form in itself.

SOURCING MUSIC

It could be argued that there has never been a better or easier time than now to source the right music for any film production made on a low budget. The advent of the Internet and fast download speeds in being able to download or listen to music has revolutionised music researching and soundtrack sourcing. Filmmakers can easily search popular music sites such as Myspace, Soundcloud, or YouTube for appropriate music to accompany their on-screen images. Both amateur and professional music producers upload original samples of their music to these and other sites; it is simple for a filmmaker to source and listen to music by using 'genre' searches. If a film requires a hard-edged sequence, searching 'rock', 'metal', or 'alt-metal' could provide the desired result. The main issue, here, could be the fact that these searches will often unearth music tracks with vocals embedded in them – and for this music to be used in a film, an instrumental mix may only be required. However, today, many genres of dance music are often instrumental; many home-based music producers can easily source software to produce this type of music. Dance music is often created with long instrumental breaks in between the vocal melodies; therefore, this particular genre could yield a 'less distracting musical palette' that may marry well with visual images. The filmmaker could simply contact the music producers through electronic media requesting the supply of mixes to suit their visuals, instrumental or otherwise – observing music ownership protocol. Downloading such music and synchronising it with film without the exclusive permission of the owner would constitute a breach of copyright, unless the copyright owner in the musical work has made it clear that their music may be used in synchronisation with film or other media. Web providers, such as Creative Commons, offer music artists (and artists of many disciplines) who upload to their service the opportunity to state their terms of licence; in other words, a music producer can upload songs to Creative Commons and state how others may have access to their works and under which terms they may exploit the work. So, a filmmaker may find music on the Creative Commons website which will allow him or her to use or synchronise music free, for a certain period of time and with certain caveats in place (www.creativecommons.org.uk). This could mean, for instance, that where a composer's music is used in a film, a credit or acknowledgement is compulsorily given. More often than not, there will be limitations in such synchronous usage.

Many amateur composers and music producers are not only keen to get their musical works noticed, they are often willing to work with film producers to develop new potential income streams on a speculative level. The budding filmmaker should not be afraid to contact the music producer or composer directly and ask for exactly what he or she wants, including any alternative mixes. When a music composer agrees to write for the screen, often they may want to see the film script in advance; sometimes, they may wish to visit the film set or location in order to get a feel for certain scenes and narratives. The composer will feel a greater personal investment and part of the production when they can meet some of the personnel associated with it. The notion of 'free music' is not a new one in the Internet age; even though the music producer may grant certain free use to the filmmaker, the composer can get paid and make money in other ways, should the film become a commercial success. Music publishing revenues are generated when a film is shown to a large public audience, and when a film or programme is screened on TV. The royalties generated are based on the duration of the music used in the film screened on TV; for instance, if a film had a song playing out through the end credits, and this lasted three minutes, then a royalty rate is returned based on the type of TV station (for example, BBC1 – UK national station), in association with the duration on a 'per second' basis. These airplay royalties would be collected by a performing rights association or organisation (PRO), and in the UK this association is PRS for music (www.prsformusic.com). In other world territories, similar PROs exist (for example, in the US, there are more than one; ASCAP, SESAC, BMI, and SoundExchange also perform this function). Therefore, in the UK, the royalties generated from performance of the musical work in a variety of media (for example, on a TV transmission) is subsequently then paid either to the composer directly – if they were a PRS for Music member – or the composer's publisher – if that song was signed to a music publisher. Understanding the music 'royalty' and its collection may seem daunting and complex to the creative filmmaker, but a basic working knowledge of all income streams due as a result of the exploitation of film in media would prove to be a valuable business asset.

PRODUCTION LIBRARY MUSIC

An alternative to sourcing bespoke music from a singer-songwriter, or commissioning a specially recorded work for use in a film, would be to obtain production library music. This type of pre-produced and themed music may sometimes seem appropriate for the task; much of the music 'trawling' task can be eradicated when using library music. A host of library music companies will commission music composers to provide music for a variety of media usage, which, more often than not, has a specific thematic title. For instance, the library music company may commission the composer to write in consideration of an appellation, such as 'industrial'. This title may suggest hard, metallic-sounding instrumentation, clanking sounds embedded in a dramatic pastiche; the music may conjure factory-like grey images to the listener, even before any visuals are synchronised. In using this post-production method, the filmmaker can search purely by library music title, thus speeding up the process of finding music that may be fully orchestrated and ready for use immediately, without the need for remixing or editing. Other possible thematic searches could include 'anthems', 'celebration', 'places', 'transport', 'inspirational', 'seasonal', and 'nostalgia' (www.carlinmusic.com). It should be noted that the library music company is often the designated publisher in the production library music selected *and* will undoubtedly own the copyright in both the original composition and in the sound recording. The filmmaker may request a library CD to be sent from the company free of charge; today, many music library companies simply post their music samples online and will supply as requested. The following issue for the filmmaker is that when the music is synchronised to the film, the music company will set out the terms of use for the music. This will vary between music companies, but, usually, the library company will make money in performing rights revenues when the film or TV programme is screened. The performing rights society (in each respective territory – in the UK, this is PRS for Music), will collect royalties when the film is screened on the TV network. The cue sheet supplied with the film will outline the different segments of library music used and the duration of each piece; the royalty returned as a result of this usage will be paid back eventually to the music library company or publisher of the music. The terms of use for library music will differ; most library music is used in smaller-scale TV or corporate video productions, and there is an endless and ever-increasing amount of library music being composed and supplied. The most positive aspect of using library music is that it can be relatively easy to find appropriate-sounding instrumental music quite quickly. For smaller productions, often permissions vary, as the music library company will make its revenues through the performing right and mechanical right when synchronised. However, it would always be advisable to check the terms of use when considering using any music available from a production music catalogue. The main issue that surrounds the use of production library music is that the music is non-exclusive to the filmmaker (for example, another film producer could easily choose the exact same music for another quite different production). This does happen often; if a good piece of high-quality or 'catchy' library music becomes available, many film producers end up using the same piece of music. This can obviously cheapen the quality of the film production and sometimes, at worst, become disconcerting when the same piece of library music keeps surfacing. In the UK, there are many well-established library music producers who provide fully comprehensive web pages to allow filmmakers to search their music catalogue for appropriate music. There is often also the opportunity to establish the terms of use in these titles online. Some popular library music company examples are Carlin Production Music, Universal Publishing Production Music (also handling BBC production music), De Wolfe Production Music, and Audio Network. It is also possible to make enquiries with any music or recording company in respect of using the music that they produce; today, many companies are aware that they must diversify in order to preserve income streams and therefore openly invite filmmakers to enquire about licensing their music. The main issue with larger companies is that, in general, a larger synchronisation fee would be required, as well as other terms that they would wish to apply. For the small independent filmmaker, the costs to use the music of a major artist are often prohibitive, so searching smaller independent composers is a cheaper, more feasible option.

USING MUSIC AND LEGAL PERSPECTIVES

The legal requirements that surround use of the musical work in film can sometimes be overlooked by the novice. A basic understanding of ownership, music copyright law, and intellectual property in music will serve to protect the filmmaker in pursuit of a final legal film artefact that he or she may then own and exploit. Similarly, as there are copyrights that exist in the film and images that the filmmaker produces, there are rights that exist in the sound recordings that would accompany them. The common terminology used when music is 'locked' to film or TV programme or video is 'synchronisation'. Therefore, when the filmmaker uses music, a synchronisation agreement must be put in place between the music supplier (composer or publisher) and the filmmaker or company. It would be prudent for the filmmaker to have a basic understanding of the ground rules that surround the use of music in synchronisation with film. Therefore, understanding the basic concepts surrounding music intellectual property law will assist the filmmaker when negotiating agreements with the music creator. The larger film or TV company will have many legal advisors (solicitors or attorneys) that will negotiate agreements between composers and music producers; but, for the smaller-scale independent with limited funds, they must negotiate the terms of music usage themselves. A basic knowledge of intellectual property (IP) will provide a greater confidence in executing negotiations for the filmmaker. The next section explains IP rules around music, and the clearances and permissions that should be sought.

INTELLECTUAL PROPERTY: OWNERSHIP IN THE MUSICAL WORK

It is important to recognise that there are two fundamental copyrights associated with the use of recorded music: copyright existing in 'the song' and copyright existing in a 'sound recording'. To understand how music may be legally synchronised to a film or TV production, these two distinct areas require further investigation. The filmmaker must ensure the correct permissions are in place to exploit the IP rights of others *before* he or she may use songs and sound recordings in his or her productions. While it could be argued that the ownership of music stems simply from those that created it, often, in music, this may be far from straightforward.

Copyright in songs

Where a singer–songwriter composes an original song, writes all lyrics, plays solo guitar (chords) and produces his or her own recording, it could be said that the songwriter owns 100 per cent of this composition. As long as this musical work is 100 per cent original, it is therefore his or hers to exploit as he or she wishes. It is important to understand 'who owns what' from the outset, and, in the solo singer–songwriter example, it is often simple to identify where the intellectual property lies. If the songwriter collaborates with other melody writers, lyricists, musicians, or arrangers, the 100 per cent share would obviously change to reflect the input from these additional inputs (Rutter, 2011: 70–92). The division of song shares is essentially an item for the songwriter(s) to negotiate – but knowing which composers did write the music *is* important in avoiding future issues after synchronisation and final post-production has occurred. When a filmmaker uses a song or composition in his or her work, he or she would need permission from all the songwriters that partook in that composition before he or she can use the song in his or her film. This would apply if the filmmaker had sourced a song online from, say, MySpace and the song had been uploaded by unpublished songwriters (of which there are literally many thousands). The imperative here is to ensure permissions are in place from *all* contributors in the musical work. However, a recurring issue in songwriting (especially where bands are concerned with several members) is that, often, multiple songwriters in any one song title may not always agree 'who wrote what', or omit others that did contribute to the song. This conundrum could become a problem for the filmmaker if a song title is released for use by the principal songwriter, without the express permission of the other contributors in the song. It would therefore be worthwhile for the filmmaker to ensure that the person releasing the composition for use in the film, signs a full agreement ensuring that they actually have the full legal rights to release the work for use in synchronisation. This measure would protect the filmmaker should another co-composer of the work surface at some stage in the future (often when the film heralds success). However, if the songwriter's material was signed to a publishing company (some songwriters set up their own independent publishing companies), then the permission to use the song would need to be sought in writing from the music publisher. If published, the administrators of the musical work could also ask for a synchronisation fee in order for the song to be used in the film. This fee could be very small (a few hundred pounds) up to hundreds of thousands of pounds, depending on the amount that the publisher thinks that they could demand from the film company. A high-profile, established song by a band such as The Beatles (for example, 'Let it Be' – administered and owned by a major publisher), would be one such title (www.Sony/ATV.com). Therefore the independent filmmaker should consider using music legally from small independent music producers that would probably cost little or nothing at all to use. Key contractual clauses outlined by film and TV companies associated with music synchronisation should be observed; an overview of how IP in the musical work is administered and contractually assigned is covered later in this chapter. The duration of copyright in songs and compositions lasts for 70 years *after* the year of death of the musical author(s) in the UK; in many other developed-world territories, the duration is similar (www.ipo.gov.uk).

Copyright in sound recordings

When lyrics are typed or written on paper, or melodies with chords are recorded on a device and mixed, resulting in a digital file or CD, a final music artefact is produced. It is this final artefact, the music production, or 'record', that highlights the *second* copyright for consideration. Just as an original song gives rise to its own copyright when it is created, so does a sound recording. The ownership in the sound recording is probably easier to understand than in a complex composition with multiple writers. Usually, the first copyright owner in the sound recording is the music producer, so in a small home-studio, computer-recorded composition, it would be easy to isolate this ownership scenario. However, in a larger music production, the copyright owner is the person who pays the music studio account. For some independent artists or major acts signed to a label, the organisation paying the studio bill is the record company; therefore, they would own the exclusive right to exploit such recordings. The Intellectual Property Office in the UK highlights IP in sound recordings (www.ipo.gov.uk). The importance of this second type of copyright for the filmmaker is that in order to use the sound recording in synchronisation with any film, permission must be granted from the owner of the recording before its use. In this case, we are assuming that the filmmaker is using the recording as sourced (for example, from an online download) and is not paying for a new soundtrack to be recorded. If the filmmaker *pays* for original music to be re-recorded (and the composer does not have signed obligations to a recording company or publisher), then the ownership in the new soundtrack would be the property of the film company. Large film companies with big budgets will commission composers and producers to record a bespoke soundtrack and therefore own the right to synchronise and exploit the music they have contracted. Some film companies may also make use of their related music company divisions, partners, and departments to supply music or even commission them to supply musical works for their productions. Keeping the film music soundtrack 'in-house' will make global exploitation easier for the large filmmaker, firmly contracting all music rights in the film for 'the world', owning all permissions and contractual extensions for the full duration of copyright. The low-budget independent filmmaker may wish to negotiate contracts, therefore, on a more localised level, negotiating rights for a set time in limited territories (for example, securing music for a European or UK film release only (not the world) and for a limited period of two years). Perhaps this style of agreement would be more attractive to the music composer/producer and, if the film went on to be a success, more favourable terms could be re-negotiated at a future stage. It is also worth considering duration of copyright in the sound recording by researching the rules around IP, which can vary in some global territories; in the EU, in September 2011, this term was extended to 70 years from the end of the year in which the recording was made (www.bbc.co.uk).

The synchronisation agreement

Film and TV companies create a synchronisation contract with the composer in order to ascertain the terms of use for the music. Film companies will also work with music supervisors, who will source music and negotiate with publishers and record companies to secure the use of pre-existing and new production music. This section outlines some of the key sections and clauses that the filmmaker should be aware of when involved in negotiations surrounding the use of original music composed and contracted in synchronisation:

- The agreement between both parties (for example, filmmaker and composer(s) or band).

- Exclusivity and limitation: ensuring that the composed music may only be used in said film or films made by the filmmaker.

- Performing rights: the composer permits the music work to be performed in all broadcast media (for example, terrestrial, online, cable in the said territory – usually worldwide).

- Appointment and delivery: the composer is appointed to create the necessary original musical compositions as directed and deliver to the company. This would include remixes and revisions as requested by the producer or director.

- Fee: the agreed payment from the film company to the composer for creating the work as necessary.

- Grant of rights: the composer undertakes to give all music permissions as required, such as allowing the film company to sell video copies worldwide and rearrange, adapt, or edit the music in the film. Note that the performing rights in the song would usually remain vested in the composer (as the film company does *not* usually act as music publisher for the composer).

- Composer's undertakings and warranties: examples in this section may include the composer declaring that the work is original and does not infringe copyrights in other musical works (for example, the composition should not contain uncleared music samples). The music may be remodelled, remixed, or extended at the request of the film company; an accurate cue sheet may be requested; the composer may be required to sign renewals and extensions in the synchronisation agreement as required.

- Liability: the film company may state that it is not duty bound to make or release the film and will not be liable for any loss of earnings on the composer's part as a result. In addition, the film company may use other musicians or composers to perform the work of the composer, in addition to, or in substitution for, the composer.

- Termination: should the composer fail to adhere to the contractual clauses, the contract may be terminated under the terms of the contract by the film company.
- Agreement: the signed and dated witnessed agreement between both parties – composer and film company.

Synchronisation agreements can be very detailed and complex; it would be the job of a film or music lawyer to ensure that the correct detail is included in such a contract. Although sample film sync agreements can be found online, it would be advisable to seek professional legal guidance in pursuit of a safe contract.

SOUNDTRACK PASTICHE

Pastiche or stylistic imitation in soundtrack production can be a helpful tool in bringing together the foundation of the music required and assisting the movie diegesis. Pastiche has always been a trigger, 'kick-starting' an appropriate film or TV soundtrack, simply by borrowing from what essentially has worked well in the past. Stereotypical soundtracks can transport the viewer quickly to where the filmmaker wants to place the audience; for instance, hearing low cello notes played simply but menacingly in the style of the 1975 thriller horror *Jaws* (Steven Spielberg) film soundtrack immediately tells the audience something sinister is about to happen. It could be argued that music in the media always relies on a stereotypical approach (for example, a daytime TV game show usually has bright lively music, a funeral film scene has slow sombre music, or a children's comedy show often contains 'wacky' music). Another strong example of simple music pastiche is the harsh discordant violin sound, used in the iconic 1960 Alfred Hitchcock movie *Psycho*, where Marion Crane (Janet Leigh's character) is attacked in the shower. The screeching violin sound taken from this scene has been used in a similar way thousands of times over, in many film and TV movie productions since; the intensity of the violin sound conjures horror, fear, or terror in the mind of the viewer. This musical pastiche has been overused so many times that, in many cases, it has also been used in comedy sketches where something sinister but also funny is about to happen. These types of predictable musical representation may suggest a lack of originality to the creative filmmaker, but giving due consideration to musical pastiche can provide a suitable starting point in creation of the soundtrack where ideas are often hard to find. For the novice film director, an awareness of pastiche can also prove very useful in guiding the composer or audio effects person when he or she is commissioned to produce the soundtrack. A filmmaker can guide those appointed to these roles by simply providing 'sound-alike' clips or online music links, if they have a strong idea what moods are required in each scene. This need not result in a completely predictable soundtrack; a good composer can use techniques known as 'plotting' to get close to the exact music required by the filmmaker. Plotting is a technique that has often been used in pop songwriting since the 1950s, whereby composers may emulate the melodies of a familiar tune or song and record them (Harding, 2010: 149). The re-tooled melody is then played against a known rhythm track, taken from a completely different but successful hit song, with a recognisable beat or rhythmic sound production. Blending these two pastiche ideas together can often create varying degrees of familiarity – a 'new take' on old ideas. Obviously, if the new song created was regarded as too close or musically similar to the original version and instantly recognisable, this would constitute a possible infringement of copyright in the original musical work. Although plotting has been used by professional songwriters many times to create new hits, plotting film soundtracks could prove litigious if too similar to other established works. Many professional film composers often 'ghost' their own works in order to create an ongoing stylistic imitation, which is expected by film companies and fans of certain film types. For instance, in each *James Bond* movie, the combined work of composer Monty Norman (www.montynorman.com) and orchestral arranging and composition by John Barry lives on in each subsequent Bond adaptation (www.johnbarry.org.uk). The audience expectation is that the same themes *will* be heard – and countless variations of these themes and pastiche arrangements have been used in John Barry *James Bond* themes and soundtracks recorded, since *Dr No* (Terence Young), released in 1962. Many composers and arrangers have since worked with these themes creating new soundtracks in each *James Bond* movie. David Arnold (www.davidarnold.com) and many others have worked on these movie scores, drawing from the original musical works of Monty Norman and John Barry. In an edited text journal for Oxford University, 'Mood Music, an inquiry into narrative film music', Simon Frith writes on the use of recognisable music in film: 'there are widely shared conventions of musical meaning and that these conventions are partly derived from people's shared experiences of film soundtracks' (Frith, 1983: 73).

The composer of original works may argue the case for using his or her own repeated motifs and stylistic techniques, which are particular to his or her own composition methods, and so similarities in soundtrack production may be used many times over, especially in a series of films. The use of pastiche should not be overlooked as a tool to help create the type of soundtrack that the audience may expect or be comfortable with. There are numerous texts that analyse the use of music and 'mood' in countless films from an in-depth theoretical perspective. Wierzbicki writes:

> What works in a fast-paced adventure such as Steven Spielberg's *Indiana Jones and the Temple of Doom* (Paramount/Lucasfilm, 1984) is a traditional symphonic score that craftily blends 'action music', 'mood music', 'scene-setting music' and 'cliché-based symbolic music' of the sort that characterised silent film features.
>
> (2009: 217–18)

Weirzbicki recognises symbolism conveyed in music in synchronisation with on-screen events, reinforcing the need for the filmmaker to consider recurring themes and, arguably, pastiche. In social theoretical circles, there are many ideologies surrounding the justification of music used in films; Grossberg points out that in contemporary youth movies, 'rock is the soundtrack of the narrative representation of youth'; in Grossberg's writings with Frith and Goodwin, Grossberg then goes on to argue 'contemporary youth movies construct a dialectic between a certain sort of alienation and a struggle for empowerment' (Frith, Goodwin and Grossberg, 1993: 198). Although the filmmaker may consider these stereotypes and representations at the planning stage, sourcing and mapping a music soundtrack usually requires immediacy – a creative gut instinct. Production schedules may affect the time permitted to examine each nuance of the diegesis in such a way, but taken from a holistic viewpoint, considering the 'stereotypical' may actually speed up the process.

CREATING SYNTHETIC MUSIC, SPECIAL EFFECTS, AND SOUNDS

In some situations, it has been known for budding filmmakers (and their collaborative production teams) to attempt to record parts of the soundtrack themselves, where time, resources, and ability permits. This would, of course, depend on the type of soundtrack required and whether simple atmospheric noises, special effects, or sounds were required – or specific appropriate instrumental music in additional accompaniment. TV programme makers operating on a low budget have been known to create their own special effects and instrumental music where a very simple soundtrack is required (for example, children's TV) by using keyboards or computer music software with auto-accompaniment and on-board composition tools. It should be noted that professional composers and movie soundtrack makers would avoid this particular method of synthetic music making – relying upon what is, in effect, computer-generated music. Music keyboard manufacturers, such as Korg, supply a series of 'professional arranger keyboards' whereby even a novice can easily create instrumental music of a standard that may be appropriate for a low-budget venture (www.korg.co.uk). There are other reputable keyboard manufacturers that also produce a range of 'arranger workstations', such as Yamaha (uk.yamaha.com) and Roland (www.roland.co.uk). Whereby investment in hardware keyboards is not an option, an online search of 'music arranger software' will also reveal free auto-accompaniment music software downloads. Non-free programs pre-loaded with instruments and music accompaniments such as Band in a Box (www.pgmusic.com) are also widely available. It should be noted that using such hardware or software would depend on how much time novice filmmakers and their teams have to experiment with the creation of their own soundtracks using such keyboard hardware or software. It would be worthwhile listening to the quality and feel of this type of music making before investing; there are many filmed demonstrations of auto- accompaniment music to be found on sites such as YouTube and also on the manufacturers' websites. The general perceived results of auto-accompaniment production music making can sometimes be regarded as under-developed, twee, and with an immature feel; its use can prove limiting and more suited to infant TV production output. However, investment in a keyboard can prove useful, as often even simple notes or effects, played in the right octave and key, can generate an appropriate background effect, in the right hands.

Jeff Rona warns of the synthetic approach to emulating an orchestral film score, in that 'Simulating an orchestra with samples and synths is a tough business. It's hard to do well; and easy to do poorly' (Rona, 2009: 138). The reason that it is so difficult to reproduce natural orchestral sounds synthetically is because of the expression delivered in an experienced musician's performance. Rona points out that 'Woodwind, brass, percussion and stringed instruments sound quite different between playing softly and loudly' (ibid.: 139). However, since the late 1980s, control over synthesisers has advanced dramatically; there are many programs, hardware and software that has witnessed improved control over velocity, sensitivity and expression in electronic sounds and instruments. Control over high-quality samples has also assisted the music soundtrack maker in making the 'synthetic' sound *real*. However, the big-budget filmmaker is almost always certain to employ a full orchestra for the soundtrack (when appropriate); an orchestra can provide an enduring soundtrack that is timeless. The filmmaker should investigate using specific music recording software to assemble the music or individual sounds – today, free software such as Audacity may prove a useful tool (audacity.sourceforge.net). There are also advanced varieties of more professional music and audio recording programs such as Pro Tools (www.avid.com) or Logic Pro (www.apple.com/logicpro), which can be used to record, edit, and assemble the audio musical parts. The parts can then later be mixed down to a stereo audio file, which then can be imported into the filmmaker's software. If the filmmaker is using Final Cut Pro software to assemble the film, audio may also be recorded live into the film edit using Final Cut Pro's 'Record Audio Interface':

> Record a musical performance or a voiceover directly into Final Cut Pro. Choose the input device, monitoring type, and volume—all in the Record Audio interface.
> (www.apple.com)

However, it could be argued that recording audio directly into film editing software in this way is better used for simpler types of sound input (for example, a simple voice-over or perhaps an atmospheric sound effect). Recording actual musical instrument sounds or blending audio should be assembled in an appropriate professional music recording software package separately. This way, greater control can be achieved over the blending process, using audio equalisation (bass or treble frequencies), panning (sound field left and right), and balance (audio level volume). When the audio files are mixed and ready for use – which may exist as separate files or audio segments – these files may easily be imported into the film editing software as required. It should also be noted that film editing software packages are often bundled with audio effect plug-ins and sound effects. Manufacturers sometimes provide these additional audio tools free or as part of program upgrades; it is therefore worthwhile researching the competition in the film software domain. Being able to use audio effects and music as part of a package (with intellectual property clearance in place as part of such package) could save the filmmaker time and money in respect of a budget production. Budgets for music and many other services and areas in support of the film have been suffering financial decline over many years, yet it is commonplace for the budget of a major US motion picture to be in the range of five to eight per cent of the final total movie spend. Using known songs by major music artists can significantly increase costs, whereby the synchronisation fee demanded by the publishers and record companies can run into hundreds of thousands of pounds.

FOLEY AND SOUND EFFECTS

Foley involves the re-creation and recording of environmental and other natural ambient sounds that would occur on the film soundtrack; these sounds are very often recorded in a dedicated Foley post-production recording studio. Historically, Jack Donovan Foley worked at Universal Studios in the US and from 1927 developed the art of mimicking sound sources that could not always be captured and recorded at the time of filming, this unique art form inheriting the 'Foley' moniker. The modern work of the professional Foley artist is succinctly outlined by Phillip Rodrigues Singer, a motion picture sound editor in the US, who categorises Foley sounds as follows:

- *Moves*. The sound of clothing rustling as an actor walks across the scene.
- *Feet*. Re-creating the sound of footsteps in exact synchronisation with the actors walk. The exact same surface (for example, a gravelled walking surface) has to be accurate also in line with the on-screen activity.
- *Specifics*. Other sounds (for example, splashing in water to emulate swimming or crinkling cellophane to emulate the sound of fire).

(www.marblehead.net)

The way in which the Foley artist works, and their collection of often-crude tools and props to create sounds, is particular to each Foley artist, although emulation techniques may have many similarities. The re-creation of these specific categories of sounds above, fall to the Foley artist, but what their role does not cover is the recording of sounds that fall into the category of other 'special effects', or SFX, as it has become known. The special effects editor is involved in the sourcing or recording of sounds that may fall into additional categories, such as helicopters, car engines, dog barks, laser blasts, or birds. It would be difficult to record and emulate these sounds in a Foley studio, so sourcing good special effects sample libraries saves much time and resources for the film company (www.marblehead.net). For budding filmmakers on a budget, a mixture of techniques could be used to create their soundtrack, but essentially there may be more reliance on a good ambient soundtrack, recorded at the time of filming – then carefully mixed at the post-production stage.

In a big-budget movie, Foley and special effects editors and recordists execute a very specialist function in remodelling certain categorical environmental sounds from scratch – considering *every* single sound that could *not* be captured by the film crew at the time of filming can be a gargantuan task. For a variety of reasons, the ambient soundtrack recorded in a city film sequence (at that particular day and time of filming), for instance, may not seem real enough or simply have the impact to give the impression of a busy, bustling city centre. Therefore, the sounds of a city centre may be recorded separately as a special effect, to include a variety of overdubbed fire engines, car horns, screeching of brakes, and general public hubbub for added authenticity. This can then be remixed into the soundtrack over speech dialogue in the film, but at a lower acceptable volume level, to allow the actors' voices to be audible over the special effects traffic noise. Re-recording certain key sounds gives the audio remixer increased control over the whole film soundtrack; in addition, certain specially recorded sounds and effects can also be boosted to give greater impact to the scene. In R. Murray Schaffer's work *The Soundscape: The Tuning of the World*, there is much to consider in the ongoing acoustic world; research into diverse environments has been conducted over many years, 'revealed through an international study entitled the World Soundscape Project, which many agencies helped to fund' (Schaffer, 1994: xi). Through this research, the filmmaker may find some of Schaffer's sound categorisations of great use, expanding discourse and thinking around environmental settings, such as the rural soundscape, towns and cities, industrial revolution, noise, and silence:

> The soundscape of the world is changing. Modern man is beginning to inhabit a world with an acoustic environment radically different from any he has hitherto known.
>
> (Ibid.: 3)

There are a growing number of audio production libraries that can supply a vast range of both atmospheric sound and special effects, both available online and in tangible format; searching by exact sound and theme or title can unearth appropriate sounds to enhance any film production. Sometimes, these sounds can be purchased for use in their entirety or licenses can be granted (for a fee) for their use in films. However, there is a danger that filmmakers using the same library production sounds (just as in the over-use of library music) will become familiar to the viewer over time, if used repeatedly. In some films, especially between the 1950s and 1970s, many film soundtrack effects became recognisable through their overuse. Large film companies can afford and will always seek originality in production of their soundtracks; they will commission the best Foley artists and special effects editors to avoid repetition and preserve individuality and distinctiveness in the soundtrack.

THE CUE SHEET

It should be noted at the outset that good housekeeping in filmmaking is advisable when using music and certain sound samples. It is important to keep a record of 'who created and produced what', just as in the roster of film production staff and crew; it is important to know who is providing (and made) the music soundtrack. On big-budget films with many songs used, a full credit list is always supplied on the end credits as the film runs to a close. Essential information is listed, including the song title, the artist performing it, the publisher of the music and the recording company – essentially, those who have granted permission for the film company to use it. This is a detailed process, but can be insisted upon by all those involved, in allowing the music to be used in association with the film. Working on a small scale is no different; full credits given at the end of a low-budget film are just as important, acknowledging those who provided the music *and* gave permission for its use – a worthwhile investment should the film become a success. The main reason for including such credit is simply to avoid future litigation; 'where there is a hit – there is a writ'! Using a 'cue sheet' is an effective way of keeping an accurate soundtrack record, ensuring that the music and special effects are logged in a time-based way throughout the film. If accurately compiled, the cue sheet will assist others, such as TV broadcasting companies, whereby composer and publisher details are also logged, in performing rights royalty payments. Where songs and published works are used in film and broadcast over a TV network, a copy of the cue sheet would be sent to the performing rights organisation concerned (in the UK, PRS for Music). This will ensure that the composer is paid for the correct duration of the music used in such screening.

PROFILE

MIKE MORAN

Mike Moran is a film composer, musician, and arranger, having scored music for films such as *Time Bandits* (Terry Gilliam, 1981) and *The Missionary* (Richard Loncraine, 1982), and also played keyboards on the soundtracks of several of the *James Bond* movies. Mike has created original music scores for over 100 networked TV productions in the UK and abroad, including ITV's *Taggart*, BBC's *Sherlock*, and 20 more feature films. Mike was awarded the Gold Badge of Merit from the British Academy of Songwriters and Composers in 2007. Mike highlights his experiences of soundtrack music composition in a career spanning several decades.

Before I start to create a soundtrack, I would usually request a full copy of the film script from the producer. Wherever the script is available, it will really help to get a good idea of the plot and have some kind of feel for the moods or emotions conveyed in each scene. More often than not, the composer is not involved in the pre-production process and comes into the process at the post-production phase. It is unlikely that the composer would visit the film set and observe the various scenes in production; therefore, the script is a good starting point. Sometimes, the film producer underestimates the sheer amount of music needed for the whole film and also in individual scenes; for instance, in a busy café scene, a radio may be playing in the background and specific composed music may be required for that purpose. At the outset, the composer really needs to get a feel for the characters and general action in all parts of the movie.

At the post-production stage, the composer needs to work with a finished movie cut wherever available; this is because the music needs to be 'frame accurate' – so, if the composer is working to an unfinished rough cut and the film is later edited, the music may not fit as originally intended. Initially in the post-production phase, the composer will meet with the film director and editor for a 'spotting' session. The purpose of this is to work with the director and editor in collaboration, looking at each scene and mutually agreeing exactly where music should occur and what will work best. When I have worked with film directors, such as Terry Gilliam on *Time Bandits*, we will discuss styles of music that will be used and other aspects – such as the period setting of the film and attributed music; sometimes contemporary modern music may actually be used in a historical period scene, depending on what the director has in mind. Often, the budget will dictate what is also possible; for instance, although full orchestral music may be suggested for certain scenes, funds may not allow this. The spotting session will also allow the composer and director time to explore and discuss thematic and other creative soundtrack ideas.

The composer will often work to a Quicktime movie file when writing to film (supplied by the film company or director) and the file could be imported into the composer's music programme, such as Logic Pro, Digital Performer, or Pro Tools. Sometimes, the film comes supplied from the editor with a 'temp track'; this version of the movie has temporary music selections dubbed on to it made by the director, to give an idea of what preferred stylistic compositions may work. Sometimes the temp

PROFILE

track can cause issues due to the fact that the director may become particularly attached to it, finding that his or her temporary music choices are what they get used to and exactly what they would like to hear in the final cut. The 'dub' is then the final stage of the process for the composer after all the music has been written and ready to be overdubbed on to the film – the composer should really try to be there in person when this happens. At this post-production editing stage, the balance of music, special effects, and dialogue is put together and is usually the last chance the composer will have to influence how his or her music is used in the movie.

Sometimes, the film director may have less knowledge about music styles and genres and may only be aware of the music that they like *personally*, which may actually be at odds with more appropriate styles of music that would work better in the movie. Often, for the composer, they will need to work speculatively with filmmakers, showing what he or she can do first before any contracts are secured, and it is worth considering that several other composers may also be pitching their compositions to secure a film music contract on that same production. Many composers also have showreels in circulation with film music supervisors, which need to be kept up to date, so this can be a continuous task for composers. As far as budgets and rates go, there is never a fixed rate for anything, and it is up to filmmakers and composers to negotiate fees on an individual basis.

GRAHAM WALKER

Graham Walker is a professional film music supervisor and music producer, having synchronised over 85 feature films, including *The Talented Mr Ripley* (Anthony Minghella, 1999), *Sleepy Hollow* (Tim Burton, 1999), and *Rules of Engagement* (William Friedkin, 2000). Graham is a classically trained musician who graduated at the Guildhall School of Music, London, and has extensive in-depth working knowledge of music production libraries, publishing, and recording, in tandem with his attributes as an arranger and conductor of popular and classical music genres.

My role in music supervision and production is to first read the script and then budget the various musical elements, including the original score. I then secure appropriate music to synchronise with the movies and produce all re-records of the various songs as required. The next step is to organise the score recording sessions in the studio within the timescale and the budget restrictions, and then supervise and mostly co-produce the score recording and mixing with the composer in accordance with the requirements of the film company and deliver all aspects on time and within budget. Depending on the movie requirements and the budget, this could be anywhere from 20 or more separate three-hour recording sessions with a 150+ piece orchestra in Abbey Road Studios, London, with all styles of lineups – jazz, rock, pop, classical, futuristic and more – down to a few three-hour sessions in Budapest, Prague, Moscow, and so on – as required artistically and as allowed within the budget. There are some music supervisors who work purely on securing music for the film, getting the best deals to fit with the budget, and with what the producer or director wants. However, I have found being a musician has been an invaluable tool personally, as my musical training has allowed me to understand the film soundtrack from a much more musical perspective, and I often become much more involved in the remodelling of the film soundtrack, when necessary. My background has also become useful in guiding the contracted film composers that I work with, pinpointing key aspects of the film score, and assisting in the creative through processes of post-production and synchronisation.

The main role of any music supervisor would be to obtain copyright clearances in respect of non-composed music in the film (for example, if several well-known 1950s pop music songs were required in a film, the music supervisor would search for and contact the music publisher to clear the copyright for use in synchronisation). If, in that same 1950s film, the original recordings were required, then the music supervisor would also contact the original rights holders in the recording (usually the record company). Sometimes, it may be appropriate to update the sound of the records using modern re-recording methods, so, in that case, permission from the recording company *may* not be required, but this must always be checked out. In essence, no filmmaker should use pre-existing music without ensuring the clearances are in place from both publisher and recording company or other master rights owner, or he or she could find himself or herself in a highly litigious position. The music supervisor *is* the music researcher for the film (for example, if jazz is required in a dancehall scene, the supervisor will research music from the era and then make appropriate suggestions to the director or producer). Music budgets are pivotal in exactly what music can be used, how much of it, and the quality of production. The music supervisor needs to develop a relationship with the music publisher who owns the rights in the songs that are sought for the film; often, it would be a case

PROFILE

PROFILE

of being candid with the publisher, outlining up front what the limitations of the music budget is and realistic figures concerning what may work for both sides. Sometimes, costs run into hundreds of thousands of pounds (or dollars) to obtain the synchronisation rights to use just a few well-known pop songs in a major movie production, and the negotiation process can be long and arduous. In this regard, it makes sense for film producers to concentrate on the creative side of filmmaking and leave the complex soundtrack clearance negotiation process to an experienced music supervisor. An awareness of music clearance is always beneficial, but the specialist knowledge a good music supervisor can provide will make the job of the filmmaker a whole lot easier when it comes to synchronising music and getting the best deals on music usage.

FURTHER READING

Books

Cooke, M., *A History of Film Music* (Cambridge, Cambridge University Press, 2008).

Cooke, M., *The Hollywood Film Music Reader* (Oxford, Oxford University Press, 2010).

Davis, R., *Complete Guide to Film Scoring* (New York, Hal Leonard Books, 2000).

Donnelly, K., *Film Music: Critical Approaches* (Edinburgh, Edinburgh University Press, 2001).

Frith, S., Goodwin, A., Grossberg, L., *Sound and Vision: The Music Video Reader* (London, Routledge, 1993).

Jones, C., *The Guerilla Film Makers Pocketbook: The Ultimate Guide to Digital Film Making*, (London, Continuum, 2010).

Kalinak, K., *Film Music: A Very Short Introduction* (Oxford, Oxford University Press, 2010).

Larsen, P., *Film Music* (London, Reaction Books, 2005).

Latham-Brown, R., *Planning the Low-Budget Film* (Chicago, Chalk Hill Books, 2007).

Lerner, N., *Music in the Horror Film: Listening to Fear* (Oxford, Routledge, 2010).

Lyons, S., *Indie Film Producing: The Craft of Low Budget Filmmaking* (Oxford, Focal Press, 2007).

Prendergast, R. M., *Film Music: A Neglected Art* (London, Norton and Co., 1997).

Redner, G., *Deleuze and Film Music: Building a Methodological Bridge between Film Theory and Music* (Bristol, Intellect, 2011).

Rutter, P., *The Music Industry Handbook* (Abingdon, Routledge, 2011),
pp. 70–92, (Lambert, S., pp. 176–82).
Ventura, D., *Film Music in Focus* (London, Rhinegold Education, 2010).
Wierzbicki, J., Platte, N., Roust, C., *The Routledge Film Music Sourcebook*
(Oxford, Routledge, 2011).

Online resources

Arnold, David. *Music composer and arranger.* Available at: www.davidarnold.
com (accessed 9 January 2012).
Art of Foley. *Phillip Rodrigues Singer (MPSE) on Foley techniques.* Available at:
www.marblehead.net/foley (accessed 9 February 2012).
Audacity. *Free music recording software.* Available at: Audacity
http://audacity.sourceforge.net (accessed 18 February 2012).
Audio editing (*in Final Cut Pro*). Available at: www.apple.com/finalcutpro/
all-features/#audio-editing (accessed 18 February 2012).
Audio Network. *Production music.* Available at: www.audionetwork.com
(accessed 6 January 2012).
Avid. *Professional audio software.* Available at: www.avid.com (accessed 18
February 2012).
Barry, John. *James Bond film soundtrack orchestral arranger and composer.*
Available at www.johnbarry.org.uk (accessed 12 February 2012).
BBC News. *Campaign to extend copyright.* Available at: www.bbc.co.uk/news/
entertainment-arts-14882146 (accessed 7 January 2012)
Beatles, The. *Let It Be* (published by Sony/ATV). Available at: www.sonyatv.
com/search/index.php/search#search=quick&page=1&quick_search=let
%2Bit%2Bbe&filters%255Bsubmit_flag%255D=1 (accessed 6 January
2012).
Carlin Music. *Music production catalogues.* Available at: www.carlinmusic.com/
music/themes (accessed 6 January 2012).
Creative Commons. *Sourcing music for use in film.* Available at: www.creative
commons.org.uk/ (accessed 6 January 2012).
De Wolfe Music. *Music production catalogues.* Available at: www.dewolfe.co.uk
(accessed 6 January 2012).
Film Music Magazine. Available at: www.filmmusicmag.com (accessed 7
January 2012).
Foley, Jack Donovan. Available at: www.marblehead.net/foley (accessed 7
January 2012).
Hitchcock, Alfred. *Psycho.* Available at: www.imdb.com/title/tt0054215
(accessed 18 February 2012).
Intellectual Property Office (UK). *Copyright in sound recordings.* Available at:
www.ipo.gov.uk/c-music-soundrec.htm (accessed 12 February 2012).
Intellectual Property Office (UK). *How long does copyright last?*
www.ipo.gov.uk/c-duration-faq-lasts.htm (accessed 18 February 2012).
Jaws (*film music*). Available at: www.imdb.com/title/tt0073195 (accessed 17
February 2012).
Korg PA50. *Auto Accompaniment*: Available at: www.youtube.com/watch?v=
S7Hk-vV1RZg&feature=related (accessed 16 January 2012).
Korg Professional Arranger Keyboards. Available at: www.korg.co.uk/products/
professional_arranger/pa_overview.asp (accessed 18 February 2012).

Logic Pro. *Professional audio software*. Available at: www.apple.com/logicpro/ (accessed 18 February 2012).

Norman, Monty. *Original bond theme composer*. Available at www.monty norman.com (accessed 12 February 2012).

Motion Picture Sound Editors (MPSE), California US. Available at: http://mpse. org (accessed 22 February 2012).

Myspace. *Sourcing original music online*. Available at: http://uk.myspace.com (accessed 12 February 2012).

PRS for Music. Available at: www.prsformusic.com/Pages/default.aspx (accessed 9 February 2012).

Silent Movie Shows. *Mood music*. Available at: www.silentmovieshows.com/ moodmusic.htm (accessed 15 February 2012).

Soundcloud. *Sourcing original music online*. Available at: www.soundcloud.com (accessed 12 February 2012).

Sound Snap. *Violin horror sounds*. Available at: www.soundsnap.com/ taxonomy/term/729/oldest (accessed 18 February 2012).

Universal Publishing. *Production music*. Available at: www.unippm.co.uk (accessed 6 January 2012).

Yamaha. *Music arranger workstations*. Available at: http://uk.yamaha.com/en/ products/musical-instruments/keyboards/digitalkeyboards/arranger_ workstations/?mode=series (accessed 18 February 2012).

YouTube. *Sourcing original music online*. Available at: www.youtube.com (accessed 12 February 2012).

Online newspapers

Hutchinson, P. *Pianists play it again at the movies*. n.d. Available at: www. guardian.co.uk/film/filmblog/2011/apr/12/pianists-silent-film-festival-musical-accompaniment (accessed 15 February 2012).

Part V

Merging and emerging media

Developing a professional specialism

CHAPTER 18

Post-film

Technology and the digital film

This chapter considers a range of technologies and techniques that are becoming popularised, if not standardised, in the age of digital. Digital affects the culture of film at the level of production, distribution, and exhibition. Consumer technology opens up the field of film practice to non-industry filmmakers who can produce, edit, and distribute films with relative ease via a number of digital tools and platforms (for example, digital cameras, editing software, and Internet hosting websites). Digital technologies equally shape industry-produced film and cinema, and this section outlines some of the key developments in filmmaking in recent years. It explores visual effects and stereoscopic 3D, and notes how computer-generated imagery and 3D both strive to produce photorealism in film.

VISUAL EFFECTS

First, we can note the field of visual effects within digital post-production, and that of special effects. Often, these terms are used interchangeably but within film production there are differences. *The VES Handbook of Visual Effects: Industry Standard VFX Practices and Procedures* notes that 'visual effects is the term used to describe any imagery created, altered, or enhanced for a film or other moving media that cannot be accomplished during live-action shooting' (Okun and Zwenman, 2010: 2). Visual effects (VFX) involve the distortion of the pro-filmic scene whereby a scene is enhanced and manipulated using technology, whereas special effects are often achieved during shooting (for example, pyrotechnics effects that are recorded). VFX are not always, however, formed in post-production. For example, visual effects can include running film at a faster or slower frame rate (in camera effects), the use of lenses, double exposure, background plates, and live-action composited scenes. Today, many of these effects are produced away from live action shooting. Animated visuals and computer-generated imagery (CGI) can be created outside of live-action shooting and later composited with a live-action image. There are a number of reasons for using visual effects to supplement live-action shooting. First, visual effects may be used where the object/scene to be represented does not exist in reality. For example, both the earlier and later films of *Godzilla* are centred upon a creature that has no basis in reality (no referent). The earlier Japanese *Godzilla* (Ishirō Honda, 1954) used models of cities and landscapes. The monster took the form of a man in a suit and, at times, a puppet.

We can compare this rudimentary form of visual effects to the later *Godzilla* (Roland Emmerich, 1998). Here, the creature was created with CGI with some use of an animatronic creature. Rotoscoping was used to integrate the live-action scenes of the New York streets with the CGI Godzilla monster. In this case, synthesis was created between the 'real' space and action and the visual effects (although there are some errors, such as a lack of motion blur). Thus, the visual effects, which blended live action and CGI, produced an image that had no 'real-life' referent and made it seem as though it interacted with a 'real-life' space. There are other reasons why visual effects might be used. There may be situations that are impossible to film live, even though they exist in reality. For example, in the film *The Perfect Storm* (Wolfgang Peterson, 2000), most of the shots contain some element of visual effects, ranging from blue screen to complete computer animation. This is because the logistics of shooting in such conditions (storms at sea) made it impractical and dangerous, if not impossible, to shoot live. It would have put cast and crew at risk. In addition, visual effects might be used to fix or improve material (Mitchell, 2004: 9). This might include continuity errors that could not be avoided during shooting (for example, changing cloud cover during outdoor shooting) or production errors, such as equipment appearing in frame. Unfortunately, visual effects are sometimes relied upon to fix a range of errors that could have been avoided during shooting and to compensate for a lack of organisation during pre-production and production. For example, it may be the case that a lack of focus on cinematography during the shoot necessitates a lot of colour grading to correct discontinuity across a number of shots or to create atmosphere where it is absent from the raw image. This often occurs in student shoots (and some professional shoots), and students would be mistaken in thinking that such errors are easily overcome in post-production. It is worth keeping in mind that visual effects are not always adequate replacements for, or supplements to, competent shooting.

COMPUTER-GENERATED IMAGERY

Computer-generated imagery has, in the last number of years, become a common element of film production, particularly in regard to the blockbuster film. Increasingly, CGI replaces other forms of camera, optical, and special effects. CGI is used in a number of ways. It can enhance photorealism – for example, through the creation of realistic backgrounds in films such as *Gladiator* (Ridley Scott, 2000) and *Lord of the Rings: The Fellowship of the Ring* (Peter Jackson, 2001). It can be used to create spectacular and fantastical imagery, such as in the folding city of *Inception* (Christopher Nolan, 2010). As Pramaggiore and Wallis note:

> CGI creates background images and objects using a three-part process: developing the spatial characteristics of an object through a 3-D model (also called the wireframe), rendering (producing the finished image), and then animating the object and simulating movement (frame by frame).
>
> (2005: 148)

CGI is often coupled with compositing, whereby a CG object is composited into a live action scene. CGI is not only used for the spectacular action of science fiction films, whereby the CGI elements are obvious. It is also used to create even the most ordinary of things such as hair, rain, and to produce photorealistic textures and movements. For example, the film *Mighty Joe Young* (Ron Underwood, 1998) used the most up-to-date technology at the time to produce CGI photorealistic fur, which is notoriously difficult to achieve. So, CGI in cinema can range from a minor element such as a feather in *Forrest Gump* (Robert Zemeckis, 1994) to entirely digital imagery such as in certain scenes of *Avatar* (James Cameron, 2009). Thus, the boundary between film and animation blurs, since both films use digitally constructed objects, scenes, and story material. Yet, while the use of such visual effects may raise questions about the difference between film and animation (Manovich, 2002), there are some who suggest that CGI is not so different from previous film practices. Scott Bukatman has suggested that the same principle governs older use of visual and special effects and CGI:

> The special effects of contemporary cinema are . . . only a more recent manifestation of optical, spectacular technologies that created immersive, over-whelming and apparently immediate sensory experiences, such as 'Renaissance' and elevated perspectives, panoramas, landscape paintings, kaleidoscopes, dioramas, and cinema- a cinema, to borrow Eisenstein's phrase, of *attractions*.
>
> (1999: 254, emphasis in original)

Stephen Prince echoes this point when he writes that 'digital tools emulate properties of human vision as well as the camera's customary way of seeing things. In this regard, the application of digital tools continues a centuries-old tradition of analogizing camera and eye' (Prince, 2011: 40). For the most part, and as Bazin (1967) suggests in 'The myth of total cinema', there is a tendency towards realism with each new technological development. While special effects and CGI are often considered to be found in mainly science fiction, action, or fantasy films, they nevertheless aspire towards perceptual realism. Prince notes how CGI, while not conforming to realism in the traditional Bazinian sense, can be used to create the perception of realism for the audience. So, while the audience undoubtedly recognises that visual effects are precisely that, they can suspend disbelief when the effects are integrated well into the fictional story world. Thus, if visual effects and CGI can be used to support the believability of the story world, then they can be considered successful and realistic (despite how unusual or fantastical the world).

COMPOSITING

Compositing refers to the blending of two or more scenes or objects that were produced separately. Typically, this might consist of an actor that is composited with a background that was shot separately. Compositing is not a purely digital effect and was a common technique of traditional filmmaking with the use of rear projection and matte painting. In the case of CGI, the composter blends live-action objects (usually actors) with CGI backgrounds or action, or vice versa, whereby a CGI object is composited into a live-action scene. At times, a CGI object may be composited with a CGI background. The act of compositing is intended to produce a seamless and perceptually realistic overall scene. There are a number of different types of compositing. Green screen or blue screen compositing has an actor or object shot against a blue or green background. The actor or object is then separated from the background using a computer and is composited with a different background. This is used quite often in TV and film and is relatively easy to achieve but difficult to master. The compositor not only separates the actor or object from the green or blue background, but also needs to ensure that the composited image blends well in terms of ratio, lighting, and so on. Compositing is also used for set extensions. For example, an actor may walk through a beautiful landscape in the script. However, it may be too expensive or problematic to shoot on location. So, a smaller scale set may be used for the shots of the actor walking, and this can be composited with either a live-action natural landscape or a CGI landscape. Crowd duplication is also now commonly used in films. It is generally very expensive to pay a large number of extras, so CGI artists can create the effect of larger crowds either by compositing images of smaller crowds across different spaces and then combining the images (direct composition) or by taking a sample of a crowd and duplicating it in an empty space (procedural composition) (Wright, 2008: 11). These are just some of the many forms of compositing.

MOTION CAPTURE/PERFORMANCE CAPTURE

Motion capture (MoCap) refers to the transformation of movement and performances into a 3D representation. As Root notes in *The VES Handbook*:

Motion capture is the process of encoding motion from the real world into the digital medium in three dimensions . . . performance capture is a term that usually refers to a subcategory of motion capture where the actor's face and body performance are recorded simultaneously.

(2010: 335)

Motion capture has become more popular in recent years due to its ability to produce more photorealistic movements than other methods or CGI alone. Films such as *The Lord of the Rings: The Fellowship of the Ring* (Peter Jackson, 2001), *King Kong* (Peter Jackson, 2005), and *Watchmen* (Zack Snyder, 2009) used motion-capture technology in order to create realistic performances by key 'actors' and characters within the film. With motion capture, actors are fitted with sensors at specific points on the body and face. The sensors send information to a computer, which maps the movement captured by the sensors on to an animation. As the actor moves, the animation then moves in sync, making the performance more perceptually real. The character of Gollum from *The Lord of the Rings* has been noted as a particular achievement in the field of motion capture. In order to create Gollum, first the character had to be defined and built. Once a 3D model was designed, anatomy such as muscles and bones were produced in order to make the texture and movement of the body more realistic. Andy Serkis, who performed Gollum, wore a suit with a multitude of sensors, and also had a number of sensors on his face. Serkis performed alongside the other actors but was removed from the scenes and later replaced with the Gollum animation. The movement captured by the sensors provided the foundation of Gollum's movement, with specific facial movements being achieved through keyframe animation. The performance of Serkis was then added to a model of Gollum.

Motion-capture technology continues to become more sophisticated, with developments such as facial and on-location motion capture producing more photorealistic and natural results. For example, in *Rise of the Planet of the Apes* (Rupert Wyatt, 2011), motion capture was used in exterior daylight locations rather than in a studio. For *Avatar*, actors wore small cameras on their heads in order to capture the facial expressions more successfully. Because dots were painted on their face (rather than with sensors), more data could be captured and this provided more photorealistic images of the Na'vi characters. It was also possible, at this time, to generate a real-time view of the data, meaning that performance could be directed more effectively (see the section on *Avatar* below for more information).

STEREOSCOPIC 3D

In the typical cinema space, the boundary between audience and screen action is clearly established with the separation between both occurring at the border of the screen frame. The flat image creates a distance between the audience and the story action (which, as we noted in earlier chapters, was overcome through the process of suturing). 3D attempts to erase this boundary by creating a more immersive experience. 3D enhances the cinematic experience through the creation of a more immersive atmosphere, whereby the flat and distant frame is given perceptual depth and the space between the audience and screen action is perceived as bridged. 3D has been popular at particular moments in cinema's history. In the 1950s, filmmakers attempted to create a more sensory cinema experience through the use of 3D, and in the 1980s 3D was once again popularised in the horror genre. Over the past decade, 3D films have once again increased with the availability of new technology. Mendinburu *et al.* point to the 'relatively varied mix of blockbusters converted to 3D, low-budget movies shot in 3D, and a flock of CGI animation rendered in 3D' (2011: 13). However, there are still not as many films shot in 3D as there are films converted in post-production. At the moment, 3D technology is still undergoing development and improvement, and it is difficult to see whether today's 3D will suffer the same fate as earlier 3D moments.

Stereoscopic vision refers to binocular vision whereby the eyes receive slightly different visual information of the same image. It allows for depth of perception (an understanding of the distance between objects). 3D vision is a human quality. Stereoscopic technology draws upon this human quality in order to create that same depth of perception in the cinematic image. Stereoscopic 3D cinema attempts to provide a richer, more 'realistic' experience by replicating the same depth of perception that is already produced by the human eyes in the real world. 3D technology is not new; in fact, it has existed since the nineteenth century. Cinema was, in a sense, always 3D, since, although the image was flat and used one lens, filmmakers produced the perception of depth through focal lenses, movement, and frame composition. 3D cinema produces the same difference of vision as the two eyes do in real life. Where the human eyes can adjust their focus, in 3D cinema special glasses do the same, bringing together the two images. The two images produced for the 3D film equate with two human eyes. This process of producing the two images is called separation and is key to 3D production of the past and of today. In the past, two projectors produced the two images but this tended to cause eye strain. Today, a single projector is often used and filters in the viewer's glasses block either the left or right eye in sync with the projector.

There are a number of different technologies employed for the effect of stereoscopic 3D: 3D animation, Real D, and IMAX 3D, with further home viewing technology available for TV viewers. Real D is a system used in existing cinema theatres. The system allows for theatres to be adapted for 3D through the use of a digital light-processing projector (DLP). The Real D Z screen and controller sits in front of the projector and acts as a polarization switch to display the left and right images. A silver screen is also used to reflect more light than a typical matte cinema screen. Finally, audience members wear passive polarised glasses to see the image on the screen. IMAX, on the other hand, uses the two-projector system and a large-format screen. This makes for a more immersive experience since the audience are required to shift their head in order to view the screen in its entirety. Coupled with 3D, then, this enhances the cinema experience even more. Like Real D and other 3D cinema formats, the audience wear glasses. However, unlike typical cinema screens, the frame is so large that the viewer feels wholly surrounded by the image.

There are a number of ways of making a 3D film. Typically, films may be produced in 2D and later converted for 3D. Films can also be shot in 3D. Converting to 3D, although common, is a complicated process that has developed and improved in the past few years. More recently, films such as *Titanic* (James Cameron, 1997), *John Carter* (Andrew Stanton, 2012), and *The Avengers* (Joss Whedon, 2012) have been converted from 2D to 3D. There are a number of practical reasons for shooting in 2D and converting in post. The camera rigs might be too problematic for the shoot, there may be a preference for shooting in film, or a film might have been shot many years ago. Even films shot in 3D might have sections of 2D, since it would have been impractical to shoot in 3D. To convert from 'mono' to 'stereo', a second 'eye' needs to be generated by a computer. Also, every frame of action needs to be converted. With each frame, a depth of contour map is created on a computer. Then, two images are produced, which results in the stereoscopic image. This is obviously an extremely laborious task, since every shot must undergo this process. For example, converting an older film may produce problems regarding the framing of action. While a character's position in the frame might not be an issue in 2D, with 3D an over-the-shoulder shot might feel odd. So, converting an older film may necessitate some reframing (as was the case with *Titanic*'s conversion). Films shot in stereoscopic 3D, such as *Avatar* (James Cameron, 2009) and *Transformers: Dark of the Moon* (Michael Bay, 2011), require different shooting and production practices. Cameras such as the Panasonic 3D camera recorder or the Red Epic are required rather than traditional film cameras. The 3D scene must be shot from at least two angles so that there will be an image for both left and right eye. Often, there are fewer edits and more camera movements in order to allow the eye to adjust to the depth. So, a different set of concerns govern the production of a 3D film, and filmmakers must have an awareness of depth perception, and how much information each shot can carry. The camera rig needs to be set up so that the two images shot will correspond to human vision.

This requires the careful consideration of camera positions in relation to each other and to the scene being shot. So, the camera needs to be set up at a distance that will make the two images similar enough, but also different enough, to correspond to a left and a right eye. Likewise, any camera movement needs to be coordinated so that the images are not out of sync with each other. Certain images are much harder to achieve in 3D. For example, close shots of action or characters are sometimes impractical due to the spacing of the cameras on the rig. Here, mirror rigs might be used to compensate so that one camera can bounce an image through a small mirror to the other camera. As 3D develops, many of these issues will be addressed. Shooting in 3D requires a paradigm shift in terms of production and direction. Filmmakers that shoot in 3D are still experimenting with the technology and, therefore, it is unsurprising that there are as many failures as successes. If audiences come to accept 3D, it is certain that the process of 3D filmmaking will become standardised; however, it is difficult to predict if this may be the case.

AVATAR (JAMES CAMERON, 2009)

James Cameron has established a reputation as an innovative filmmaker in terms of visual effects technology. His earlier films such as *The Terminator* (1984), *The Abyss* (1989), and *Titanic* (1997) all used ground-breaking visual effects, which have marked important points in the evolution of visual effects and CGI in cinema. Cameron does not have a large portfolio of films given the length of his tenure in Hollywood, yet many of his films represent years of work into visual effects design. For example, *The Abyss* used CGI to produce the effect of the morphing of alien creatures. Through the collaboration with Industrial Lights and Magic (ILM) and benefiting from the technology developed by the likes of Pixar, *The Abyss* produced the most photorealistic blending of CGI and live action for that time (Pierson, 2002: 47). The technology was also used in *Terminator 2* (1991). In the case of *Avatar* (2009), this blending of CGI and live action was developed even further. Stephan Bugaj goes as far to suggest that films such as *Avatar* lean more towards animation with elements of live action (Okun and Zwerman, 2010: 737). The film was developed over 10 years and cost around $300 million to make. Not only were the creatures – the Na'vi – visually designed, but also the entire world of Pandora, including the landscape, flora and fauna, and other creatures that contributed towards the believability of the world. Among the range of techniques used were performance capture and real-time feedback, as well as 3D.

Performance capture is related to motion capture, yet Cameron uses the term 'performance', since actors do not simply generate motion. Performance capture aims to capture all of the other performance elements rather than just motion; body movement, expression, and emotion. As well as capturing the general body motion with regular motion capture, the actors who performed the Na'vi characters had cameras mounted on their heads that recorded their facial movements. In order to capture the motion and performance in as much detail as possible, these cameras would record the actors from a range of angles. The performance-capture technology removed the need for facial sensors and markers (which tend to impede the performance of the actor). The camera instead captured the performance from the head – a rig and a small camera that was fitted directly before the actor's face. Motion capture was used for the other creatures that formed part of the world of Pandora, as well as other moving objects. *Avatar* also utilised Simul-cam and Virtual Camera, which, along with the Stereoscopic 3D Fusion camera system, allowed for live viewing of the blended CGI and live action scenes during filming. This meant that Cameron could direct the film almost as if it were a live action film, since the CGI and live action blend could be viewed on set as it occurred. For example, the

Simul-cam allowed the director to film actors in a green screen stage that would have digital set extensions and then view the composited footage live. This has changed the nature of visual effects filmmaking, since, previous to this, the composited image could only be viewed in post-production.

THE HOBBIT: AN UNEXPECTED JOURNEY (PETER JACKSON, 2012)

At the 2012 CinemaCon, Peter Jackson introduced a 10-minute preview of his upcoming *The Lord of the Rings* prequel, *The Hobbit* (due for release in December 2012). There has been much discussion and speculation about the film and, although there was some positive feedback on the 10-minute preview, there was also a good deal of negative feedback. Much of the speculation and negative feedback related to the film's visual effects. While *The Lord of the Rings* trilogy had won awards and commendations for visual effects, there were feelings among those at the preview that Jackson had perhaps gone too far. The debate that was generated by *The Hobbit* preview related to the use of 48 frames per second (fps) format. The industry standard is 24 fps, so this marked a 100 per cent increase in the normal frame rate. In addition, *The Hobbit* has been shot in stereoscopic 3D with Red Epic cameras. It was released on a wide variety of formats, including 2D, 3D, IMAX 3D, 24 fps, and 48 fps.

The justification for using 48 fps is that the image appears to be smoother and more realistic. Such a high frame rate is arguably more valuable for widescreen, spectacular films. In 24 fps, the wider screen image produces displacement. Therefore, 48 fps should offer a more immersive experience. However, the feedback from the CinemaCon preview indicated that people found it fake and unrealistic; in other words, the opposite of what the higher frame rate was intended for. Some of this criticism can be attributed to the print that was screened. The footage had not been colour corrected, and some VFX were missing. However, the criticism also recalls the reaction to other attempts at higher frame rate (Labrecque, 2012), with films such as *Leonardo's Dream* (Douglas Trumbull, 1989). Here, viewers found the film's 'ultra-realism' off-putting. In essence, 48 fps is more perceptually realistic but in the sense that the realism undoes the suspension of disbelief for the viewer. 48 fps does not necessarily make the story more realistic; rather, it foregrounds the artifice of the filmmaking process. One critic, Peter Sciretta, responding to *The Hobbit*'s preview, noted:

> It looked uncompromisingly real – so much so that it looked fake . . . Hobbiton and Middle Earth didn't feel like a different universe, it felt like a special effect, a film set with actors in costumes. It looked like behind the scenes footage. The movement of the actors looked . . . strange. Almost as if the performances had been partly sped up . . . it didn't look cinematic.
>
> (Frazer, 2012)

However, such reviews only had a short sequence of the film to base judgement on. Jackson and other advocates of faster frame rates (such as James Cameron) argue that frame rates of 48 fps or even 60 fps work better for 3D, as it reduces the amount of strobing and blurring.

Ultimately, the debates about the differences between 24 fps and 48 fps are the same types of debates that have haunted many emerging technological innovations from moving image itself, to sound, colour film, and digital cameras. Like other innovations, its success is not simply a matter of art or storytelling, but one of commerce. Although *The Hobbit* is shot in 48 fps and 3D, the film was available in 24 fps and 2D. This is due to the additional costs that cinema theatres must bear in upgrading for both 48 fps and 3D. There are debates about how much the 48 fps upgrade might cost cinemas. Sony has recently announced a software upgrade for 48 fps that is estimated to cost $10,000. While some of the main first-run theatres will probably upgrade, it is difficult to see many other theatres following suit. As with 3D upgrades, the 48 fps upgrade places an extra cost burden on cinema theatres, which may be passed on to customers. Thus, the transition to 48 fps, despite the feedback, will be more an issue of commerce and maths, than an artistic issue.

CHAPTER 19

Post-film

Production, distribution, and consumption in the digital age

POST-FILM

What is meant by post-film? How can we be 'post-film' when cinema remains such a prominent cultural product? To be post-film can refer to the decline of celluloid as the primary tool of filmmaking. It can also refer to the transformations that have taken place in the wake of digital technologies. We can think of the post-film era in a number of ways. For example, we can think of it in terms of the digital age, where digital technology is increasingly replacing film technology both as a method of production and exhibition. As we'll see, digital technology has had a huge impact on the production, distribution, and consumption of film. Not only does it have an impact on film practice, where a film can be made for much less than has previously been possible (through DV cameras, non-linear editing technology, web-based technologies), but it also has an impact on film form and aesthetics. Some question and consider the mourning of the 'end of film' as a historical practice and as a format (Hanson, 2004; Lewis, 2001; Willis, 2005). Some note that the distinct aesthetic of film, its graininess, its capacity for high contrast, is being lost to the inferior successor of digital, which has not yet reached the standard of film (for example, poor contrast ratio; Fossati, 2009). Similarly, others refer to the rise in digital effects usage (composting, layering, and so on), which are said, in various ways, to detract from or add to a film's 'realism' (Prince, 1996; Lister and Dovey, 2009). One might think of the effects used for the folding and shifting cities in the film *Inception* (Christopher Nolan, 2010).

Lev Manovich goes as far as to suggest that contemporary cinema is a subset of animation, such is the extent of digital effects (2002). Yet, others suggest that little has changed fundamentally about film or cinema, and that it was always transformative (Young, 2006). For example, we can question the degree to which the move towards digital production and exhibition has altered the film spectator's experience of a film. Although there are debates about the immediate impact of 'digital' on film audiences and cinema culture, there are a number of ways in which the industry has changed; some as a direct result of the digital era, others in a less obvious way.

CONVERGENCE

A key term in the debates about film in the digital age is convergence. Although media convergence is not a direct result of digitisation, there is a relationship between the two. Henry Jenkins defines it as:

> the flow of content across multiple media platforms, the cooperation between multiple media industries, and the migratory behaviour of media audiences who will go almost anywhere in search of the kinds of entertainment experiences they want.
>
> (2006: 2)

Recent years have seen a growth in media conglomeration. The once relatively distinct film industry is now part of the broader entertainment industry. So, media industries operate together. A film production company may be part of a music production company, which may be part of a print media company. These, in turn, are owned by the same company that develops hardware such as DVDs, DVD players, televisions, music players, and so on. Sony is an example of this. Convergence occurs at three levels – that of content (whether it is music, a film, a game), platform (Internet, television, phone), and distribution (in terms of how it is received on the platform). So, one conglomerate may be able to deliver all through their various subsets. You could have a Sony mp3 or TV, or buy a Sony film on a Sony DVD to play on your surround sound Sony home theatre. Convergence means the delivery of various forms of communication on to or through one or multiple devices. Yet, convergence is not limited to the media producer; it also refers to relationship between the consumer and the media. The consumer no longer accesses media in the same way as 70 years ago. For example, in the early years of cinema, the audience could only really access the film by attending a cinema. The consumption of a text was limited to a certain space and environment. The spectator was immobile. Thus, we could discuss the screen-spectator relationship in relatively fixed terms. Today, however, the consumer can access the same film text through a number of different platforms: TV, DVD, and PC; even PSP or smartphone. These changes in platforms inevitably alter the previous conceptions of spectatorship. Much of the theorisation of film has centred upon the screen-spectator relationship. We come to understand film meaning in terms of how the spectator is situated in relation to the text (for example, theorists have employed psychoanalytic theory in order to account for the spectator's participation in the film event, to understand how the subject is interpolated; Metz, 1982; Mulvey, 1989).

But these theories are based upon a particular mode of exhibition and a mode of reception. If we now experience the film text in very different ways (for example, we are not isolated in a darkened auditorium), we may not commit to the entire text, then we need to re-think certain aspects of film theory. This is, to date, a grey area. Theorists such as Jenkins and Manovich are offering re-readings of film and spectatorship (Jenkins, 2006; Manovich, 2002). So, what does convergence do to film viewing?

Even before the age of digital, converging media platforms were changing modes of cinema spectatorship. In fact, cinema spectatorship, after the era of television, became only one element of the film-viewing experience. Where TV had been defined as a 'live' media, one determined by presence, cinema was said by Ellis, for example, to offer narrative images of specificity (Ellis, 1992). The convergence of both mediums, particularly where film was broadcast on TV, has led to various debates about the nature of film reception. For example, where television spectatorship is presumed to be fractured (where the viewer may partake in other activities along with viewing), and television broadcast defined by segmentation, cinema spectatorship is considered more complete; in other words, the spectator will immerse himself or herself in the film for its duration (ibid.; Fiske, 1987; Williams, 1974). However, these days, cinema spectatorship is no longer confined to the cinema. The box office receipts of any film represent only a fraction of a film's returns, which are now mainly made up of DVD, Blu-ray, TV distribution rights, and Internet distribution and streaming (Polan, 2012; Malloy, 2009). In addition to this convergence, technologies such as the remote control and VCR (now DVD, Blu-ray, and so on) enable the spectator to 'interact' in some ways, to control film viewing – if not content, then temporality. Peter Greenaway, the filmmaker, even called the introduction of the remote control 'the death of cinema', since the director no longer had full control over the film viewing (Kirby, 2009: 172).

CONVERGENT SCREENS

As Henry Jenkins (2006) notes in *Convergence Culture*, various forms of media content are converging on the one platform. Similarly, one form of media content, the film, is now accessible through a variety of platforms. In this sense, the traditional cinema screen represents only one screen on which a film may be played. Lev Manovich traces the history of the screen from the classical screen (the still, rectangular image, still used today), through to the dynamic screen of the moving image. For him, both of these screens strive for 'complete illusion and visual plenitude' where the viewer will engage in a suspension of disbelief and identify with the on-screen image (Manovich, 2002: 96). This image typically fills the screen space. For example, many people feel frustrated when a widescreen film is shown on a standard TV. There are, indeed, different expectations of the film screen, the TV screen, and the small mobile screen. Today, one can watch a film on smaller and smaller screens, yet for the most part films are not made for such screens. Think about how difficult it may be to watch *Avatar* (James Cameron, 2009) on an iPhone or PSP. Manovich sees the turn to such screens as the possible death of the dynamic screen of cinema. After all, the viewer is no longer immersed in the image to the same degree. Manovich notes that screen culture is now governed by the computer screen, by a windows culture. This is not only recognisable in the way we 'use' a computer screen, but also in how we may navigate TV channels, switch in and out of a film on TV or between TV programmes. We now interface rather than immerse. The image can be changed in real time, unlike cinema, where the image was changed in the past, always already done. The user can interact with the computer screen, change windows, and view multiple windows simultaneously. As Friedberg notes, 'spectators are "user" . . . with an "interface"', rather than viewers of a screen (Friedberg, 2004: 914). The user/spectator is now more sophisticated. They can process a large amount of alternative information at any given time: Word document, web page, film. This does not simply reflect a computer user, but a change in media literacy. One can equally navigate a number of pages on TV, and flick backwards and forwards between DVD menu pages, or commentary and film. The user/spectator is more interactive than the dynamic screen spectator. More and more, films seem to speak to this interactive audience in a number of ways.

CONTEMPORARY SCREEN AESTHETICS

While interactivity is still relatively rare in cinema, there are a number of ways in which film has been influenced by these new screen-spectator relations, both within the film text and the wider world of film culture in general. Non-linear narratives are one example of this. These non-linear structures can also be understood in terms of the changing nature of filmmaking practices, and film and media literacy. For example, Klinger (2006) suggests that while such non-linear practices existed prior to the advent of 'digital language', in the contemporary media and social sphere, there is now a correspondence between industry and consumer appropriation of technology. It has been assimilated on both sides. Both filmmakers and audiences are Windows users. 'Hyperlink cinema' describes such films, which may be told out of sequence, have multiple screens playing simultaneously, and manipulate traditional narrative form. Others, such as Manovich (2002), refer to these films as 'databases'. These are films that have a number of distinct strands, such as *Rashomon* (Akira Kurosawa, 1950), *Timecode* (Mike Figgis, 2000), and *Run, Lola, Run* (Tom Twyker, 1998). Interactivity occurs where the user can interact with the screen or the film experience. The multiple split-screen images, as in *The Tracey*

Fragments (Bruce McDonald, 2007), require a small degree of interactivity, since the viewer must decide upon which image to prioritise.

Lev Manovich calls these sequences of split screen 'spatial montage' (Manovich, 2002: 322). He notes that, often, temporal unity is maintained. For example, split screen is often used to show two people talking on the phone. Manovich feels that spatial montage offers a kind of macro-cinema, and is becoming increasingly popular in media in general. Viewers of news channels (such as Sky News or CNN) and people who use computers, or play video or multiplayer games, are already familiar with spatial montage (where two screens occupy the same space). He notes the wide use of multiple windows of GUI (graphic user interface – menus, docs, mouse, and images) and says that GUI and spatial montage are not all that different. Although windows on a PC might not be related to each other, we can navigate them easily, switching between different tasks. Montage, which is the relationship between two separate images, usually occurs in a sequential manner – one after the other. Spatial montage asks the viewer to watch the two images concurrently. But since our eye is usually drawn to one character or piece of action, this means that we could miss something. Conventional narratives usually retain only information important to the story. Dialogue reveals something about the character's personality or something about the story. Background *mise en scène* might reveal further clues. Audiences are almost conditioned to pay attention to all of the action. So, what does this mean for the viewer of the spatial montage film? Manovich points to Foucault:

> 'Of other spaces' Michel Foucault writes: 'We are now in the epoch of simultaneity: we are in epoch of juxtaposition, the epoch of near and far, of the side-by-side, of the dispersed . . . our experience of the world is less of a long life developing through time than that of a network that connects points and intersects with its own skein . . .'
>
> (2002: 324–5)

Others argue that we are used to dealing with highly dense information surfaces regularly, and that we can filter information more quickly in this media-dense age (Jenkins, 2006).

CONTEMPORARY SCREEN CULTURE

In addition to such alternative film forms and narratives, contemporary films are increasingly taking the form of other media formats. While this is not to suggest that dominant narrative is a thing of the past, a good deal of recent films can be understood in terms of remediation. The concept of remediation basically refers to one media's borrowing or referencing of another media. For Bolter and Grusin, who write extensively on remediation in the contemporary visual arts, it is 'a defining characteristic of the new digital media' (1999: 5). For example, films such as

His Girl Friday (Howard Hawks, 1940) included sequences of news print, while *Natural Born Killers* (Oliver Stone, 1994) draws upon a whole host of media, as does *Redacted* (Brian De Palma, 2007). What is particularly noticeable in many recent films is the incorporation of another media in its entirety. Certain films use the format of other visual media, even print media.

An early example might be the film *La Jetée* (Chris Marker, 1962), which is almost exclusively shot in still photographs. Another recent example would include *The Blair Witch Project* (Daniel Myrick and Eduardo Sanchez, 1999), which is shot as documentary, something many horrors do, including *Rec* (Jaume Balaguero and Paco Plaza, 2007), *The Zombie Diaries* (Michael Bartlett and Kevin Gates, 2006), and *The Fourth Kind* (Olatunde Osunsanmi, 2009). These films can be defined in terms of: (1) immediacy, where the spectator feels like he or she can access the object directly (in other words, the documentary look gives the impression that the events are authentic and are being experienced); and (2) hypermediacy, where the media very overtly draws attention to itself. We can, then, begin to think about such films and their relationship to the hyperreal and to simulation, since these films appear more realistic when they draw from 'factual' media. Do we feel that they are more realistic because they appear to be news footage or documentary? For example, the film *Series 7: The Contenders* (Daniel Minihan, 2001) is shot as a television series, something like *Survivor*, where instead of voting other team members off, they must kill each other. There is no reference to this being a film. It mimics a TV show throughout – all episodes including the final showdown.

DISTRIBUTION

Similarly, we can note another pattern that has emerged in the wake of digitalisation and windows culture – viral marketing campaigns. Marketing campaigns undoubtedly play a huge role in mainstream film exhibition. So, what, if any, relationship exists between such campaigns and the post-film era? We can look at two films, in particular, that demonstrate a shift in marketing strategy: *The Blair Witch Project* (Daniel Myrick and Eduardo Sanchez, 1999) and *Cloverfield* (Matt Reeves, 2008) (more recent examples include *2012* (Roland Emmerich, 2009) and *Super 8* (J.J. Abrams, 2011)). Both of these films relied heavily in pre-filmic build up. *The Blair Witch Project*, for example, did not advertise itself as a film, but rather as a documentary. First, we can note how the marketing campaign materialised. The first mention of the film came with the tagline 'In October of 1994, three student filmmakers disappeared in the woods near Burkittsville, Maryland, while shooting a documentary . . . A year later, their footage was found'. This approach was maintained throughout the film's production and exhibition – that this was a real event and a real documentary film. The filmmakers promoted the factuality of the film not only to audiences, but also to other media outlets, interweaving various media in its campaign. Other media producers also became complicit in the 'lie'. Not only was there confusion about its source among media consumers, but also among the producers themselves. This lack of consensus about the 'authenticity' of the footage helped to create the hype over the film. Word began to spread over the Internet about the film, and users were directed towards the blairwitch.com website. This website (Figure 19.1) confirmed the film's apparent authenticity. It had news reports of the events, brief clips of the footage, photos of the location, details of the town, and interviews with the families and friends of the missing people.

There was even a 'real' documentary broadcast on the Sci-Fi channel about the missing students. The film demonstrates the closing gap between separate media forms and the interweaving of different forms of pleasure. The extra-filmic media provides a backstory to the film, rather than being simply an advertisement for it. The spectator/user can immerse himself or herself in these extra-filmic environments, much like the player of a game, and this provides alternative, non-cinematic pleasures for the film audiences. Likewise, *Cloverfield* had an elaborate campaign that included Myspace pages for each of the characters, a strange connection to an ecological disaster that occurred in Japan, which made reference to a mysterious drink Slusho – the extra-filmic mystery providing alternative forms of engagement for those who actively took part in the campaign. *Cloverfield* could be seen as a postmodern media text, a hybrid of various forms, and a converged media text. Its advertising poster resembled previous films such as *The Day After Tomorrow* (Roland Emmerich, 2004), but also has an uncanny likeness of the 9/11 footage witnessed by many people around the globe. The film also took on the style of amateur handheld footage, something once again experienced in the unending replays of the 9/11 events. This kind of film experience requires more participation and interaction from the film consumer. This aspect of participation is one of the key features to emerge in the post-film or post-cinema era.

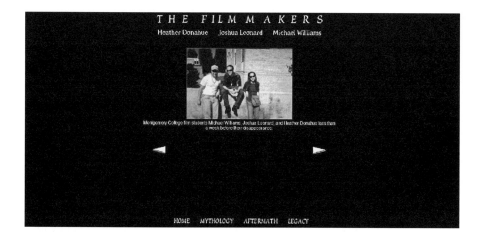

FIGURE 19.1
The Blair Witch Project website

GRASSROOTS AND PARTICIPATORY MEDIA

So, the previous part of this section focused on feature-length 'professional' film; the next part will focus on user- or consumer-made shorts. Here, we will discuss how audiences can now respond to film texts. They can respond using the same medium. We can also consider the significance of fan cultures, and, indeed, fans as authors. We will note the popularity of the parody short, and consider the case of *Star Wars Episode IV: A New Hope* (George Lucas, 1977) in relation to these.

We will note some early examples of desktop films, which were made using the most basic of filmmaking hardware and software. These are examples of participatory media. Participation is an essential aspect of convergence. Henry Jenkins says that the consumer (the media user) is driving convergence (Jenkins, 2006). The consumer/user makes the connections between the various media and continues to give the media a forum (through continuous consumption and interaction), perhaps allowing for a certain democratisation of film culture. They also have the opportunity to become media producers, since they are involved in the media through their use of it. Consumers/users can go online and discuss a film on chat rooms. They can write reviews, create blogs, and produce responsive media such as Internet memes. They can respond to media in a much more public way – they become 'noisy' consumers rather than quiet, passive ones. Jenkins notes the proliferation of DIY media forms in which users either respond to a media message (through manipulation) or create alternative media products as a reaction to an original (ibid.). What happens is the amateur or non-professional (someone who doesn't enter media as a career choice or profession) becomes a producer. There is an intersection between, or a blurring of, media producer and consumer. This is one of the primary features of participatory culture in general.

A number of trends have appeared in relation to film and participatory culture:

- the response to, or engagement with, a pre-existing text (for example, *Star Wars*, *Star Trek*), and also manipulation or interactivity (for example, General Motors and the interactive ad that backfired);
- the dominance of the comedy short film (which Klinger, 2006 discusses in detail);
- a significant drop in production cost and quality (due to infancy of technology);
- the rise of social documentary (for example, www.documentary-film.net); and
- the user becomes a media distributor (either legally or illegally – YouTube or file sharing).

PARTICIPATORY CULTURE AND RESPONSES TO A TEXT

It is worth remembering that there is a huge ongoing conflict between the controlling media institutions and producers (in the form of concentration of ownership) and control by the public (as 'users' rather than passive consumers, as publicly responding to media). Rather than seeing one as being dominant, we have to look at the relationship between both media producer and user producer. Jenkins sees the rise of participatory media as a return to pre-consumer or pre-industrial days, where folklore and myths circulated freely (Jenkins, 2006: 119). They were built and extended upon through the centuries. No one owned them, and everyone could participate in their circulation. The rise of individualism (in the form of authorship, intellectual property rights, and the decline of community) limited the circulation of stories and myths. IP rights and copyright created a dichotomy of producer-consumer. Jenkins sees media participation as challenging this. The consumer is also a contributor. Barbara Klinger notes how this is manifested in the web shorts that respond to existing film texts. Klinger links the rise of such web shorts to rise of web technologies, such as streaming software, as well as the wider availability of broadband and the turn in filmmaking practices towards online editing and post-production (Klinger, 2006: 200). All of these are relatively cheap and accessible. Coupled with this is the growth of general Internet surfing as a form of entertainment. Klinger also notes the dominance of the parody short on websites such as Atomfilms. For example, when Klinger was discussing Atomfilms, the website was host to a variety of short film genres, which included comedy/parody. Today, Atomfilms has been replaced with video-sharing websites such as Funny or Die. Today, YouTube surpasses Atomfilms for its wide variety of parody shorts. As Klinger notes, these user-generated parody films demonstrate the 'mass cultural competence' of the user generation, where consumers are not simply capable of imitating genres, but can create layered intertextual systems in each short (ibid.: 228). Jenkins looks at the multiple alternative versions of *Star Wars* available over the Internet. The film does not have a limited lifespan; rather, it continues as a media product beyond simple exhibition of the original. This has obvious benefits for the filmmaker/media maker. Lucas has engaged with fan culture and profited from it. He has held competitions for the best *Star Wars* amateur films on Atomfilms, allowing users to manipulate, parody, and re-interpret the original work in shorts such as *Chad Vader: Day Shift Manager* (Aaron Yonda and Matt Sloan, 2006). But there is a certain amount of tension between 'official' filmmakers and media producers and unofficial users. The relationship is often not as perfect as it first appears. Jenkins notes:

> If many advocates of digital cinema have sought to democratize the means of cultural production, to foster grassroots creativity by opening up the tools of media production and distribution to a broader segment of the general

public, then the rapid proliferation of fan-produced *Star Wars* films may represent a significant early success story for that movement.

(2004: 283)

To put it in context, some of these fan films have been viewed more times than many big-budget films. Lucas has publicly praised and supported the user-generated films that have developed the *Star Wars* or Lucas theme. One of the most popular, *George Lucas in Love*, was a winner at a number of film festivals and had the approval of Lucas.

However, the scope of support for this type of participation is limited. When the *Star Wars* fan contest was first held (the fan movie challenge), a large number of the most popular *Star Wars*-inspired films were excluded. For example, comedy spoofs were allowed, but serious films that extended the *Star Wars* story were not. Part of the reason why spoofs are often circulated where serious 'homages' are not is that parody is protected under most laws, whereas copyright laws protect everything else. There is also a big fear among the producers of particular texts that ownership or authority over the product will be lost. For example, the critical reaction to *Star Wars Episode I: The Phantom Menace* (George Lucas, 1999) was extreme. Fans felt that Lucas had interfered with *their* product, that he had let them down or tarnished the *Star Wars* culture. Re-edited versions of the film appeared, such as *The Phantom Edit*, which Lucas was wary of and attempted to restrict (McDermott, 2006: 252). It seems the prime issue at stake is appropriation. The user-filmmaker is not limited to mere consumption of the text, but wants to respond to and to be more deeply involved in the text (whether it be in a favourable or critical way). The ability to respond using the same media may be a source of empowerment for the user, creating a sort of even playing field (in spite of the obvious differences). But it is precisely this disruption of the boundaries between media producer/owner and user/consumer that has caused the most trouble. Many of these parodies do not revere the original text; in fact, they may critique it. As Klinger suggests:

> We can see that the more iconoclastic parodies engage in self-reflexive play to challenge the original. In so doing, they question the right and the ability of institutions to control meaning-in these cases, to dictate how a mainstream film will circulate and acquire significance for viewers . . . some e-films can be considered as critical responses to the empire of corporate capitalism and the media mythos that supports it.

(2006, 225)

THE DEMOCRATISATION OF FILM

While Klinger is cautious not to view the e-parody as entirely subversive or revolutionary, there are other forms of filmmaking practices that attempt to break down the barrier between producer and consumer. The e-parody allows the user to become the producer, yet is always dependent upon an already-existing dominant text. Participatory film is a product of both producer (industry) and consumer (participant). Many of these filmmaking exercises are politicised to a degree. In other words, the project of many such films is to give voice to those typically left out of representation or the filmmaking process itself. In many cases, cameras are given to a group of people who go on to record their own experiences of a particular event. The footage is then edited by a production team. Such an approach may challenge the hegemonic nature of dominant cinema, since authorship is not solely in the hands of the producer. Such film practices are undoubtedly enabled by the availability of technology, particularly digital media, as well as the high degree of media saturation in the West. *Voices of Iraq* ('People of Iraq', 2004) and *The War Tapes* (Deborah Scranton, 2006) circumnavigate traditional modes of documentary film (for example, both do not rely on journalists, directors, or traditional voices of authority), but also demonstrate that the user-filmmakers (the citizens/soldiers reporting their experiences of war) are conditioned in such filmmaking practices. They use narrative and storytelling devices typical of the documentary format. Similarly, those fan–filmmakers of the Beastie Boys' *Awesome I Fuckin' Shot That* ('Nathanial Hornblower', 2006) tend to employ the conventions of stadium photography, which might suggest that such practices are not as radical as they might initially seem.

CONCLUSION

As John Lewis notes, the term the 'end of cinema' was coined by Godard in the 1960s and taken up by scholars in the 1980s (2001: 1). Each cinema era, it seems, predicts its own downfall. It is far too pessimistic to assume the end of cinema as an institution, and possibly way off the mark. What we can note is the changing landscape of the cinema and film worlds. While cinema may still be controlled by the ever-familiar dominant corporations and institutions, there are grassroots 'movements' emerging. These movements, if we can call them that, are enabled by the easy availability of digital technology and electronic communications. As a result, there are challenges and resistances to the traditional hierarchies. Likewise, the current media landscape, in which traditionally separate media platforms converge upon each other, means that film does not necessarily exist as a distinct form. There are the obvious technological and economic reasons for this – film can be bought and sold online, viewed online, and on multiple other platforms. At the same time, we must acknowledge the audience/users participation in these changes. After all, this active audience is responsive to such things as Internet promotion, DVD extras, fan forums, and user-generated short videos.

CHAPTER 20

Mapping a career path

As you progress through your university film production studies, you will be considering and working towards fostering and developing your creative aims and aspirations. As you journey through to reach your creative goals, you *need* to be focusing on a particular specialism of film practice, one that you are both passionate about and adept at. You need to be investigating and trying out creative problem-resolution practices connected to the film field specialism that you are developing and honing, whether in cinematography, editing, scriptwriting, sound, directing, or producing. Additionally, the theory/practice skills you cultivate during your educational journey will not only serve you well to develop a career either at a film production/post-production company (or, indeed, your own independent production company), but also carries great weight in developing transferable skills for peripheral job positions within the film/media industry. These *transferable skills* greatly increase the likelihood of you securing work or creative careers in a range of diverse areas, such as: film archiving (British Film Institute, American Film Institute), entertainment law, television field production, production management, human rights media, museums/galleries, and arts councils/funding agencies.

CREATING A DEMO REEL AS A CALLING CARD

As you complete your educational film productions, you need to be planning which projects that you have worked on can be effectively utilised to compile a demo reel to highlight your particular specialist skills. Generally, your final-year short film should be the centrepiece of what your filmic talents demonstrate. You may also have materials from projects you worked on during your second year (and possibly your first year, as well) that you could select from to highlight any outstanding specific creative work (for example, a particular scene or sequence that demonstrates creative command of direction, cinematography, and editing, and/or sound design). I would suggest that your demo reel be no longer than 10 minutes in duration (unless you are working in documentary, then I would limit it to no more than 15 minutes). I would recommend that you insert a graphic of your name and your production role before the images begin and after they are completed (for example, director, cinematographer, sound, editor, scriptwriter). This is useful so that your prospective employer has a clear indication of whose material they are viewing and so they don't have to spend time figuring out what your role is. This is good practice, as many times young filmmakers' demo reels have only the original title list from their production(s). Film/production company owners and producers don't have the time to search out your name and role in your film's end credits, so it's in your interest to make it easiest for your prospective employer, as it sheds good light on who you are and your professional creative role in a succinct and accessible manner. Your completed demo reel greatly complements your résumé as an important marketing device. It is also worth developing and writing out a personal *mission statement*, which outlines your aims and goals for your creative journey, desires, and role within the film industry or as a filmmaker. A mission statement will help focus your thinking and accentuate your personal creative abilities in furtherance of finding your place in the film world. Write out, in a paragraph, how you see yourself developing as a creative practicioner, your personal vision of what you want your particular film specialism to be, and what you want to creatively contribute to and explore on film.

FINDING A JOB IN THE FILM INDUSTRY

Securing a gig in the world of film is not only a challenge, but a talent. This notion results from the fact that the world of film production operates as a market out of everyday sight.

Production companies depend on networking, industry character, and personal references as the main form to communicate and interconnect. Production jobs and roles are designated well in advance of the production. Word of mouth travels fast within the film industry, with previous affiliations affecting who gets hired by production managers and commissioning editors. Forging a relationship with various production managers is your primary task to get a foot in the door as a runner or production assistant. These introductory roles comprise the bulk of where student film graduates find industry jobs. Having a creative demo reel and well-tuned curriculum vitae is also vital. I would highly recommend obtaining the *Guardian Media Guide* and other industry 'who's who' publications that list production companies and studio names and contact details in the United States, Canada, and Australia. Many contacts can also be found by searching on the web. It is a good idea to send an email or make a direct telephone call, if possible, to introduce yourself before sending in your résumé and demo reel. As it goes without saying, any industry contacts you have already cultivated (including relatives or friends of relatives) will be indispensable to assist you with getting your foot in the door. It is a very competitive job marketplace, so every attention to detail will contribute a piece of the job puzzle to help create a good picture of who you are and the creative talents you have to offer.

Generally, directors, cinematographers, editors, sound recordists, producers, and many of the production team are hired per film project and last for the duration of pre-production, the shoot, and post-production. Only a few large companies or studios ever retain any sort of crew as full-time employees. Most employment in the film business springs forth from what you are currently working on, not necessarily on what you know or whom you know. Not 'burning bridges' is imperative to maintain and secure the next job. Word of mouth spreads fast within the film community, so you need to be diligent, smart, hard-working, proactive, and have a positive attitude as you take on your initial jobs, likely to be as runners or production assistants. If you are really fortunate, you might find an experienced crew member to take you on as a trainee. Or, perhaps, you can negotiate an internship (unpaid placement) with a company or, say, a cinematographer or editor who is looking to be a guide or mentor to someone up and coming with talent and passion. The key, here, is to be creative and resourceful in your pursuit. Moreover, you must do more than just send out unsolicited blanket mailings with your résumé, as they will likely end up in someone's over-burgeoning file folder or as part of a growing pile sitting on a shelf somewhere in the recesses of an office. Being proactive and getting into the groove of formulating relationships within the industry is the likeliest recipe for success in getting your foot inside the door. Once you're up and running, job-wise, some of you will want to carry on making your own films and developing storyline ideas. I would suggest working out a schedule-calendar to compartmentalise your time so that you allot specific days and hours to work on your own personal scripts and film projects. This includes time for you to investigate the various Arts Council funding agencies in your area that support emerging filmmakers, particularly those wanting to make short films or films that push and challenge filmic conventions and practices. Many successful filmmakers developed their filmic 'voices' and *personal signatures* by obtaining film arts grants from various funding institutions, such as the British Film Institute, the American Film Institute, the National Endowment for the Arts, European Culture Foundation, Canada Council for the Arts, and Australia Council for the Arts. Early filmmaking career examples who have received arts support include David Lynch, Atom Egoyan, Guy Maddin, Derek Jarman, and Danny Boyle. Here is an example of what's on offer from the BBC in support of the development of young filmmakers (there are many more to be found with a little digging online): www.bbc.co.uk/filmnetwork/filmmaking/guide/before-you-start/funding.

FOSTERING CREDITS ON FILM PRODUCTIONS

Securing that initial job to get you on the 'film ladder' should entail a three-pronged approach: (1) demonstrating capability via your personality, CV, and demo reel; (2) volunteering to take on any task and completing it to a high standard; and (3) developing your contacts to obtain an internship. Once you're in the door, you can develop further contacts on the production itself by being a go-getter (albeit a humble and polite one) to cultivate relationships with the potential to turn one of them into a possible mentorship. Anything is possible! The strongest chances for a break are generally with smaller companies and independent productions. Contact them and offer your services as a volunteer. As you achieve credits, your CV indicates gained experience, and you can approach larger companies and bigger-budgeted productions. One important element to have on your résumé is to indicate that you have a driver's license. This is almost imperative to have as your likely first few film jobs may entail some sort of delivery or 'running' of errands for the company at hand. You may even be designated to 'pick up' talent (that is, main actors) from their accommodation or, perhaps, as their designated driver if it is a larger studio production.

Other places to investigate include any regional film commissions, as many cities, counties, states, and provinces in the UK, Europe, the United States, Australia, and Canada have government-sponsored film development and funding agencies, generally found under 'Arts' categories. These commissions are a great source of contacts, particularly when large international or national studio productions choose a particular regional locale to film in. In these cases, the company production managers always liaise with the local film commission to secure local logistical, location, crew, and talent support. Having your résumé on file and maintaining communication with the appropriate contact person at the various film commissions (and checking their websites regularly) is a definite plus to potentially getting a job on one of these productions. Production managers (they do the main hiring of on-locale crew) will also distribute information and crew-hiring needs to these regional commissions so it is in your interest to be vigilant and proactive on this account.

THE INTERVIEW

Prior to any initial interviews, it will be to your advantage to rehearse what you could potentially be asked to respond to relative to the job at hand. Use a buddy or relative to ask you a series of questions, written out by you, related to available job position. The practice of expressing yourself is crucial so that you don't stumble or mumble through answers, and works to progress how you articulate yourself. As well, you must maintain good posture and ey contact with those you are speaking with – no slouching or unfocused attention. If you have a camera handy, record your session, then review with your questioner on a monitor to analyse how you are coming across. Then fine-tune any speech anomalies, body positioning, or gestures and go through it again. Pay attention to your facial expressions, how you are seated, how you gesture, your eyeline engagement, and your ability to relax and converse naturally. When you're comfortable and confident with your 'performance', you're ready to go! Another useful tip is to research the production (or post-production) company you are applying to in terms of what films they have produced or worked on previous (and, of course, you should watch their films so that you can complement or speak to them in the course of your interview). Be prepared to discuss films that you're passionate about and to demonstrate a good basic knowledge of the industry and what the crew or job role at hand requires. Always have a question prepared to ask the interviewer about the company, the project, or the shoot in general. This demonstrates a positive and proactive attitude on your part, and sits well with those who have to make the choice on who to bring on-board.

THANK YOU RESPONSES

To set you apart from the majority, a good habit to get into is the valuable practice of sending out thank you emails or letters by post. The use of personal notes to acknowledge when you have received industry guidance, recommendations, or information from those in the industry is an excellent way to cultivate relationships in the film industry. This practice serves positive notice to those who receive them in terms of you being remembered and appreciated for the time and effort you took to communicate. You will be more likely to be considered for jobs or given helpful information, references, or guidance as a result of sending out letters or notes of appreciation to your industry contacts. Additionally, you should send out notes directly after a job interview, after a job offer, and after any film production you're working on completes principal photography (send a thank you note to the producer and director, or editor if you're on the post-production team, as well as the production manager).

HAVE CONFIDENCE IN YOURSELF

Ensuring confidence and belief in yourself is a primary attribute you will need to personally develop and refine. Self-assurance must be conveyed when you are being interviewed for a job. You must reflect conviction and honesty during your interview, otherwise you will be on the receiving end of being passed over for the job. Confidence is not arrogance, as you don't want to 'over-sell' yourself, but you need to maintain an attitude or buoyance of why you are right for the job. It is not up to the person interviewing you to say why you are good for the job, as this is your role, and it must be approached in a professional, up-tempo, and sincere manner. For those seeking a more independent filmmaking route, be confident in your creativity and be bold and boundary-pushing when seeking funding or producing partners for your productions. If you are hell-bent on developing yourself as an independent filmmaker, work to obtain a peripheral job within the industry and then plan to spend your non-day-job hours writing/developing script ideas and putting the pieces of the puzzle together to get that next short film (or first feature) up and off the ground. There are a myriad of ways and means to partake in of our society's great tradition of cinematic storytelling; that is, which creative specialism do you have the passion to pursue? How will you develop your craft to create a personal signature as a filmmaker that extends, provokes and challenges the boundaries of image-making? How will you contribute to furthering cinematic language? Can you make a difference to the world around us with your passion for cinematic storytelling? It's up to you!

Glossary

Absolute film A film that is non-representational, using form and design to produce its effect, often described as 'visual music'.

Abstract film A film that presents recognisable images as 'poetic' rather than narrative.

Abstract form A manner of image organisation where the parts relate to each other through repetition and variation of directed movement, rhythm, colour, and shape. See **associational form**.

Academy ratio A term for standardised dimensions of the film frame for theatrical release as established by the Academy of Motion Pictures and Arts and Sciences (Los Angeles). In the original ratio, the frame was 1⅓ times as wide as it was high (1.33:1); later, the width was normalised at 1.85 times the height (1.85:1).

Actualities An old term for documentaries.

Adaptation (story) *Literal*: adaptation to film from previously published materials where the action and dialogue is translated cinematically in, generally, complete form. *Faithful*: adaptation to film from original literary material that encompasses the original's substantive qualities. *Loose*: adaptation to film drawing on only inconsequential remnants of the primary literary material.

Aerial perspective A cue for suggesting represented depth in the image by presenting objects in the distance less distinctly than those in the foreground.

Affective fallacy Used in literary criticism to suggest that it is an error to judge a work of art (including film) on the basis of its results, especially its emotional effect.

Affective theory Theory that deals with the effect of a work of art (including film) rather than its creation.

Aleatory technique An artistic technique that utilises chance conditions and probability. In aleatory film, images and sounds are not planned in advance.

Allegory A story in which every object, event, and person has an immediately discernible abstract or metaphorical meaning.

Ambient light The natural light surrounding the subject, generally considered as 'soft light' (not harsh or garish in intensity).

Ambient sound Sounds natural to any film scene's environment.

Anamorphic lens A particular camera lens designed for creating widescreen films using the regular Academy ratio frame size of 1.85:1. The camera lens takes in a wide field of view and squeezes it on to the frame, and a similar projector lens 'un-squeezes' it on to a wide theatre screen. Cinemascope and Panavision are models of anamorphic widescreen processes.

Angle of framing See **camera angle**.

Animation Any process whereby artificial movement is created by recording/ capturing a series of drawings or computer images one by one.

Artisanal production/artisan A production in contrast to the mass production of studio production. A filmmaker, producer, and crew devote their energy to making a single film.

Aspect ratio The relationship of the frame's width to its height. A term used to define the shape of the screen, presented in the form width:height. Virtually all pre-1950s films and all standard (non-widescreen) televisions have an aspect ratio of 4:3 (also described as 1.33:1 or Academy ratio); widescreen films have an aspect ratio of 1.85:1 and anamorphic widescreen films are usually 2.35:1. Widescreen televisions have an aspect ratio of 16:9 or 1.77:1 and are the approximate mid-point between the two standard widescreen ratios. Some filmmakers still use the original standard cinematic ratios, though rarely. A recent example is the 2012 Academy Award-winning film *The Artist* (Michel Hazanavicius, 2011), a tribute and a harking back to the silent era of cinema; it was shot in the 4:3 format (1.33:1) in black and white.

Associational form A type of organisation in which the film's parts are juxtaposed to suggest similarities, contrasts, concepts, emotions, and expressive qualities.

Asynchronous sound Sound that is not matched with image, as when dialogue is out of sync with lip movements.

Attraction Eisenstein's theory of film analyses the image as a series or collection of attractions, each in a dialectical relationship with the others. In this theory, attractions are thus basic elements of film form.

Auteur/auteurism French term for the author of a film, generally the director who has a specific approach and methodology; a personal style that demarcates the film through his or her mise en scène practice, as opposed to just a metteur en scene, whose direction is considered more like craftsmanship, in particular formulaic studio pictures. The term has a particular cultural and political background, beginning with the *politique des auteurs*, a manifesto written in the 1950s by French film directors and critics in *Cahiers du Cinéma*, which fêted the role and position of the director as the 'creative visionary' of a film, particularly in relation to the 'Hollywood studio system'. The argument is that films parallel paintings and books through their creation by a distinct artist, which discloses a personal vision encompassing style, theme, and the conditions of production.

Avant-garde Artists who are more intellectually or aesthetically advanced than are their contemporaries (if we assume that art is progressing). Avant-garde films are generally non-narrative in structure and push boundaries of storytelling, image, editing, and *mise en scène*; an experimentation with form and content outside traditional narrative cinema practices and 'norms'.

Axis of action In the continuity editing system, the imaginary line that passes from side to side through the main actors, defining the spatial relations of all the elements of the scene as being to the right or the left. It is also called the 180° line. When the camera crosses this axis at a cut, those spatial relations are reversed, thereby confusing the audience. It is one of the cardinal rules of continuity editing not to cross this axis during a sequence.

Backlighting Lighting cast on to the figures from the side opposite the camera. It creates a thin outline of light on a figure's or character's edge.

Back projection (also known as rear projection) Pre-filmed images utilised as backdrop to the action, generally to show moving exterior scenery through a travelling vehicle's windows, in particular the back window (in actuality, the vehicle and actors are static within the confines of studio). Back projection may be outdated and over the top by today's standards, but it was used into the early 1970s, as camera equipment was bulky and awkward. Today, the range and reduced size of equipment allow the camera into the car; see, in particular, Quentin Tarantino's *Death Proof* (2007). However, these techniques have been used by a range of recent directors, including Oliver Stone in *Natural Born Killers* (1994), where back projection is used as an aesthetic device to depict an 'unnatural' world that the young serial killers traverse.

Bird's-eye view A shot in which the camera photographs a scene from directly overhead.

Boom An extended pole where the microphone is affixed and is held over and above the action being filmed, allowing for flexibility and directional re-positioning as the characters move about the scene.

Brechtian Known as 'Brechtian alienation' or 'Brechtian distanciation'. Radical theatre playwright and acting teacher Bertolt Brecht (1898–1956) left Germany during the Nazi era but was summarily excommunicated from America during the McCarthy anti-Communist witch hunts. Brecht developed a series of stage techniques using song and the practice of speaking directly to an audience as a means to prevent an empathising with the characters or immersing themselves within the narrative and potentially losing sight of the dramatic political substance. Brecht's notions were embraced by directors, notably French New Wave filmmakers such as Jean-Luc Godard, who turned cinematic convention and narrative inside-out. Other examples include films that adopt the use of both black and white and colour scenes or the interspersing of surreal scenes within a traditional narrative. A Brechtian sensibility can be said to be operating at the level of the 'reflexive' documentary; examples include Michael Moore and Nick Broomfield who, arguably, push the boundaries of 'objective truth' by calling attention to, and overtly parading, documentary practice.

Bridging shot A shot used to cover passing time or setting or other discontinuity (for example, hands of a clock, calendar pages flipping, swirling newspaper headlines, train wheels, changes of season, book pages turning, and sand in an hourglass.

Cahiers du Cinéma A seminal French film journal founded by Andre Bazin, Lo Duca, and Jacques Doniol-Valcroze in 1951. Godard, Truffaut, Chabrol, Rohmer, and Rivette, among others, also wrote film criticism for the magazine and themselves became filmmakers. This time period (the 1950s), and its collection of French directors, came to be known as the *Nouvelle Vague* (New Wave); as a collective, they developed the notion of the auteur policy.

Camera angle The position of the frame relative to the depicted subject matter. A high angle is when camera is above facing downward, and low angle points upward from closer to the ground.

Camera movement On-screen notion that the framing is shifting in terms of the filmed scene; achieved by camera being moved (track/dolly), zooming, or visual effects.

Caméra-stylo 'Camera-pen', a catch-phrase coined by French film scholar and director Alexandre Astruc, equating the flexibility and scale of cinema to traditional arts (for example, the essay and novel).

Canted framing A 'slanted' view where the framed image is not uniformly horizontal, with one frame side lower, which depicts scene elements as angled.

Cell animation Hand-drawn animation done as a series of single drawings; these are individually filmed to give the representation of a moving object, character, and/or setting.

CGI/computer-generated imagery Realistic computer animation and 3D graphics, which blends in seamlessly with live action footage; a simulated environment that 'looks and feels' genuine and convincing. See, for example, Terrence Mallick's *Tree of Life* (2011) and Martin Scorsese's *Hugo* (2011).

Characters (on screen) *Dynamic*: Experiences of characters who transform through the progression of the narrative. In particular, transformations of the internal life of the character, not in their external environment. As such, shifts in awareness or perception of personal ethics, principals, or beliefs. *Flat*: Banal or unsurprising characters; unoriginal in personal behaviour or sophistication in terms of psychological or emotional gravity. *Round*: Figures who are challenging and who don't fit particular types or classifications; these characters project a certain measure of equivocality and multifariousness. *Static*: Unchanging characters that do not evolve or have any epiphany or internal realisations. *Stock*: Secondary figures; personified by clichéd occupations, with typical traits who reproduce expected acts and deeds on screen.

Cheat cut When employing continuity editing structure, an edit that portrays uninterrupted shot-to-shot time but disconnects object and character placement within the scene or frame.

Cinéaste A French term co-opted by the film industry; an aficionado of cinema or someone involved in cinematic practice.

Cinéma-vérité A cinema that utilises lightweight and mobile equipment, two-person crews (camera and sound), and free-form interview techniques. It is also now often used loosely to refer to any kind of documentary technique; a film that shows ordinary people in actual activities without being controlled by a director. See **direct cinema**.

Climax See **story structure**.

Closed (film) form Stylised frame compositions, meticulously matched, that create an alluring and dynamic aesthetic; utilised to imply an autonomous and self-reliant world.

Closure The degree to which the ending of a narrative film reveals the effects of all the causal events and resolves all lines of action.

Colour palette The selection of particular colours (colour scheme) by the director to subconsciously convey a range of story and character facets and traits to an audience.

Continuity editing A methodology of image cutting that preserves cinematic narrative action in a sustained, logical, and 'real-time' way; image-linking to harmonise time, character/object placement, and screen movement to create spatial and temporal associations from one shot to another.

Contrast The difference between the darkest and lightest areas within the cinematographic frame, as determined and designed by the Director of Photography (DP).

Crane shot When the camera rises or drops, forcing the framing perspective to shift/change, by means of a mechanical jib-arm that can be raised or lowered by the camera team (referred to as a 'grip').

Cross-cutting Synchronised cutting of two or more lines of scene action transpiring at various locations.

Cut-in An abrupt, immediate change from close framing to a distant vista or vice versa; an unexpected frame modification.

Decoupage French term for the organisation and composition of a film's design through its 'seamless' assemblage of shots.

Deep focus Cinematographic term for all of a frame's elements being in complete focus, from objects in the foreframe, through to the middle, and extending to the far background. The intensity of light sources and particular lens usage determines the focal length of which everything depicted within the scene stays sharp. Historically, Orson Welles's *Citizen Kane* (1941) is the seminal film that has been singled out as a prime example of deep-focus cinematography.

Deep space An organisation of *mise en scène* that creates a vast expanse from the nearest camera plane to the one most distant; here, all or some of the elemental planes can be in focus.

Dénouement See **story structure**.

Depth of field The extent of the closest and most distant planes of the camera lens where all objects will be in clear focus (for example, a depth of field from 6 to 20 feet means those framed elements less than 6 feet in distance from the lens and those past 20 feet will be not be in focus and will appear 'soft').

Dialectics A thought system that centres on contradictions between conflicting views. Cinematically, it connects to Eisenstein's film editing notion of image juxtaposition, where two distinct elements 'collide' to form a new or alternate meaning, a meaning that doesn't exist in the original two images. See **montage**.

Dialogue overlap When editorially constructing a scene or sequence, positioning the cut so that a short portion of dialogue or sound emanating from shot 1 can be heard underneath shot 2, whether from another character or *mise en scène* element.

Diegesis In a narrative film, the 'world' of the film's story, the prior events, actions, and spaces implicit off-screen. This moving-image 'world' text is denoted not only by what is literally seen or of sounds heard and produced from the direct on-screen action and/or objects (for example, screeching car tyres, car crash), but also by off-screen sounds emanating from the 'world' being shown (for example, clock tower, ocean surf). Non-diegetic sound is generally sound effects or music not representative in the world of the film; they are inserted on the audio track to signify the state of mind of a particular character or to create a reaction from an audience. See **diegetic sound** and **non-diegetic sound**.

Diegetic sound Any voice, musical passage, or sound effect presented as originating from a source within the film's world. See **non-diegetic sound**.

Direct cinema Prominent documentary form that started in the 1960s. Similar to *cinéma-vérité*, but does not use narration nor include the filmmaker on-screen or as a presence; this style of documentary allows the characters and action to 'directly' unfold. Classic examples include Frederick Wiseman's *Titicut Follies* (1967) and the Maysles brothers' *Salesman* (1968).

Direct sound Background, voice, and music recorded from original filming location; antithesis of post-synchronisation, where sound is added during the editing phase.

Discontinuity editing In opposition and in direct conflict with 'acceptable' continuity editing practices (for example, disjointed spatial and temporal links, breach of the axis of action, sound disparity). See **elliptical editing**, **intellectual montage**, and **non-diegetic insert**.

Dissolve Transition between two shots where one image fades out while the next image fades in; for an instant, the two images overlap in **superimposition**.

Distance of framing Perceived distance of the frame from the *mise en scène* elements. Also termed 'camera distance' and 'shot scale'. **Close-up** and **medium long shot** are examples of terms referring to distance of framing.

Dolly Camera platform with interchangeable wheels for use on a set of rails or directly on the ground, to create a tracking or moving shot.

Dominant The frame area within the scene that draws the eye of the audience to convey particular story or character information.

Double exposure An old in-camera film technique whereby one action is recorded then the film is re-wound and another separate action is captured or superimposed over the original. Nowadays, this is easily accomplished during digital post-production; however, if you are shooting with 16 mm Arri or Bolex cameras, it is accomplished through the rewind mechanism found on the camera body. This technique is utilised, today, more by experimental film artists.

8 mm These film stocks have been re-issued and are available. *Standard (Regular) 8*: 16 mm film stock that is wound on a 25-foot spool; only half the film emulsion is exposed to light through the aperture, then once the spool is finished, it is 'turned over' and re-threaded to expose the other half of the film; the 16 mm exposed footage is then slit down the middle after it is processed at the lab and one end is spliced onto the other, forming a continuous 50-foot (three minutes) worth of running time. Standard 8 mm cameras are arguably superior to the later-developed Super 8 cameras, as they have a built-in film pressure plate that gives better imaging. *Super 8*: 8 mm film cartridge system produced by Kodak starting in 1965; easy one-touch loading that was developed for the domestic market and mass pro-duced. The image area is also larger, as the gate was widened to allow a greater use of the film stock area as only one side had to have the sprocket holes (as on the standard 8 mm system, both sides of the stock had to have sprocket holes to accommodate the 'turning-over' of the stock to expose the other half of the film). Two types of film stock are available for 8 mm: **negative stock** and **reversal stock**.

Ellipsis Diminishing of narrative time achieved by excluding periods of story time.

Elliptical editing Shot transitions that exclude elements of an action, producing an ellipsis in narrative temporality.

Establishing shot A shot that depicts the spatial relations among the main characters, objects, and setting in a scene; generally framed encompassing a distant or long-ranging perspective.

Exploitation film Designed to serve a particular need or desire of the audience (for example, blaxploitation, sexploitation, transgressive).

Exposition See **story structure**.

Exposure The measurement indicating the quantity or intensity of light that hits the film emulsion; in the case of digital capture, the amount of light striking the camera's CCD (charge-coupled device). An image that is 'over-exposed' represents an over-bright light, washed out dreamy quality, while an image that is 'under-exposed' creates a shot that is dark, bleak, and ominous.

Expressionism/expressionist Use of the 'distortive' and personalised imagination of a filmmaker's vision. See **German expressionism** and **formalism**. The name given to a particularly stylised form of cinema, in which the elements of shooting and editing are mobilised primarily to evoke powerful feeling in an audience. Originating in Germany in the 1920s – the first major example being *The Cabinet of Dr Caligari* (Robert Wiene, 1920) – the trademarks are high contrast of light and dark (and later, colour), extreme camera angles and shot composition, and powerful music. The melodrama in the 1940s and 1950s, right up to contemporary horror films and even some soap operas, all are indebted to expressionism.

External diegetic sound Sound represented as coming from a physical source within the story space and that we assume characters in the scene also hear. See **internal diegetic sound**.

Extreme close-up Framing in which the scale of the object is very large; generally, a small object or a part of the body; also known as a detail shot.

Extreme long shot A framing in which the scale of the object shown is very small; a panoramic view of an exterior location photographed from a considerable distance, often as far as a quarter of a mile away.

Eyeline match A cut obeying the axis of action principle, in which the first shot shows a person looking off in one direction and the following shot shows a nearby space containing what he or she sees. If the person looks left, the following shot should imply that the looker is off-screen right.

Fade *Fade-in*: a dark screen that gradually brightens as a shot appears. *Fade-out*: a shot gradually darkens as the screen goes black (or brightens to pure white or to a colour).

Fast motion The film is shot at less than 24 frames per second so that when it is projected at normal speed, action appears to move much faster. (A slow motion is achieved when film is shot faster than 24 frames and projected at normal speed.) Also called accelerated motion.

Fill light Lighting from a source less bright than the key light, used to soften deep shadows and illuminate areas not covered by key light. Also called filler light. See **three-point lighting**.

Film noir French for 'dark film', a term applied by French critics to a type of American film, usually in the detective or thriller genres, with low-key lighting and a sombre – often fatalistic – mood, especially common in the late 1940s and early 1950s. Term originally applied (after the French term for a gothic novel, *roman noir*) to a series of notably dark and cynical Hollywood films mostly made during the 1940s and 1950s. Arguments continue as to whether *film noir* constitutes a genre or a style, but the established features of the form include a crime or underworld milieu; a troubled hero, often haunted or tormented by mistakes in his past; a bleak urban setting, typically at night; and a sense of the inevitability of fate. *Femmes fatales* also feature heavily. Stylistically, *films noirs* tend to be characterised by high-contrast black and white photography, with heavy use of shadows to expressionist effect and the employment of unusual or distorted camera angles to emphasise the psychological disturbance of their characters. Although *film noir* is primarily an American form, its influence can be found in filmmaking as diverse as the French New Wave and Japanese yakuza movies.

Film stock The strip of material upon which a series of still photographs is registered; it consists of a clear base coated on one side with light-sensitive emulsion.

Filter Translucent glass or gelatine placed in front of camera or printer lens to alter the quality (colour) or quantity of light striking the film in aperture; distortion of light quality.

Flashback Alteration of story order in which the plot moves back in time to show events that have taken place earlier than the one already shown.

Flash cutting Editing the film into shots of very brief duration that succeed each other rapidly.

Flash-forward Alteration of story order in which the plot moves forward to future events, then returns to the present.

Flash frame A shot of only a few frames' duration, which can just barely perceived by the audience.

Focal length Distance from the centre of the lens to the point at which the light rays meet in sharp focus. The focal length determines the perspective relations of the space represented on the flat screen.

Focus The degree to which light rays coming from the same part of an object through different parts of the lens re-converge at the same point on the film frame, creating sharp outlines and distinct textures.

Focus in, out A punctuation device in which the image gradually comes into focus or goes out of the focus.

Foils (narrative) Characters whose physicality, conduct, manner, traits, thoughts, attitude, and way of life contrast each other and function to delineate and demarcate their personas.

Foley track/Foley artist The construction or approximation of sound effects using sources other than those represented on screen. Examples would include a knife piercing a watermelon to approximate a stabbing sound, or the use of coconut shells to approximate the sound of horses' hooves. The Foley artist is the person responsible for sourcing and making these sounds.

Following shot A shot with framing that shifts to keep a moving character on-screen (that is, a shot that follows a moving character).

Forelengthening Linear distortion caused by a wide-angle lens; the perception of depth is exaggerated.

Foreshortening Distortion caused by a telephoto lens; the illusion of depth is compressed.

Form The general system of relationships among the parts of a film. In *closed* form, the frame drastically limits the space of the scene and suggests that the limits of the frame are the limits of artistic reality. In *open* form, *mise en scène* and design elements of the frame conspire to make the audience aware of the continuous space beyond the limits of the frame, suggesting that reality continues outside the frame.

Formalism A theoretical term that considers the notion of 'meaning' exists primarily in the form or language of discourse rather than in the content or subject; developed in 1920s by the Soviet movement of that period.

Formative theory Theory that deals with form rather than function or subject.

Frame That singular element, either on film or digital capture, depicting a single image. When a series of frames are projected on to a screen in rapid succession (normally 24 frames per second for film), an illusion of movement is created; the shape and size of the image on the screen when it is projected at the cinema or screened on a monitor; the compositional unit for film design.

Framing The use of edges of the film to select and compose what will be visible on-screen.

Free Cinema Term coined by British directory Lindsay Anderson, taken from a poem by Dylan Thomas, to name a short season of films shown at the National Film Theatre in May 1956; it represented an informal movement of (mostly) documentary filmmakers. The three films in the first Free Cinema season were Anderson's *O Dreamland*, Lorenza Mazzetti's *Together*, and Tony Richardson and Karel Reisz's *Momma Don't Allow*. The filmmakers accompanied their productions with a 'manifesto', which suggested that they constituted a coherent movement, although the films had been made independently over a period of four years. The Free Cinema 'style' is characterised by a low-budget aesthetic, using cheap, hand-held 16 mm cameras and non-sync sound, usually without narration, and a focus on ordinary, often working-class subjects, in an attempt to convey what Anderson called the 'poetry of everyday life'. The filmmakers rejected the documentary orthodoxy associated with John Grierson and the British documentary movement of the 1930s and 1940s. The founders ended up gravitating to feature filmmaking and developed into groundbreakers in the 'British New Wave' of the late 1950s and early 1960s.

Freeze-frame A freeze shot, which is achieved by printing a single frame many times in succession to give the illusion of a still photograph when projected.

Frequency In a narrative film, the aspect of temporal manipulation that involves the number of times any story event is shown in the plot.

Frontal lighting Lighting directed into the scene from a position near the camera.

Frontal projection Method of combining images. Live action is filmed against a highly reflective screen on which an image from a slide or movie projector is projected by means of mirrors along the axis of the taking lens so that there are no visible shadows cast by the actors. When the screen is exceptionally reflective and the live actors are well lit, no image from the projector should be visible on the actors or props in front of the screen.

Full shot A shot of a subject that includes the entire body and not much else.

Function The role or effect of any element within the film's form.

Futurism An early twentieth-century movement and manifesto, emanating from Italy, that sought to use reality directly as analogy in filmmaking practice; to develop and promote cinema as an 'expressive' medium where 'the universe will be our vocabulary', and dramatising 'states of mind'.

Gauge The width of the film strip, measured in millimetres. 35 mm is the most commonly used film stock for theatrical film production by the major studios. Also used, but rarer due to its prohibitive cost, is 65 mm (70 mm) for 'cinemascope' releases (particularly favoured on large-budgeted Hollywood studio productions in the 1950s and 1960s); today, '70 mil' is utilised for **IMAX** productions. 16 mm (and Super 16 mm) stock has been historically used by low-budget filmmakers (and for television broadcast dramas); here, the negative can be 'blown up' to 35 mm for theatrical release (for example, *El Mariachi*, Robert Rodriguez, 1992; *Clerks*, Kevin Smith, 1994; *Pi*, Darren Aranofsky, 1998). 8 mm and Super-8 mm are 'home-movie' formats that were developed for the domestic market and amateur cinema-makers (currently, this gauge is now claimed for use by experimental film artists or for filmmakers seeking a particular aesthetic, see **8 mm**).

Generation When shooting on film, the stock in the camera when the shot is taken is 'first generation'. A print of this negative will be 'second generation'. An inter-negative made from this positive will be 'third generation', and so on. Each generation marks a progressive deterioration in the quality of the image so that by the time it reaches the cinema, it is a number of processes removed from the in-camera original.

Generative theory A theory that deals with the phenomenon of the production of a film rather than the consumption of it. See **affective theory**.

Genre/genre theory Various 'types' of films that audiences and directors recognise via familiar narrative conventions. Common genres are drama, comedy, horror, musical, gangster, and western films. A way of categorising different types of moving image texts. Genre is studied via reference to narratives, iconography, themes, and characters that crop up relatively predictably within individual examples of a particular genre. Additionally, it is crucial to consider the role of the spectator when study-ing genre, as audiences enjoy both the repetition of what is familiar in any example of a genre; however, there is also an expectation to witness fresh and original approaches to genre filmmaking practices.

German expressionism A style of film developed in Germany in the 1920s, characterised by dramatic lighting, distorted sets, and symbolic action and character.

Graphic match Two successive shots joined so as to create a strong similarity of compositional elements (for example, shape, colour, character position, horizon).

Hard-key lighting Lighting that creates comparatively little contrast between the light and dark areas of the shot; shadows are relatively transparent and brightened by fill light.

Hard lighting Lighting that creates sharp-edged shadows.

Height of framing The height of the camera above the ground, regardless of camera angle.

High-angle shot Camera shot positioned over eye level and looking or pointing downward; this framing creates the image perspective of reducing the subject or object's significance or value within the scene.

High-contrast lighting Dynamic use of lighting to create stylised use of shadow, darkness, and channels of light, generally in the form of particular patterns (for example, in *film noir*, the use of window shades to create shafts of light and dark).

Iconography Refers to single visual elements of a shot that resonate beyond their literal meaning or representation. Thus, a particular kind of motorcycle in films such as *Easy Rider* (Dennis Hopper, 1969) has come to signify a whole counter-cultural movement. Iconography refers to a whole system of icons with the same range of reference, also referred to as a 'semantic field'. For example, John Ford's western films feature iconography that includes cowboy hats, boots, guns, landscape (desert, buttes, big sky), and wagon horses. These re-occurring material elements have come to be culturally linked to mid-nineteenth-century American western frontierism.

Ideology A personal system of beliefs, values, or ideas shared by like-minded individuals or a group; particular filmmakers may tend to promote their life views and opinions through dramatic narrative or documentary form.

IMAX A large-format film camera that utilises 65 mm (70 mm) film negative to capture an image *horizontally* (as opposed to traditional vertical capture) resulting in film projection that is super-wide in scope and scale. Images have far greater sharpness and definition than can be shown in conventional cinemas; the film is usually projected on a gigantic screen several storeys high. The format was invented in 1969, but only really took off in the 1990s. Partly because the format lends itself better to spectacular location shots than conventional dramatic editing, and partly because many IMAX cinemas can be found in or alongside museums, the vast majority of IMAX films are documentaries or 3D presentations.

Intellectual montage The juxtaposition of a series of images to create an abstract idea not present in any image. See **montage**.

Internal diegetic sound Sound represented as coming from the mind of a character within the story space. Although we and the character can hear it, we assume that the other characters cannot. See **external diegetic sound**.

Interpretation The viewer's activity of analysing the implicit and symptomatic meanings suggested in a film.

Iris A round, moving mask that contracts to close down to end an scene (*iris-out*) or emphasize a detail, or opens to begin a scene (*iris-in*), or to reveal more space around a detail.

Irony The collocation of visual opposites as a cinematic method to create or under-score a particular story or character point; the use of irony is utilised to contribute to the narrative's thematic.

Jump cut An *elliptical* cut that appears to be an interruption of a single shot. It occurs within a scene, rather than between scenes, to condense the shot. Either the figures seem to change instantly against a constant background, or the background changes instantly while the figures remain constant.

Key light In the three-point lighting system, the brightest light coming into the scene. See also **backlighting** and **fill light**.

Language In semiotics, cinema is considered a language because it is a means of communication, but it is not necessarily a language system because it does not follow the rules of written or spoken language.

Leitmotif A recurring notion or idiom by a character that develops into a facet or attribute that demarcates that particular individual.

Linearity In a narrative, the clear motivation of a series of causes and affects that progress without significant digressions, delays, or irrelevant actions.

Long shot A framing in which the scale of the object shown is small; a standing human figure would appear nearly the height of the screen.

Long take A shot that continues for an unusually lengthy time before the transition to the next shot.

Loose framing A wide and free-range *mise en scène* that encompasses a considerable area of filmic space where the characters can move about with minimal limitation.

Low-angle shot The camera positioned below eye level that 'looks up' at a particular character or object; this framing (often employing a wide-angle lens) embellishes or amplifies the relevance or dominance of what or who is being filmed.

Low-key lighting Lighting that creates strong contrast between light and dark areas of the shot, with deep shadows and little fill light.

Mask An opaque screen placed in the camera that blocks off selected elements of the frame and alters the shape of the captured image, leaving part of the frame a solid colour. As seen on the screen, most masks are black, although they could be white or coloured. This effect is also more commonly utilised at the post-production stage through the use of digitally created masks.

Match cut A cut in which two shots joined are linked by visual, aural, or metaphorical parallelism. For example, at the beginning of Stanley Kubrick's *2001: A Space Odyssey* (1968) an ape (the 'dawn of man') tosses an animal bone up into the air (in slow motion), then when the bone begins to fall it match cuts to a falling space ship 2,000 years later.

Materialist cinema A contemporary movement, mainly in avant-garde cinema, that celebrates the physical fact of film, camera, light, projector, and in which the materials of art are its main subject matter. Examples include the cinema of Jean-Luc Godard and Roberto Rossellini, who combine a strong conception of political change as dialectically materialistic (that is, as rooted in the basic conflict of concrete economic realities).

Matte shot A type of process shot in which different areas of the image (usually actors and setting) are photographed separately and combined in the film lab to create a combined, seamless image.

McGuffin Alfred Hitchcock's term for the device or plot element that catches the viewer's attention or propels the reasoning of the plot, but often turns out to be insignificant or is to be ignored after it has served its purpose. Examples in Hitchcock's work include the mistaken identity of Cary Grant's character at the start of *North by Northwest* (1959) and the Janet Leigh 'stolen money' subplot of *Psycho* (1960).

Meaning (in film narrative) *Referential*: allusion to particular pieces of shared prior knowledge outside the film that the audience is expected to recognise. *Explicit*: meaning expressed overtly, usually in language and generally at the film's beginning or end. *Implicit*: meaning left inferred or implied, for the viewer to discover upon analysis or reflection. *Symptomatic*: meaning that the film divulges, often 'against its will', by virtue of its historical or social context.

Medium close-up A framing in which the scale of the object shown is fairly large; a human figure seen from the chest up fills most of the screen.

Medium long shot A framing at a distance that makes an object about four or five feet high appear to fill most of the screen vertically. See **Plan Americain**, the special term for a medium long shot depicting human figures.

Medium shot A framing in which the scale of the object is of moderate size; a human figure seen from the waist up would fill most of the screen.

Melodrama Initially just meant drama with music, in particular a form of nineteenth-century drama focussing on physical action/theatricality/plot rather than character; specifically, a type of nineteenth-century drama centring on unsophisticated struggles or clashes among protagonists and antagonists. A type of drama portraying an impractical, over-the-top style, generally inclusive of amplified emotion; the narrative tends to avoid realism and has been critiqued as such.

Method acting A form of dramatic performance developed in the 1930s by the Russian theatre director Konstantin Stanislavsky. His techniques were taught and took hold in America during the 1940s, particularly in New York under Lee Strasberg who developed the notion and moniker of 'the method' (utilising emotional 'recall'), which has been adopted by Western actors in both theatre and cinema through to today. 'Method' draws on the performers' close personal identification with the scripted character by associating their own experiences and feelings to those of the character. Variations of 'the method' were developed by other teachers, including Stella Adler (who taught Marlon Brando and Robert De Niro) and Sanford Meisner (the 'Meisner technique'), who broke away from Strasberg and developed acting concepts based on precise behaviour expression that emanated from the performer's actual responses to the other characters, the environment, and the situations at hand.

Microcosm (in film) An autonomous and sequestered setting, place, or individual character action that is representative of the human condition, state of mind, or conduct on a global or stereotypical scale.

Mimesis/mime Greek for 'imitation', a term important in the realist school. Although mime is a theatrical tradition that goes back centuries, if not millennia, in a specifically film and television context the term refers to the practice of pretending to be producing a sound that is, in fact, being generated elsewhere. Good examples of miming can be seen in most music videos, where bands pretend to be performing what are in fact pre-recorded versions of their music.

Minimal cinema A form of extreme, simplified realism best exemplified by the films of Carl Dreyer, Robert Bresson, and early Andy Warhol; minimal dependence on the technical capacity of the medium.

Mise en scène All the elements (the composition of character position, props, setting, lighting, sound, colour) situated within the camera frame to be photographically captured either on location or on set. Differentiated from montage, which is composed during the edit stage. Originally a French theatre term that literally signifies 'what is placed in the scene'.

Mise en shot The design of an entire shot, in time as well as space.

Mixing Multiple compilations of individual sound elements (or tracks) interwoven to comprise a single film soundtrack (with output in various forms – mono, stereo, surround).

Mobile frame The effect on the screen of moving camera, a zoom lens, or special effects shifting the frame in relation to the scene being filmed.

Modality A term coined to unpack the notion of 'realism'. Modality refers to how close to reality the producer intends a particular text to be. For example, the makers of *Shrek* (Andrew Adamson and Vicky Jenson, 2001) obviously intended their animation to be some distance from realistic – to have 'low modality'. In contrast, for example, observational documentaries promote a particular account of reality (that is, 'high modality'). Each text will include clues as to how high or low the modality is. For example, 'modality markers' may comprise whether shots are extended or still, if the soundtrack includes music, or if the editing embraces a certain style.

Monochromatic colour design Colour design that emphasises a narrow set of shades of a single colour.

Montage A synonym for *editing*; an approach to editing developed by the Soviet filmmakers of the 1920s; it emphasises dynamic, often discontinuous, relationships between shots and the juxtaposition of images to manifest ideas not inherently existent within each of the shots. Also termed the *montage of attraction*; a stylised method of cutting images together that conveys of a prodigious amount of information within short duration.

Montage sequence A segment of film that summarises a topic or compresses a passage of time into a brief symbolic or typical image. Frequently, dissolves, fades, superimpositions, and wipes are used to link the images in a montage sequence.

Motif A recurrent thematic element in a film that is repeated in a significant way; the repetition of particular notions, imagery, designs that connect with the overall thematic.

Motivation The justification given in film for the presence of an element.

Multiple exposure A number of images printed over each other.

Multiple image A number of images printed beside each other within the same frame, often showing different camera angles of same action, or separate actions. Also termed split-screen.

Mumblecore A term coined in the early 2000s to represent a film movement that is pared-down in its approach to production and infused with an intensified naturalism. These films are economically produced with simplicity of aesthetic and rudimentary vernacular. The narratives explore issues of sexuality and interpersonal relationships among the twenty-somethings and are filmed (generally) in a handheld documentary-type style, which has been referred to as 'neo neo-realism'.

Narration The process through that the plot conveys or withholds story information. It can be more or less restricted to character knowledge and more or less deep in presenting characters' mental perceptions and thoughts.

Narrative film A film that tells a story, as opposed to a **poetic film**.

Narrative form A type of filmic organisation in which the parts relate to each other through a series of causally related events taking place in a specific time and space.

Naturalism A theory of literature and film that supposes a scientific determinism such that the actions of character are predetermined by biological, sociological, economic, or psychological laws. Not to be confused with **realism**.

Negative space The use of void or unoccupied space within the *mise en scène*; this uninhabited space is utilised as counterpoint to specified or particular components within the shot.

Negative stock A film stock from which the resultant images are reversed from the original image. This type of stock cannot be projected, and requires a positive (or reversal) print created from the original negative or else can be telecined (transferred to a digital format).

Neo-realism A style of filmmaking developed by Italian directors (for example, Vittorio De Sica, Roberto Rossellini, and Luchino Visconti), who, in the 1940s, made films employing non-professional actors, location shooting, handheld camera work, and political ideology; a system of film production with a 'documentary' feel and aesthetic, not within the confines of a studio.

New Wave A group of French filmmakers (Godard, Truffaut, Chabrol, Rohmer, Rivette) who began as critics on *Cahiers du Cinéma* in the 1950s and who were influenced by Andre Bazin. Also termed *Nouvelle Vague*. Originally coined in the

1950s to label a collection of French critics-turned-film directors, such as François Truffaut and Jean-Luc Godard. During this time, British filmmakers, in particular Lindsay Anderson, Karel Reisz, and Tony Richardson, followed in the *Nouvelle Vague* wake and the British New Wave emerged. These filmmakers worked against the grain of mainstream narrative techniques to push cinematic storytelling practices through experimentation with content and technical innovation.

Nickelodeon The earliest film cinemas, the term stemming from the admission price of the American monetary coinage of 'five cents' or 'nickel'.

Non-diegetic insert A shot or series of shots cut into a sequence, showing objects represented as being outside the space of the narrative.

Non-diegetic sound Sound represented as coming from outside the space of the narrative, such as mood music or a narrator's commentary.

Non-simultaneous sound Diegetic sound that comes either earlier or later than the accompanying image of the source.

Oblique angle A skewed camera position where the shot image appears tilted or slanted on screen.

Off-screen sound Simultaneous sound from a source assumed to be in the space of the scene but in an area outside what is visible on-screen.

Off-screen space The six areas blocked from being visible on the screen but still part of the space of the scene: to four sides of the frame, behind the set, and the behind the camera.

180° rule The continuity approach to editing that dictates that the camera should stay on one side of the action to ensure consistent spatial relations between objects to the right and left of the frame. Also called the **axis of action**.

One-reeler A film of 10 to 12 minutes in duration.

Open form A casual or relaxed mode of framing the action, configuration, or composition of elements within the *mise en scène* generally induced by modern handheld camera technique that tends to haphazardly 'mis-frame' characters or the action at hand.

Order In a narrative film, temporal manipulation of the sequence in which the chronological events of the story are arranged in the plot.

Overlap A cue for suggesting depth in the film image by placing closer objects partly in front of more distant ones.

Overlapping editing Cuts that repeat part or all of an action, thus expanding its viewing time and plot duration.

Pan Camera movement from left to right, or vice versa, positioned on a tripod. On the screen, it produces a mobile framing that scans the space horizontally; not to be confused with a **tracking shot** or **dolly** shot.

Pantheon The system of rating directors in hierarchical categories common to the auteur policy; pantheon directors are the highest rated.

Period piece Screenplay/film set within a particular historical era.

Persona From the Latin for 'mask'; a character in a literary, cinematic, or dramatic work. More precisely, the psychological image of the character that is created, especially in relation to the other levels of reality.

Pixellation A form of single-frame animation in which three-dimensional objects, often people, are made to move in staccato bursts through the use of stop-action cinematography, thereby breaking the illusion of the continuous movement.

Plan Americain French term to indicate framing in which the scale of the object shown is fairly small; the human figure seen from the shins to the head would fill most of the screen; so named by the French critics who argue that it is the most utilised framing device in American films. Also referred to as a **medium long shot**, particularly when human figures are not shown.

Plan-sequence French term for a scene handled in a single shot, usually a long take; often referring to complex shot including complicated camera movements and actions. Also called sequence shot.

Plot In a narrative film, all the events that are directly presented in the film, including their causal relations, chronological order, duration, frequency, and spatial locations; as opposed to story, which is the viewer's imaginary construction of all the events in the narrative.

Poetic film Non-narrative film, often experimental. Jonas Mekas's phrase to distinguish new American cinema from commercial, narrative film.

Point-of-view (POV) shot A shot taken with the camera placed approximately where the character's eyes would be, representing what the character sees; usually cut in before or after a shot of the character looking.

Portmanteau film A compendium of several distinct stories, generally comprised of a connecting narrative throughout the film. For example, see the classic British productions *Dead of Night* (Alberto Cavalcanti, Charles Crichton, Basil Dearden, and Robert Hamer, 1945) and *Quartet* (Ralph Smart, Harold French, Arthur Crabtree, and Ken Annakin, 1948). A more recent example is *The Acid House* (Paul McGuigan, 1998), based on three short stories by Irvine Welsh (author of *Trainspotting*).

Post-synchronisation Process of adding sound to images after they have been shot and assembled; includes dubbing of voices and inserting diegetic music or sound effects. It is the opposite of **direct sound**.

Process shot Any shot involving re-photography to combine two or more images into one, or to create special effects. Also called a **composite shot**.

Proxemic patterns The ostensible relationship of distance between the subject/object within the *mise en scène* and the camera; the relation of space and spaces of the characters within the frame. Good examples of proxemic patterns in film include *Last Year at Marienbad* (Alain Renais, 1961 – see p. 14) and Michel Antonioni's *L'avventura* (1960) and *The Passsenger* (1975).

Pull-back shot A tracking shot or zoom that moves back from the subject to reveal the context of the scene.

Pushover A type of wipe in which the succeeding image appears to push the preceding one off the screen.

Rack focus Shifts the area of sharp focus from one plane to another during a shot, thereby directing the attention of the viewer forcibly from one subject to another.

Rate In shooting, the number of frames exposed per second; in projection, the number of frames thrown on the screen per second. If the two are same, the speed of action appears normal, while a disparity will create slow or fast motion. The standard rate in sound cinema is 24 frames per second for both shooting and projection (for silent film, it used to be between 16 and 18 frames per second.)

Reaction shot A shot that cuts away from the main scene or speaker in order to show a character's reaction to it.

Realism In film, attitude opposed to *expressionism* that emphasises the subject as opposed to the director's view of the subject; usually concerns topics of a socially conscious nature, and uses a minimal amount of technique.

Red Cinematography A high resolution camera whose sensor captures images in excess of 4K. 'Red' cameras afford the use of master prime lenses and have extended dynamic colour range and latitude in low-light conditions. They are the digital replacement/complement to 35 mm film.

Re-establishing shot A return to a view of an entire space after a series of closer shots following the **establishing shot**.

Reframing Short panning or tilting movements to adjust for the figures' movements, keeping them on-screen or centred.

Reversal stock A film stock from which the resultant images are positive when viewed; viewed through a projector or when telecined (to a digital format ready for editing).

Rhetorical form A type of filmic organisation in which the parts create and support an argument.

Rhythm The perceived rate and regularity of sounds, series of shots, and movements within the shots. Rhythmic factors include beat (or pulse), accent (or stress), and tempo (or pace).

Roll The rotation of camera around the axis that runs from the lens to the subject as a means to disorientate the audience in relation to the character's point of view; accomplished by tracking camera movement by dolly or Steadicam.

Rotoscope A machine that projects live-action motion picture film frames one by one on to a drawing pad so that an animator can trace the figures in each frame. The aim is to achieve more realistic movement in an animated cartoon.

Rushes Prints of takes that are made immediately after a day's shoot so that they can be examined before the next day's shooting begins.

Scene A segment in a narrative film that takes place in one time and space (or that uses cross-cutting to show two or more simultaneous actions).

Screen direction The right-left relationship in a scene set up in an establishing shot and determined by the position of characters and objects in the frame, by the directions of movement, and by the character's eyeline. Continuity editing will attempt to keep screen direction consistent between shots. See **axis of action**, **eyeline match**, and **180° rule**.

Segmentation The process of dividing a film into parts for analysis.

Semiology, semiotics Theory of criticism pioneered by Roland Barthes in literature and Christian Metz, Umberto Eco, and Peter Wollen in film. It uses the theories of modern linguistics, especially Ferdinand de Saussure's concept of signification, as a model for the description of the operation of various cultural languages, such as film, television, body language, and written and spoken languages.

Sequence Term commonly used for a moderately large segment of a film, involving one complete stretch of action and consisting of one or more scenes.

Shallow focus Restricted depth of field, which keeps only those planes close to the camera in sharp focus; the opposite of **deep focus**.

Shallow space Staging the action in relatively few planes of depth; the opposite of **deep space**.

Short A film generally less than 30 minutes in running time.

Shot In shooting, one uninterrupted run of the camera to expose a series of frames. Also called a **take**; in the finished film, one uninterrupted image with a single (static or mobile) framing.

Shot/reverse shot Two or more shots edited together that alternate characters, typically in a conversation situation. In continuity editing, characters in one framing usually look left, and, in the other framing, right. Over-the-shoulder framings are common in shot/reverse-shot editing.

Side lighting Lighting coming from one side of a person or an object, usually in order to create a sense of volume, to bring out surface tensions, or to fill in areas left shadowed by light from another source.

Sign In semiology, the basic unit of signification composed of *signifier* (which carries the meaning) and *signified* (which is the concept or thing signified). In written language, for example, the word 'tree' is the signifier, and the idea of the tree the signified; the whole sign is comprised of both elements. In cinema, the signified, the idea of tree, remains the same, but the signifier, the image (or even the sound) of the tree is much more complex. See **semiology**.

Simultaneous sound Diegetic sound that is represented as occurring at the same time in the story as the image it accompanies.

Size diminution Cue for suggesting represented depth in the image by showing objects that are further away as smaller than foreground objects.

Slapstick Type of comedy, widely prevalent during the silent film era, which depends on broad physical action and pantomime for its effect rather than verbal wit.

Soft lighting Lighting that avoids harsh bright and dark areas, creating a gradual transition from highlights to shadows.

Sound bridge As the scene starts, the sound from the previous scene carries over briefly before the sound from the new scene begins. Or, conversely, at the end of a scene, the sound from the next scene is heard, leading into that scene.

Sound over Any sound that is not represented as being directly audible within the space and time of the images on the screen. This includes both **non-simultaneous sound** and **non-diegetic sound**.

Sound perspective The sense of a sound's position in space, yielded by volume, timbre, and pitch; in stereo or surround systems, a multiplicity of aural information across channels.

Space At minimum, any film displays a two-dimensional graphic space, the flat composition of the image. In films that depict recognisable objects, a three-dimensional space is represented as well, which may be directly depicted as on-screen space, or suggested as off-screen space. In narrative film, one can also distinguish between story space, the locale of the totality of the action (whether shown or not), and plot space, the locales visibly and audibly represented in the scenes.

Special effects General term for various photographic manipulations that create fictitious spatial relations in the shot, such as **superimposition**, **matte shots**, and **rear projection**.

Story structure *Exposition*: The place within the narrative that presents or reveals who the characters are, their connections to each other, and locates the setting and the time period of where the story occurs. *Climax*: Occurs at the height of the narrative's action where oppositional characters or elements confront the conflict that has been building between them, generally protagonist versus antagonist, nature, or himself or herself. *Dénouement*: Near the conclusion of the film narrative, when the air of stability or equipoise reoccurs.

Subsidiary contrast Secondary elements of the *mise en scène*, either dissimilar or supplementing the principal image.

Subtext Inferences or thematic notions implied underneath the script's text but disassociated from the literal spoken text. For example, in Alexander Payne's *Sideways* (2004), the main protagonist discusses his love of wine with a woman whom he has just met. Although he speaks literally about which particular wines disagree with him, he is actually 'talking' and expressing his feelings about his failed relationships with women, which connects with the thematic of the overall film.

Superimposition In essence, placing one image on top of another image, whereby both images are viewable to create a particular visual or emotional effect. The super-imposing of imagery is not meant to indicate a particular transition from one scene to another but rather to impart multiple character points-of-view or pieces of information to the audience.

Surrealism A movement of painters and filmmakers during the 1920s; in particular, artist Salvador Dalí and filmmaker Luis Buñuel, who teamed up to make *Un Chien Andalou* (1929); a film style reminiscent of that movement, either fantastic or psychologically distortive. Although the term 'surreal' has (too) often been used merely as a synonym for 'weird', surrealism is a fully fledged philosophical movement created by French intellectuals in Paris in the 1920s, whose central feature was the exploration and championing of the workings of the unconscious mind. Key surrealist artists include the writers André Breton and Paul Eluard, the painters Salvador Dalí, René Magritte, and Max Ernst, and the filmmaker Luis Buñuel. Although Britain did not produce any high-profile surrealist filmmakers as such, Humphrey Jennings and Lindsay Anderson have been cited, and it is not uncommon for films to show surrealist touches.

Symbol Within the *mise en scène*, a concrete object, movement, deed, or moniker that represents a non-concrete or intangible notion or concept.

Synchronous sound Sound that is matched temporally with movements occurring in the images, as when dialogue corresponds to lip movement or footsteps across a floor.

Take A version of a shot; in filmmaking, the shot produced by one uninterrupted run of the camera. One 'shot' in the final film may be chosen from among several 'takes' of the same action.

Technique Any aspect of the film medium that can be chosen and manipulated in making a film.

Telephoto lens A lens of long focal length that affects a scene's perspective by enlarging distant places and making them seem closer to the foreground planes. In 35 mm filming, a lens of 75 mm length or more. A normal lens for 35 mm filming would be a lens of 35 mm to 50 mm; the telephoto diminishes the illusion of depth.

Three-point lighting Common positioning utilising three directions of light on a scene: from behind the subject (**backlighting**), from one bright source (**key light**), and from a less bright source balancing the key light (**fill light**).

Tight framing Utilisation of the frame edge to 'ensnare' or 'confine' characters who have minimal or no autonomy to move; the *mise en scène* is precisely calculated and balanced.

Tilt Camera movement by swivelling upward or downward on a stationary support; creates a mobile framing that scans space vertically.

Top lighting/hair light Lighting coming from above a person or object, usually in order to outline the upper areas of the figure or to separate it more clearly from the background.

Tracking shot Mobile framing that travels through space forward, backward, or laterally. It could move on tracks or dolly, or handheld; also termed a 'travelling shot'.

Typage A performance technique of Soviet montage cinema whereby an actor seeks to represent or characterise a social class or other group.

Under-lighting Lighting from a point below the characters in the scene.

Unity The degree to which a film's parts relate systematically to each other and provide motivations for all the elements used.

Variation In the film form, the return of an element with notable changes.

Verisimilitude The quality of appearing to be cinematically truthful or real.

Visceral An emotional reaction created within the audience in response to the interaction of objects and/or subjects within the frame; classic examples include *Un Chien Andalou* (Luis Buñuel, 1929), where a close shot of a straight razor slits the eye of a female character, or in *The Exorcist* (William Friedkin, 1973), where the main character twists into physical contortions, including the use of projectiles and sound to create a physical and emotional 'reaction' within the spectator.

Voice-over narration Utilisation of a separate voice on the soundtrack that is not synced to a character on screen; usually in the form of a narrator or first-person account. A narrative device that adds a further layer or knowledge to the narrative. For example, in Sydney Pollack's *Out of Africa* (1985), the film's protagonist (Meryl Streep), a famous writer, reads from her prose and diary about her relationship with a hunter and adventurer (Robert Redford) that she meets while living in Africa in the early part of the twentieth century.

Whip pan Extremely fast movement of the camera from side to side that blurs the image into a set of indistinct horizontal lines briefly; often, an imperceptible cut joins two whip pans to create a trick transition between scenes.

Wide-angle lens A lens of short focal length that affects the scene's perspective by distorting straight lines near the edges of the frame and by exaggerating the distance between foreground and background planes. In 35 mm filming, a wide-angle lens is 30 mm or less. Produces the opposite effect of a **telephoto lens**.

Wipe Transition between shots in which a line or image passes across the screen, eliminating the first shot as it goes and replacing it with the next one.

Zapruder film Arguably the world's most famous 8 mm colour film footage, a 26-second strip that captures the assassination of American President John F. Kennedy on 22 November 1963. The film was kept from public view until 1975 before being screened on television for the first time. It was taken by amateur filmmaker Abraham Zapruder, a Dallas dressmaker, who brought his Bell and Howell 414 home-movie camera to film the president's visit to Dallas, Texas. The original footage was incorporated into Oliver Stone's 1991 docu-narrative film, *JFK*, which considered the Zapruder film as prima facie evidence of a conspiracy (see *JFK*, Oliver Stone, 1991; *Executive Action*, David Miller, 1973).

Zoom lens A large-format lens with a focal length that can be changed during a shot. A shift towards the telephoto range enlarges the images and flattens its planes together, giving an impression of moving into the scene's space, while a shift towards the wide-angle range does the opposite.

Bibliography

Aaron, Michelle (2006) *New Queer Cinema: A Critical Reader*. Brunswick, NJ: Rutgers University Press.

Acland, Charles R. (2003) *Screen Traffic: Movies, Multiplexes and Global Culture*. Durham, NC: Duke University Press.

Adler, Stella (1990) *The Technique of Acting*. New York: Bantam Books.

Aitken, Ian (2002) *European Film Theory and Cinema*. Bloomington, IN: Indiana University Press.

Balio, Tino (1985) *The American Film Industry*. London: University of Wisconsin Press.

Barthes, Roland (1974) *S/Z: An Essay*. Trans. Richard Miller. New York: Hill and Wang.

Barthes, Roland (2009) *Mythologies*. Trans. Annette Lavers. London: Vintage.

Baudrillard, Jean (1983) *Simulacra and Simulation*. Trans. Paul Foss, Paul Patton, and Philip Beitchman. New York: Semiotext(e).

Baudry, Jean-Louis (1985) 'Ideological effects of the basic cinematographic apparatus', in Bill Nichols (ed.) *Movies and Methods. Vol. 2*. Berkeley, CA: University of California Press, pp. 531–42.

Bazin, André (1967) *What is Cinema? Vol 1*. Berkeley, CA: University of California Press.

Bazin, André (2009) 'From what is cinema? The evolution of the language of cinema', in Leo Braudy and Marshall Cohen (eds) *Film Theory and Criticism*. New York: Oxford University Press, pp. 41–53.

Benshoff, Harry and Griffin, Sean (2009) *American on Film: Representing Race, Class, Gender and Sexuality*. Malden, MA: Wiley-Blackwell.

Benson, Thomas W. and Snee, Brian J. (2008) *The Rhetoric of the New Political Documentary*. Carbondale, IL: Southern Illinois University Press.

Bolter, David. J and Grusin, Richard (1999) *Remediation: Understanding New Media*. Cambridge, MA: MIT Press.

Boorstin, Daniel J. (1992) *The Image: A Guide to Pseudo-Events in America*. New York: Vintage Books.

Bordwell, David (1985) *Narration in the Fiction Film*. Madison, WI: University of Wisconsin Press.

Branigan, Edward (2006) *Projecting a Camera: Language-games in Film Theory*. Abingdon: Taylor & Francis.

Braudy, Leo and Cohen, Marshall (eds) (2009) *Film Theory and Criticism*. New York: Oxford University Press.

Brecht, Bertolt (1966) *Brecht on Theatre: The Development of an Aesthetic*. New York: Hill & Wang.

Brenner, Robin E. (2007) *Understanding Manga and Anime*. Westport, CT: Libraries Unlimited.

Brunette, Peter (1996) *Roberto Rossellini*. Berkeley, CA: University of California Press.

Bruzzi, Stella (2006) *New Documentary: A Critical Introduction*. London: Routledge.

Bukatman, Scott (1999) 'The artificial infinite: on special effects and the sublime', in Annette Kuhn (ed.) *Alien Zone II: The Spaces of Science-Fiction Cinema*. London: Verso, pp. 249–75.

Butler, Alison (2007) 'Avant-garde and counter-cinema', in Pam Book (ed.) *The Cinema Book*. Third edition. London: BFI, pp. 89–96.

Butler, Judith (1990) *Gender Trouble: Feminism and the Subversion of Identity*. London: Routledge.

Carroll, Noël (1998) *Interpreting the Moving Image*. Cambridge: Cambridge University Press.

Cashill, Robert (2003) 'Classic Hollywood horrors', *Cineaste* 28(3): 48–9.

Caso, Frank (2008) *Censorship*. New York: Infobase Publishing.

Cavallaro, Dan (2010) *Anime and the Art of Adaptation: Eight Famous Works from Page to Screen*. Jefferson, NC: McFarland & Co.

Clute, Shannon S. and Edwards, Richard L. (2011) *The Maltese Touch of Evil: Film Noir and Potential Criticism*. Boston, MA: Dartmouth.

Cook, Guy (1992) *The Discourse of Advertising*. London: Routledge.

Cook, David A. (2004) *A History of Narrative Film*. New York: Norton.

Corrigan, Timothy (ed.) (2012) *American Cinema of the 2000s: Themes and Variations*. New Brunswick, NJ: Rutgers University Press.

Crofts, Stephen (2002) 'Reconceptualizing national cinema/s', in Alan Williams (ed.) *Film and Nationalism*. Brunswick, NJ: Rutgers University Press, pp. 25–51.

Crook, T. (2012) *The Sound Handbook*. Abingdon: Routledge, pp. 11–17.

Davies, Steven Paul (2008) *Out at the Movies: A History of Gay Cinema*. Harpenden: Kamera Books.

Deleuze, Gilles (2009) *Cinema I: The Movement Image*. London: Continuum.

Deleuze, Gilles (2005) *Cinema II: The Time Image*. London: Continuum.

Denzin, Norman K. (1991) *Images of Postmodern Society: Social Theory and Contemporary Cinema*. London: Sage.

De Saussure, Ferdinand (1916) *Course in General Linguistics*. Reprint 1983. London: Duckworth.

De Valck, Marijke and Hagener, Malte (2005) *Cinephilia: Movies, Love and Memory*. Amsterdam: Amsterdam University Press.

Doane, Mary Anne (1987) *The Desire to Desire: The Woman's Film of the 1940s*. Bloomington, IN: Indiana University Press.

Dulac, Germaine (1987) 'The essence of cinema', in Catherine Gallagher and Thomas Laqueur (eds) *The Avant-Garde Film: A Reader of Theory and Criticism*. Berkeley, CA: University of California Press, pp. 36–48.

Dyer, Richard (2001) *Stars*. London: BFI.

Dyer, Richard (2002) *Only Entertainment*. London: Routledge.

Eisenstein, Sergei (1974) 'Montage of attractions: for "enough stupidity in every wiseman"', *The Drama Review: TDR* 18(1): 77–85.

Eisenstein, Sergei (2009) 'From film form', in Leo Braudy and Marshall Cohen (eds) *Film Theory and Criticism*. New York: Oxford University Press, pp. 13–40.

Ellis, John (1992) *Visible Fictions: Cinema, Television, Video*. London: Routledge.

Elsaesser, Thomas (2004) 'The pathos of failure: American films of the 1970s – notes on the unmotivated hero', in Thomas Elsaesser, Alexander Horwath, and Noel King (eds) *The Last Great American Picture Show*. Amsterdam: Amsterdam University Press, pp. 279–92.

Erza, Elizabeth and Rowden, Terry (2006) *Transnational Cinema: The Film Reader*. London: Routledge.

Eurimages (2011) 'Eurimages supports 19 European co-productions', available at: https://wcd.coe.int/ViewDoc.jsp?id=1857885&Site=DC (accessed 22 January 2011).

Featherstone, Mike (1995) *Undoing Culture: Globalization, Postmodernism and Identity*. London: Sage.

Film Council (2011) 'UK box office: 16–18 December 2011', available at: www.ukfilm council.org.uk/article/17701/UK-Box-Office-16—-18-December-2011 (accessed 22 January 2011).

Fiske, John (1987) *Television Culture*. London: Methuen.

Fossati, Giovanni (2009) *From Grain to Pixel: The Archival Life of Film in Transition*. Amsterdam: Amsterdam University Press.

Foucault, Michel (1998) *The History of Sexuality: The Will to Knowledge*. London: Penguin.

Foucault, Michel (2007) *The Archaeology of Knowledge and the Discourse on Language*. Trans. A.M. Sheridan Smith. London: Routledge.

Frazer, Bryant (2012) 'The Hobbit, the "soap opera effect", and the 48fps (and faster future of movies', 30 April 2012, available at: www.studiodaily.com/2012/04/the-hobbit-the-soap-opera-effect-and-the-48fps-and-faster-future-of-movies/ (accessed 3 June 2012).

Friedberg, Anna (2004) 'The end of cinema: multimedia and technological change', in Leo Braudy and Marshall Cohen (eds) *Film Theory and Criticism*. Sixth edition. New York and Oxford: Oxford University Press.

Frith, S. (1983) *Mood Music: An Enquiry into Narrative Film Music*, available at: http://screen.oxfordjournals.org/content/25/3/78.full.pdf+html (accessed 15 February 2012).

Giddens, Anthony (1990) *The Consequences of Modernity*. London: Polity Press.

Grant, Barry Keith (2007) *Film Genre: From Iconography to Ideology*. London: Wallflower Press.

Gray, Gordon (2010) *Cinema: A Visual Anthropology*. Oxford and New York: Berg.

Gunning, Tom (2009) 'Narrative discourse and the narrator system', in Leo Braudy and Marshall Cohen (eds) *Film Theory and Criticism*. New York: Oxford University Press, pp. 473–6.

Hagan, Uta (1991) *A Challenge for the Actor*. New York: Scribner.

Hall, Stuart (1997) *Representation: Cultural Representations and Signifying Practices*. London: Open University Press.

Hallam, Julia and Marshment, Margaret (2000) *Realism and Popular Cinema*. Manchester: Manchester University Press.

Hanson, Mark (2004) *The End of Celluloid: Film Futures in the Digital Age*. Hove: Rotovision.

Harding, P. (2010) *PWL: From the Factory Floor*. London: Cherry Red Books.

Hayward, Susan (2006) *Cinema Studies: Key Concepts*. Third edition. London: Routledge.

Heath, Stephen (1976) 'Narrative space', *Screen* 17(3): 68–112.

Heath, Stephen (1981) *Questions of Cinema*. Bloomington, IN: Indiana University Press.

Higson, Andrew (2000) 'The limiting imagination of national cinema', in Mette Hjort and Scott Mackenzie (eds) *Cinema and Nation*. London: Routledge, pp. 63–74.

Hillstrom, Kevin and Collier Hillstrom, Laurie (1998) *The Vietnam Experience: A Concise Encyclopedia of American Literature, Songs, and Films*. Westport, CT: Greenwood Press.

Hollows, Joanne (2003) 'The masculinity of cult', in Mark Jancovich, Antonio Lazaro Rebol, Julian Stringer, and Andrew Willis (eds) *Defining Cult Movies: The Cultural Politics of Oppositional Tastes*. Manchester: Manchester University Press, pp. 35–53.

Horwath, Alexander (2004) 'The impure cinema: new Hollywood 1967–1976', in Thomas Elsaesser, Alexander Horwath, and Noel King (eds) *The Last Great American Picture Show*. Amsterdam: Amsterdam University Press, pp. 9–18.

Hutchings, Peter (1995) 'Genre theory and criticism', in Joanne Hollows and Mark Jancovich (eds) *Approaches to Popular Film*. Manchester: University of Manchester Press, pp. 59–78.

Iwabuchi, Koichi (2002) *Recentering Globalization: Popular Culture and Japanese Transnationalism*. Durham, NC: Duke University Press.

Jacobs, Steven (2007) *Wrong House: The Architecture of Alfred Hitchcock*. Rotterdam: 010 Publishers.

Jameson, Fredric (1998) *The Cultural Turn: Selected Writings on the Postmodern, 1983–1998*. New York: Verso.

Jenkins, Henry (2004) 'Quentin Tarantino's Star Wars? Digital cinema, media convergence, and participatory culture', in David Thorburn and Henry Jenkins (eds) *Rethinking Media Change: The Aesthetics of Transition*. Cambridge, MA: MIT Press, pp. 281–312.

Jenkins, Henry (2006) *Convergence Culture: Where Old and New Media Collide*. New York: New York University Press.

Jerslev, Anne (2002) *Realism and 'Reality' in Film and Media*. Copenhagen: Museum Tusculanum Press.

Kaplan, E. Ann (1994) *Women and Film: Both Sides of the Camera*. London: Routledge.

Kearney, Mary Celeste (2006) *Girls Make Media*. New York: Routledge.

King, Noel (2004) 'The last good time we ever had: remembering the new Hollywood cinema', in Thomas Elsaesser, Alexander Horwath, and Noel King (eds) *The Last Great American Picture Show*. Amsterdam: Amsterdam University Press, pp. 19–36.

Kirby, Alan (2009) *Digimodernism: How New Technologies Dismantle the Postmodern and Reconfigure our Culture*. London: Continuum International Publishing Group.

Klinger, Barbara (2006) *Beyond the Multiplex: Cinema, New Technologies, and the Home*. Berkeley, CA: University of California Press.

Kracauer, Siegfried (1960) *Theory of Film: The Redemption of Physical Reality*. New York: Oxford University Press.

Kramer, Peter (2005) *The New Hollywood From Bonnie and Clyde to Star Wars*. London: Wallflower Press.

Krauss, Rosalind (1993) *The Optical Unconscious*. Cambridge, MA: MIT Press.

Kruger, Robert (2000) 'Paul Rotha and the documentary film', in Robert Kruger and Duncan J. Petrie (eds) *A Paul Rotha Reader*. Exeter: Exeter University Press, pp. 16–44.

Kubrick, Stanley (2001) *Stanley Kubrick: Interviews*, ed. Gene D. Phillips. Jackson, MS: University Press of Mississippi.

Kuhn, Annette (1994) *Women's Pictures: Feminism and Cinema*. London and New York: Verso.

Labrecque, Jeff (2012) '"2001: A Space Odyssey" tech pioneer on "Hobbit" footage: "A fabulous and brave step in the right direction"', 2 May 2012, available at: http://insidemovies.ew.com/2012/05/02/douglas-trumbull-hobbit-frame-speed (accessed 3 June 2012).

Langford, Barry (2005) *Film Genre: Hollywood and Beyond*. Edinburgh: University of Edinburgh Press.

Lévi-Strauss, Claude (1962) *The Savage Mind*. Reprint 1974. London: Weidenfeld & Nicolson.

Lévi-Strauss, Claude (1976) *Structural Anthropology, Vol. II*. Trans. Monique Layton. New York: Basic Books.

Lewis, John (2001) *The End of Cinema as We Know it: American Film in the Nineties*. New York and London: New York University Press.

Lister, Martin and Dovey, Jon (2009) *New Media: A Critical Introduction*. Abingdon: Routledge.

Lugowski, David (2005) 'Great directors: James Whale', available at: http://sensesof cinema.com/2005/great-directors/whale (accessed 4 August 2011).

McDermott, Mark (2006) 'The menace of the fans to the franchise', in Matthew Wilhelm Kapell and John Shelton Lawrence (eds) *Finding the Force of the Star Wars Franchise: Fans, Merchandise, and Critics*. New York: Peter Lang, pp. 243–64.

MacDonald, Scott (1993) *Avant-Garde Film: Motion Studies*. Cambridge and New York: Cambridge University Press.

Malloy, Tom (2009) *Bankroll: A New Approach to Financing Feature Films*. Studio City, CA: Michael Wiese Productions.

Maltby, Richard (2003) *Hollywood Cinema*. Second Edition. Oxford: Blackwell Publishing.

Manovich, Lev (2002) *The Language of New Media*. Cambridge, MA: MIT Press.

Mayne, Judith (2002) *Cinema and Spectatorship*. New York: Routledge.

MEDIA (2011) 'Funding', available at: www.mediadeskuk.eu/funding (accessed 22 January 2011).

Meisner, Sanford and Longwell, Denis (1987) *Sanford Meisner on Acting*. New York: Random House.

Mendinburu, Bernard, Pupulin, Yves, and Schklair, Steve (2011) *3D TV and 3D Cinema: Tools and Processes for Creative Stereoscopy*. Waltham, MA: Focal Press.

Metz, Christian (1982) *The Imaginary Signifier: Psychoanalysis and the Cinema*. Trans. Celia Britton, Annwyl Williams, Ben Brewster, and Alfred Guzzetti. Bloomington, IN: Indiana University Press.

Metz, Christian (1986) *The Imaginary Signifier: Psychoanalysis and the Cinema*. Bloomington, IN: Indiana University Press.

Miller, Jacques-Alain (1977) 'Suture (elements of the logic of the signifier)', *Screen* 18(4): 24–34.

Miller, Toby, Govil, Nitin, McMurria, John, and Maxwell, Richard (2001) *Global Hollywood*. London: BFI.

Mitchell, A.J. (2004) *Visual Effects for Film and Television*. Burlington, MA: Focal Press.

Mitter, Shomit (1992). *Systems of Rehearsal: Stanislavksy, Brecht, Grotowski and Brook*. Abingdon: Routledge.

Monaco, James (2003) *The Sixties: 1960–1969*. Berkeley, CA: University of California Press.

Mulvey, Laura (1975) 'Visual pleasure and narrative cinema', *Screen* 16(3): 6–18.

Mulvey, Laura (1989) *Visual and Other Pleasures*. Bloomington, IN: Indiana University Press.

Mulvey, Laura (2009) 'Visual pleasure and narrative cinema', in Leo Braudy and Marshall Cohen (eds) *Film Theory and Criticism*. New York: Oxford University Press, pp. 711–22.

Musterberg, Hugo (1992) 'The photoplay: a psychological study', in Gerald Mast, Marshall Cohen, and Leo Braudy (eds) *Film Theory and Criticism*. Oxford: Oxford University Press.

Neale, Stephen (1993) 'Masculinity as spectacle', in Steven Cohen and Ina Rae Clark (eds) *Screening the Male: Exploring Masculinities in Hollywood Cinema*. London and New York: Routledge, pp. 9–22.

Neale, Stephen (2000) *Genre and Hollywood*. London and New York: Routledge.

Nelmes, Jill (2003) *An Introduction to Film Studies*. Third edition. London: Routledge.

Nichols, Bill (2001) *Introduction to Documentary*. Bloomington, IN: Indiana University Press.

Okun, Jeffrey A. and Zwerman, Susan (2010) *The VES Handbook of Visual Effects: Industry Standard VFX Practices and Procedures*. Burlington, MA: Focal Press.

O'Pray, Michael (2003) *Avant-Garde Film: Forms, Themes and Passions*. London: Wallflower Press.

O'Regan, Tom (1996) *Australian National Cinema*. London and New York: Routledge.

Oudart, Jean-Pierre (1977) 'Cinema and suture', *Screen* 18(4): 66–76.

Peirce, Charles Sanders (1931–58) *The Collected Papers of C.S. Peirce*. Vols. 1–6, Charles Hartshorne and Paul Weiss (eds); Vols. 7–8, A.W. Burks (ed.). Cambridge, MA: Harvard University Press.

Petrie, Duncan J. (2000) 'Paul Rotha and film theory', in Robert Kruger and Duncan J. Petrie (eds) *A Paul Rotha Reader*. Devon: Exeter University Press.

Pierson, Michele (2002) *Special Effects: Still in Search of Wonder*. New York: Columbia University Press.

Plantinga, Carl (2009) 'Documentary', in Paisley Livingston (ed.) *The Routledge Companion to Philosophy and Film*. Abingdon and New York: Routledge, pp. 494–504.

Polan, Dana (2012) 'Movies, a nation, and new identities', in Tim Corrigan (ed.) *American Cinema of the 2000s: Themes and Variations*. New Brunswick, NJ: Rutgers University Press.

Pramaggiore, Maria and Wallis, Tom (2005) *Film: A Critical Introduction*. London: Laurence King Publishing.

Prince, Stephen (1996) 'True lies: perceptual realism, digital images, and film theory', *Film Quarterly* 49(3): 27–37.

Prince, Stephen (2011) *Digital Visual Effects in Cinema: The Seduction of Reality*. Piscataway, NJ: Rutgers University Press.

Ray, Robert B. (1998) 'Impressionism, surrealism, and film theory: path dependence, or how a tradition in film theory gets lost', in John Mill and Pamela Church Gibson (eds) *The Oxford Guide to Film Studies*. Oxford: Oxford University Press, pp. 67–76.

Real, Michael R. (1996) *Exploring Media Culture: A Guide*. London: Sage.

Reekie, Duncan (2007) *Subversion: The Definitive History of Underground Cinema*. London: Wallflower Press.

Renoir, Jean (1989) *Renoir on Renoir*. Trans. Carol Volk. Cambridge: Cambridge University Press.

Renov, Michael (1993) *Theorizing Documentary*. New York: Routledge.

Ritzer, George (1993) *The McDonaldization of Society*. London: Sage.

Röhl, Alexander (2009) *Forms and Functions in Documentary Filmmaking: American Direct Cinema*. Munich: GRIN Verlag.

Rona, J. (2009) *The Reel World, Scoring for Pictures*. New York: Hal Leonard Books.

Root, John (2010) 'What is motion capture?', in Jeffrey A. Okun and Susan Zwerman (eds) *Visual Effects Society Handbook: Workflow and Techniques*. Oxford: Focal Press.

Ryan, Michael and Kellner, Douglas (1990) *Camera Politica: The Politics and Ideology of Contemporary Hollywood Film*. Bloomington, IN: Indiana University Press.

Salt, Barry (1992) *Film Style and Technology: History and Analysis*. Second edition. London: Starword.

Schaffer, Murray, R. (1994) *The Soundscape, Our Sonic Environment and the Tuning of the World*. Vermont: Destiny Books.

Schatz, Thomas (1988) *The Genius of the System: Hollywood Filmmaking in the Studio Era*. New York: Pantheon Books.

Schatz, Thomas (1993) 'The new Hollywood', in Jim Collins, Hilary Radner, and Ava Preacher Collins (eds) *Film Theory Goes to the Movies*. New York: Routledge, pp. 8–36.

Shiel, Mark (2006) 'American cinema 1965–1970', in Linda Ruth Williams and Michael Hammond (eds) *Contemporary American Cinema*. London: Open University Press, pp. 12–40.

Silverman, Kaja (1983) *The Subject of Semiotics*. New York: Oxford University Press.

Sontag, Susan (1977) *On Photography*. New York: Anchor Books.

Spence, Louise and Navarro, Vinicius (2011) *Crafting Truth: Documentary Form and Meaning*. Piscataway, NJ: Rutgers University Press.

Stam, Robert, Burgoyne, Robert, and Flittermas Lewis, Sandy (1992) *New Vocabularies in Film Semiotics: Structuralism, Post-Structuralism and Beyond*. New York: Routledge.

Stanislavski, Constantin (1989) *An Actor Prepares*. Trans. Elizabeth Reynolds Hapgood. New York: Routledge.

Stanislavski, Constantin (1994) *Building a Character*. Trans. Elizabeth Reynolds Hapgood. New York: Routledge.

Stiglitz, Joseph E. (2002) *Globalization and its Discontents*. New York: W.W. Norton.

Strasberg, Lee (1988) *A Dream of Passion: The Development of the Method*. New York: Bloomsburg.

Suarez, Juan Antonio (2002) 'Pop, queer, or fascist? The ambiguity of mass culture in Kenneth Anger's Scorpio Rising', in Wheeler W. Dixon and Gwendolyn Audrey Foster (eds) *Experimental Cinema: The Film Reader*. London and New York: Routledge, pp. 115–38.

Tudor, Andrew (1989) *Monsters and Mad Scientists: A Cultural History of the Horror Movie.* Oxford: Blackwell.

Verrone, William E. (2011) *The Avant-Grade Feature Film: A Critical History*. Jefferson, NC: McFarland & Company.

Vitali, Valentina and Willemen, Paul (eds) (2006) *Theorising National Cinema*. London: BFI.

Wartenberg, Thomas E. (2001) 'Humanising the beast: King Kong and the representation of black male sexuality', in Daniel Bernardi (ed.) *Classical Hollywood, Classical Whiteness*. Minneapolis, MN: University of Minnesota Press, pp. 157–77.

Wees, William Charles (1992) *Light Moving in Time: Studies in the Visual Aesthetics of Avant-Grade Film*. Berkeley, CA: University of California Press.

Wierzbicki, J. (2009) *Film Music – A History*. Oxford: Routledge.

Williams, Raymond (1974) *Television: Technology and Cultural Form*. London: Fontana.

Willis, Holly (2005) *New Digital Cinema: Reinventing the Moving Image*. London: Wallflower Press.

Wood, Robin (1985) 'An introduction to the American horror film', in Bill Nichols (ed.) *Movies and Methods*. *Vol. 2*. Berkeley, CA: University of California Press, pp. 195–319.

Wood, Robin (1986) *Hollywood from Vietnam to Reagan*. New York: Columbia University Press.

Wright, Steve (2008) *Compositing Visual Effects: Essentials for the Aspiring Artist*. Burlington, MA: Focal Press.

Young, Paul (2006) *The Cinema Dreams its Rivals. Media Fantasy Films from Radio to the Internet*. Minneapolis, MN: University of Minnesota Press.

Zaniello, Tom (2007) *The Cinema of Globalization: A Guide to Films about the New Economic Order*. Ithaca, NY: IRL Press.

Filmography

8½, 1963. Federico Fellini. Italy/France. Columbia Pictures.
12 Angry Men, 1957. Sidney Lumet. USA. United Artists.
2012, 2009. Roland Emmerich. USA. Columbia Pictures.
Abyss, The, 1989. James Cameron. USA. 20th Century Fox.
Age d'Or, L', 1930. Luis Buñuel. France. Corinth Films.
Akira, 1988. Katsuhiro Otomo. Japan. Toho.
Alice Doesn't Live Here Anymore, 1974. Martin Scorsese. USA. Warner Bros.
All the President's Men, 1976. Alan J. Pakula. USA. Warner Bros.
Alphaville, 1965. Jean Luc Godard. France. Athos Films.
Alvin and the Chipmunks: Chipwrecked, 2011. Mike Mitchell. USA. 20th Century Fox.
American Gigolo, 1980. Paul Schrader. USA. Paramount Pictures.
Anthem, 1991. Marlon Riggs. USA. Frameline.
Apocalypse Now, 1979. Francis Ford Coppola. USA. Zoetrope Studios.
Arthur Christmas, 2011. Sarah Smith. UK/USA. Sony Pictures.
Artist, The, 2011. Michel Hazanavicius. France. Entertainment Film Distributors.
Astro Boy, 1963–75. Osamu Tezuka. Japan. Fuji TV.
Avatar, 2009. James Cameron. USA. 20th Century Fox.
Avengers, The, 2012. Josh Whedon. USA. Walt Disney Pictures.
A Very Harold & Kumar 3D Christmas, 2011. Todd Strauss-Schulson. USA. Warner Bros.
Awesome I Fuckin' Shot That, 2006. 'Nathanial Hornblower'. USA. THINKFilm.
Barry Lyndon, 1975. Stanley Kubrick. USA. Warner Bros.
Batman Dracula, 1964. Andy Warhol. USA. Undistributed.
Battleship Potemkin, 1926. Sergei Eisenstein. Soviet Union. Goskino.
Between the Lines, 1977. Joan Micklin. USA. Vestron Video.
Bicycle Thieves, 1948. Vittorio De Sica. Italy. Ente Nazionale Industrie Cinematografiche
Birthday Party, The, 1968. William Friedkin. UK. Continental Motion Picture Corp.
Birth of a Nation, The, 1915. D.W. Griffith. USA. David W. Griffith Corporation.
Black Cat, The, 1934. Edgar G Ulmer. USA. Universal Pictures.
Blade Runner, 1982. Ridley Scott. USA. Warner Bros.

Blowout, 1981. Brian DePalma. USA. MGM.

Blair Witch Project, The, 1999. Daniel Myrick and Eduardo Sanchez. USA. Artisan Entertainment.

Blue Velvet, 1986. David Lynch. USA. De Laurentiis Entertainment Group.

Body as Montage, The: A Spectacle of Punishment, 2010. Mark de Valk. UK/Canada. Falcon Film Prods.

Body Snatchers, The, 1945. Robert Wise. USA. RKO Radio Pictures.

Bonnie and Clyde, 1967. Arthur Penn. USA. Warner Bros-Seven Arts.

Bowling for Columbine, 2002. Michael Moore. USA. United Artists.

Breathless, 1960. Jean-Luc Godard. France. Rialto Pictures.

Bride of Frankenstein, 1935. James Whale. USA. Universal Pictures.

Bringing Up Baby, 1938. Howard Hawks. USA. RKO Radio Pictures.

Bus 174, 2002. Jose Padilha and Felipe Lacerda. Brazil. Zazen Produções.

Cabinet of Dr. Caligari, The, 1920. Robert Wiene. Germany. Decla-Bioscop A.G.

Camp, 1965. Andy Warhol. USA. The Andy Warhol Museum.

Carrie, 1976. Brian De Palma. USA. United Artists.

Catfish, 2010. Henry Joost and Ariel Schulman. USA. Universal Pictures.

Cat People, 1942. Jacques Tourneur. USA. RKO Radio Pictures.

Chad Vader: Day Shift Manager, 2006. Aaron Yonda and Matt Sloan. USA. Accessed 5 May 2012 www.youtube.com/watch?v=4wGR4-SeuJ0.

Children of Men, 2006. Alfonso Cuaron. USA/UK. Universal Pictures.

Chinatown, 1974. Roman Polanski. USA. Paramount Pictures.

Citizen Kane, 1941. Orson Welles. USA. RKO Radio Pictures.

Cleo From 5 to 7, 1962. Agnes Varda. France. Criterion Collection.

Cloverfield, 2008. Matt Reeves. USA. Paramount Pictures.

Conversation, The, 1974. Francis Ford Coppola. USA. American Zoetrope.

Creature from the Black Lagoon, The, 1954. Jack Arnold. USA. Universal International.

Crisis: Behind a Presidential Commitment, 1963. Richard Leacock. USA. New Video.

Dark Days, 2000. Marc Singer. USA. Oscilloscope Laboratories.

Day After Tomorrow, The, 2004. Roland Emmerich. USA/Canada. 20th Century Fox.

Deliverance, 1972. John Boorman. USA. Warner Bros.

Dog Star Man, 1961. Stan Brakhag. USA. The Criterion Collection.

Dolce Vita, La, 1960. Federico Fellini. Italy/France. Koch-Lorber Films.

Doodlebug, 1997. Christopher Nolan. UK. Cinema 16.

Double Indemnity, 1944. Billy Wilder. USA. Universal Pictures.

Dracula, 1931. Tod Browning. USA. Universal Pictures.

Easy Rider, 1969. Denis Hopper, 1969. USA. Columbia Pictures.

Edward II, 1991. Derek Jarman. UK. Image Entertainment.

English Patient, The, 1996. Anthony Minghella. UK/USA. Miramax Films.

Enter the Void, 2007. Gasper Noe. France. Wild Bunch Distribution.

Eraserhead, 1977. David Lynch. USA. Libra Films.

Eternal Sunshine of the Spotless Mind, 2004. Michel Gondry. USA. Universal Pictures.

Executive Action, 1973. David Miller. USA. Wakeford/Orloff Prods.

Exorcist, The, 1973. William Friedkin. USA. Warner Bros.

eXistenZ, 1999. David Cronenberg. Canada/UK. Dimension Films.

Fahrenheit 9/11, 2004. Michael Moore. USA. Lions Gate Films.

Festen, 1998. Thomas Vinterberg. Denmark. Blue Light.

Fight Club, 1999. David Fincher. USA. 20th Century Fox.

Fireworks, 1947. Kenneth Anger. USA. Mystic Fire Video.

Fish Tank, 2009. Andrea Arnold. UK. IFC Films.

Five Easy Pieces, 1970. Bob Rafelson. USA. Columbia Pictures.

Flaming Creatures, 1963. Jack Smith. USA. Film-Makers Cooperation.

Fog of War, The, 2003. Errol Morris. USA. Sony Pictures Classics.
Forrest Gump, 1994. Robert Zemeckis. USA. Paramount Pictures.
Fourth Kind, The, 2009. Olatunde Osunsanmi. USA. Entertainment Film Distributors.
Frankenstein, 1931. James Whale. USA. Universal Pictures.
Full Metal Jacket, 1987. Stanley Kubrick. USA. Warner Bros.
Gimme Shelter, 1970. Albert and David Maysles. USA. 20th Century Fox.
Girl Power, 1992. Sadie Benning. USA. Video Data Bank.
Girlfriends, 1978. Claudia Weill. USA. Warner Bros.
Gladiator, 2000. Ridley Scott. USA. Universal Pictures.
Godfather, The, 1972. Francis Ford Coppola. USA. Paramount Pictures.
Godzilla, 1954. Ishirō Honda. Japan. Toho
Godzilla, 1998. Roland Emmerich. USA. Sony Pictures Entertainment.
Go Fish, 1994. Rose Troche. USA. Samuel Goldwyn Company.
Graduate, The, 1967. Mike Nichols. USA. United Artists.
Grande Illusion. Le, 1937. Jean Renoir. France. Janus Films.
Grapes of Wrath, The, 1940. John Ford. USA. 20th Century Fox.
Great Train Robbery, The, 1903. Edwin S. Porter. USA. Edison Manufacturing Company.
Guess Who's Coming to Dinner, 1967. Stanley Kramer. USA. Columbia Pictures.
Halloween, 1978. John Carpenter. USA. Compass International Pictures.
Happy Feet 2, 2011. George Miller. Aus, Warner Bros.
Harlan County, USA, 1976. Barbara Kopple. USA. First Run Features.
Haunting, The, 1963, Robert Wise. UK. Metro-Goldwyn-Mayer.
Heartbreak Kid, The, 1971. Elaine May. USA. 20th Century Fox.
Hearts and Minds, 1974. Peter Davis. USA. Rialto Pictures.
High School, 1968. Frederick Wiseman. USA. Zipporah Films.
Hills Have Eyes, The, 1977. Wes Craven. USA. Vanguard.
His Girl Friday, 1940. Howard Hawks. USA. Columbia Pictures.
Hobbit, The: An Unexpected Journey, 2012. Peter Jackson. New Zealand. Warner Bros.
Hôtel du Nord, 1938. Marcel Carné. France. Soda Pictures.
House of Frankenstein, 1944. Erle C. Kenton. USA. Universal Studios.
Housing Problems, 1935. E.H. Anstey and Arthur Elton. UK. BFI.
Hugo, 2011. Martin Scorsese. UK/USA/FR. Paramount Pictures.
Hunchback of Notre Dame, 1923. Wallace Worsley. USA. Universal Pictures.
Idiots, The, 1998. Lars von Trier. Denmark. Tartan.
I'm Still Here, 2012. Casey Affleck. USA. Magnolia Pictures.
Inception, 2010. Christopher Nolan. USA. Warner Bros.
Inglourious Basterds, 2009. Quentin Tarantino. Germany/ France/USA. Universal Pictures.
Intolerance, 1916. D.W. Griffith. USA. Triangle Distributing Corporation.
Invisible Man, The, 1933. James Whale. USA. Universal Pictures.
Irreversible, 2002. Gasper Noe. France. Mars Distribution.
Island of Lost Souls, 1932. Erle C. Kenton. USA. Paramount Pictures.
It's a Wonderful Life, 1946. Frank Capra. USA. Paramount Pictures.
Ivan's Childhood, 1962. Andrei Tarkovsky. USSR. Mosfilm.
I Walked With a Zombie, 1943. Jacques Tourneur. USA. RKO Radio Pictures.
Jetée, La, 1962. Chris Marker. France. The Criterion Collection.
JFK, 1991. Oliver Stone. USA. Warner Bros.
John Carter, 2012. Andrew Stanton. USA. Walt Disney Pictures.
King Kong, 1933. Merian C. Cooper and Ernest B. Schoedsack. USA. Turner
    Entertainment.
King of Kong: A Fistful of Quarters, 2007. Seth Gordon. USA. Picturehouse.
Klute, 1971. Alan J. Pakula. USA. Warner Bros.
Koyaanisqatsi, 1983. Godfrey Reggio. USA. New Cinema.

Last Year at Marienbad, 1961. Alain Resnais. France. Cocinor.

Lawrence of Arabia, 1962. David Lean. USA. Columbia Pictures.

Leonardo's Dream, 1989. Douglas Trumbull. Italy. Showscan.

Living End, The, 1992. Gregg Akari. USA. Strand Home Video.

Lord of the Rings, The: The Fellowship of the Ring, 2001. Peter Jackson. New Zealand. New Line Pictures.

Lost in Translation, 2003. Sophia Coppola. USA/Japan. Focus Features.

M, 1931. Fritz Lang. Germany. Nero Film A.G.

Madres de La Plaza de Mayo, Las, 1985. Susana Munoz and Lourdes Portillo. Argentina. Women Make Movies.

Man Who Wasn't There, The, 2001. Joel Coen. USA. Gramercy Pictures.

March of the Penguins, 2005. Luc Jacquet. France. Warner Bros.

MASH, 1970. Robert Altman. USA. 20th Century Fox.

Matrix, The, 1999. Larry and Andy Wachowski. USA. Warner Bros.

Me and Rubyfruit, 1989. [Online Video] Sadie Benning USA. Accessed 5 May 2012. www.youtube.com/watch?v=UqG3GRjkPNo.

Medium Cool, 1969. Haskell Wexler. USA. Paramount.

Melancholia, 2011. Lars von Trier. Den/Swe/Fr. Nordisk Film.

Memento, 2000. Christopher Nolan. USA. Summit Entertainment.

Meshes of the Afternoon, 1943. Maya Deren. USA. Mystic Fire Video.

Metropolis, 1927. Fritz Lang. Germany. UFA.

Midnight Cowboy, 1969. John Schlesinger. USA. United Artists.

Mighty Joe Young, 1998. Ron Underwood. USA. Walt Disney Pictures.

Mildred Pierce, 1945. Michael Curtiz. USA. Warner Bros.

Mother, 1926. Vsevolod Pudovkin. Soviet Union. Tartan Video.

Mummy, The, 1932. Karl Freund. USA. Universal Pictures.

My Neighbour Totoro, 1988. Hayao Miyazaki. Japan. Toho.

My Own Private Idaho, 1991. Gus Van Sant. USA. Fine Line Features.

My Week With Marilyn, 2011. Simon Curtis. UK/USA. Entertainment.

My Winnipeg, 2006. Guy Maddin. Canada. IFC Films.

Naked, 1993. Mike Leigh. UK. Fine Line Features.

Natural Born Killers, 1994. Oliver Stone. USA. Warner Bros.

New Year's Eve, 2011. Gary Marshall. USA. Warner Bros.

Night and Fog, 1955. Alain Resnais. France. Argos Films.

Night of the Living Dead, 1968. George A. Romero. USA. The Walter Reade Org.

Nil By Mouth, 1997. Gary Oldman. France/UK. Sony Picture Classics.

Nitrate Kisses, 1992. Barbara Hammer. USA. Frameline.

October, 1928. Sergei Eisenstein. Soviet Union. Sovkino.

Old Dark House, The, 1932. James Whale. USA. Universal Pictures.

Ordinary People, 1980. Robert Redford. USA. Paramount Pictures.

Orlando, 1992. Sally Potter. UK. Sony Pictures Classics.

Ossessione (Obsession), 1943. Luchino Visconti. Italy. Industrie Cinematografiche Italiane.

Parent Trap, The, 1961. David Swift. USA. Buena Vista Distribution.

Paris is Burning, 1991. Jennie Livingston. USA. Miramax Films.

Pépé le Moko, 1937. Julien Duvivier. France. Criterion Collection.

Perfect Storm, The, 2000. Wolfgang Peterson. USA. Warner Bros.

Phantom of the Opera, The, 1943. Arthur Lubin. USA. Universal Pictures.

Pipe, The, 2009. Risteard O' Domhnaill. Ireland. Filmbuff Distribution.

Pleasantville, 1998. Gary Ross. USA. New Line Cinemas.

Plow that Broke the Plains, The, 1936. Pare Lorentz. USA. U.S. Resettlement Administration.

Poison, 1991. Todd Haynes. USA. Zeitgeist Films.
Police State, 1987. Nick Zedd. USA. Nick Zedd Prods.
Pretty Woman, 1990. Gary Marshall. USA. Touchstone Pictures.
Primary, 1960. Richard Leacock. USA. Docudrama.
Princess Mononoke, 1997. Hayao Miyazaki. Japan. Miramax Films.
Psycho, 1960. Alfred Hitchcock. USA. Paramount Pictures.
Puss in Boots, 2011. Chris Miller. USA. Paramount.
Raging Bull, 1980. Martin Scorsese. USA. United Artists.
Raiders of the Lost Ark, 1981. Steven Spielberg. USA. Paramount Pictures.
Rashomon, 1950. Akira Kurosawa. Japan. RKO Radio Pictures.
Rec, 2007. Jaume Balaguero and Paco Plaza. Spain. Fox Searchlight Pictures.
Redacted, 2007. Brian De Palma. USA/Canada. Magnolia Pictures.
Requiem for a Dream, 2000. Darren Aronofksy. USA. Artisan Entertainment.
Return to Reason, 1923. Man Ray. France. Image Entertainment.
Rise of Planet of the Apes, 2011. Rupert Wyatt. USA. 20th Century Fox.
Rocky, 1976. John A. Avildsen. USA. United Artists.
Roger & Me, 1989. Michael Moore. USA. Warner Bros.
Rome, Open City, 1945. Roberto Rossellini. Italy. Minerva Film Spa.
Room, The, 2003. Tommy Wiseau. USA. Wiseau Films.
Rope, 1948. Alfred Hitchcock. USA. Universal Pictures.
Rules of the Game, The, 1939. Jean Renoir. France. Janus Films.
Run, Lola, Run, 1998. Tom Twyker. Germany. Sony Pictures Classic.
Saddest Music in the World, The, 2003. Guy Maddin. Canada. Manitoba Production
    Centre.
Salesman, 1969. Albert and David Maysles. USA. Maysles Films.
Saturday Night Fever, 1977. John Badham. USA. Paramount Pictures.
Schindler's List, 1993. Stephen Spielberg. USA. Universal.
Science of Sleep, The, 2006. Michel Gondry. France/Italy. Gaumont.
Sciuscià (Shoeshine), 1946. Vittorio De Sica. Italy. Scalera Studios Roma.
Scorpio Rising, 1964. Kenneth Anger. USA. Fantoma.
Scream, 1995. Wes Craven. USA. Dimension Films.
Se7en, 1995. David Fincher. USA. New Line Cinema.
Searchers, The, 1956. John Ford. USA. Warner Bros.
Secrets & Lies, 1996. Mike Leigh. UK. October Films.
Series 7: The Contenders, 2001. Daniel Minihan. USA. USA Films.
Shaft, 1971. Gordon Parks. USA. Warner Bros.
Sherlock Holmes: A Game of Shadows, 2011. Guy Ritchie. UK/USA. Warner Bros.
Shipyard, 1935. Paul Rotha. UKA. BFI.
Shutter Island, 2010. Martin Scorsese. USA. Paramount Pictures.
Snow White and the Seven Dwarfs, 1937. David Hand supervisor. USA. RKO Radio
    Pictures.
Spirited Away, 2001. Hayao Miyazaki. Japan. Walt Disney Pictures.
Stagecoach, 1939. John Ford. USA. United Artists.
Staircase, The, 2004. Jean-Xavier De LeStrade. France. Maha Productions.
Stalker, 1979. Andrei Tarkovsky. USSR. Mosfilm.
Star Wars Episode I: The Phantom Menace, 1999. George Lucas.
Star Wars Episode IV: A New Hope, 1977. George Lucas. USA. 20th Century Fox.
Strike!, 1925. Sergei Eisenstein. Soviet Union. Kino Video.
Super 8, 2011. J.J. Abrams. USA. Paramount Pictures.
Survivor, 2000– [TV Series] Charlie Parsons. USA. CBS.
Suspicion, 1941. Alfred Hitchcock. USA. RKO Pictures.
Sweet Sixteen, 2002. Ken Loach. UK. Germany. Spain. Lionsgate.

Sweet Sweetback's Baadasssss Song, 1971. Melvin Van Peebles. USA. Cinemation Industries.

Tape, 2001. Richard Linklater. USA. Lionsgate.

Tarnation, 2003. Jonathan Caouette. USA. Wellspring Media.

Tarzan and Jane Regained . . . Sort of, 1963. Andy Warhol. USA. The Andy Warhol Museum.

Taxi Driver, 1976. Martin Scorsese. USA. Columbia Pictures.

Terra Trema, La, 1948. Luchino Visconti. Italy. Image Entertainment.

Terminator, The, 1984. James Cameron. USA. Orion Pictures.

Terminator 2: Judgement Day, 1991. James Cameron. USA. TriStar Pictures.

Thelma and Louise, 1991. Ridley Scott. USA. Metro-Goldwyn-Mayer.

Thin Blue Line, The,1988. Errol Morris. USA. Miramax Films.

Thin Red Line, The, 1998. Terrence Malick. USA. 20th Century Fox.

Third Man, The, 1949. Carol Reed. UK. British Lion.

Timecode, 1948. Mike Figgis. USA. Screen Gems.

Titanic, 1997. James Cameron. USA. 20th Century Fox.

Titicut Follies, 1967. Frederick Wiseman. USA. Zipporah Films.

Tongues Untied, 1989. Marlon Riggis. USA. Frameline.

Touch Of Evil, 1958. Orson Welles. USA. Universal Pictures.

Tracey Fragments, The, 2007. Bruce McDonald. Canada. THINKFilm.

Transformers: Dark of the Moon, 2011. Michael Bay. USA. Paramount Pictures.

Trip to the Moon, A, 1902. [Online Video] Geroges Méliès. France. Accessed 5 May 2012. http://video.google.com/videoplay?docid=-5523481985091852675#.

Twilight Saga: Breaking Dawn, The – Part 1, 2011. Bill Condon. USA. eOne Films.

Umberto D, 1952. Vittorio De Sica. Italy. Janus Films.

Un Chien Andalou, 1929. Luis Buñuel. France. Les Grands Film Classiques.

Underground, 1976. Emile De Antonio. USA. Sphinx Productions.

Variety, 1983. Bette Gordon. USA. Kino International.

Vertigo, 1958. Alfred Hitchcock. USA. Paramount Pictures.

Voices of Iraq, 2004. 'People of Iraq'. USA/Iraq. Becker Film International.

Wanda, 1970. Barbara Loden. USA. Parlour Pictures.

War Tapes, The, 2006. Deborah Scranton. USA. Scranton-Lacy Films.

Wavelength, 1967. Michael Snow. USA. Image Entertainment.

Wedding Party, The, 1969. Brian DePalma. Oudine Prods.

Weekend, 1968. Jean-Luc Godard. France. Athos Films.

Welfare, 1975. Frederick Wiseman. USA. Zipporah Films.

Wings of Desire, 1987. Wim Wenders. Germany. Road Movies Filmproduktion.

Winter Soldier, 1972. Winterfilm Collective. USA. Millarium Zero.

Wolf Man, The, 1941. George Waggner. USA. Universal Pictures.

Workers Leaving the Factory, 1895. [Online Video] Lumière Brothers. France. Accessed 5 May 2012. www.youtube.com/watch?v=DEQeIRLxaM4.

Zombie Diaries, The, 2006. Michael Bartlett and Kevin Gates. UK. Revolver Entertainment.

Index